Praise for Robin

"Defining Russian conservatism . . . Robinson offers an absolutely scrupulous dissection of its manifestations from 1800 to 2017."
—*Times Literary Supplement*

"Robinson's fascinating book is a must-read for anyone who wants to understand the socio-cultural dynamic and history behind Russia's great-power ambition."
—*The Federalist*

"*Russian Conservatism* is a magisterial work, and a must-read for students of Russia's past as well as those of her present, and certainly those eager to divine her future."
—*New Books Network*

"Among this book's notable contributions are ideational cameos of little-known Russian conservative thinkers."
—*Choice*

"As an overview of Russia's leading conservative thinkers, Robinson's succinct survey is an excellent introduction. Those who teach courses on the history of Russian thought will be obligated to include his book in their syllabi. It will also help us understand political thinking in today's federation."
—*Canadian Slavonic Papers*

"This important, timely book fills a void. The book is an insightful primer, introducing readers to conservatism as a part of the ideological landscape and national conversation across two centuries."
—*Slavic Review*

"Paul Robinson's comprehensive and timely *Russian Conservatism* locates contemporary Russian politics within the historical continuum of conservative thought. With a balanced, systematic approach, Robinson guides his reader through a complex and at times contradictory set of beliefs from the early 1800s to the present day."
—*BASEES*

"Robinson's book facilitates an understanding of just how conservatism has triumphed in Russia."
—*Journal of European Studies*

RUSSIAN LIBERALISM

A VOLUME IN THE NIU SERIES IN

SLAVIC, EAST EUROPEAN, AND EURASIAN STUDIES

Edited by Christine D. Worobec

For a list of books in the series, visit our website at cornellpress.cornell.edu.

RUSSIAN LIBERALISM

PAUL ROBINSON

NORTHERN ILLINOIS UNIVERSITY PRESS
AN IMPRINT OF
CORNELL UNIVERSITY PRESS
Ithaca and London

First published 2023 by Cornell University Press

Library of Congress Cataloging-in-Publication Data

Names: Robinson, Paul, 1966– author.
Title: Russian liberalism / Paul Robinson.
Description: Ithaca [New York] : Northern Illinois
    University Press, an imprint of Cornell University
    Press, 2023. | Series: NIU series in Slavic,
    East European, and Eurasian studies |
    Includes bibliographical references and index.
Identifiers: LCCN 2023022461 (print) | LCCN 2023022462
    (ebook) | ISBN 9781501772146 (hardcover) |
    ISBN 9781501772177 (paperback) |
    ISBN 9781501772160 (pdf) | ISBN 9781501772153 (epub)
Subjects: LCSH: Liberalism—Russia. | Liberalism—Soviet
    Union. | Liberalism—Russia (Federation) | Political
    culture—Russia. | Political culture—Soviet Union. |
    Political culture—Russia (Federation)
Classification: LCC DK510.6 .R64 2023 (print) |
    LCC DK510.6 (ebook) | DDC 320.510947—dc23 / eng
    / 20230520
LC record available at https://lccn.loc.gov/2023022461
LC ebook record available at https://lccn.loc.gov/
    2023022462

CONTENTS

ACKNOWLEDGMENTS

I would like to thank all those who have helped in the production of this book, notably Chione and Clemency Robinson, Oksana Drozdova-Bélanger, Amy Farranto, Viktoria Lavriniuk, Randall Poole, Alison Rowley, Richard Sakwa, Guillaume Sauvé, and Srdjan Vucetic.

NOTES ON DATES AND TRANSLITERATIONS

All dates in this book are new style. In the notes and bibliography, I have strictly followed the Library of Congress system for transliterating Russian words and names. In cases where I have used translations from Russian, the transliteration of names may vary, so that one author's name may appear in several versions. In the main text, I have altered the Library of Congress system in a number of ways to reflect normal English usage and to bring it closer to how words sound in English. For this reason, I have translated the Russian *ë* as *yo* not *e*. Because Russians whose names end in *uй* are popularly rendered as ending in *y* not *ii*, I have used the former—Kerensky, not Kerenskii. I have also generally used a *y* for the Russian soft sign—thus Ilyin not Il'in—although on some occasions I have omitted the soft sign entirely—Tretiakov, not Tret'iakov. Where there is a generally accepted transliteration for a Russian name, I have used that, e.g., Yeltsin, not El'tsin. The names of Russian emperors and empresses are given in English—Alexander I, Nicholas I, and so on. Again, this is to reflect common practice.

Introduction

Liberalism is an ideology, a political movement, and a set of cultural, political, and economic practices aimed at maximizing personal potential by putting into effect a distinct set of values, such as liberty and pluralism, through a distinct set of institutions, such as free markets and representative government. Liberalism has been called "the most influential political philosophy of the last 300 years" and is the dominant ideology in that part of the world known collectively as "the West."[1] In recent years, however, it has become common to speak of a "crisis of liberalism," with many commentators believing that liberalism is under threat from both within and without the West. Among the most important players said to be challenging liberalism's global dominance is Russia.

Ideological differences are just one of the causes of the current political tensions between Russia and the West. Nevertheless, these tensions have taken on an ideological hue. Western leaders portray themselves as representing the forces of liberalism and democracy against conservatism and autocracy. Meanwhile, their Russian counterparts pose as the champions of an alternative to the Western-led liberal world order. Thus, in a 2019 interview, Russian president Vladimir Putin (b. 1952) remarked that "the liberal idea has become obsolete. It has come into conflict with the interests of the overwhelming majority of the population."[2]

At the time of writing, in early 2023, as Russia fights a war in Ukraine, is the target of Western sanctions, and clamps down on political expression and freedom at home, Russian liberalism is in an extremely parlous state. This is far from untypical in Russian history. Indeed, Russian liberalism has rarely fared well. Liberals have held power for only two short periods of time—very briefly in 1917 and then for a few years during the 1990s. Determining why what is considered the primary mode of political thought and practice in the West has failed to achieve similar success in Russia is a matter of considerable contemporary relevance.

This is far from easy. Daniel Field notes that "it is not clear . . . what 'liberal' and 'liberalism' mean with reference to nineteenth-century Russia."[3] One can say something similar for the twentieth and twenty-first centuries, with additional complications arising when one tries to fit all three eras within the same framework. As V. A. Gutorov comments, "Defining liberalism was an extremely knotty problem in Russian social thought from the very beginning . . . and has remained so until today. . . . Creating a contemporary typology of our country's liberalism, taking into account its historical and contemporary peculiarities, is an extremely difficult task."[4]

This problem is not unique to Russia, in part due to the fact that liberalism overlaps with other political beliefs and practices and can be professed together with beliefs and practices that are illiberal, or at the very least nonliberal.[5] The term liberalism encompasses a huge variety of different viewpoints, many of which appear to be entirely contradictory.[6] This puts the student of liberalism in a difficult position. On the one hand, its existence and importance cannot be denied. On the other hand, it is not at all clear what it is.

Another problem is that understandings of liberalism have changed over time. Some historians date liberalism's origins back many hundreds of years.[7] However, most consider that as a formal ideology and political movement, liberalism emerged in Western Europe in the early nineteenth century.[8] In its initial manifestation, liberalism was a movement that sought to limit arbitrary government and carve out a private sphere of life into which the state should not intrude.[9] Politically, early liberalism of this sort was associated with demands for civil liberties (such as freedom of speech) and with a preference for free trade and markets over protectionism and state regulation of the economy. These became the tenets of what is now known as "classical" liberalism.[10]

As the nineteenth century progressed, classical liberalism attracted criticism from socialists and other radicals, who argued that the freedom sought by liberals was of no benefit to those who were too poor to make use of it. As the Russian writer Nikolai Chernyshevsky (1828–1889) commented, "Liberalism conceives freedom in a very narrow, purely formal way. . . . Neither I nor you, reader, is forbidden to dine off a golden dinner service; unfortunately neither you nor I has or, in all probability, ever will have the means with which to put this refined idea into practice; for this reason I say frankly that I place no value whatever on my right to have a golden dinner service and am ready to sell this right for a silver ruble or less. All those rights for which liberals plead are exactly like that for the common people."[11]

In the face of such criticism, European liberals shifted their position toward a more positive understanding of liberty, arguing that what mattered was not so much freedom "from" as freedom "to," and particularly the freedom for individuals to fulfill their potential. To do this they required assistance from the state, in matters such as education, economic opportunity, and health care.[12] Victorian-era British philosopher T. H. Green (1836–1882) declared that "when we speak of freedom as something to be so highly prized, we mean a positive power or capacity of doing or enjoying something worth doing or enjoying, and that, too, something that we do or enjoy in common with others."[13] Green's views have been described as "social liberalism" (a term occasionally used to describe some post-Soviet Russian liberals) and had a strong influence on what in Britain became known as "New Liberalism," an interventionist philosophy that saw the state as a major provider of social benefits.[14] The boundaries between liberalism and socialism began to blur, especially as the twentieth century progressed and the scale of state intervention in social and economic life grew.

Over time, therefore, liberals became more and more associated with "big government." Old-style classical liberalism did not, however, disappear. During the Cold War, some in the West looked to classical liberalism as a counterweight to communism. Drawing on the ideas of thinkers of the Austrian school of economics such as Friedrich von Hayek (1899–1992) and Ludwig von Mises (1881–1973), neoliberalism (not to be confused with the aforementioned New Liberalism) reaffirmed the value of personal freedom and free markets.[15] By the late twentieth century, the term "liberal" could refer either to supporters of big government or to supporters of limited government, although in political terms these groups stood very much in opposition to one another. European and American understandings of the word also vary: in Europe the emphasis is on free markets, whereas in the United States, "liberal" has become closely associated with support for government intervention, although this distinction is not rigid.

In the past thirty years or so, liberalism has moved in yet another direction, defined by philosopher Charles Taylor as the "politics of difference." Its proponents argue that human dignity requires that the unique identity of the individual be recognized and safeguarded. Since that identity is often connected to membership of a group, safeguarding it may also require recognition of group rights. The focus of this liberalism thus shifted from demanding identical rights for all individuals to accommodating differences. As Taylor puts it, "Where the politics of universal dignity fought for forms of nondiscrimination that were quite 'blind' to the ways in which citizens differ, the politics of difference often redefines nondiscrimination as requiring that we make these distinctions the basis of differential treatment."[16] Seeking accommodation manifests itself in what are commonly called identity politics.[17]

Liberalism has thus changed considerably over the past 200 years. As Rostislav Kapeliushnikov says, the result of this process of change is that "liberalism has long since ceased to be a strictly defined concept with clearly outlined semantic boundaries, and has turned into a bunch of multicolored associations that often have nothing in common with one another. . . . It is appropriate to compare it to a gigantic ship to whose bottom, after long years of sailing, there has stuck an inconceivable quantity of all kinds of odds and ends."[18]

Scholars to date have only partially analyzed the Russian aspect of this story, with some eras of history having attracted far more attention than others. Western historians have focused mainly on the period before the revolutions of 1917.[19] Studies include biographies of leading Imperial Russian liberals, and analyses of certain aspects of liberal thought and of liberal parties and organizations.[20] Some key liberal texts of the era have been translated into English.[21] By contrast, a mere handful of scholars have examined Russian liberalism during the period of the civil war and subsequently in emigration.[22] Likewise, with a few notable exceptions, the reemergence of liberal ideas during the Soviet period has been largely ignored, creating the impression that liberalism appeared fully formed out of nowhere in the late 1980s.[23] Given the weakness of liberalism in contemporary Russia, it has also been deemed not worthy of significant attention from Western scholars, whose focus in recent years has been overwhelmingly on Putin and the system that he leads.[24]

A similar pattern appears in the writings of Russian authors. During the Soviet era, they largely ignored liberalism, but following the collapse of the Soviet Union, Russian scholarship on liberalism of the imperial period exploded, with a vast literature being produced on liberal movements, parties, and personalities.[25] Particularly notable are historians Valentin Shelokhaev (b. 1941) and Aleksei Kara-Murza (b. 1956), who have produced a prodigious number of works on Russian liberalism from the late eighteenth century to the end of the civil war.[26] A small number of authors have continued the story of Russian liberalism into emigration, but the Soviet period is again a relative void.[27]

Consequently, prior to this book there has been no study that examines Russian liberalism as a whole, from its origins in the late eighteenth century through the Soviet era to post-Soviet Russia, including also the interwar Russian emigration. Furthermore, there is no consensus in the existing literature on numerous issues. These include the origins of Russian liberalism; the definition of liberalism, and who and what should be considered liberal in a Russian context; and the relationship of Russian liberalism to Western liberalism.

Following a brief analysis of theories of liberalism, the next chapter addresses these issues in order to set the scene for the ten chapters that follow. Four cover the prerevolutionary era. One examines the revolution and civil war. One looks at the Russian emigration. Two study the Soviet period. And finally, two chapters cover the post-Soviet era. This book thereby provides the first comprehensive survey of Russian liberalism from its origins in the late eighteenth century through to the present day.

CHAPTER 1

Defining Russian Liberalism

Despite the differences between them, there is general agreement that some common thread does unite liberalism's many variations. The intellectual challenge is to identify what this is. This chapter therefore begins with a brief overview of theoretical literature on the general topic of liberalism, before moving on to discuss the specifics of liberalism in Russia.

One may view liberalism as composed of three concentric rings. In the central ring is the person or individual. This focus is not unique to liberalism. Many other political ideologies, as well as religions, give a central importance to the human person. Thus, while it is true that the person is the "foundational liberal principle," this is not sufficient by itself to distinguish liberalism from other doctrines and practices.[1] To do that one must identify other principles that unite the various forms that liberalism has taken and that constitute the unique way in which liberalism considers that the interests of the person should be promoted. These form the second and third rings. In the second are certain principles pertaining to how the interests of the person may best be served. And in the third and outermost ring are the institutions through which these principles are given practical expression. It is not necessary for all of these principles and institutions to be present for somebody or something to be considered liberal. Moreover, different people will attach different meanings and different relative values to the various elements. The result is that different versions of liberalism may appear to be at odds with one another.

Principles

Philosophers disagree on what exact set of principles constitutes liberalism's core. To Adam Gopnik, "The critical liberal words are not *liberty* and *democracy* alone—vital though they are—but also *humanity* and *reform*, *tolerance* and *pluralism*, *self-realization* and *autonomy*."[2] To M. Steven Fish, "individual rights, tolerance and pluralism constitute the hard core."[3] And John Gray says of liberalism that "it is *individualist*, in that it asserts the moral primacy of the person against the claim of any social collectivity; *egalitarian*, in as much as it confers on all men the same moral status . . . *universalist*, affirming the moral unity of the human species . . . and *meliorist* in its affirmation of the corrigibility and improvability of all social arrangements and political institutions."[4]

Edmund Fawcett provides a different list of four "broad ideas" which he claims "have guided liberals in their history," namely "acknowledgment of conflict's inescapability," "distrust of power," "faith in human progress," and "civic respect."[5] By contrast, Michael Freeden identifies seven "core elements" of liberalism—liberty, rationality, individuality, progress, sociability, the general interest, and limited and accountable government—but stresses that "the proportionate weight attached to each of these concepts within the family of liberalisms may differ."[6]

Russian scholars produce even longer lists. According to E. E. Grishnova, liberalism has ten core elements: "the absolute value of the human person," "the autonomous individual will," "the essential rationality and goodwill of mankind," "the existence of definite inalienable human rights," "the creation of the state on the basis of consensus," "the contractual nature of the relationship between the state and the individual," "the supremacy of law," "limitation of the scope and sphere of state action in the name of the free market, free competition and accumulation," "the defense (above all from the state) of peoples' private lives," and "the existence of higher truths of reason which are accessible to the thinking individual."[7] Another Russian scholar gives nine elements of liberalism's "irreducible ideological basis," namely, "the primacy of individual freedom and rationalism," "the priority of the individual over society," "recognition of the fundamental importance of human rights," "a market based on competition and private property," "constitutionalism," "separation of powers," "inviolability of private property," and a "guarantee that citizens' interests will be represented."[8]

These lists often mix together core principles that guide liberals in how they interpret the interests of the person (liberty, equality, and so on) with the institutional manifestations of these principles (such as democracy). They also contain potentially contradictory elements: for instance, universalism and pluralism.

And they are all different. There are, however, some ideas which appear over and over again, most notably liberty, autonomy, equality, pluralism, universalism, progress, and reason.

Liberty and Autonomy

The name "liberalism" derives from liberty, and with that the idea that the interests of the person require the person to be free.[9] Michael Freeden comments, "It is simply unimaginable to entertain, and empirically impossible to find, a variant of liberalism that dispenses with the concept of liberty."[10]

What, then, is meant by liberty? Scholars commonly answer this question by referring to the distinction between negative and positive liberty, between "liberty from" and "liberty to." Negative liberty is "not being interfered with by others."[11] By contrast, positive liberty is more a matter of "self-mastery," or self-realization.[12] The latter is sometimes expressed in terms of "autonomy." The idea is that "what is distinctive and valuable about human life is our capacity to decide for ourselves what is valuable in life, and to shape our lives in accordance with that decision."[13]

In brief, negative liberty consists of "being let alone, not being interfered with,"[14] and positive liberty of "being self-determining, master of one's destiny."[15] Proponents of negative liberty will tend to favor limited government, economic freedoms (such as private property and free markets), and political and civil rights (freedom of speech and association, and so on). By contrast, proponents of positive liberty may put more emphasis on social and economic rights (such as the rights to work and to education).

Equality

Some philosophers prefer to focus on equality. Ronald Dworkin, for instance, maintains that liberals are much more concerned with equality than with liberty.[16] "A certain conception of equality . . . is the nerve of liberalism,"[17] he writes. Paul Kelly similarly comments that political liberalism is "guided by that basic philosophical commitment to equality."[18]

To some extent this is true. All types of liberalism accept in principle (if not always in practice) the idea that all persons are of equal moral value. From this there tends to arise a belief that all citizens should be equal before the law. This, however, is not the same as a belief in equality of outcome. Historically many liberals have been antiegalitarian.[19] Political liberals have often argued that political rights should be confined to those with the property, leisure, or education to make suitable use of them. Economic liberals have also attacked the idea of equality as meaning anything other than equality before the law. As von Hayek writes: "From the fact that people are very different it follows that, if we treat them equally, the result must be inequality in their actual position, and the only way to place them in an equal position would be to treat them differently. Equality before the law and material equality are therefore not only different but are in conflict with one another; and we can achieve either one or the other, but not both at the same time."[20] In theory, therefore, one may say that liberalism contains a commitment to the moral and legal equality of all persons. But what this means in practice is less straightforward.

Pluralism and Universalism

Equality, as Hayek pointed out, can contradict liberty. Two other liberal principles—pluralism and universalism—also appear to contradict one another.

Pluralist liberalism connects with Fawcett's idea of the "acknowledgment of conflict's inescapability." It considers that there is no single "good" toward which all should be aiming, or that if there is, we are not in a position to agree on what it is. Either because diversity is considered desirable in itself, or simply because of the requirement for people with different versions of the good to live in peace together, pluralist liberalism implies tolerance of different beliefs and lifestyles.

By contrast, universalist liberalism endorses the idea that there is a single version of the good that all should in principle follow. John Gray argues that modern Western liberalism has inherited Christianity's "teleological interpretation of history as a process with a preordained destination."[21] This can make it intolerant of alternatives. There is "an imposed, even coercive, consensus in order to ensure that no choice other than liberalism can ever be legitimately and effectively exercised," claims Adrian Pabst. "As such, the notion of illiberal liberalism is not wholly unwarranted."[22]

Progress and Reason

"Liberals," says Gopnik, "believe . . . in reform. But liberals also believe in the *necessity* of reform."[23] As E. M. Spirova writes, liberalism "above all views history as a progressive process that is subject to rational direction. Liberal ideology is infused with a progressivist spirit and is deeply rationalistic. That is to say that it derives from a belief in progress and the power of human reason."[24] This connects to a historical determinism that sees history as marching inevitably toward a universal future, as well as to Gray's idea of meliorism—the concept that human beings and their institutions can be improved through the application of reason.

As with liberalism's other core principles, this is not unique to it. However, the liberal's commitment to change may be seen to differ in some regards from that of others. The conservative wishes to change cautiously and in accordance with existing traditions. The radical wishes to change rapidly in accordance with some abstract ideal. The liberal, by contrast, is said to prefer a middle way between conservatism and radicalism, advancing like the radical in accordance with abstract principles but like the conservative in a gradual, cautious way.[25] While this may be generally true, there are exceptions. Russian liberals of the late 1980s and early 1990s, for instance, rejected gradualism in favor of "shock therapy." Liberals can be revolutionaries.

Institutional Expressions of the Principles

Liberals differ in how they think the principles above should be put into practice. Still, one can identify some institutions that are commonly favored by liberal actors. Several stand out which deserve discussion. These are: private property, free markets and free trade; popular representation and democracy; the rule of law; civil and political rights; economic, social, and cultural rights; and civil society.

Private Property, Free Markets, and Free Trade

Many classical liberals see private property, free markets, and free trade as essential components of a liberal order. "Free markets represent the only non-coercive means of coordinating activity in a complex industrial society," writes Gray; "private property is the embodiment of individual liberty in its most primordial form and market liberties are indivisible components of the basic liberties of the person."[26]

Nevertheless, even the most liberal societies do not regard property rights as absolute, nor is there any society in which markets are entirely free. Every state taxes its citizens to some degree, expropriates private property when necessary for the provision of public goods, and regulates economic activity. The difference between an economically liberal society and an economically non-liberal society is one of degree.

Popular Representation and the Rule of Law

If economic liberalism is associated with private property and free markets, political liberalism is commonly associated with popular representation and the rule of law.

Support for these institutions arose among liberals in the nineteenth century as a means of limiting arbitrary government. As popular representation expanded to include the entire population, liberalism became increasingly associated with democracy, to the extent that many consider liberalism and democracy to be inseparable. As Valentin Shelokhaev puts it, "Liberalism cannot be considered apart from democracy, which is a litmus test for the classification of genuine liberals, one that distinguishes them from para-quasi-pseudo-liberals."[27]

This is too absolute. Liberalism favors democratic government, except when it doesn't. Many nineteenth-century Russian liberals viewed representative institutions with considerable suspicion, and Russia has a strong tradition of conservative liberalism that has supported autocratic rule. Similarly, after the revolutions of 1917, many liberals became fervent advocates of military dictatorship, while in the late 1980s and early 1990s some Russian liberals favored the "Pinochet option"—dictatorship combined with free market reform. One can be an economic liberal but politically illiberal, just as one can be politically liberal but economically not.

Rights

Liberalism is often viewed as a philosophy of rights.[28] These are often divided into two sets: civil and political rights (such as freedom of speech and assembly, and the right to vote); and economic, social, and cultural rights (such as the rights to work, to health care, and to education). Historically, liberalism has tended to be more concerned with the former than the latter. It is no accident that the International Covenant on Civil and Political Rights, which was adopted in 1966, is legally enforceable, whereas the International Covenant on Economic, Social and Cultural Rights, adopted in the same year, is not. It is relatively easy for states to guarantee negative civil and political rights simply by refraining from interfering with them. By contrast, economic, social, and cultural rights are positive rights, which require the state to take action and spend money. Furthermore, many liberals, especially classical economic liberals, have tended to look on social and economic rights as undesirable from the point of view of economic efficiency.

By contrast, socialists have prioritized economic and social rights over civil and political ones. One might say, therefore, that the relative importance given to the different types of rights helps to differentiate liberalism from socialism. On the whole, though, societies that promote economic, social, and cultural rights are seen as more liberal than societies that do not. For instance, a country that prohibits trade unions or limits the right to strike would likely be considered by most observers as less liberal than one that does not. While liberalism may favor civil and political rights, it does not entirely ignore economic, social, and cultural ones.

Civil Society

It is often asserted that liberalism and civil society are mutually dependent. Definitions of civil society range from those including all voluntary activity taking place beyond the control of the state to those including only those actors and activities that are "supportive of liberalism."[29] With regard to Russia, the latter definition leads to a tendency "to equate Russia's civil society with the liberal opposition to Putin's government."[30]

Civil society is not, however, necessarily liberal, let alone oppositional. Much charitable and other voluntary activity is apolitical, and those involved may even be illiberal in their attitudes. While the first definition above is overly broad, the second is too limited. Nevertheless, the various definitions share a core understanding, namely that there is a realm of activity that is neither that of the state nor of commercial enterprise, an independent sector in which citizens can organize themselves (sometimes referred to as the "third sector" operating between the state and the market).[31]

Civil society is said to "support liberalism" for two main reasons. First, it helps to limit government and to hold it to account, bringing to light abuses of authority through a free press, human rights organizations, and so on.[32] Second, it helps to inculcate in the population the kind of values and political and legal culture required to sustain a liberal order.[33] In the Russian instance, the fact that the Soviet government brought most forms of communal activity under the control of the Communist Party has persuaded those seeking to promote liberalism and democracy in postcommunist Russia that the creation of a powerful, and liberal, civil society is a priority.

Approaching Russian Liberalism

Historians disagree about the starting point of Russian liberalism.[34] A common thesis proposes that liberalism emerged in Russia in the late eighteenth century during the era of Catherine II.[35] The most often cited proof is the *Instruction* (*Nakaz*) issued by Catherine for the Legislative Commission that she summoned in 1767, but reference is also commonly made to the writings of men such as Aleksandr Radishchev (1749–1802) and Nikolai Novikov (1744–1818) during Catherine's reign.[36] The ideas of liberalism are thus seen as predating the appearance of liberalism as a political movement by some time.[37]

Other historians place the origins of Russian liberalism later. Julia Berest argues that the beginnings of Russian liberalism "should be sought in the early decades of the nineteenth century, when legal education and especially courses in natural law awoke many Russians to the notions of civil and political rights."[38] But while liberal ideas were beginning to emerge in this period, historians note that these ideas came together to form a program for political and social change only from the mid-1850s onward.[39]

Even this is too early for some historians, who argue that it is almost impossible to find anybody in Russia who could properly be labeled liberal until the late nineteenth or even early twentieth century.[40] Vanessa Rampton, for instance, claims that it was not until 1900 "that a self-consciously liberal movement took shape," and says that, "prior to the early twentieth century, there was not a definite form of liberalism in Russia, only a set of philosophical ruminations about freedom that recognized the conflict between rights."[41]

One way to resolve these differences is to divide Russian liberalism into various periods, each with its own variety of liberalism. Russian historians see prerevolutionary liberalism as breaking into three such periods. The first runs from the late eighteenth century through to the mid-1850s. This era saw the gradual emergence of liberal ideas and coincided with a form of enlightened autocracy in which Russia's rulers put some of these ideas into practice. The second period lasted from the mid-nineteenth century through to the 1890s, an era that witnessed the gradual development of a liberal political movement. And the third period, from the 1890s through to 1917, saw liberals moving into direct opposition to the Russian autocracy.[42]

This periodization stops at 1917. Few scholars have tried to take it further. One exception is Andrei Medushevsky, who divides the history of Russian liberalism into five periods. According to his scheme, the first period lasted until 1917, during which time liberals' primary concern was to Europeanize Russia. The second was the period of the interwar Russian emigration, which involved "a rethinking of the entire liberal program." The third spanned the Cold War years and involved a "critical analysis of the liberal tradition" to see whether the Soviet Union could be reformed in a liberal direction. The fourth period was the final years of the Soviet Union and the early years of post-Soviet Russia. This era witnessed a "romantic interpretation of liberalism" that abandoned the traditions of Imperial Russian liberalism in favor of Western economic neoliberalism. And the fifth and current stage has seen a "correction of the ideas of the liberal model in the post-Soviet period," in light of the perceived failures of Russian liberalism in the 1990s.[43]

Another point of disagreement is which people, organizations, and policies in Russian history deserve the label liberal. The problem is complicated by the fact that Russian liberals have often preferred to call themselves by other names. For instance, in the late Imperial period they tended to use the title "constitutionalists" or referred to themselves as "society" (*obshchestvo*), while in the late Soviet and post-Soviet eras they have preferred the moniker "democrats."[44]

One way of deciding whom to designate as "liberal" is to follow John Gray's idea that liberalism is an "integral outlook," and that it is possible to identify a set of core features, all of which must be present for someone or something to be liberal.[45] If one takes this line, then the obvious approach for a study such as this is to include only those people, arguments, and policies that can be shown to display the core features in question.

An alternative approach is that taken by Michael Freeden, who argues that the various layers of liberalism are in "a constant state of mutual arrangement," producing "continuously fluctuating combinations," and sometimes pulling people in "irreconcilable directions."[46] For this reason, it is probably a mistake to speak of liberalism, in the singular. The best one can do is speak of liberalisms, plural, that are "all part of a broad family exhibiting both similarities and differences."[47] Duncan Bell, meanwhile, argues that the liberal family has grown so broad that all one can truly say is that "the liberal tradition is constituted by *the sum of the arguments that have been classified as liberal, and recognised as such by other self-proclaimed liberals, across time and space.*"[48] In essence, liberalism is whatever people who have called themselves liberals have said it is. If one follows this line, one would include in a study of liberalism those people, arguments, and policies that have previously been identified, or have self-identified, as liberal. From that, one could draw a definition of liberalism. In this second approach, the study ends with a definition rather than begins with one.

The first approach has the benefit of consistency. However, it excludes many things that would be considered liberal were another list of core features chosen, and excludes everything that is only partially liberal. This is the approach taken by many historians of Russian liberalism, and it has had some perverse consequences.

A notable example is Victor Leontovitsch's book *The History of Liberalism in Russia*, which examines the topic from the reign of Catherine II up to 1917. Leontovitsch declares, "[I] regard conservative liberalism as true liberalism."[49] This belief leads him to make what many might consider to be strange decisions as to who and what is liberal in Russian history. For instance, according to Leontovitsch, historian Nikolai Karamzin (1766–1826), often considered one of the founding figures of Russian conservatism, was a liberal.[50] By contrast, Leontovitsch claims that the Constitutional Democratic (Kadet) Party, normally considered the archetypal liberal organization, was not.[51]

Other commentators have similarly sought to rewrite the canon of Russian liberalism. Aileen Kelly, for instance, argues that Boris Chicherin (1828–1904), who is normally considered one of the central figures in the history of Russian liberalism, does not deserve the liberal label.[52] On the other hand, she considers that populist thinker Aleksandr Herzen (1812–1870), generally considered a radical, does merit it.[53] Similarly, Daniel Field argues that Konstantin Kavelin (1818–1885), like Chicherin usually considered a key personality in Russian liberal history, was in fact not a liberal at all.[54]

These differing conclusions flow naturally from the different definitions of liberalism chosen by the authors in question. So too do the conclusions of modern Russian historians. Perhaps out of a sensitivity to the complaint that liberalism is a Western import without deep roots in Russian society, Russian scholars have sought to expand the definition of liberalism to include as large a group of people and ideas as possible. To this end, they start with the person (*lichnost'*) as the focus of liberal thought, and stress the principle of personal freedom.[55] "The problem of the status of the Person is the central problem of liberalism," writes Shelokhaev, adding that liberalism's aim is to maximize peoples' ability to fulfill their potential.[56] "Liberalism in all its manifestations is a doctrine defending the freedom of the person," agree Lidiia Novikova and Irina Sizemskaia.[57]

With the definition of liberalism limited largely to the person and to personal freedom, the door is open to include within the parameters of Russian liberalism a huge spectrum of people and ideas. Anybody who was, or is, in some way committed to the value of the person and personal freedom fits within the definition. This is the case even if they imagined that the interests of the person could best be served by the application of principles and institutions other than those mentioned above. Aleksei Kara-Murza's huge encyclopedia of Russian liberal "Ideas and People" contains biographies of a vast range of figures, including some usually considered deeply conservative (such as Karamzin and the journalist Mikhail Katkov [1818–1897]); Slavophiles (such as Ivan Aksakov [1823–1886]); radicals and revolutionaries (such as Herzen); bureaucrats (such as Nikolai and Dmitry Miliutin [1818–1872 and 1816–1912, respectively]); and others whom one might more obviously expect to find in a list of Russian liberals (such as certain members of the Kadet Party).[58] What they all have in common beyond some vaguely defined commitment to personal freedom is not obvious.

In brief, much of the literature on Russian liberalism suffers from the manner in which it adopts the first approach mentioned above—that is to say, starting with a narrow definition of liberalism and working from there. The second approach above has the advantage of accepting liberalism's complexities. It allows one to examine liberalism through "a description of its historical manifestations" rather than by reference to theory.[59] Consequently, it is this approach that this study will adopt. In line with Bell's definition, the book will examine both actors who have self-identified as liberal and ideas and policies that have been widely recognized as liberal, even when those putting them forward would not have considered themselves liberal or have been recognized as such by others. The latter includes, for instance, so-called enlightened bureaucrats—that is to say, state officials who have promoted liberal policies for reasons that have often had little or nothing to do with liberal theory.

By taking this approach, the book adopts Freeden's concept of a family of liberalisms. In so doing it avoids limiting the study to those who seem to suit a single narrow definition of liberalism. Instead, it includes a broad mixture of actors, ideas, and policies which fit in some way within the overall "family." In the process, it illustrates the decided complexities and contradictions within Russian liberalism, as well as its national peculiarities.

The National Peculiarities of Russian Liberalism

The identification of the values and institutions of liberalism mentioned above has come almost entirely from studies of Western European and North American liberalism. It is a matter of dispute among historians of Russian liberalism whether there is such a thing as "Russian" liberalism which is distinct from its Western counterpart. A common complaint raised against Russian liberalism is that it has been imposed "from above without taking into account national peculiarities."[60] Russian liberalism has been described as "a copy" of Western liberalism that is fundamentally "un-Russian."[61] Russian liberalism, according to this view, is not and never has been "an indigenous creed in Russia," but rather has been thoroughly "derivative in nature."[62]

Perhaps aware that this line of argument can be used to politically delegitimize liberalism in their country, many modern Russian scholars reject the idea that Russian liberalism is a Western import, claiming that Russia "has given birth to its own national versions of liberalism."[63] Russian liberalism is not "a Western European surrogate" but a truly "Russian child," says Shelokhaev. From the very start, he claims, Russian liberals understood that Western ideas could not be transplanted to Russia and thus Russian liberalism always had a national character.[64] From this Shelokhaev concludes that, "the typology used to study West European liberalism is hardly applicable to Russian liberalism."[65]

Some Western historians agree. Writing of the late nineteenth and early twentieth centuries, Vanessa Rampton notes that "if one defines liberalism as

a list of characteristics derived from Western experience . . . it is next to impossible to find any recognizable Russian liberals."[66] Alfred Rieber similarly argues that "the language of politics spoken in nineteenth-century Russia and
subsequently adopted by most historians is borrowed from the West European
experience. In the Russian context the terminology is confusing, misleading,
and politically highly charged. . . . Linguistically and structurally, the Russian
political scene requires a different vocabulary."[67]

It serves the interests of contemporary Russian liberals to paint themselves as
the heirs of a long, native tradition. But the extent to which Russian liberalism
truly is distinct from that of the West is debatable. Consequently, this will be one
of the issues addressed in the pages that follow through an analysis of various
types of liberal thought and practice, namely cultural liberalism, political liberalism, and social-economic liberalism. The three categories on occasion overlap.
Issues of nationalism, for instance, fit within both cultural liberalism and political liberalism. Nevertheless, distinguishing between the categories makes it possible to clearly compare how Russian thinkers have addressed similar problems
in different time periods. The sections on cultural liberalism examine issues such
as liberals' understanding of the nation and of Russia's relationship with the
West. These in turn connect to issues such as liberals' sense of progress, universalism, and historical determinism. In these ways, cultural liberalism to some
degree coincides with the second ring in the model of liberalism above. By contrast, the categories of political and economic liberalism fit more closely in the
third ring; that is to say, they relate to issues of political and economic institutions, such as democracy, the rule of law, and free markets.

Cultural Liberalism

In Western Europe, the rise of liberalism was associated with the development
of capitalism and the growth of a large and powerful bourgeois class. In the
Soviet Union, historians adopted this model in their analyses of Russian liberalism, and viewed it as a class-based ideology, representing the interests of the
bourgeoisie.[68] This line of argument has mostly been abandoned by Russian
and Western analysts in the post-Soviet era. Liberal ideas arrived in Russia at
a time when a capitalist bourgeoisie was largely absent. Consequently, says
Greg Gaut, Russian liberalism developed in "its own unique way," producing
a "different kind of liberalism with a different social base," with liberalism
emerging as "a movement of ideas rather than commercial self-interest."[69]

Prerevolutionary Russian liberalism is nowadays generally seen as having
been the purview of a relatively small layer of Westernized noblemen and professionals, notably lawyers and university professors.[70] As the leader of the

liberal Kadet party, Pavel Miliukov (1859–1943), put it, "Russian liberalism was not *bourgeois*, but *intellectual*."[71] A similar dynamic has persisted in later periods. In the Soviet Union, liberal modes of thinking were associated primarily with a narrow elite within the scientific community (referred to as the "technical intelligentsia").[72] Nowadays they are commonly associated with urban professionals, or what are sometimes called the "creative classes" (*kreativnye klassy* in Russian, giving rise to the disparaging term *"kreakly"*).

Several features unite these various groups through time. The first, as Gaut notes, is a lack of clearly defined commercial interests. With certain important exceptions, this has often induced liberals to prioritize cultural and political concerns over economic ones. Second, Russian liberalism has been a decidedly elite phenomenon with few connections with the mass of the Russian people. As such it has very much reflected the culture of that elite.

This culture has been oriented toward the West. It has also tended to be positivist and rationalist in outlook. As this book shows, this outlook has produced a view of human society as driven by scientifically determinable rules, and of history as an inexorable process toward a known end—a liberal society in line with Western models.

Consequently, Russian liberalism has been, and still is, as much a cultural as a political or socioeconomic phenomenon. Its aim is to culturally transform Russia to make it what is often called a "normal" country, by which is meant a Western one. Liberalism in a Russian context is closely associated with the concept of Westernization. It is a common liberal theme that Russia is deficient compared to the West (however defined) and needs to reform itself to more closely emulate the Western ideal. "The Russian liberal is a thoughtless fly buzzing in the ray of the sun; that sun is the sun of the West," said Pyotr Chaadaev (1794–1856) in the early nineteenth century.[73] Similar criticisms can be heard today.

The idea that the West represents an ideal whose norms all other civilizations should adopt is reinforced by a historical determinism which regards Westernization as an inevitable process. As Miliukov puts it, "The Europeanization of Russia is not a product of adoption but an inevitable consequence of inner evolution, which is basically the same in Europe and in Russia."[74] "National self-consciousness clings to particular features of national existence, such as dress, dwelling, social habits, political institutions, and old forms of the popular creed. But in the long run these features cannot be preserved."[75] In this vision, Russia is destined to merge with the West, and anything that stands in the way of this convergence should be removed.

A certain contradiction lies within this attitude. On the one hand, it rests on a belief that Russia and the West are not fundamentally different. On the other hand, the very idea of Westernization implies that Russia *is* different, that Russia isn't Western but that it *ought* to be. This "ought" has been a driving force of Russian liberalism throughout its history.

The wish to combat the efforts of Russian conservatives to associate the Russian nation with the Orthodox church, "traditional values," and the autocracy (or later communism), has forced Russian liberals to create a different form of nationalism resting on different values and institutions. This has taken a variety of forms, including civic nationalism, ethnonationalism, and imperialism. It has therefore been said that "during the most influential periods in the history of Russian liberalism, nationalism and/or imperialism were fundamental to the liberal project. . . . The history of Russian liberalism is, therefore, in many ways a history of state and nation-building."[76]

Nevertheless, many critics of Russian liberalism have agreed with the philosopher Nikolai Berdiaev (1874–1948) that "the national idea lacks deep roots in Russian liberalism; for the mass of Russia liberals, patriotism is a question of political tactics."[77] The close association of Russian liberalism with Westernization leads to charges that Russian liberals lack patriotic feeling. For though they may love Russia in the abstract, their desire to change it into something different suggests that they dislike it as it actually is. There is a strong "perception that liberal principles are antithetical to Russian national interests and a cohesive national identity."[78] Whereas so-called national liberalism acquired significant support in some nineteenth-century European states, such as Germany, it has never gained great traction in Russia (apart perhaps from a short period in the early twentieth century—see chapters 5 and 6). Arguably, this has greatly weakened liberalism's political appeal.

Allied to the idea that liberals do not like the Russian reality is a belief that they do not much like the Russian people either. Liberals have sometimes adopted a manner that could be called "condescending" or "patriarchal," looking down on the people as needing the guidance of the intelligentsia to raise them up from their cultural inferiority.[79] In its worst manifestations, this attitude has taken the form of contempt of the people, who have been seen as lacking education and a proper understanding of freedom. As we shall see in the final chapter of this book, many modern liberals view their country's problems as lying in the alleged psychological failings of the masses. Liberalism's task is seen as developing a new culture that will make the people suited for a liberal order.

Various approaches have been taken to this problem. One is educational— the spread of education is seen as essential for the development of an appropriate culture. Another involves supplanting one set of cultural symbols with another (in modern times, this involves debates around decommunization).

And yet another is institutional. This last approach advances from a belief that institutions shape culture, and that what has held the people back are the repressive social and political institutions of the existing system. This implies, therefore, that political reform is essential for the country's cultural progress.

Political Liberalism

Russian liberals' complex relationship with the Russian people has led to an equally complex relationship with the state and the idea of political reform. On the one hand, the liberal commitment to freedom has led many liberals to endorse the idea of a democratic order. On the other hand, a fear of the mob and a belief that the people lack the appropriate culture to sustain a democratic order has led others to view democracy with skepticism and even to prefer authoritarian government.

Roughly speaking, one can split Russian political liberalism into two main streams—radical liberalism and conservative liberalism. The former has sought, and still seeks, to radically transform, or even overthrow, the existing system. The latter prefers to work with it and within it and to enact change gradually.

In this way, the two streams differ in their attitude to the existing form of the state. Overall, though, they differ little in their view of the state per se. Russian liberals have rarely shared classical liberalism's distrust of the state, but instead have looked to the state as the means by which liberal reform will be carried out. Furthermore, liberals have also generally supported the Russian model of a highly centralized system of authority, with power concentrated in the hands of the executive branch of government, be that the tsarist autocracy or the 1993 Constitution of the Russian Federation. Overall, Russian liberalism is considered to have a "statist orientation."[80]

Liberal reforms in Russia have more often been carried out from above by rulers who have recognized their utility than forced on those rulers by pressure from below.[81] In this way, liberal ideas have often been used for "a function that was not natural to them."[82] Liberal ideology and liberal practice are not the same.

As well as believing in a strong state and centralized authority, Russian liberals have also been firm supporters of what is often referred to as a "law-based" state. Referring to the Imperial period, Andrzej Walicki states that "the main concern of Russian liberal thinkers was the problem of the rule of law, and the most precious legacy of Russian liberalism was precisely its contribution to the philosophy of law."[83] Law, says Walicki, was "the core value in the liberal view of the world. . . . It is no exaggeration to say that the entire history of liberal thought in Russia revolved around the problem of the rule of law and the rule-of-law state."[84]

Marc Raeff notes, however, that the establishment of the rule of law in the Western sense has been impossible within the confines of the existing political order, given its rejection by successive rulers. Consequently, "introduction of real legality could only mean the overthrow of the existing regime." This has resulted in a "blurring of the line between radicalism and liberalism."[85]

Social-Economic Liberalism

Unlike Russian political liberalism, Russian economic liberalism has been little studied.[86] This may well be because, with the exception of the early 1990s, the economic aspect of Russian liberalism has generally been of lesser importance than the cultural and political ones, perhaps because Russian liberalism has not been strongly rooted in economic interests.

Nevertheless, Russian liberals have not neglected social and economic questions. Imperial Russia and the interwar emigration contained classical free market liberals such as Boris Chicherin and Boris Brutskus (1874–1938), as well as those who supported an approach to economic and social issues that bears some resemblance to the English New Liberalism mentioned above. In Soviet times, a slightly different dynamic prevailed, in that liberal-minded intellectuals remained wedded to communist ideas of social justice. The "technical intelligentsia" mentioned above preferred to think in terms of adjusting the socialist economy rather than replacing it.

This changed in the final years of the Soviet Union and in the immediate post-Soviet period. The radical liberal reformers of that era have been accused of putting economic concerns above all else,[87] reversing earlier priorities. For a brief while, economic liberalism trumped political liberalism. Since then, there has been some adjustment. As we shall see, some contemporary liberals remain wedded to the free market model, while others have adopted a more social-democratic one.

At the heart of liberalism lies the concept of the person. Beyond that, liberalism rests on a mixture of principles such as liberty and equality that are given expression in a variety of institutions such as private property, representative government, and human rights legislation. None of these elements can alone be said to constitute liberalism's essential core. Moreover, the elements can contradict one another, and it is rare to find them all combined in one person, one political doctrine, or one political practice.

This is as true in Russia as anywhere else. As Riccardo Cucciolla comments, "In Russia, there is no universal paradigm of liberalism and it has taken the form of monist radicalism in certain periods and of moderate pluralism in others . . . economic and political liberalism often appeared disjointed or in opposition to each other."[88] In this way, it resembles liberalism in general. There are many Russian liberalisms—nationalist and antinationalist; democratic and authoritarian; free market and interventionist; and so on. No single one can be said to be Russian liberalism, but together they form a single family, which in some ways resembles Western liberalism and in some ways does not. The commonalities and contradictions within this family are explored in the chapters that follow.

CHAPTER 2

Early Russian Liberalism

The history of Russian liberalism begins in the second half of the eighteenth century, during the reign of Catherine II (reigned 1762–1796), when Enlightenment ideas of reason and progress made their way into Russia. Freemasonry also arrived in Russia, bringing with it humanist ideas about the innate dignity of the human person. It is estimated that there were at least 2,500 Freemasons in Russia during Catherine's reign.[1] These included some of the people of the highest rank in the nation, most notably Catherine's foreign minister, Nikita Panin (1718–1783), and her personal secretary and director of court theater, Ivan Elagin (1725–1794). Russian nobles began to talk and think about natural law, a constitutional order, and the rights of the person.[2] Thereafter, liberalism developed in fits and starts as Russian rulers swung back and forth between reform and reaction.

Catherine's reign was typical in this regard. In its early years, Enlightenment thinking appeared to be ascendant. An example is Catherine's *Instruction* to the Legislative Commission that she summoned in 1767. The *Instruction* has been described as "the first official proclamation of human rights . . . not only in Russia, but in Europe as a whole."[3] The commission was suspended without completing its work, but it did induce a flourishing of intellectual activity, as shown in the writings of authors such as Semyon Desnitsky (1740–1789), Nikolai Novikov, and Aleksandr Radishchev. Before too long, though, political threats to Catherine's rule persuaded her to change tack. First, her position was shaken by a major peasant rebellion known as the Pugachev Revolt, which lasted from 1773 to 1775. Second, the French Revolution, which broke out in 1789, created the danger of the spread of revolutionary ideas into Russia. Catherine turned in a more conservative direction.

The reign of Alexander I (1801–1825) followed a similar pattern. After ascending the throne, Alexander formed an "unofficial committee" of himself and close friends to examine the possibility of reform. It produced few results. Next, Alexander asked his state secretary, Mikhail Speransky (1772–1839), to produce a program to restructure the system of government, but only some elements of it were instituted. A key turning point was the French invasion of Russia in 1812 and the subsequent war that ended with Russian troops marching into Paris in 1814. The war helped to create a more conservative political atmosphere in Russia. Nevertheless, Alexander's reign did see some of the first efforts to bring constitutional government to Russia. These included the granting of a constitution to the Kingdom of Poland in 1815 and the drafting of a constitution for the Russian Empire (which was never enacted) in 1819.

In 1825, Alexander died without legitimate issue. His younger brother Constantine had renounced his claim to the throne some years earlier, although this was not widely known. The crown passed to another brother, Nicholas I (reigned 1825–1855). Nicholas was unpopular with some elements of the Russian officer corps, who launched an abortive coup, known as the Decembrist Revolt. The Decembrists were divided into two groups—the Northern Society and the Southern Society. Many members of both groups had served in the Russian army in its campaigns against France. Despite its failure, the revolt is considered by many to have been an important stage in the history of Russian liberalism.

The subsequent years of Nicholas's reign are often portrayed as a period of darkest reaction. Nevertheless, some historians date Russian liberalism's origins to this period. Russia's first law faculties were opened, producing a new generation of Russians committed to the idea of the rule of law. This was a period of considerable intellectual debates, the most famous being the dispute between the Westernizers and the Slavophiles. Westernizers such as Moscow University's Timofei Granovsky (1813–1855) played an important role in propagating ideas that would be central to later Russian liberalism.

It would be hard to identify any single person or set of ideas in this period as liberal in the sense of combining all the elements of the model presented in chapter 1. Different aspects of liberalism emerged bit by bit, mixing with other practices and modes of thoughts. Nevertheless, it was in this era that the foundations of Russian liberalism were laid.

Cultural Liberalism

In the late eighteenth and early nineteenth centuries, Russian thinkers began to work out what one might call a liberal theory of Russian nationhood. In this, the nation consisted of free individuals bound together by common institutions rather than ethnicity or culture. It was believed that Russia had yet to develop into a nation of this sort but was destined to do so in line with the logic of history displayed in the West.

An early example is the writing of Radishchev, best known for his 1790 book *Journey from St. Petersburg to Moscow.* Andrzej Walicki notes that "Radishchev had a wholly rationalist and nominalist view of the nation as a 'collection of citizens' rather than a super-individual whole endowed with a 'collective soul.'"[4] Influenced by social contract theory, Radishchev described the nation as "a collection of individuals [who] have come together in order to safeguard their interests. . . . Since all men, however, are by nature free . . . the setting up of society always assumes real or tacit agreement."[5]

The Decembrists of the early 1820s held a somewhat similar view. According to Susana Rabow-Edling, the Decembrists advocated a "civic form of nationalism, as seen in their vision of a political community of equal rights-bearing citizens."[6] Their attitude was well expressed by the economist Nikolai Turgenev (1789–1871), who supported the Decembrist Revolt but was out of the country when it happened and so avoided arrest. "If one were to ask in which direction the Russian people is destined to march, I would say that the question has already been answered: it must march towards European civilization," Turgenev wrote.[7]

Speaking to interrogators after their failed coup, many Decembrists spoke of the Western inspiration for their rebellion. "I was first infected by liberal ideas during the campaigns in France," said one Decembrist, Kondraty Ryleev (1795–1826).[8] "I acquired my insane liberal ideas during my stay in foreign countries . . . that is, during and after the war of 1813–14," said another, Aleksandr Muravyov (1793–1862).[9] "The first notions of free thought and liberalism I acquired during our stay in Paris in 1814," said a third, Matvei Muravyov-Apostol (1793–1886).[10]

Though united in their Westernism, the Decembrists differed on how to govern a multiethnic, multicultural society and proposed two models—federative and unitary. In his *Project for a Constitution*, Nikita Muravyov (1796–1843) of the Northern Society called for the establishment of a federal system.[11] By contrast, Pavel Pestel (1793–1826) wrote in his manifesto for the Southern Society, entitled *Russian Law*, that "races which because of their weakness are subject to a larger state . . . may not invoke the right to nationhood, for in their case it is fictitious and nonexisting." The peoples of the Russian Empire, he said, "will never be able to constitute separate states. . . . The Russian state is one and indivisible."[12] A federal structure, wrote Pestel, would inevitably result in the empire splitting apart, and so would be "utterly ruinous and wholly evil."[13]

During the reign of Nicholas I, the initiative in creating a liberal notion of Russian nationhood passed to historians. While conservative historians such as Mikhail Pogodin (1800–1875) sought to display Russia as having followed a line of historical development distinct from Western Europe, Westernizers endeavored to show Russia as subject to the same historical rules and heading in the same inevitable direction as the West.

Particularly notable was Timofei Granovsky, a professor of history at Moscow University who delivered an influential series of lectures in the 1840s. Granovsky, influenced by Hegel, viewed history, in the words of his biographer Priscilla Roosevelt, as "purposeful and progressive, constantly moving forward towards a more rational future for mankind."[14] Granovsky associated this future with the development of the state.[15] Drawing on the example of Western Europe, he argued that new social forms inevitably replace old ones in a progressive process, leading eventually to the liberation of the person.[16] This law of history applied equally to Russia and the West. Granovsky remarked: "The masses, like nature or the Scandinavian god Thor, are thoughtless or thoughtlessly good-natured. They become apathetic under the burden of historical and natural determination that only the thinking individual can throw off. This individualization of the masses through the power of ideas is the essence of historical progress. The goal of history is the moral, enlightened individual, emancipated from the fatalistic pressure of external determinations."[17]

Granovsky's statement succinctly summarizes what has been a common liberal view of the people. While liberals have sought to develop the "moral, enlightened individual," their desire to do so reflects a belief that the masses are in need of cultivation. Granovsky was concerned that, as he put it, "the victory of the masses would bring about the destruction of the best fruits of civilization."[18] This was far from a unique position among Westernizers.

Granovsky established close links with officials in the imperial administration and had a strong influence on many of his colleagues and students, most notably Konstantin Kavelin. In 1847 Kavelin produced an essay entitled "A Brief Survey of Juridical Relations in Ancient Russia," which has been described as "one of the defining statements of Russian Westernism."[19]

Kavelin argued that Russian history passed through various stages—communal, tribal, and family—before reaching the era of the state. In the earlier stages, he wrote, "the principle of personality [*lichnost'*] did not exist." Strong blood ties meant that people did not distinguish between themselves and others.[20] History involved the gradual development of the principle of personality. Kavelin wrote: "Personhood, recognizing its own endless unconditional worth, is the essential condition for the spiritual development of the people. . . . This defines the law of development of our inner life. It must consist of a gradual education and appearance of the principle of personality, and so also a gradual negation of the exclusive blood tie in which personhood cannot exist."[21]

Kavelin rejected the idea of an eternal Russian nature that was distinct from that of the rest of Europe. "Our history consists of a gradual *changing* of forms, and not of their repetition," he wrote. "In this sense we are a European people, capable of perfection and of development."[22] "The difference [between the West and Russia] lies solely in the preceding historical facts; the aim, the task, the aspirations, the way forward are one and the same," said Kavelin.[23] Whatever Russia's past differences from the West, its future lay in the same direction.

Political Liberalism

Catherine II's *Instruction* has been described as promising "to turn Russia into a law-abiding state that would respect the natural rights of all." Some historians claim that Catherine's commitment to the "principles of liberalism" was sincere, and that the *Instruction* "opened the doors in Russia to the liberal ideas of the European Enlightenment."[24] Others are more circumspect. Marc Raeff, for instance, accuses Catherine of only toying with liberalism, and dismisses the *Instruction* as "mere window dressing and propaganda."[25]

In the *Instruction*, Catherine stated that the government should not "take away the natural liberty of subjects."[26] Gary Hamburg comments that Catherine understood liberty as involving "obedience of conscience" and of the law.[27] The *Instruction* stated that "liberty cannot consist in anything but the possibility to do what one ought to do and in not being forced to do what one should do," and that "liberty is the right to do everything that the law allows."[28] Hamburg concludes that this circumscribed view of liberty "reduced it to the 'natural liberty' to act in the common interest, and thus to obedience to the state whose task it was to defend that common interest."[29]

Catherine was rather less of a liberal than her supporters maintain. Nevertheless, her *Instruction* did provide an impetus to Russians to come forward with ideas which might more properly merit the liberal label. An example was a statement sent to the Legislative Commission by a professor at Moscow University,

Semyon Desnitsky, whom Walicki calls "probably the most outstanding and perhaps also the most original Enlightenment thinker of his generation."[30]

Desnitsky's "Proposal on the Establishment of Legislative, Judicial, and Executive Authority in the Russian Empire" recommended the establishment of a permanent advisory body, the Senate, that was to be elected by landowners, merchants, artisans, and teachers in higher educational institutions.[31] The Senate was to draft legislation that would be passed to the empress for approval. Desnitsky proposed the introduction of jury trials and suggested that judges be appointed for life.[32] As Desnitsky's Senate was to be advisory only, his proposal left the absolute monarchy in theory intact. Nevertheless, it represented an attempt to blend elements of Russian absolutism with liberal institutions such as representative government.

Desnitsky also promoted the concept of natural rights, arguing in a 1768 lecture that justice required recognition of such rights.[33] Among others who popularized the idea of natural rights in Catherine's reign was Nikolai Novikov, best known as a publisher of satirical journals. Strongly influenced by Freemasonry, Novikov published in 1777 an article entitled "On Human Dignity in Relation to God and the World." In this he argued that all humans, regardless of their social status, deserved to be treated with respect as they were all God's creations.[34] Although Catherine tolerated Novikov for a while, in 1785 she ordered his arrest. He remained in prison until after Catherine's death.

More extreme than Novikov was Aleksandr Radishchev, whose status in the canon of Russian liberalism is disputed. Some historians consider Radishchev a radical. Others disagree. Gary Hamburg, for instance, says that "it is also possible to classify him [Radishchev] as a would-be reformist, or perhaps even a proto-liberal."[35] Indeed, Radishchev's book *Journey from St. Petersburg to Moscow* has been described as "one of the classics of Russian liberal thought."[36] According to the Kadet party leader Pavel Miliukov, it contained "the first political program of Russian liberalism. . . . In the book of Radishchev Russian liberalism thus came of age."[37]

Radishchev described autocracy as "the condition most repugnant to human nature."[38] Hamburg notes that "Radishchev's doctrine of resistance to tyranny did not constitute advocacy of armed revolution," but also remarks that his ideas "seemed to point toward the possibility of revolution."[39] Radishchev's protoliberalism can be seen in his support for natural law as well as his belief in the natural equality of all people. Like Novikov, Radishchev fell foul of the empress, and was exiled to Siberia. Released by the emperor Paul, he committed suicide in 1802.

Alexander I's ascent to the throne in 1801 opened up opportunities for reform in Russia. Alexander had received a liberal education courtesy of his

French tutor Frédéric-César de La Harpe (1754–1838). In 1797, he wrote to La Harpe, "Once my turn comes, it will be necessary to work, little by little, to achieve a national representation that will be directed to make a free constitution, after which my power will cease absolutely."[40] Reality proved to be rather different.

On becoming emperor, Alexander announced an amnesty for political prisoners and entrusted Aleksandr Vorontsov (1741–1805) with drafting a Charter Addressed to the Russian People, to be modeled on the French Declaration of the Rights of Man. On receiving the draft, however, Alexander got cold feet. Surrendering his power proved less attractive in practice than in theory. The charter was never published.[41]

Instead, Alexander established the "unofficial committee," to which various reform proposals were submitted. Some of these proposals suggested the creation of an elected assembly.[42] The committee rejected them. W. Bruce Lincoln notes that Alexander and his friends on the committee "embodied both authoritarian and libertarian elements," and that although they spoke in the language of Western liberalism, they "gave these terms meaning in the context of Russian, not European, experience." For instance, they viewed the separation of powers not as a means of restricting the power of the executive but as a means "of achieving an efficient state administration."[43] The committee limited itself to approving minor administrative changes.

Alexander did not entirely drop the idea of reform. He instructed Mikhail Speransky to draw up a plan to restructure the Russian government. Speransky worked from the assumption that nations developed in a consistent pattern, with the institutions of state evolving to fit changing social and economic conditions. In his view, Russia lagged behind Europe in adapting its institutions, and needed to reform them so that they better matched its level of development.[44] In this sense his views fitted well with the concept of historical determinism discussed in the previous section, and his aim can be seen as "bring[ing Russia] closer to the European model."[45]

In 1809 Speransky presented the emperor with a plan that would have created an indirectly elected legislative assembly, the State Duma, based on a property franchise. This was to be an entirely advisory body, able to present petitions to the emperor but not to initiate legislation. Speransky also proposed judicial reform, suggesting that the Duma elect juries to try cases, in this way separating the judiciary from the executive branch of government. The executive, legislative, and judicial branches of government would be united at the top in the person of the emperor, supported by a second, appointed, advisory chamber, the State Council.[46] Receiving these proposals, Alexander once again balked, and rejected most of them. Only the State Council was ever instituted.

Speransky differentiated between civil liberties (such as freedom of speech) and political ones (such as the right to vote), and envisioned a form of enlightened autocracy that guaranteed the former but not the latter.[47] Marc Raeff concludes that Speransky's' reforms "should not be construed as implying a liberal and constitutional orientation of [Russia's] government."[48] "Speransky was basically conservative."[49] Other historians assess Speransky's proposals differently. Marie-Pierre Rey agrees that "there was no question of installing in Russia a constitutional government," but argues that "Speransky wished to implement a system that was liberal in inspiration . . . to guarantee a certain number of freedoms to individuals, to legally ensure the people against the excesses or weaknesses of bureaucracy."[50] Similarly, John Gooding describes Speransky as "a convinced, if of necessity somewhat stealthy, liberal," while Andrzej Walicki calls him the personification of "a specific variation of Christian liberalism."[51] These debates highlight the difficulty of defining Russian political ideology.

Alexander's rejection of most of Speransky's proposals did not entirely end reform. In 1815, Alexander granted a constitution to the Kingdom of Poland. Speaking to the Polish parliament in March 1818, Alexander told the representatives that "you have thus offered me the means to show my country what I have long been preparing for it, and which it will obtain, when the elements of such an important task have reached the necessary development."[52] In line with this logic, Alexander tasked Nikolai Novosiltsev (1761–1838) with drafting a constitution for the Russian Empire. Novosiltsev presented Alexander with his draft in October 1819. This proposed giving the emperor what have been called "extremely extensive powers" but sharing his legislative authority with an elected parliament. It granted citizens freedom of speech and worship, guaranteed the inviolability of private property, and asserted the equality of all citizens before the law.[53] Once again, Alexander failed to act, and the constitution never came into force.

Despite the lack of action, ideas of natural law, civil and political rights, and constitutionalism gained ground among Russia's educated elite. One of the more notable figures in propagating these ideas was Aleksandr Kunitsyn (1873–1840), who taught at the Lyceum in Tsarskoe Selo and later at the Main Pedagogical Institute in St. Petersburg. "Kunitsyn's classes," says his biographer Julia Berest, "undoubtedly contributed to opening the minds of his students to liberal ideas."[54] According to Berest, "Kunitsyn taught his students that man's primary natural right is the right to one's person, by virtue of which 'every individual can demand from others that they treat him not as a mere tool to their ends but as a person endowed with reason and will.'"[55] To Kunitsyn, the purpose of the state was to secure peoples' freedom. "Freedom," he wrote, "is the right of each person to act according to his will in all matters that do not harm others."[56]

In his 1818 book *Natural Law*, Kunitsyn argued that the most fundamental right, "the right to one's person," presupposed "the right to exist," "the right to act," and "the right to achieve wellbeing."[57] Since human desires varied, so too did understandings of wellbeing. Thus, in an early Russian exposition of the liberal principle of pluralism, Kunitsyn concluded, "each person has a right to choose the way of life and occupation which he finds conducive for his wellbeing."[58]

Following from this, Kunitsyn argued in favor of limited government. The state should restrict its sphere of activity to providing security and justice. "The subjects agree to obey the supreme power only for the sake of safety; therefore in all their private matters they remain free," he wrote.[59]

Kunitsyn influenced the thinking of the Decembrists, several of whom had taken his courses on natural law.[60] The Northern Society's plan for a constitutional monarchy proposed that the emperor would hold executive power, control foreign policy and the military, and appoint ministers. Legislative authority would be given a two-chamber parliament, the lower house of which would be elected using a property-based franchise.[61] The plan stated that "all Russians are equal before the law" and that "everyone has the right to express his ideas and feelings without hindrance."[62]

By contrast, the Southern Society wished to overthrow the monarchy and establish a republic. The society's leader, Pavel Pestel, stated that all class distinctions should be eliminated and all citizens guaranteed freedom of speech and worship. Unlike the Northern Society's property-based parliament, Pestel envisioned a single-chamber legislature based on a universal franchise.[63] In this sense, his proposal was in theory more democratic. However, Pestel qualified his commitment to individual rights with a statement that "every right must be based on a prior obligation. . . . A right without a prior obligation is nothing."[64] He added, "the wellbeing of society must be regarded as more important than individual happiness, and if the two conflict then the former should take priority."[65] Moreover, Pestel's democratic republic was not to come into being immediately. Rather, a provisional government with dictatorial powers was to be established, which would last for a least a decade before it would hand over power to the proposed new legislature.[66]

The failure of the Decembrist Revolt put an end to political reform for the three decades that followed under the rule of Nicholas I. Consequently, there is a tendency to accept Miliukov's judgement that the years 1825 to 1855 mark "an interruption in the history of Russian liberalism."[67] This is not entirely true. The oppressive nature of Nicholas's reign, especially the tight censorship regime, made freedom the rallying cry of intellectuals across the political spectrum. These years were therefore an important stage in the development of liberal thought.

One such development came from the writer Aleksandr Herzen, whose journal *The Bell*, published in exile abroad and smuggled into Russia, was widely read by members of Russia's educated class. Herzen declared that, "the liberty of the individual is the greatest thing of all, it is *on this and this alone* that the true will of the people can develop."[68] "Since the age of thirteen," he said, "I have served one idea, marched under one banner—war against all imposed authority—against every kind of deprivation of freedom, in the name of the absolute independence of the individual."[69]

Many subsequent members of the liberation movement and Kadet party in the early twentieth century greatly admired Herzen. For instance, Fyodor Rodichev (1856–1923) proclaimed, "Herzen represented for me the living tradition from the first heralds of free thought, from Novikov and Radishchev, from the Decembrists to the men of the sixties. He was the vital link between Russian liberation and the European movement. But above all and beyond all else, the value of Herzen is in the freedom of his spirit."[70]

Aileen Kelly argues that "Herzen's ideas correspond better to liberal conceptions of freedom than do those of his opponents, the Russian Westernizers."[71] However, as Andrzej Walicki notes, "Herzen was never a liberal in the sense of believing in the rule of law, the parliamentary system, and economic freedom."[72] He rejected the idea that Russia must follow the same path of development as Europe, and he put his faith in a form of socialism founded on the peasant commune. Vanessa Rampton concludes: "Herzen's exultation of individual liberty . . . bear[s] witness to his support for the idea of negative liberty. . . . Yet, Herzen remains a controversial figure in the liberal canon. His criticisms of the record of the Western institutions of his time, including parliamentary democracy and the rule of law, are unsettling for those who associate liberalism with the protection of liberty by legal, political, and institutional safeguards."[73]

Something similar might be said about the Slavophiles. The Slavophiles supported the emancipation of the serfs and the abolition of the death penalty, and were fervent proponents of free speech.[74] But they rejected the outer layer of liberal institutions such as the rule of law, the separation of powers, and representative government. Consequently, their beliefs have been defined by one historian as "untraditional liberalism."[75]

Rather than the Slavophiles, the liberal tradition in Russia is more often associated with their rivals, the Westernizers, though they too were less than fully committed to liberal institutions, notably representative government. At the more radical end of the Westernizers was Vissarion Belinsky (1811–1848).

"The fate of the subject, the individual, the personality is more important than the fate of the whole world," he declared.[76] In an 1840 letter, he wrote: "From now on the words *liberal* and *man* are one and the same to me, as are absolutist and wielder of the knout. The aim of liberalism is rational and Christian in the highest degree, for its aim is to restore the rights of the individual and reinstate man's dignity, and Christ himself came into this world and suffered on the cross for the sake of the *individual*."[77]

Belinsky's commitment to freedom led him on occasion to support the idea of revolutionary violence against the autocracy. "My heroes in history are those destroyers of the past such as Luther, Voltaire, the Encyclopedists, the terrorists," he wrote, adding that "people are so stupid that you have to lead them to happiness. And of what significance is the blood of a few thousand when compared to the degradation and suffering of millions?"[78]

More moderate Westernizers such as Granovsky had a different attitude. Granovsky saw the state as the driver of historical progress. Democratic institutions, he believed, could work only once the people had acquired the necessary degree of education and political and legal consciousness. Since the Russian people as yet lacked these qualities, Russia should remain an absolute monarchy.[79] Kavelin shared this point of view. "I believe completely in the necessity of absolutism in present-day Russia, but it ought to be progressive and enlightened," he wrote.[80]

Granovsky was in close contact with government officials, most notably the brothers Dmitry and Nikolai Miliutin, both of whom would go on to lead reforms in the governments of Emperor Alexander II. Granovsky provided a link between the theorizing of the Westernizers and the practical politics of reform. Another link was the spread of higher education during Nicholas I's reign, with universities and law schools producing a new generation of graduates who entered government and joined the ranks of what has been termed the "enlightened bureaucracy."[81] The number of civil servants employed by the Russian state more than quadrupled in the first half of the nineteenth century.[82] The bureaucracy played an increasingly important role in policy making.

Nicholas wanted Russia to operate like a well-oiled machine, and put a great emphasis on the idea of lawfulness (*zakonnost'*). "I want to place all the forces and strictures of the laws at the base of the system of state and government," he declared.[83] A first step to achieving this aim was a codification of Russian laws completed by Mikhail Speransky in 1833. Another step was a major expansion in legal education. The University Statute of 1835 created law faculties within the universities, and in the same year a separate law school, the School of Jurisprudence, opened its doors. Many of its graduates joined the

Ministry of Justice, resulting in the "growth of a corps of officials with loy-
alty to the ministry rather than to local executive authorities."[84] This new generation was committed to the idea of law and some of them went on to draft
the legal reforms that came into force in the 1860s. In this way, Nicholas inad-
vertently helped to lay the foundations for Russia's advance toward something
more closely, if imperfectly, resembling the liberal model of a law-based state.

Social-Economic Liberalism

One of the major issues of this era was the future of Russia's largest class, the
peasantry, which consisted of two main groups—state peasants and serfs,
the latter of whom had financial or labor obligations towards the owners
of the lands that they worked. In an early attempt to address the issue of serfdom, Catherine II asked the Free Economic Society, which had been established in 1765, to discuss whether peasants should be given property rights.[85]
This led to a proposal from the jurist Aleksei Polenov (1738–1816), according
to which land would remain the property of its current owners but peasants
would obtain the right to lease in perpetuity the land they tilled, paying a
percentage of the crop to the owner.[86] Nothing came of this proposal.

Catherine herself is said to have held "liberal opinions in the field of economic policy." In her 1767 *Reflections on the Manufacturers*, she wrote that,
"Nothing is more dangerous than drawing up regulations for everything." Government should "neither forbid nor compel" industry, she added.[87] She extended the property rights of landowners, giving them ownership of mineral
deposits under their land as well as the right to exploit them.[88]

Particularly popular in this era were the ideas of Adam Smith (1723–1790).
Desnitsky, who had spent time studying under Smith in Glasgow, was among
those who propagated the Scotsman's ideas.[89] Gary Hamburg remarks that
"the degree of Smith's influence on Desnitsky's economic thinking was striking: hostility towards consumption taxes, preference for progressive taxes, the
desire to avoid a heavy state presence in economic life, and the concern for
production as the source of national wealth."[90] Desnitsky did not propose abolishing serfdom, but did suggest that peasants be given certain property rights,
such as the "right to buy and sell moveable property."[91] He also argued for a
redistribution of the tax burden, saying that taxes should be related to the ability to pay.[92]

The first translation of Smith's *The Wealth of Nations* appeared in Russia in
four parts from 1802 to 1806, and is said to have strongly influenced Russian
government thinking in the first decade of Alexander's rule.[93] In 1803, the Rus-

sian minister of internal affairs spoke of the need for "removing all constraints" from trade and industry, a policy which Nikolai Mordvinov (1754–1845), appointed head of the Department of State Economic Affairs in 1810, attempted to put into action.[94] "Property is the cornerstone," wrote Mordvinov, "without it, without the permanence of the rights that guarantee it, neither laws nor the fatherland, nor the state can be of use to anyone."[95]

Among those who admired Smith was Kunitsyn, whose "unbounded enthusiasm for economic liberalism" has been described as "rather unusual for the time."[96] Kunitsyn favored the elimination of the tax exemptions enjoyed by the nobility, and argued that high tariffs hurt agricultural producers, who had to pay higher prices for goods. He also spoke out against serfdom, saying that it was economically inefficient.[97] By contrast, Speransky's attitude toward serfdom has been called "extremely cautious."[98] Speransky limited himself to proposing that relations between serfs and masters be based on a clearer contractual relationship, and to arguing that the peasant commune should give way very gradually over time to a model of individual farming.[99] Marc Raeff argues that this shows that Speransky should not be considered a liberal. John Gooding, however, disagrees, noting that in the first draft of his 1809 reform plan Speransky suggested giving the peasants their freedom "without any gradualness whatsoever."[100] This proposal disappeared in the final version, a fact Gooding suggests can be explained only by the intervention of the emperor.[101]

As for economic theory more generally, Speransky saw a free market as a desirable eventual goal, but not entirely appropriate in Russia's current circumstances. He wrote: "The rule is now accepted that need and private interests can direct human activity in industry and the economy better than all government measures. Therefore, the government should be only a spectator of private efforts in this field. . . . When the national industry . . . will have reached . . . its full maturity, it can and must be allowed to proceed alone. . . . But in its early beginnings . . . the government has the obligation to guide it . . . and even . . . to give it subsidies."[102]

Later, classical liberal economic theory exerted some influence on the thinking of the Decembrists, whose ideas have been described as based on a "sprinkling of poorly digested economic liberalism along the lines of Adam Smith."[103] Nevertheless, the Decembrists have been accused of being indifferent to industrial development. Pestel, for instance, felt that Russia's competitive advantage was in agriculture, and that it should therefore focus on that, not on developing industry.[104] Pestel declared that serfdom should be abolished and that:

> It is known that the best means to foster flourishing prosperity consists in granting *freedom* and in having the government pay attention to

the national economy only for the sake of spreading the knowledge and information necessary for industry and enlightenment and for removing those obstacles that exceed private means. . . . Economic enterprise itself should be freed, to the maximum extent possible, from all difficulties and obstacles which are the result not only of poorly conceived regulations but also of external actions and causes, in such a manner that government decisions be not obstacles to the success of economic enterprise.[105]

The economist most closely associated with the Decembrists was Nikolai Turgenev, who, like Kunitsyn, opposed serfdom as economically inefficient. Turgenev remarked that, "factories and manufacturing . . . cannot prosper if labour is not free."[106] In his 1818 *Essay on the Theory of Taxation*, Turgenev praised Adam Smith and wrote that "everything that is good comes from freedom." He argued in favor of an income tax and the elimination of the tax privileges of the nobility.[107] He also supported the emancipation of the serfs, the abolition of the peasant commune, and free trade, but opposed giving the emancipated peasants any land, and viewed industrial development rather negatively.[108]

During the reign of Nicholas I, the influence of classical economic theory somewhat declined. Nevertheless, important work on economic reform began within the bureaucracy. Two important figures in this regard were Nikolai Miliutin, then an official working on issues of municipal government, and Andrei Zablotsky-Desiatovsky (1808–1881), head of the Statistical Section of the Department of Rural Economy. Miliutin led a discussion circle that took control of the Royal Geographical Society. The society set about collecting accurate statistical data about the rural economy, without which it was felt that no rational reform of agriculture was possible.[109] In 1851, Zlabotsky-Desiatovsky published *Memorandum on the Shortcomings of Communal Landholding and the Advantages of Private Ownership of Land by the Peasants*. In this he stopped short of calling for the emancipation of the serfs but did call communal landownership a "stumbling block to any attempt at improvement" of the rural economy, and wrote that "without the confidence of the peasant in the continual ownership of those [lands] which he tills, there can never be never be any successes in agriculture." He concluded by urging that state peasants be given ownership of the land that they worked.[110] In this way, the foundation was laid for more radical reform a decade later.

It would be difficult to say that there was a single identifiable Russian liberalism in this period. There were instead a multiplicity of liberalisms, or perhaps protoliberalisms, some of a more radical and others of a more moderate kind.

In particular, liberal-minded thinkers began to construct a model of the Russian nation that was different than that of Russian conservatives. This model viewed Russia as an essentially European country and as such bound to follow the same path of development as its Western neighbors. From this moment on, Russian liberalism became closely associated with Westernism.

Throughout the period, ideas of natural law, the innate dignity and equality of all humans, and their consequent right to equal treatment in the eyes of the law, gained ground. In political terms, such beliefs drove some in a radical, revolutionary direction, while others remained committed to defending Russia's absolutist monarchy, seeing it both as necessary to defend against anarchy and as the historical motor of progressive reform.

Economically speaking, classical liberalism had strong support during the reigns of Catherine II and Alexander I. Support for the emancipation of the serfs grew. Meanwhile, a new generation of educated bureaucrats took office, who were committed to enacting change. The reforms that followed Nicholas's death in 1855 sprouted in fertile ground.

CHAPTER 3

The Great Reforms

In October 1853, war broke out between Russia and an alliance of France, Britain, and the Ottoman Empire. The Crimean War, as it became known, ended in a humiliating defeat for Russia in March 1856. By then, Nicholas I had been dead for a year, having been succeeded as emperor by his son Alexander II (reigned 1855–1881).

In 1856, Russia was an overwhelmingly rural society. The vast majority of the population were peasants, divided roughly equally into state peasants and serfs. State peasants owed obligations to the state and serfs to their masters, in the form of either labor or payment, of money or in kind. Masters also had significant legal power over the serfs.

The basic social unit of the peasantry was the household. Households were grouped together in communes. Communes divided the land that the peasants worked into strips that they would occasionally redistribute to reflect changes in household sizes. Beyond that, communes were responsible for determining what crops were planted, ensuring the payment of taxes and the provision of conscripts for the army, providing social welfare to members, and punishing criminal behavior.

The Crimean War revealed serious deficiencies in this system. Russia lacked the industry required to sustain modern military operations, and the existing method of conscription was unable to provide the army with the quantity and quality of recruits that it needed. The war convinced the new emperor of the need for reform, starting with the abolition of serfdom. That, however, would upend the entire system of local government and require changes to local administration and the justice system. The result was a succession of measures that together go by the name of the Great Reforms.

In March 1856, Alexander gave a speech in Moscow promising to free the serfs, a promise that he put into effect in 1861. The emancipation of the serfs was followed in 1864 by an overhaul of the judicial system and the creation of a new system of local government, in the form of elected institutions known as zemstva. These had responsibility for matters such as education and health care. The culmination of the reform process was the establishment of a system of compulsory military service by defense minister Dmitry Miliutin in the 1870s.

By that time, a number of factors had led to a conservative turn in Russian politics. The first was a rebellion that broke out in Poland in 1863. The second was a rise of revolutionary terrorism, an early example of which was an attempt to assassinate the emperor in 1866. Disaffected elements in Russian society began to advocate the violent overthrow of the monarchy. Perhaps the best known were Sergei Nechaev (1847–1882) and Mikhail Bakunin (1814–1876), who in 1869 published a manifesto entitled *Catechism of a Revolutionary*, which argued that the ends justified the violent means. In 1876, Bakunin's followers established Land and Liberty, a secret organization dedicated to the destruction of the imperial state. In 1879, this split into two, with one group advocating peaceful politics and the other forming the terrorist organization People's Will.

Toward the end of his reign, Alexander made one last effort to reform Russian politics, asking his minister of the interior, Count Mikhail Loris-Melikov (1824–1888), to draft proposals for a new political order. Loris-Melikov did so in early 1881. Alexander approved the scheme, but before it could be put into effect, terrorists from People's Will assassinated him, bringing the age of reform to an end.

Alexander's reign is often seen as the high-water mark of nineteenth-century Russian liberalism. The extent to which the reforms were driven by liberal ideas rather than by pragmatic interests of state is debatable, and the officials who put them into action often bypassed the more liberal segments of Russian society when drafting legislation. The era might be seen as one of enlightened bureaucracy rather than of liberalism per se.

Meanwhile, the intellectual debates that surrounded the reform process generated paradoxical policy ideas. While those who are generally identified as liberals supported the emancipation of the serfs, they often chose to approach the practicalities of emancipation in a conservative fashion, arguing in favor of maintaining the peasant commune as a means of preserving order in the countryside. They were suspicious of proposals to create a national elected legislature, believing that it would be dominated by reactionary nobles and would stand in the way of future reform. Many liberals supported the maintenance of monarchical absolutism, seeing the monarchy as the main driver of change.

Some conservatives favored more radical solutions. Members of what is known as the "aristocratic opposition," an informal collection of wealthy landowners, proposed the abolition of the commune, the reorganization of the rural economy on free market, capitalist principles, and the creation of an elected legislature. Daniel Field notes that in the circumstances of mid-nineteenth-century Russia, "Doctrines naturally clustered together in Western Europe were in conflict in Russia . . . the espousal of constitutionalism or laissez-faire economics was regarded, often correctly, as an attempt to perpetuate the dependence of the peasantry and the dominance of the nobility. . . . [A reformer] could not . . . embrace the whole bundle of liberal doctrines. Different men, grasping different parts of the bundle, naturally came into conflict."[1]

These ideological disputes took place within a very narrow social group—members of Russia's nobility—and stemmed from different understandings of how their interests could best be defended. The aristocratic opposition sought to maintain the nobility's control over Russian society and government by means of rapid institutional change. The liberals believed that their interests would be better served by expanding citizens' personal liberty, albeit in a gradual manner that would ensure stability. Meanwhile, the enlightened bureaucrats within the government believed that they alone were able to govern in the interests of the country. While the fate of the peasantry took center stage in the debates of this period, liberals in the reign of Alexander were noblemen, not peasants. The forms liberalism took reflected this reality.

Cultural Liberalism

By the mid-nineteenth century, liberalism and nationalism had become closely connected in European thought, with the nation-state being regarded as the ideal form of organization.[2] The nation-state was held to provide a means of liberating people from foreign oppression, guaranteeing their sovereignty, and creating a community of interests. Liberalism could act as a means of binding a nation together and was seen as unleashing the potential of the people, thereby enabling the country to develop.

A Russian exemplar of liberal nationalism from this period was Aleksandr Gradovsky (1841–1889), a professor of law at St. Petersburg Imperial University. In Gradovsky's opinion, the development of the state went hand in hand with the development of national consciousness,[3] and the nation-state was the natural and inevitable result of historical processes.[4] His example has been called "a clear-cut case of liberal withdrawal from engagement with the problem of diversity as a result of an intellectual choice in favor of a nation-centered paradigm of liberalism."[5]

Another liberal nationalist was the journalist Mikhail Katkov, who is best known as a voice of conservative thought in the reign of Alexander III, but who at the start of his career was noted for his "outspoken liberalism."[6] Katkov was a great admirer of England, but rejected the blind application of foreign ideas to Russia, writing in 1858 that "we, on our part, consider every borrowing from abroad, every imitation, not only futile but even harmful."[7]

The turning point for Katkov was the Polish rebellion of 1863. This convinced him that a stable state was impossible without a unifying national idea, which in Russia could be provided only by the Russian people, its language, and its culture. In an 1863 article, he wrote: "We do not want coercion or persecution or restraint against ethnic peculiarities . . . but we do indeed propose that Russian government be solely Russian throughout the whole expanse of the possessions of the Russian power."[8] Katkov insisted on the elimination of education in non-Russian languages, such as German-language education in Russia's Baltic provinces.[9] His support of Russian ethnonationalism is one of the factors that lead historians to categorize him as having moved into the reactionary camp after 1863, but his shift was not unique among Russian liberals.

Like Katkov, the political philosopher Boris Chicherin regarded Russia as essentially European but also distinct. "The Russian people are now part of the European family," he wrote in 1857.[10] At the same time, he noted that Russians historically had had a different relationship with the state than had Western Europeans. Chicherin was deeply concerned about the loss of international status that Russia had suffered in the Crimean War. To Chicherin, the roots of Russia's defeat lay in the illiberal manner in which Russia was governed. States, he argued, could not prosper in the international system without the advantages that freedom gave them.[11]

Chicherin is said to have had "a somewhat instrumental approach to liberalism. . . . Nation-building was a prerequisite for progress and in order to realize it, liberalization was needed."[12] He thought that the system operating in Russia suppressed civic spirit, as an unfree people felt no sense of obligation either to each other or to the state. A liberal order, by contrast, would create active citizens and so would allow the nation to advance.[13] As Chicherin put it, "Only political freedom is capable of inspiring new life in the Russian people, to educate its political sense . . . and create the milieu that produces state-minded people."[14] Cultural factors were thus all-important in Chicherin's worldview. As he put it, the primary task was not to reform institutions but rather to "work on ourselves."[15]

Others had a similar view of the importance of developing the people's moral character. The novelist Ivan Turgenev (1818–1883), for instance, wrote that "the role of the educated class in Russia is to transmit civilization to the people, in order that they may themselves hereafter decide what they shall accept and repudiate."[16] Turgenev represented a moderate liberalism that equally disliked both tsarist autocracy and revolutionary nihilism. He was also a thoroughgoing Westernizer: "I am a European, and I love Europe; I pin my faith on its banner, which I have carried since my youth," he declared.[17]

Turgenev's pro-European orientation reveals itself in his novel *Smoke*. This takes place in the town of Baden in Germany among two sets of Russians: a group of aristocratic generals and a group of radical Slavophile socialists. Turgenev mocks both: the generals for their reactionary views and the radicals for their rejection of Europe in favor of some idealized understanding of Russia's uniqueness. The character in the novel generally believed to reflect Turgenev's own views, Sozont Potugin, denounces Russia's "lack of culture and civilization."[18] "Servile habits are too deeply ingrained in us. . . . Slaves through and through. Both slavish pride and slavish debasement," says Potugin, adding: "I'm a Westernizer, that is to say I'm devoted to Europe."[19] As for Russia, he says, "I love her passionately, and hate her passionately."[20] *Smoke* infuriated Russian conservatives, most notably the writer Fyodor Dostoevsky (1821–1881), who felt that it indicated Turgenev's "lack of patriotism."[21]

Smoke appeared in the March 1867 edition of the journal *Vestnik Evropy* (Herald of Europe), which had been founded the previous year by the journalist Mikhail Stasiulevich (1826–1911), and in time became Russia's leading liberal journal. Stasiulevich was convinced that Europe and Russia had a common historical development. "Universal history is called *universal* because it supposes a *common* human nature in all peoples," he wrote.[22] His dream, he said, was "for the border between us and the West to entirely disappear."[23]

Vestnik Evropy's contributors viewed the Western European nation state as the natural form into Russia would in due course evolve and so considered nationalism a progressive phenomenon.[24] But they also expressed concern that nationalism could be exploited by reactionary governments for their own purposes.[25] This concern was reflected in the journal's attitude to Pan-Slavism, namely the idea that Russia and the Slavs of Eastern Europe had a natural affinity and that Russia should support the national aspirations of Slavs in the Austro-Hungarian and Ottoman empires. *Vestnik Evropy*'s Aleksandr Pypin (1833–1904) argued that support for the liberation of national minorities within the Austro-Hungarian and Ottoman empires could be seen as progressive, but he also pointed out that Pan-Slavism could put Russia on a collision course with Western Europe, thereby damaging "common European ideals."[26]

Although *Vestnik Evropy* looked to Europe as the ultimate goal, its contributors held a somewhat conservative view of the path that Russia should follow to get there, advocating "the acquisition of civic responsibilities through local self-government instead of the leap of an inexperienced population into mass politics. Local socioeconomic concerns thus acted as the catalyst of civic consciousness."[27] Expansion of the activities of the new *zemstva* was preferred to national constitutional projects. The *zemstva* served a cultural purpose, namely the transformation of popular culture and the creation of an engaged, active, and responsible citizenry.

Political Liberalism

Alexander II's 1856 statement of intent to free the serfs unleashed an unprecedented wave of political debate. Alexander asked for ideas from Russia's nobility about the form the emancipation should take, and committees of nobles were formed in each of Russia's seventy provinces to draw up proposals. Emancipating the serfs had political consequences. Local government had previously relied on noble landowners, who would be deprived of their legal powers over the serfs once they were freed. Consequently, members of the provincial committees rapidly started making proposals of a political nature.

Especially forward were members of the provincial committee of Tver province, 100 miles northwest of Moscow, which proposed a new system of local administration consisting of assemblies at the local (*volost'*), district (*uezd*), and provincial levels. Representatives would be elected by all classes, albeit with a franchise that was weighted in favor of the nobility.[28] This and similar proposals from provincial committees got short shrift from the Editing Commission that the emperor had put in charge of drawing up the legislation for emancipating the serfs. One of its leading members, Nikolai Miliutin, declared his position clearly, saying: "Never, never, as long as I have the power will I allow the nobility to claim any initiative in matters regarding the interests and needs of the people as a whole. Concern for their welfare belongs to the government. The initiative in undertaking any reforms for the good of the country belongs to the government and only to the government."[29]

Unhappy with how the Editing Commission had drafted the emancipation decree, in February 1862, a year after the serfs had been freed, the Tver provincial committee met again, and demanded "the institution of an independent and public judiciary," and the "introduction of full publicity into all branches of official or public and other administrations."[30] The Tver nobles believed that it would serve their interests better in the long term to give other classes a share of the responsibility for the administration of the country. Not only would this relieve them of some of the burden of government but it could also reduce the possibility of social tension. The Tver committee drafted a petition to the emperor that read in part: "SOVEREIGN. . . . We are convinced that all reforms remain unsuccessful because they are undertaken without the permission or knowledge of the people. The summoning of elected representatives from all the Russian land represents the only means for the satisfactory solution indicated, but not effected, by the legislation of 19 February [i.e., the emancipation declaration]."[31]

Other proposals for constitutional change quickly followed. In 1863, Alexander asked the minister of the interior, Pyotr Valuev (1815–1890), to draw up proposals for including a representative element in the system of government. This resulted in a memorandum by Valuev suggesting a reform of the State Council so as to turn it into an advisory assembly incorporating representatives of the nobility and townspeople.[32] Alexander shelved the proposal, but it was indicative of how even conservative members of Russia's ruling class, such as Valuev, were coming round to the idea of creating some type of representative institution.

Although Alexander rejected reform of the central government, he did accept change at a local level in the form of the creation of the *zemstva*. The process of reforming local government was put first under the control of Nikolai Miliutin and then, from 1861 onward, Valuev. Miliutin believed that by making the *zemstva* elected institutions, the state could provide a means of channeling energies into productive administrative work. This would, he said, "serve to counter anarchistic intellectual ferment," and also help create a sense of civic responsibility.[33] "The most vital state interests . . . urgently demand that the new rural institutions . . . be given an effective and serious meaning," he said.[34]

The emancipation also led to a requirement for changes in the judicial system. The result was the judicial reform of 1864. This created a system of independent courts, public trials, and trial by jury. It also introduced oral proceedings and an adversarial trial process. It fell short of establishing a unified system of law for all Russian subjects, as civil cases between peasants were under the jurisdiction not of the new justices of the peace created by the reform but of local "volost courts" that were allowed to make reference to local custom.[35] Nevertheless, the reform is considered to have been a major step toward the rule of law in Russia.[36]

One fact that drove judicial reform was that noble landowners wanted stronger legal protection of private property.[37] Having lost control over the serfs, they had also lost the ability to enforce contracts, collect debts, and so on. The reform thus looked to replace the landowner's authority with the authority of the courts. The dynamic was well expressed by one of the young lawyers who drew up the reform, Konstantin Pobedonostsev (1827–1907), who remarked that "the first concern of the law should be the protection of the *creditor*, for his legal interests are the interests of *property*, and the interests of property are inseparably tied to the internal security and internal prosperity of the state itself."[38]

In due course, Pobedonostsev would acquire a reputation as an arch-reactionary. His role in the judicial reform process shows how it had strong "conservative appeal."[39] Liberal measures that promoted a key liberal institution—the rule of law—reflected the interests of Russia's ruling class and were only weakly connected to liberal theory.

Miliutin's hope that the *zemstva* would reduce "intellectual ferment" proved illusory. Zealous *zemstvo* officials, desiring to use their position to better their communities, sought to expand their activities and to pay for this with increased taxes. They also asserted their right to run their local administrations as they desired. Meanwhile, a modernizing national bureaucracy sought to control, centralize, and homogenize. Almost inevitably, clashes resulted between local *zemstvo* reformers and central government officials.

One of the most notable figures in this process was Ivan Petrunkevich (1843–1928), a member of the Chernigov provincial *zemstvo* in Ukraine. Frustrated at resistance to his proposals for social and economic reform, Petrunkevich moved into political opposition to the central government, drafting a declaration by the Chernigov *zemstvo* that condemned the use of political repression to defeat revolutionary terrorism.[40] The declaration argued that revolutionary feelings could only be eliminated by giving Russian citizens the freedom to express their opinions.[41]

Petrunkevich set about trying to find allies in *zemstva* elsewhere in the Russian Empire, organizing a conference in Moscow in March 1879 of *zemstvo* representatives from Chernigov, Tver, Kharkov, and Kiev.[42] Soon afterward, Petrunkevich was punished for his activities by being expelled from Chernigov and sent to internal exile in Tver.

The end of Alexander II's reign saw one last effort to change the political system. This followed Alexander's instructions to Count Loris-Melikov to draft reform proposals. Loris-Melikov set up a commission to which Sergei Muromtsev (1850–1910), a law professor at Moscow University, submitted a document that was signed by twenty-five prominent Muscovites. Muromtsev's memorandum asserted that the primary cause of revolutionary terrorism was "the absence of conditions for the free development of public opinion and the free exercise of public activity."[43] The document concluded that

> the only way of extracting our country from its current situation is the creation of an independent assembly of representatives of the *zemstva* and offering this assembly the opportunity to participate in the management of the nation and of working out the necessary guarantees of personal rights, and of freedom of thought and speech. This freedom will stimulate the activity of the most capable social forces, will awake the slumbering spirit of the people and develop the abundant productive forces of the state. Freedom, much more than the strictest repressive measures, will assist in eliminating anarchical elements, hostile to the state.[44]

Muromtsev's memorandum showed that liberals were beginning to come together to press common demands. However, appeals for representative government were more often associated with conservative elements of Russian society than with liberal ones. Following the emancipation of the serfs, many Russian nobles felt that the central government was not interested in their concerns. "The thought comes to mind that the Sovereign is the sworn enemy of the nobility," said Count Vladimir Orlov-Davydov (1809–1892), reflecting a common view among the aristocratic opposition.

The solution some nobles developed to this problem was to press for an elected representative assembly to share legislative power with the emperor. Basing the right to vote on a property requirement would ensure noble dominance in the assembly, and would thereby allow the nobility to retain control of the affairs of state.

Members of the aristocratic opposition produced a number of proposals to this end. Orlov-Davydov, for instance, suggested the creation of a parliamentary chamber modeled on the British House of Lords. Orlov-Davydov was yet another Anglophile. He had studied at the University of Edinburgh and served in the Russian embassy in London. His example shows the difficulty of classifying political thought in this era, for he consciously adopted liberal English models in both politics and economics, but at the same time clearly acted not on the basis of liberal principles but of class interest.

A similar proposal to Orlov-Davydov's was put forward by the head of the Gendarmes (and thus head of internal security), Pyotr Shuvalov (1827–1889). In 1872 Shuvalov proposed allowing the *zemstva* a say in the legislative process and also creating a second legislative chamber consisting of provincial "marshals of the nobility" (who were elected by nobles in every province).[45]

Somewhat confusingly, therefore, some conservatives supported representative government, while some liberals rejected it. Among the latter were Kavelin and Chicherin. In 1855 the two men, signing themselves as "A Russian liberal," wrote an anonymous "Letter to the Editor" to Aleksandr Herzen's journal *Golosa iz Rossii* (Voices from Russia). In this Kavelin and Chicherin criticized the exiled Herzen for peddling dangerous revolutionary ideas. "Your revolutionary theories . . . arouse only indignation and disgust in us," they wrote.[46] Instead of revolution, they said, "We are ready to rally round any remotely liberal government and support it with all our might, for we are firmly convinced that we can only act and achieve any results through the government. But you propagate the destruction of all government and consider anarchy the ideal of the human race."[47]

For Kavelin, the state was the primary driving force of progress.[48] He believed that in Russia constitutional government would serve the narrow class interests of the nobility rather than the interests of the state as a whole.[49] He wrote that "constitutional institutions in the European sense are unthinkable and impossible here. We should admit this with complete truthfulness and total frankness. Our situation is too serious to continue living a life of illusions."[50]

In an 1862 article entitled "The Nobility and the Liberation of the Serfs," Kavelin noted that Russia had only two significant classes—the nobility and the peasants—without any meaningful middle class. The nobility "could not imagine any interests other than their own" and could not be trusted with power. As for the peasants, Kavelin said, "nobody who knows them even a little can consider them an element which is ready for representative government."[51] Consequently, wrote Kavelin, "representative government is impossible here; thinking about it is an idle dream."[52]

In 1875 Kavelin returned to the theme of constitutional government in an article entitled "What Should We Be?" The situation had never been worse, he wrote, and "the government has lost all our respect and trust."[53] The solution did not, however, lie in the sort of political reforms proposed by the aristocratic opposition. Kavelin wrote: "A constitution makes sense only when a well-organized and authoritative wealthy class supports and protects it. Without such a class a constitution is a worthless scrap of paper, a lie, a prelude to the most dishonest and dishonorable deceit. . . . By itself, a constitution doesn't give or guarantee anything, absent these conditions it is nothing, but a harmful nothing because it deceives with the external form of political guarantees."[54]

Kavelin's beliefs may be described as a conservative liberalism that looked to the autocratic monarchy as the driver of progress and sought to initiate political change at the local level, only gradually moving up to the national level as the necessary political culture developed. This conservative liberalism is even more strongly associated with Boris Chicherin, who attempted to balance the need for freedom against the need for a strong state.[55] In an 1858 essay entitled "Contemporary Tasks in Russian Life," Chicherin noted that "the government has always been a driving force in our development and progress."[56] At the same time, he cautioned that "government activity must not preclude the autonomy of the people, for popular autonomy is a basic precondition of public life. . . . For the government to establish norms of behavior and opinion and to bend everything to these norms . . . is to kill any life and to destroy one of the fundaments of society."[57]

Unfortunately, said Chicherin, this was precisely what the government had done, establishing a "frightful dominance over national life."[58] It followed that change was necessary. "We need freedom!" he wrote, "We want the opportunity to freely express and develop our thoughts, so the Tsar will know what Russia is thinking and can govern us with a clear understanding of social and economic conditions."[59]

"Liberalism! This is the slogan of every educated and sensible person in Russia," wrote Chicherin. In practice this meant "freedom of conscience," "emancipation from servile status," "freedom of speech," "freedom of the press," "academic freedom," "publication of all government activities," and "public legal proceedings." "In liberalism . . . is Russia's future; it alone can awake Russia to new life," concluded Chicherin.[60]

Chicherin was unusual not only in referring to himself as a liberal but also in drawing up a definition of what he meant by liberalism. This he did in an article published in 1862 entitled "Various Forms of Liberalism," in which he identified three types of liberalism, the first two of which he rejected, and the third of which he supported. These were, respectively, "street liberalism," "oppositional liberalism," and *"okhranitel'nyi* liberalism." The last is normally translated as "conservative liberalism," but this does not do justice to the adjective *okhranitel'nyi* which may be translated as "protective" or "guardian," and in the context of Russian politics has a decidedly statist flavor (the imperial Russian security service was known as the Okhrana).

The street liberal, said Chicherin, "loves noise; he needs unrest for unrest's sake. . . . It never occurs to him that respect of authority is respect of thought, of labor, of talent, of everything that gives mankind higher reason."[61] Meanwhile, "oppositional liberalism understands freedom in a purely negative way. . . . The first and necessary condition is to have no contact with the authorities, to stay as far away from them as possible. . . . Everyone knows that every decent person must without fail stand in opposition."[62] In contrast to these deviant forms of liberalism, Chicherin posited his ideal: *okhranitel'nyi* liberalism. He wrote: "The essence of *okhranitel'nyi* liberalism consists of reconciling the principle of freedom with the principles of power and law. In political life its slogan is 'liberal measures and strong government': liberal measures that enable society to act independently, that guarantee the rights and personhood of citizens, that protect freedom of thought and conscience, that allow one to express all lawful desires; and strong government, the guardian of state unity, that connects and restrains society, preserves order, severely ensures obedience of the law, and punishes any breaches of it."[63]

Chicherin's long-term goal was for Russia to become a constitutional monarchy.[64] In the short term, though, he believed that the country was not yet ready for this, and he therefore supported the retention of the autocratic system, albeit with expanded civil liberties.[65] In his book *On Popular Representation*, Chicherin argued that free institutions brought many benefits, but their significance should not be exaggerated, since "Enlightened absolutism . . . contributes much more to the development of popular welfare than do republics torn by factionalism."[66] Political liberty, Chicherin said, was dependent upon a certain political and legal culture, associated with the ownership of property. He wrote, "There is therefore nothing ethically troubling in denying political rights to poor people."[67] Chicherin concluded: "Under a given set of circumstances, and taking into account the political sophistication of a people, one must decide whether the advantages [of political liberty and representation] outweigh the disadvantages. The conclusion will not always be the same, and, for this reason, representative government is not always appropriate."[68]

Social-Economic Liberalism

The most important event in the social-economic history of this era was the emancipation of the serfs in 1861. The members of the Editing Commission who drew up the emancipation legislation varied in their political and economic perspectives. Many were members of the Royal Geographical Society, in which capacity they had worked for several years on collecting statistical data about the countryside; eight had participated in Nikolai Miliutin's liberally oriented discussion circle in the 1850s; and six had participated in Slavophile circles.[69]

The commission sought a pragmatic compromise between the emperor's command to free the serfs and the desire to compensate landowners for their losses, bearing in mind also the requirement to provide the freed peasants with the means to sustain themselves and the need to ensure social stability in the countryside. To these ends, the commission produced a decree that freed the serfs from their obligations to their former masters and provided them with a limited amount of land for which they had to compensate the landowners by means of a redemption tax paid gradually over a period of many years. The land did not, however, become their personal property but belonged to the peasant commune, which was retained as a means of regulating rural society.

The emancipation decree left many people dissatisfied—landowners were unhappy with their loss of power, while the peasants felt that they had received too little land and resented the redemption payments. The retention of the commune severely limited peasants' rights—for instance, they needed the commune's permission in order to leave their village to work elsewhere. Rights within the commune continued to rest with the household rather than the individual. And the creation of the *volost'* courts meant that peasants were subject to a different legal system from other classes. In these ways, although the emancipation was a notionally liberal measure, freeing millions of peasants from bondage, it failed to put key liberal institutions into effect, such as legal equality and private property.

Possibly the lone economic liberal in the commission was Nikolai Bunge (1823–1895), a professor of economics at Kiev University who became minister of finance in 1881. One of his predecessors in this job was Mikhail Reutern (1820–1890), who served as finance minister from 1862 to 1878. Reutern had been much impressed by what he had seen on a trip to the United States and took various steps to try to liberalize the Russian economy. These included abolishing the state monopoly on the mining and sale of salt, eliminating contracts with private individuals to collect taxes on alcohol, and making government finances more transparent by publishing a list of the state's revenues and expenditures.[70]

Under Reutern, the Russian government "lowered taxes on industry and made it easier for individuals to take up commercial and industrial occupations."[71] Reutern also encouraged railroad construction. Rather than having the state build railroads (as would become the norm under Alexander III), Reutern encouraged private companies, offering "profit guarantees to the entrepreneurs to whom it granted concessions for the building and operation of railroads." The result was an "enormous railroad boom."[72]

Apart from Bunge and Reutern, the one prominent thinker of this era associated with economic liberalism was Chicherin, who wrote that "inequality predominates in human communities." This was in part due to natural differences among humans and in part due to the fact that freedom inevitably produces inequalities as a result of the different choices people make. According to Chicherin, "Freedom by its nature, leads to inequality. In the sphere of property this rule shows itself fully operative, yet one cannot destroy this inequality without destroying its root—that is human liberty."[73] This led

Chicherin to oppose social security programs, such as the one introduced in Germany by Otto von Bismarck (1815–1898) in the 1880s. According to Chicherin, the state did not have the right to force people to save for their pensions, insure themselves against unemployment, and so on, as this would infringe on their freedom of choice.[74]

Chicherin remarked that "only free labor, only activity driven by the mainspring of personal gain, only these things can significantly advance an industry."[75] This attitude led to him to be a fervent opponent of serfdom, which he called "a ball and chain which we drag behind ourselves and which confines us to virtual immobility while other nations forge inevitably ahead."[76] "If you desire the Russian peasant to become more industrious, then it is necessary first to remove his fetters," he added.[77]

In Slavophile mythology, the commune was an ancient form of Russian social organization that reflected the collective identity and morality of the Russian people. Chicherin disagreed, arguing that the commune was a relatively recent historical institution.[78] He did not argue that the state should forcibly abolish the commune, but he did believe that it should cease trying to preserve it, so that over time it would wither away. With that, the separate legal status of peasants would disappear and they would turn into citizens with the same rights and obligations as others.[79] The replacement of the commune with individual property-owning farmers would, Chicherin argued, provide a stable basis for Russian society and so prevent revolution. As he wrote, "A property holder, always anxious about his property, fears disturbances most of all. This is especially true of landed property owners, who are tied to the land and who love stable, unchanging circumstances. They are the most conservative element that one can imagine."[80] To Chicherin, the emancipation of the serfs was a conservative measure, in that its purpose was to ensure the stability of the countryside and thus ultimately of the state.[81]

Also critical of the commune were members of the aristocratic opposition, although for different reasons. Count Orlov-Davydov, for instance, supported the abolition of the commune and the reorganization of landholding on the principle of private property. His ideal was the large landed estates of the British aristocracy. In 1857, prior to the emancipation, he proposed that the peasants be freed without being given any land and that the rural economy be reorganized in the shape of large estates (owned by nobles such as himself), from which the peasants could rent the land they needed. This would leave some peasants landless, but that would have the advantage of creating the pool of cheap labor that Russian needed to industrialize.[82] Orlov-Davydov argued that the commune encouraged socialism, whereas independent peasant farmers operating outside of the commune would form a rural middle class that would be naturally conservative. The commune, he said, also inhibited the development of industry, whereas the concentration of land in the hands of large landowners would increase their revenues and generate the capital needed for industrialization.[83] Similarly, in 1871 another member of the aristocratic opposition, Nikolai Lobanov-Rostovsky (1826–1887), complained that the communal control of land "prevents any individual enterprise—the basis of progress—destroys the significance of the family . . . [and] the desire to work, because property is insufficiently guaranteed."[84]

Russian conservatives could, therefore, favor a form of economic liberalism. By contrast, Russian liberals could be quite conservative on economic matters. Kavelin, for instance, argued that progress did not require the transformation of communal property into private property. He wrote that: "Private property . . . is a source of movement, of progress, of development; but it becomes of source of death and destruction, it corrodes the social organism when its extreme consequences are not moderated and balanced by other landowning principles. . . . I see communal landowning as one such principle."[85]

Kavelin also expressed a suspicion of capitalism and industrialization, which he believed produced social tensions that would, he said, "lead every society, sooner or later, to social revolution and destruction."[86] The commune provided a counterweight to this process, protecting the rural masses from the worst consequences of capitalist development and "from the monopoly of private property."[87]

The reign of Alexander II was a period of enormous change in Russia. The logic of the reforms was in many respects utilitarian—in other words, they were undertaken because of the perceived benefits for the state. The bureaucrats who administered the reforms did so with very pragmatic goals in mind and in keeping with the practical realities of mid-nineteenth-century Russia rather than on the basis of abstract liberal principles.

Nevertheless, the reforms did advance liberalism in Russia, freeing millions from serfdom, laying the fundaments of a law-based state, and instituting a form of elected local self-government. Initially, liberals supported the emancipation of the serfs, while conservative nobles opposed it. However, some liberals took a conservative approach to enacting it, reflecting a suspicion of industrial capitalism as well as a desire to maintain order in the countryside. By contrast, the aristocratic opposition took a more radical approach, embracing free market principles and industrial development.

In political terms, the loss of power associated with the emancipation of the serfs convinced some conservative nobles to support the creation of a constitutional form of government, featuring a noble-dominated representative assembly. In this way, conservatives promoted a liberal institution, albeit with limits. By contrast, liberal thinkers tended to favor the preservation of the absolute monarchy, while also calling for the expansion of civil liberties. Russia was deemed to lack the political culture required to sustain a democratic order. Rather than try to introduce constitutional government prematurely, liberals pinned their hopes on gradually developing the necessary political culture by granting the people civil liberties and engaging them in local government.

Liberalism in this period was therefore fairly conservative in nature. It sought to enhance liberty in the nation, but in a gradual way, aiming both to strengthen the state and to protect the interests of the nobility against the threats of social tension and political revolution. However, by the end of Alexander II's reign some in the liberal ranks were growing impatient with this moderate approach. Following Alexander's death this impatience would grow into open dissent.

Chapter 4

The Era of Counter-Reform

Alexander III's accession to the throne in 1881 introduced a more conservative phase in Russian politics that continued into the reign of his successor, Nicholas II (1894–1917). Alexander and Nicholas rejected the idea of surrendering any of their absolute powers. An 1889 law revamped local administration by creating "land captains," to whom local institutions, including peasant communes, were subordinated. An 1890 law increased noble representation in the *zemstva*, and an 1892 statute reduced the autonomy of city councils. The result was increasing tension between central and local government.

From the 1880s onward, Russia industrialized rapidly, a process often associated with the policies of finance minister Sergei Witte (1849–1915). As the economy grew, Russian civil society grew also. The late nineteenth and early twentieth centuries witnessed an enormous expansion in voluntary associations, of which there were more than 10,000 by 1900.[1] These included charities, educational establishments, mutual aid societies, religious groups, artistic institutions, sports clubs, and women's groups. For the most part, these were not involved in political activity.[2] Nevertheless, relations between the government and parts of civil society became increasingly strained as time went on. As Joseph Bradley notes, "Autocracy equated privately organized activity in the public realm with ideas of constitutions and limited government, thereby driving more and more ordinary citizens into confrontation with the state."[3]

Despite the rapid industrialization, Russia remained an overwhelmingly rural country, divided into distinct estates (nobles, merchants, peasants, etc.) who were subject to different legal rules. Meanwhile, the benefits of economic growth largely bypassed the countryside. In 1891, Russia experienced a severe famine. The central government proved incapable of launching a well-organized relief effort, and much of the burden of providing aid fell on social organizations and local government. The experience convinced many within the liberal community that the state needed to cede more powers to what they called "society."

These factors combined to increase opposition to the imperial autocracy. A key moment was the establishment in 1902 of the opposition newspaper *Osvobozhdenie* (Liberation) and in 1903 of a liberal opposition organization known as the Union of Liberation. Furthermore, terrorists carried out a number of high-profile assassinations, including the murders of interior minister Viacheslav von Plehve (1846–1904) and Alexander III's brother, Grand Duke Sergei Aleksandrovich (1857–1905).

External problems worsened Russia's domestic situation. In the 1870s and early 1880s, the Russian army had occupied much of Central Asia but by the mid-1880s this process was complete. Thereafter Russia enjoyed twenty years of peace until February 1904, when Japan launched an attack on Russian forces in the Far East. Russia's military suffered a series of defeats in the Russo-Japanese War, which ended in September 1905 with the signing of the Treaty of Portsmouth.

These defeats undermined the prestige of the Russian monarchy and helped to provoke a series of revolutionary outbursts throughout 1904 and 1905. These included rural disturbances in which peasants seized land and burnt down nobles' houses; industrial strikes; and revolutionary terrorism. In January 1905, troops in St. Petersburg gunned down a group of protestors, killing around 100 people in what became known as "Bloody Sunday." This galvanized opposition to the government, and violent disorder spread across the country. Liberals became increasingly radicalized and Russian liberalism acquired a revolutionary air.

Cultural Liberalism

The prevailing intellectual current of this era may be described as positivism. Deriving from the theories of writers such as Auguste Comte (1798–1857), positivism holds that the only valid knowledge is that which can be empirically verified. According to this mode of thought, religion or morality should not determine truth or what should be done, as they are not scientifically verifiable. Positivism also suggests that human societies are subject to scientifically determinable laws, and it tends toward "an optimistic view of history," according to which societies gradually progress toward more and more rational forms of social organization.[4] As what is rational for one is rational for all, it follows that societies will gradually converge toward one common model of organization. This view was well expressed by the historian Pavel Miliukov, who would later lead the liberal Constitutional Democratic party (often referred to as the "Kadets" in light of the party's initials, "K. D."). Miliukov declared that "free forms of political life are as little national as are the use of the alphabet or of the printing press, steam or electricity. . . . The adoption of these forms becomes necessary when public life becomes so complicated that it can no longer be contained within the framework of a more primitive public structure. When such a time arrives, when a new era of history knocks at the door, it is useless to place restraints and delays in its path."[5]

Positivists such as Miliukov rejected the idea that Russia had a unique culture, distinct from that of Europe. "Civilization makes nations, as it makes individuals, more alike," Miliukov said.[6] He then turned an "is" into an "ought." Because, in his opinion, it was an observable fact that nations developed in the same way, he concluded that Russia ought to reform itself in order to accelerate its progress in that direction. Confronted by the complaint that Western European models did not apply to Russia, he replied that Russia had to obey "the laws of political biology."[7]

The same "laws" could be used to justify war and imperial expansion. Taking their cue from the Social Darwinist ideas of Herbert Spencer (1820–1903) and other Western philosophers, some Russian liberals viewed war between states as an inevitable, even desirable, product of international competition, one that helped to promote the "survival of the fittest" among nations. Given that the most advanced nations had a tendency to subdue the less advanced ones, Russian imperial expansion could be considered not only justifiable but even necessary. According to V. M. Khevrolina, "Liberals vigorously argued in favor of assimilating the Far East," and after Japan defeated China in the Sino-Japanese War of 1894–1895, "liberals joined the choir calling for action to prevent Japan from gaining a foothold on the mainland."[8]

Fear of the threat from the east grew as the nineteenth century came to an end. Among those who expressed concern was the philosopher Vladimir Solovyov (1853–1900). In his poem "Pan-Mongolism," Solovyov wrote about the tribes of the east, "countless as locusts, and as ravenous," destroying Russia, whose "tattered banners [would be] passed like toys among yellow children."[9]

In other respects, though, Solovyov was highly critical of the positivist logic described above, and held a very different view of nationality and nationalism.

As with so many figures in this book, Solovyov's status as a liberal is much contested.[10] Solovyov urged voluntary subordination to the good, as defined by God's will, which, he said in his book *The Justification of the Good*, has a "universal character."[11] The rational human, he wrote, "must put himself into a filial position in relation to the supreme principle of life, that is, gratefully surrender himself to its providence and submit all his actions to the 'will of the Father.'"[12] Solovyov did not advocate liberal democracy, but rather a "free theocracy," in which Russia and Europe were to be united under the authority of the Russian tsar and the pope. Nevertheless, his philosophy led him to some liberal positions.[13] Greg Gaut argues that although Solovyov was "not a liberal in the Western European sense," his worldview "allowed him to find a practical unity with Russian liberalism,"[14] on which he was to exert a considerable influence.

In particular, Solovyov published numerous articles in the 1880s and 1890s in the liberal journal *Vestnik Evropy*. In these, he attacked nationalism and the positivist view that international politics was merely a matter of competing national interests, with no place for morality. In an article entitled "Morality and Politics," Solovyov declared: "A complete separation of morality and politics is one of the predominant mistakes and evils of our time. From a Christian point of view and within the boundaries of the Christian world, these two areas—moral and political—although they cannot entirely coincide, must nonetheless be tightly bound together. Just as Christian morality has in mind the accomplishment of the Kingdom of God within an individual person, so too should Christian politics prepare for the arrival of the Kingdom of God for all humankind as a whole and its major parts, peoples, tribes, and states."[15]

Nationality was an integral part of people's identity, Solovyov argued. It was impossible to respect others' personal dignity without respecting their nationality. This meant, he said, that "we must love all nationalities as our own."[16] Nationality and nationalism were not the same: "Nationality is a positive force, and every people, according to its own special character, is appointed for a particular service. Different nationalities are different organs in the entire body of humanity . . . but . . . the desire to separate oneself [from the body] can arise. And with such a desire, the positive force of nationality turns into the negative force of nationalism. . . . Taken to extremes, nationalism destroys the people who have fallen into it, making them an enemy of mankind."[17]

Solovyov's insistence that politics must have a moral foundation had a powerful influence on political philosophers of the late nineteenth and early twentieth centuries, some of whom sought the "replacement of positivism by *neo*-idealism as the theoretical foundation of liberalism."[18] An important event in this process was the publication in 1903 of an edited volume entitled *Problems of Idealism*, which attacked the principles of positivism. The basic theme of the book was well expressed in the first chapter, written by the philosopher and economist Sergei Bulgakov (1871–1944). Bulgakov wrote: "No matter how well developed, positive science will always remain limited by its object—it studies only fragments of a reality that widens constantly before the eyes of the scientist . . . we must also obtain answers to questions that fall completely outside the field of vision of positive science . . . not only *how*, but also *what*, *why* and *what for*? Positive science has no answers to these questions."[19]

Answers to these questions could come only from religion, argued Bulgakov, besides which, "It is obvious that 'ought' can in no way be substantiated from 'is.'"[20] Other contributors to *Problems of Idealism* took a very similar line. "The basic idea and also the basic error of positivism consists in subordinating 'what ought to be' ('ought') to 'what is' ('is') and in deriving the first from the second," wrote Pyotr Struve (1870–1944).[21]

In another essay, Pavel Novgorodtsev (1866–1924), a professor of law at Moscow University, denounced historical determinism for speaking of the "imperceptibly acting forces of history . . . of the necessity for individual persons to bow down before this general course of history and recognize its inevitability and beneficence."[22] Historical determinism, he said, implied that "the general course of events is everything and the individual is nothing."[23]

Another contributor to *Problems of Idealism*, Pyotr Struve, constructed a liberal theory of nationalism. "The people and society live in the person and in persons. . . . It would be foolish, or worse, hypocritical to talk of the free creativity of the national spirit if the people lack their rights," he wrote.[24] Thus, concluded Struve, "true nationalism cannot be anything other than unconditional respect of the person, the natural and real bearer and subject of the spiritual principle on earth."[25]

According to Richard Pipes, Struve was first and foremost a nationalist, whose liberalism derived from his belief that only freedom would enable Russia to develop and strengthen. Liberalism was "a matter of national survival" in the dog-eat-dog arena of international competition.[26] The same logic also made Struve a proponent of imperial expansion.[27] "Every vibrant state always has been, and always will be, infused with imperialism," he wrote.[28]

When war broke out with Japan in February 1904, it divided the liberal community in Russia. More moderate elements came out in support of the war effort.[29] By contrast, the Union of Liberation longed for Russia's defeat. "Marshal Oyama [the commander of the Japanese army] is the best ally in the struggle for the liberation of Russia," declared an article in the journal *Os-vobozhdenie*.[30] "What will the Russian people lose if their army and navy are routed in the Far East?" asked another article, answering that "they will lose the assurance that Tsarist power is indestructible. . . . But . . . if their army is victorious . . . they will lose everything."[31]

Struve at first tried to take a compromise position, along the lines of "oppose the government but support the troops."[32] But as the news from the front went from bad to worse, he began to demand an immediate end to the war.[33] The patriotic mood that had captured moderate liberals rapidly faded. The idea that political opposition should be postponed until the fighting was over was almost universally abandoned and liberalism in Russia found itself in the contentious position of cheering on the country's foreign enemies.

Political Liberalism

The process by which Russian liberalism ended up seeking the overthrow of the government in time of war was a long one. In the 1880s and early 1890s, Russian liberalism remained in loyal opposition to the government, and was largely confined to the local politics of the *zemstva*. This era of "gentry liberalism" is generally viewed as moderate in nature, favoring the gradual transformation of Russia in a liberal direction. After the accession of Nicholas II, liberalism moved into less loyal opposition. At the same time, liberalism's social base somewhat changed. As more and more nobles took up employment as lawyers, academics, doctors, and the like, liberalism became associated with what is known as the "intelligentsia." Meanwhile, the *zemstva* employed thousands of men and women as teachers, healthcare workers, agronomists, statisticians, and so on, collectively known as the "third element." These people provided another pool of liberal recruits, and liberalism's social base shifted from the nobility toward a new professional middle class.[34] However, liberalism still had almost no representatives from the peasants, who made up 80 percent of the Russian population, nor from the expanding urban working class.

Until 1900, liberals devoted themselves largely to practical work at the local level in the *zemstva* and to theoretical debate. Very roughly speaking one can divide the liberals of the late nineteenth century into three groups. The first group was the "constitutionalists," who sought the abolition of the autocracy and the creation of a constitutional system of government.[35] The second group was the so-called Slavophile liberals, the most notable of whom was Dmitry Shipov (1851–1920), who became head of the Moscow provincial *zemstvo* board in 1893. The Slavophiles supported the preservation of the absolute monarchy, while also defending the autonomy of local self-government.[36] And third was a group of moderate "gentry liberals," who were somewhat close to the Slavophiles in that they rejected grand schemes of constitutional reform at the national level, and focused on expanding civil liberties and developing local self-government. They differed from the Slavophiles, however, in their strong European orientation.

The main journal of the moderate liberals was *Vestnik Evropy*. In April 1882 this published a "liberal program" by the lawyer and journalist Konstantin Arsenyev (1837–1919). Arsenyev called for freedom of the press and of conscience, and argued in favor of a gradual transformation of popular political culture through the spread of education and the creation of a new form of elected local self-government at a level below that of the *zemstva*.[37] This gradualist approach reflected the journal's general political philosophy—*Vestnik Evropy* emphasized local government, civil liberties, and the rule of law.

Vladimir Solovyov was to play an important part in revising liberal understandings of the rule of law, in particular by helping to resurrect the notion of natural law. By the late nineteenth century, the positivist theory of law had become the prevailing legal doctrine. According to this, law has nothing to do with morality. Rather what makes a law is the fact that it has been deemed to be a law by a recognized authority that has the power to enforce it. Legal rights are therefore rights because the state has declared them to be rights, not because they exist in some metaphysical sense. Solovyov challenged this view. In an essay entitled "Morality and Law," he remarked that "the concern of the state . . . is not that each achieve his private objectives . . . but only that . . . each not violate the balance with the advantages of the other, not eliminate another's interests within the boundaries in which interest is right. . . . Therefore, law is not determined by the concept of utility, but contains within itself a formal moral principle."[38]

Further to this, Solovyov remarked that law is the implementation of the natural right to freedom, constrained by the necessity to live in a society.[39] Law is "an expression of a proper balance between individual liberty and the good of the whole," said Solovyov.[40] He concluded, "The rule of true progress is this, that the state should interfere as little as possible with the inner moral life of man, and at the same time should as widely as possible secure the external conditions of his worthy existence and moral development."[41]

Following in Solovyov's wake, other philosophers challenged legal positivism. Struve wrote that natural law "lies at the heart of any true liberalism. . . . Natural law is not only the ideal but also the desirable law . . . it is absolute law, rooted in an ethical understanding of the concept of the person and its self-determination."[42] Meanwhile, legal scholar Leon Petrazycki (1867–1931) developed what has been called a "psychological theory of law."[43] According to Petrazycki, "moral and legal norms and obligations represent nothing actually and objectively outside the minds of those individuals asserting or denying their existence."[44] As important as positive law, therefore, was the population's legal consciousness. It was essential, wrote Petrazycki, that positive law not diverge too far from what he called "intuitive law," that is, people's intuitive understanding of right and wrong. If it did, pressures for change would build up, which if not dealt with would result in an "explosion: a revolution."[45] By implication, this was the situation that Russia found itself in—if it failed to reform, revolution would result.

According to Petrazycki, rights played a key role in raising the population's legal consciousness. For it was the recognition that they had rights that led people to recognize that others had rights too, and so led them to treat other people with respect.[46] Petrazycki concluded: "The evolution, in the masses, of a 'citizen' type of a special and ideal character—possessing economic efficiency, energy, and initiative—depends upon the structure of the law and the direction of legal policy, and in particular and especially upon developing the principle of legality and a system of subjective rights which are strong, stable, and guaranteed against arbitrary conduct."[47]

The concept of legal consciousness also influenced Pavel Novgorodtsev. In a 1901 lecture, Novgorodtsev placed Solovyov's thinking in the context of a "crisis of legal consciousness" brought about by "decades of dominating legal Positivism that had reduced [law] to positive law, i.e. order of the state authority." This, said Novgorodtsev, had produced a "legal nihilism," in which people had no respect for the law because they regarded it as being entirely "the product of force."[48] The solution, said Novgorodtsev, was a "revival of natural law."

These developments in legal thought had important implications in terms of creating a theory of rights and also, as shown in the next section, of justifying a new form of interventionist economic policy. For the meantime, however, they remained matters of intellectual debate rather than practical politics. It took a number of events in the 1880s and 1890s to move liberals to action.

First, the limitations on the authority of the zemstva and the creation of the land captains, mentioned above, had the effect of severely straining the states' relations with liberal nobles. Second, the government's inept response to the famine of 1891 convinced many zemstvo members that the government was incompetent and should cede more authority to them. And third, liberals blamed Russia's continuing problems with revolutionary terrorism on the government's repressive policies. The only way to eliminate terrorism, they concluded, was to address its root cause—in other words, to give people more freedom.

Liberals looked to Nicholas II with hope when he ascended the throne. The nobles of Tver sent an address to Nicholas that voiced a desire that Russians could express their opinions to the emperor by means of "representatives of the Russian people."[49] Nicholas responded to this appeal by calling the Tver nobility's aspirations "senseless dreams."[50] With this, hopes for a more liberal policy under the new emperor were dashed.

Matters rapidly deteriorated thereafter. During the 1890s, the *zemstva* and municipal governments greatly expanded their activities. As they did so, they came up against resistance from a central bureaucracy that resented what were seen as encroachments into its sphere of competence. Tensions between the *zemstva* and the central government increased, and liberals became more and more radicalized. They began to organize themselves into a formal opposition.

An early step in this direction was the formation in Moscow in 1899 of the *Beseda* (Conversation) discussion circle, nearly all of whose members were active in the *zemstva*.[51] Even more significant was the founding in 1902 of the newspaper *Osvobozhdenie*, edited by Struve. Russian liberals began to push openly for the overthrow of the state. As Shmuel Galai writes, the Liberation movement "was not interested in partial reforms . . . guaranteed by a constitution granted from above. What it aimed at the was the destruction of autocracy by pressure exerted from below."[52]

This change of direction to some degree reflected the change in liberalism's social base. Leadership passed from the landed nobility into the hands of intellectuals such as Struve and Miliukov.[53] Viktor Leontovitsch contends that consequently Russian liberalism became more and more "doctrinaire" and "not in the least interested in an understanding with the monarch or the forces of the old system in general."[54] The practical realities of Russian life were forgotten, claims Leontovitsch, in favor of abstract theory and a conviction that a constitution would solve all Russia's problems.[55]

At first *Osvobozhdenie* attempted to keep the *zemstvo* oppositionists united by avoiding direct references to a constitution, lest such a reference drive out Slavophile liberals such as Shipov.[56] Before long, however, Miliukov, Struve, and other contributors tired of compromise.[57] This coincided with the creation of the Union of Liberation, which held its first congress in St. Petersburg in January 1904. At this, it adopted a resolution declaring that "the first and main aim of the Union of Liberation is the political liberation of Russia . . . the Union will seek before all else the abolition of autocracy and the establishment in Russia of a constitutional regime."[58] This was to be done by means of a constituent assembly elected by universal, equal, secret, and direct elections (known as the "four-tail" franchise).[59]

By this point, long experience of the imperial government had convinced many members of the Union of Liberation that the regime would never agree to any compromise with educated society unless subjected to intense pressure from below.[60] As a 1904 article in *Osvobozhdenie* remarked, the liberation movement was "fundamentally antagonistic toward autocracy, for the latter is organically unable to incorporate legitimate activities and social groups."[61]

From this, *Osvobozhdenie* drew the conclusion that "constitutionalists must not miss any opportunity that offers the chance of intensifying or provoking conflict between the organs of autonomous social action and the autocratic regime."[62] The Union of Liberation threw its weight behind revolutionary forces. "The revolutionary parties unite the best, the most active, and the most self-sacrificing elements of the younger generation of the incessantly growing intelligentsia. This [is] the intellectual and moral flower of the nation," wrote Struve.[63]

The Union's position was now that there were "no enemies on the left," and more and more members became willing to condone revolutionary violence.[64] In October 1904, Struve wrote in *Osvobozhdenie* that "as long as the stronghold of autocracy has not been destroyed, anyone also fighting against it represents not a great danger, but a great blessing. . . . In Russia there is no internal enemy apart from autocracy. . . . Solidarity between all our oppositional forces . . . constitutes the first commandment of a sensible political struggle."[65]

In late 1904, the Union of Liberation took two steps to further its cause. The first was the adoption of a draft constitution for Russia, written by a group of prominent liberal lawyers. This proposed the establishment of a constitutional monarchy, with an elected parliament but with the emperor retaining substantial powers, including the ability to veto legislation and to dissolve parliament. The constitution was to be confirmed by means of a constituent assembly elected by the four-tail suffrage.[66]

Second, the Union of Liberation organized a series of meetings designed to mobilize civil society against the government. To provide cover for what were actually political gatherings, the meetings took the form of banquets, each organized by members of a specific professional group. For instance, in November 1904, St. Petersburg lawyers held a banquet with the notional objective of celebrating the fortieth anniversary of the 1864 judicial reform. The meeting passed a resolution demanding that (a) citizens be granted certain "inalienable rights," namely "personal inviolability, freedom of conscience, speech, press, assembly, and association"; (b) "all class, national, and religious restrictions be removed and that a real equality before the law be established"; and (c) "all laws be issued and taxes established only with the participation of representatives freely elected by the people." To this end the banquet goers demanded the "immediate convocation of a constituent assembly."[67]

Meanwhile, the *zemstva* were also moving into opposition to the state. In November 1904 *zemstvo* members from across Russia met for a national congress in St. Petersburg. The congress demanded "inviolability of the individual," "freedom of conscience and religion, freedom of speech and press, and also freedom of assembly and association," the abolition of legal differences between estates, and an expansion of the powers of local self-government.[68] Congress delegates proposed that the emperor summon a representative assembly, but avoided mention of a constitution.[69]

The massive increase in social unrest which followed Bloody Sunday swung liberal opinion further in a revolutionary direction. Struve wrote in *Osvobozhdenie*: "Tsar Nicholas II has openly become an enemy and an executioner of the people. . . . He has destroyed himself in our eyes and there can be no return to the past. . . . We must neither think nor write about anything except revenge and freedom."[70] Miliukov was even more outspoken: "All means are now legitimate against the terrible threat latent in the very fact of the continued existence of the present government."[71]

The *zemstva* held further national congresses in February, April, May, and July 1905. The tone of each was more radical than the last. By July 1905, the *zemstvo* congress had firmly moved into the constitutional camp, adopting a draft constitution written by Sergei Muromtsev and Fyodor Kokoshkin (1871–1918). Article 1 of what is often called the "Muromtsev Constitution" stated that "the Russian Empire shall be governed on the firm foundations of laws that have been promulgated in accordance with procedures stipulated in the present fundamental law."[72] The document proposed two houses of parliament—an elected lower chamber and an upper chamber representing local institutions—*zemstva* and town councils. But, as in the draft constitution adopted by the Union of Liberation, it left very considerable power in the hands of the executive, centered on the person of the emperor. It therefore sought to introduce a form of constitutional government, but one that conformed to Russian traditions and institutions.[73]

Despite their radical language of revolutionary change, Russian liberals' aims were, in fact, somewhat modest. They sought not a republic but something close to the German constitution of the time, in which civil liberties and representative institutions were combined with strong monarchical authority. Underlying this aspiration was a belief that once the Russian people acquired civil and political liberties, they would abandon any revolutionary inclinations. Struve wrote:

The only way to direct the enormous social movement stirring Russia's urban and rural population into the channel of lawful struggle for their interest is to invite the entire population, on equal rights, to share in the political life—that is to institute universal franchise. Give political freedom and political equality, and life itself will freely sweep away all that which is premature and unrealizable in radical programs. . . . Universal franchise . . . will bring no horrors and no miracles; the masses, called on to participate in political and social construction, will astonish us neither with their obscurantism nor their radicalism. . . . Under the universal franchise, the masses, having become responsible members of their own destiny, will understand what is necessary and what is not.[74]

In their revolutionary zeal, Russian liberals temporarily abandoned their traditional suspicion of the masses. Some also took the view that liberalism and socialism were converging, and that if provided with a democratic government, socialists would abandon their revolutionary political pretensions in return for economic and social reforms that would improve the lives of their constituents.[75] Miliukov told an American audience: "The scope of divergence among different shapes of opposition is steadily diminishing. . . . In studying the history of the liberal and socialistic currents, we have found that the chasm existing between them at their inception was perpetually narrowing . . . the utopian element . . . slowly but steadily vanishing from the socialistic programs."[76]

With the benefit of hindsight, Struve's and Miliukov's statements appear extraordinarily naïve. It appears that liberals believed that having turned on the revolutionary movement, they could just as easily turn it off again once they got what they wanted. As subsequent events were to show, this was not the case.

Social-Economic Liberalism

Insofar as free market economics had a champion in this era it was Nikolai Bunge, who served as finance minister from 1881 to 1886. An admirer of Adam Smith, Bunge moderated his free market views to fit Russian circumstances, gradually accepting some degree of limited state involvement in the economy.[77] He has been described as a "conditional interventionist," in that he believed that the state should retain control of certain key sectors, such as communications, but that it should generally avoid supporting private businesses.[78] Bunge wrote: "The state would be embarking on a dangerous path if it . . . engaged in those branches of industry that private entrepreneurs have successfully pursued, if it took into its head to monopolize mining, mills, and factories. . . . The intrusion of the state into industrial enterprise would mark the start of the unlimited power of the administration to set prices, a power hitherto unknown and one which, of course, would be far mightier than any combination of capitalists."[79]

Bunge sought to expand property rights among the peasantry by establishing the Peasant Bank. This provided cheap loans to peasants who wanted to purchase land outside of the commune.[80] Perhaps Bunge's most notable reform was a series of factory laws that placed limits on the use of female and child labor in industry; laid out procedures for the hiring and firing of workers, the payment of wages, and so on; and created factory inspectors whose job it was to enforce the relevant legislation.[81] Bunge's support for the factory laws did not make him a supporter of socialism, which he described as "an evil that would destroy morality, duty, liberty, and the individual." Rather the factory laws were an attempt, as Bunge put it, "to eliminate discord and conflicts of interest between capital and labor, on the one hand, and among the workers themselves, on the other."[82] Bunge has been described as an "economic liberal in terms of supporting the development of an economy based on both property rights and private capital."[83] He wrote: "There is no doubt that without monetary capital, humans could never have got out from a primitive state, and all that makes us proud of contemporary civilization: knowledge, science, art, the use of the forces of nature—would then have been inaccessible."[84]

Struve was also a firm supporter of capitalism, arguing that it brought not just economic growth but also political liberation and cultural progress, "the very foundations of culture."[85] To function properly, capitalism required individual freedom, an educated population, and the rule of law.[86] Struve wrote that "the positive, creative work of the capitalist process of development, as represented by industrial growth and rationalization of agriculture, will in Russia, as everywhere else, outstrip its negative, destructive work," and that "the development of capitalism, that is, economic progress, constitutes the first condition of the improvement of the lot of the Russian population."[87]

Struve's praise of capitalism was rather unusual among liberal intellectuals, many of whom viewed it with suspicion. In the 1880s and 1890s, the Russian economy underwent a massive expansion as a result of a policy of state-led industrialization. To pay for this, the state resorted to foreign loans, protectionist tariffs, and indirect taxes. The burden fell on consumers, who had to pay more for both imported and domestic products. Since most consumers were peasants, this led to criticism that the government's industrial policy was favoring heavy industry at the expense of the countryside. This endangered future growth by suppressing demand, and created a risk of social tension due to the impoverishment of the peasantry.

Among the critics of the industrialization policy was Miliukov, who complained that it increased the prices of commodities without creating a corresponding increase in the purchasing power of consumers."[88] He added that "the agricultural crisis is at the bottom of the other crises, and the diminution of the purchasing power of the peasant is at the bottom of the agricultural crisis."[89]

Miliukov's views echoed those of Leonid Slonimsky (1849–1918) who published many articles on economics in *Vestnik Evropy*. Slonimsky denounced Russian capitalism as "rapacity and speculation, barbarity, intellectual darkness."[90] In an 1888 article, he argued that the interests of agriculture should take precedence over those of industry.[91] Slonimsky wrote that "the foundations of national economies have little to do with commodity trade but lie much deeper; they depend first of all on agricultural relations, which determine a country's economic life and give the national economy a general tone regardless of the industrial system."[92]

Contributors to *Vestnik Evropy* made various proposals to improve the economic condition of the countryside. For instance, Konstantin Arsenyev argued that Russian liberalism should support communal landholding to protect peasants from becoming landless; provide more land to peasants; create microcredit institutions for peasants; reduce the redemption payments imposed during the emancipation of the serfs; and redistribute the tax burden away from the peasantry toward Russia's wealthier classes.[93] To achieve this goal, *Vestnik Evropy* supported lower indirect taxes and import duties and the introduction of a progressive income tax.[94]

In some respects, the *Vestnik Evropy* program resembled that of conservative economists such as Sergei Sharapov (1855–1911), who similarly argued that Russia should focus on the countryside.[95] What distinguished one from the other and made *Vestnik Evropy* "liberal" was its contributors' belief that successful development depended on expanding the rights of the peasantry and the role of the *zemstva* in the economic management of the countryside. Arsenyev, for instance, argued that the 1891 famine showed the effectiveness of local initiative in responding to local needs and concluded that "zemstvo influence on economic life had to increase."[96] Anton Fedyashin notes that *Vestnik Evropy* believed that "socially stable and economically successful modernization would produce long term results only if the state extended the rights and responsibilities of local self-government and made the Russian people a participant in modernization, not a subject of economic experiments."[97] The result might be slower economic growth, but it would ensure social stability.[98]

Vestnik Evropy's economic views fell somewhere between free market liberalism and socialism, favoring what has been called "social liberalism."[99] This received a major theoretical boost in the writings of Vladimir Solovyov. In an 1897 essay entitled "The Social Question in Europe," Solovyov declared:

> The principle of equality in its true sense is that all men are equal . . . each represents intrinsic value, and possesses an inalienable right to an existence corresponding to his human dignity. The raison d'être of society in relation to its members is to assure for each not solely a material livelihood, but moreover a *dignified* livelihood. Now it is clear that poverty beyond a certain threshold . . . is contrary to human dignity and therefore incompatible with true public morality. Therefore, society must insure all its members against this degrading poverty in securing for each a *minimum* of material resources.[100]

Solovyov's conception that the state should provide all of its citizens with the minimum required for a dignified existence was to have a strong influence on liberal thinking. His views on some other matters were rather at odds with the tenor of the times, and to modern eyes Solovyov appears rather more liberal than the notional liberals of his own era.

An example of his liberalism is in the realm of criminal justice. The harsh measures favored by many in the liberal intelligentsia (described below) provoked Solovyov's wrath. "We ought *to pity both* the victim and the criminal," he wrote, adding that "society has a right to safety; the criminal has a right to correction and reformation."[101] The idea that criminals were incorrigible, as the theorists discussed below supposed, was "absolutely arbitrary," claimed Solovyov.[102] Punishing criminals to deter others was wrong, he said, because it treated criminals as means rather than as ends in themselves.[103] Likewise, the death penalty was a "profane, inhumane, and shameful act," while punishments such as "life sentences, hard labor, long-term exile" involved "unnecessary violence and torture."[104]

In discussing crime and punishment, Solovyov targeted the medical profession and liberal academics of the era. The latter were strongly influenced by the theories of the Italian criminologist Cesare Lombroso (1835–1909), who maintained that while criminality, alcoholism, and other supposed "degenerate" character traits initially had social causes, once acquired they became hereditary characteristics and were transferred from generation to generation.[105] From this starting point, liberals drew some quite illiberal conclusions.

Because degeneracy was a product of social conditions, it followed that radical social change was necessary to eradicate it.[106] Criminologist Dmitry Dril

(1846–1910) remarked that the "physical and mental-moral degeneration of the species" was intimately connected to society's "economic foundations" and it was therefore necessary "to rework the current iniquitous order in the genuine interests of the common good."[107] This logic led many doctors into opposition to the autocratic state, seeing it as the cause of the nation's physical and psychological decline. But it also led many to support repressive social policies. Since criminality and other types of degeneracy were also, according to this logic, hereditary, it followed that society needed to protect itself by removing criminals and other supposed degenerates and preventing them from breeding or from passing on their degeneracy to others by a process of "moral contagion." They were therefore to be "isolated . . . in special institutions" in a form of "indefinite preventive detention," and subjected to "coercive healing in labor colonies."[108] Consequently, writes Daniel Beer, Russian liberalism became in some respects decidedly "coercive," even "draconian" with respect to crime.[109]

Liberals' approach to family policy was more progressive. Late imperial Russia was patriarchal. Husbands and fathers had considerable legal powers over their wives and children. As William Wagner notes, "A wife was obligated to live with her husband and to obtain his consent before undertaking a number of activities . . . while children required parental consent to marry, and . . . to enter employment."[110] Liberals, notably the jurist Aleksandr Borovikovsky (1844–1905), sought to eliminate many of these patriarchal regulations. Discussing the drafting of a new civil law code, Borovikovsky argued that it should "clearly and categorically state that the marital union is founded on the principle of the equal rights of spouses and that possible disagreements between them [i.e., the spouses] must be resolved in accordance with the interests of the family."[111] Borovikovsky supported the expansion of personal rights but also sought to protect the family as an institution. Wagner therefore concludes that he and other liberals displayed "a combination of individualist and communitarian ideals."[112]

Proposals to diminish husbands' powers over their wives were steps toward gender equality in Russia. That said, liberals were not all committed to complete legal equality. The Union of Liberation did promise to extend the vote to women, but the Muromtsev constitution restricted it to men. William Rosenberg notes that "gender . . . was almost entirely ignored" by liberals.[113] He concludes: "Insofar as it constructed citizenship by universalizing personal rights (with "traditional" exceptions for women, some insisted) [Russian liberalism] privileged individual over collective identities and created the necessary environment for individual human development. That men and women might develop differently, and that most liberal visions of modernity preserved male hegemony in various ways was not, for many, a serious issue. What mattered was not gender equality (or social equalities in other ways) but the sanctity and inviolability of the person."[114]

For much of this period, liberals adopted a relatively moderate position, seeking the expansion of local self-government and the slow transformation of Russian society toward a new understanding of personal rights and liberties. Similarly, their views on economic development were initially fairly conservative, opposing the rapid industrialization promoted by the state and instead looking to slowly develop the rural economy, while preserving the peasant commune as a bastion of social stability in the countryside.

Once Nicholas II came to the throne, liberals moved sharply leftward. On economic issues, they rejected socialism (that is to say, collective ownership of the means of production) but increasingly embraced a form of social liberalism that saw a significant role for the state in the economy. Socialism and liberalism were seen as converging in both the political and economic realms. Sergei Bulgakov remarked that "not only must liberalism never be opposed to socialism, but they must not even be separated from one another. According to their basic ideal they are identical and indivisible. [Hence] in contrast to what many people fear, socialism does not threaten liberalism. Socialism comes not to destroy but to fulfil the legacy of liberalism."[115]

Unfortunately for Russian liberals, they were to discover in due course that Russian socialists had a rather different view of their relationship. In the meantime, as they became more radicalized, Russian liberals hoped that revolution could serve their purposes in forcing the state to grant a constitution. Once that was done, they thought that revolution could be set aside. Miliukov declared, "Yes, we are for revolution, as far as it serves the goals of political liberation and social reform; but we are against those who propose 'permanent' revolution, because we believe that this permanent revolution—revolution come what may—serves the aims of reaction."[116]

At the heart of this viewpoint was a belief that the cause of revolution was the existence of the absolute monarchy. Once this was abolished, liberals believed, revolution would soon lose steam. This belief would dictate much of what they did in the decade that followed.

CHAPTER 5

Between Revolutions

In 1905, disorder spread throughout Russia, in the form of political protests, strikes, and attacks on nobles' homes. Peace with Japan was followed by a wave of mutinies in the army. In October 1905 Nicholas II decided that he needed to make political concessions. He issued a manifesto promising to create an elected legislature, the State Duma, and to expand the civil liberties of Russian citizens. With this October Manifesto, Russian politics entered a new era.

The October Manifesto did not immediately eliminate the threat of revolution. In the short term it encouraged further acts of violence, by creating the impression that the regime was weak and that one final push could destroy it. Russian society remained extremely unequal; wealth was concentrated in the hands of a small part of the population, and the nobility enjoyed many more rights than peasants and workers, who were expected to treat the nobility with deference. The rural economy was struggling, as the population rapidly grew but the land available to peasants did not. In the cities, conditions for the expanding working class were poor, workers had few legal protections against their employers, and trade unions were forbidden. While these problems were largely economic, many Russians believed that political reform was a precondition for addressing them.

The October Manifesto went some way toward meeting popular demands but created new problems. From 1906 onward, all legislation had to be approved by the Duma, but the emperor appointed government ministers, who were responsible to him, not to the parliament. Consequently, the system allowed for a situation in which the Duma and the ministers were entirely at odds with one another. This is exactly what transpired.

Duma members were elected using a complex indirect system. This was weighted in favor of Russia's wealthier classes but still gave a considerable voice to the peasantry and urban working class. Socialist parties boycotted the elections to the First Duma in 1906, and liberal parties won many seats. The liberals then pushed a legislative program that Nicholas and his ministers considered unacceptable. After just a couple of months, the emperor abruptly dissolved the Duma.

The Second Duma, convened at the start of 1907, proved even more confrontational. This time, socialist parties participated in the election, giving the Second Duma a more radical complexion than the first. Three months later it, too, was dissolved. At this point, Russia's prime minister, Pyotr Stolypin (1862–1911), rewrote the electoral law so as to weaken the representation of the poorer elements of the Russian population. Consequently, the Third Duma, which began work in November 1907, proved more acceptable to the government, and was able to complete its entire mandate. A Fourth Duma was elected in 1912. This operated until the Russian Revolution of 1917.

Appointed prime minister in July 1906, Stolypin sought to stabilize the country through a two-pronged strategy of repression and reform. To deal with revolutionary violence, he established a system of field courts martial that tried people whose guilt had supposedly already been determined beyond all doubt. Over 3,000 people were sentenced to death by these field courts martial. Stolypin also introduced a wide-ranging plan of reform, the centerpiece of which was legislation that allowed peasants to leave the commune and consolidate their land into a unified plot that was their own personal property.

Stolypin largely succeeded in restoring order, but some terrorist violence continued and in 1911 he was assassinated by a socialist revolutionary, Dmitry Bogrov (1887–1911). Under Stolypin's successors, reform came to a halt, and relations between the state and Russian liberals worsened. An important factor in this was the central bureaucracy's efforts to limit the scope of local government. In his study of the Moscow city council in this era, Robert Thurston notes how the council's efforts to expand its activities in realms such as education and health care ran into continual opposition from a central state that did not want local government to amass too much power. This caused considerable resentment. Aleksandr Guchkov (1862–1936), leader of the Union of 17 October (the Octobrist party), remarked that the root of tensions between liberal society and the state was precisely "the attitude of the government to the organs and to the very idea of local government."[1]

Guchkov's party was the largest in the Third Duma. It was committed to supporting the constitutional order created by the October Manifesto, and is often described as a liberal party, albeit one on the conservative end of the liberal spectrum. This is a somewhat difficult position to defend. The Octobrists were noted for "Great Russian chauvinism," supported Stolypin's repressive policies, and engaged in antisemitic rhetoric.[2] Consequently, Shmuel Galai concludes that, "the Octobrists could not be considered a liberal party in the true sense of the word."[3]

Rather, the dominant liberal force was the Constitutional Democratic (Kadet) Party, founded in August 1905. Several other liberal parties were also established, such as the Progressive Party, the Party of Peaceful Renewal, and the Party of Democratic Reform.

The Kadet party has been described as a "party of professors." Its central committee's members were almost all professionals—especially academics, lawyers, and journalists. The party had almost no members among the peasantry, the urban proletariat, or the merchant or business classes.[4] The Kadet party was also overwhelmingly male—there was just one woman, Ariadna Tyrkova-Williams (1869–1962), in the central committee. Overall, as Dittmar Dahlmann notes, "women were completely underrepresented in the party, in contrast to the socialist parties."[5]

From 1905 to 1907, the Kadet party stood clearly in opposition to the imperial monarchy. In 1914, after the outbreak of the First World War, it initially decided to put aside its political differences with the government. Liberal activists took a leading role in setting up local and national organizations designed to provide the Russian army with much-needed supplies. These included war industry committees, which aimed to increase the production of essential war materials, and the Union of Towns and Zemstva, which among other things provided medical care to wounded soldiers. These civil society organizations established close contacts with senior military officers and in due course took on a political role, seeking to persuade Russian generals to influence the emperor to share with society the management of the country.

After the Russian army suffered a series of defeats in summer 1915, many liberals came to the conclusion that the government was incapable of running the war effort effectively. Some even concluded that the country's defeats were the result of treason at the highest levels. They demanded that the state cede more authority to society and that Nicholas II appoint a government enjoying the confidence of the State Duma. Nicholas refused to yield.

The strains of war caused serious problems for the Russian economy, and basic supplies ran short in the major cities. As the economic situation worsened, and as casualties mounted at the front, the political atmosphere became increasingly tense. When huge protests erupted in the capital Petrograd (as St. Petersburg had been renamed) in early 1917, and Nicholas II was swept from power, liberals welcomed the opportunity to establish what they hoped would be a better political and social order.

Cultural Liberalism

Liberalism's social base—urban professionals—gave it a particular culture, distinguished by "its very high degree of Westernization."[6] According to Peter Enticott, "the Kadet leaders were not ashamed to admit that they had, as it were, taken Western liberalism 'off the peg.'"[7] Thus, Kadet Duma member Gabriel Shershenevich (1863–1912) introduced a bill to guarantee freedom of assembly by saying, "I do not think we have our own arbitrary distinctive method of solving this problem. I think that the models of Western political life will serve as our models for a long time to come."[8]

For the Kadet party, the most important issue was constitutional change, which was viewed as the key that would unlock all the other benefits that its members were seeking. More moderate liberals opposed this approach and argued that cultural change had to precede political reform. The philosopher Evgeny Trubetskoi (1863–1920), for instance, quit the Kadets in protest at their antigovernment stance and joined the Party of Democratic Reform. Trubetskoi argued that "every government is a product of its social environment."[9] Changing the leaders would simply lead to the replacement of one set of corrupt people with another. He believed that liberals should return to a strategy of "small deeds," similar to that previously followed by the zemstva, promoting education, health care, and cultural institutions.[10] Other liberals, however, objected that this approach had been tried and had failed. Absent political reform, they argued, no progress was possible.

Still, liberals of all sort invested a significant amount of time in educational projects. These included setting up "people's universities," of which sixteen were operating by 1911.[11] A notable project was the Ligovsky People's House in St. Petersburg, established by Countess Sofia Panina (1871–1956). This contained a theater, cafeterias, libraries, classrooms, and a legal aid clinic, and provided day care, adult education, and other services for members of St. Petersburg's working class.[12] According to Adele Lindenmeyr, Panina believed in the "transformative power" of "European and Russian high culture," and sought "to prepare Russia's masses . . . for their future responsibilities in a democratic polity."[13]

Lindenmeyr notes that Panina's "belief in the feasibility of cross-class understanding and collaboration echoes themes found often in the history of Russian liberalism."[14] An important principle in liberal thinking of this time was the idea of *nadklassnost'*, that is, of being above classes. As the jurist Sergei Gessen (1887–1950) put it, "The state's task is to be an above-class [*nadklassnym*] intermediary between classes."[15] The Kadet party insisted that it did not represent any particular class, but rather the nation as a whole.[16] "The Kadet party—is the party of freedom *for the people*. The political freedom it demands is for *all of the people*, for *all citizens*, regardless of the social group or economic class to which they might belong," said party election materials.[17]

While many liberals took the intelligentsia's leading role in society for granted, the 1905 revolution led some to conclude that it was time for a rethink. Among these was Pyotr Struve, to whom the 1905 revolution demonstrated that the masses were more to be feared than the government, due to their "political immaturity, naivete and credulity, their susceptibility to any demagogic appeal that responded to their prejudices, resentments, needs and wishes."[18] Overall, concluded Struve, what Russia needed was a cultural rather than a political revolution. He wrote: "The purely political approach has proven futile . . . we can now assert that no political program is possible without cultural progress. . . . To reduce everything to a critique of the government would mean infinitely to exaggerate the importance of a given government and of authority in general. The source of the failures, disappointments, and defeats which have afflicted Russia lies much deeper."[19]

In 1909, Struve joined a group of liberal intellectuals to publish a volume entitled *Vekhi* (Landmarks), attacking the intelligentsia. In this, philosopher Nikolai Berdiaev complained that the obsession with overthrowing the autocracy meant that the intelligentsia was willing to bend truth in any way that served its political purpose.[20] Other contributors made similar complaints. Sergei Bulgakov, for instance, attacked "intelligentsia maximalism . . . its historical impatience . . . its denial in practice of the evolutionism it professes in theory."[21] Bogdan Kistiakovsky (1863–1920) complained of the intelligentsia's lack of respect for the law.[22] And Semyon Frank (1877–1950) accused it of "nihilistic moralism."[23] "The intelligentsia must reexamine its entire attitude," concluded Struve.[24]

Vekhi did not go down well with liberal intellectuals. In a volume of responses entitled *Intelligentsiia v Rossii* (The Intelligentsia in Russia), Miliukov denounced *Vekhi* as reactionary. "The seeds which the authors of *Vekhi* are sowing . . . are poisonous seeds, and the work which they are doing . . . is dangerous and harmful," he wrote.[25] Miliukov objected to the idea that the intelligentsia should look inward and work on self-improvement. "The role of the educated class in Russia is to be the transmitter of civilization to the people," he argued.[26]

Many liberals, like Miliukov, thought of civilization in terms of European culture. Nevertheless, some, notably Struve, developed a strong attachment to Russian nationalism. Struve claimed that, with the exception of the Poles and the Finns, the non-Russian nationalities within the Russian empire did not have fully developed cultures, and he opposed concessions to national minorities, such as the right to education in their own language. He wrote: "I am deeply convinced that, for instance, creating middle and high schools in the Malorussian [i.e., Ukrainian] language would be an artificial and entirely unjustifiable waste of the population's psychological forces. . . . A Russian can be an educated person and participate in national life without understanding a word of Malorussian, but the Malorussian who doesn't understand Russian is simply illiterate in relation to the nation and the state."[27]

Miliukov's perspective was different, favoring cultural but not political autonomy for national minorities. He drafted an amendment to a government education bill to permit education in minority languages in districts where there were at least fifty children of that minority. "The principle of the equality of nationalities is the Alpha and Omega of all good government," he declared.[28] Miliukov feared that Great Russian nationalism would result in the Kadet party losing support among the empire's minorities.[29] He argued in favor of "nationalities living together in the framework of a single state," adding that, "the Russian people will not lose anything if it ceases to be the 'dominant nation,' because it never had anything, but instead it will win, for it will win the state."[30]

Kadet party policy reflected Miliukov's position rather than Struve's. The party program stated that "the basic law of the Russian Empire must guarantee all the peoples of the Empire, as well as full civil and political equality, the right of free cultural self-determination, such as complete freedom of the use of different languages and dialects."[31] The Kadets believed that cultural autonomy would reduce discontent among minorities and so eliminate the threat of separatism.[32] Politically, however, the Kadets were committed to a unitary model of the state, and with the exceptions of Poland and Finland, they rejected the granting of political autonomy to national minorities, as they feared that federalism could lead to the unraveling of the empire.[33]

While Struve and Miliukov differed on issues of domestic policy, they shared an imperialistic outlook when it came to foreign policy. In a 1908 essay entitled "Great Russia," Struve argued that weak states risked being swallowed by up stronger ones, and it was therefore essential for every state to increase its power on the international scene. "A great people cannot . . . sit quietly by in a world that is moving forward and growing amidst uninterrupted struggle," he wrote.[34] In a 1911 article, Struve remarked: "If by imperialism we mean caring for the state's external power, and by liberalism caring for justice in its internal relations, then it is a feature of the nineteenth and twentieth centuries that everywhere those states have triumphed which have the most completely combined and embodied both these ideas."[35]

Following its defeat by Japan, the Russian state was in no position to adopt an assertive imperial policy of the sort that Struve desired. In 1908, Russia had to stand by and do nothing when Austria-Hungary annexed Bosnia, in what was seen as a blow to Russia's prestige. Similarly, Russia remained on the sidelines when war broke out between various Balkan states in 1912 and then again in 1913. During the Russo-Japanese War, Russian liberals had opposed the state's imperial policies. Now, however, their attitudes underwent a remarkable transformation and they attacked the state for its apparent weakness on foreign policy issues.

Among those who criticized Russia's foreign policy as weak was one of the leading members of the Kadet party, Vasily Maklakov (1869–1957). In a December 1912 speech, he attacked the government for the "meek" language it had used regarding the First Balkan War, saying that it "should not fall to the temptation to lower Russia" in the eyes of Europe.[36] "We should be ready for war," he added.[37] When war broke out in the Balkans in 1912, many liberals took a firmly anti-Turkish line and discussed the possibility of Russia taking control of the Dardanelles straits. Lawyer Fyodor Kokoshkin remarked that "the straits are a vital interest for Russia. . . . Our sympathies must be on the side of the Slavs. We cannot forget that a struggle is taking place between countries with democratic constitutions against countries that are military despotisms. . . . We shouldn't accept the point of view that war should be avoided at any price."[38]

Unlike in 1904, when war came to Russia in August 1914, liberals committed themselves to seeing it through to a successful conclusion regardless of the cost. They also adopted decidedly aggressive goals. In a 1915 article, Miliukov argued that Russia's war aims should be the annexation of Galicia and Turkish Armenia, the unification of Poland as part of the Russian empire, and control of the Dardanelles.[39]

One difference between the Russo-Japanese War and the First World War was that the latter was fought close to the Russian heartland whereas the former was not.[40] Another was liberals' attitudes to their enemies. There was little enmity toward Japan, but an intense dislike of Germany, which was seen as militaristic and despotic. The fact that Russia was allied with the democratic powers of France and Britain strengthened liberals' perception that the First World War was a struggle of good against evil. As Miliukov told the Duma in January 1915:

"We are marching hand in hand with mankind's most enlightened nations. . . . We value no less that profound moral meaning which the world war is acquiring thanks to the participation in it of the two most advanced democracies of contemporary mankind. We believe that this participation will guarantee to us the full realization of the liberating goals of this war."[41]

Meanwhile, in a lecture entitled "The National Question, Constantinople and St. Sophia," Evgeny Trubetskoi argued that capturing Constantinople and the cathedral of Hagia Sophia (converted by the Turks into a mosque) was a matter of extraordinary spiritual significance. "Every question of Russian life raised by the present war turns upon this one central question. Will Russia succeed in restoring the desecrated church and again show the world the light extinguished by the Turks?" he asked.[42] Despite its brutality, war, said Trubetskoi, reveals "the wholeness of person, nation, and humanity . . . in war the feeling of universal human solidarity achieves an extent hardly possible in peace."[43] This, he concluded, was "the spiritual meaning of the war."[44]

Political Liberalism

Early twentieth-century liberals' aim was a "law-based state" (*pravovoe gosudarstvo*). This objective led theorists such as Novgorodtsev, Maksim Kovalevsky (1851–1916), Bogdan Kistiakovsky, and Fyodor Kokoshkin to devote a considerable amount of time to debating the relationship between the state and the law. They divided into two main groups—positivists and supporters of natural law.[45] But whatever their theoretical disagreements, liberal thinkers agreed that the law-based state was their goal. "The law-governed state is the highest form of social organization ever elaborated by human beings," said Kistiakovsky.[46] To him, the rule of law necessarily involved the codification of inalienable rights that would serve to limit the power of the state over individuals.[47] Meanwhile, Kovalevsky remarked, "The guarantee of the recognition of so-called personal rights is the possibility of summoning to court everybody, no matter who they are, who has caused harm and loss through actions that contradict the law. Legal responsibility is therefore the foundation of personal rights . . . [the] responsibility of each and every person, from the lowest to the highest."[48]

Liberal thinkers agreed that the Russian state fell far short of this ideal. This weakened its legitimacy, paving the way for popular revolution. Kovalevsky denounced Stolypin's rewriting of the electoral rules for the Duma in 1907 as a "coup d'état" and complained that "arbitrariness from above is always accompanied by arbitrariness below. . . . Ministers themselves break the law and

the constitution . . . [and thereby] prepare the ground for the death of the order that they are meant to protect."[49] Maklakov denounced Stolypin's field
courts martial, saying, "If you defeat the revolution this way, you will at the
same time defeat the state, and in the collapse of revolution you will find not
a rule-of-law state but only solitary individuals, a chaos of state breakdown."[50]

Liberals' attitude toward the state put them in a difficult position. On the
one hand, they wished to strengthen the state, which was seen as the provider
of law, order, and justice. On the other hand, they opposed the existing form
of the state, and felt that they had to weaken it in order to force it to change.
Many liberals therefore believed that it was necessary to ally with revolutionary forces. "Nothing has changed, the struggle goes on," said Miliukov on hear-
ing news of the October Manifesto.[51] This set the tone for liberal politics for
most of the decade that followed.

To put the October Manifesto into effect, in 1906 Nicholas II issued a set of
"fundamental laws." These laid out citizens' rights, such as freedom of the
press and association, guaranteed the independence of the judiciary, and established a bicameral parliament consisting of an indirectly elected Duma and
an appointed State Council. The emperor retained considerable powers, including control of foreign policy and the military and the right to appoint ministers. The existence of the State Council and the fact that ministers were
responsible to the emperor, not to parliament, meant that the new system of
government fell short of what liberal constitutionalists had sought, namely a
constitutional monarchy with a single parliamentary chamber that was to have
the right to initiate legislation and to hold ministers to account.

The Kadet party opposed the indirect voting system established to elect the
new Duma and demanded that the parliament be elected by the four-tail suffrage.[52] There were some divisions within the party about whether this would
mean giving the vote to women. Women played only a small role in the party,
whose members came largely from professions from which women were
barred, such as academia and law.[53] Those opposed to giving the vote to women
noted that female suffrage had not been adopted in the West, and also claimed
that women's illiteracy and irrationality would lower the level of political debate.[54] Among the most prominent opponents of female suffrage was Miliukov, who argued that supporting it would lose the Kadet party the votes of
conservative-minded peasants. This put him in opposition to his wife, Anna
Miliukova, who persuaded the first party congress to pass a resolution endorsing votes for women. Miliukov then counterattacked by successfully proposing an amendment that designated Miliukova's resolution nonbinding.[55] At the
Kadet party's second congress in January 1906, however, Miliukov's amendment was overturned, and votes for women became official party policy.[56]

Believing that the state could not be trusted, liberals turned down repeated offers to cooperate with the government, insisting on almost complete acceptance of their demands as a condition for collaboration. In October 1905, prime minister Sergei Witte met with leading members of the Kadet party to discuss whether they might join the government. The Kadets demanded that as a condition of doing so, the government should summon a constituent assembly elected by four-tail suffrage, and also grant an amnesty to political prisoners. Witte refused.[57] Rather than compromise with the state, Kadets preferred to rely on revolutionary pressure from the left to coerce the government into concessions. Ivan Petrunkevich, by now a member of the Kadet central committee, noted, "I do not fear revolution and consider myself and all of us to be revolutionaries. . . . I see now that it is possible to hold out our hand to the socialists since we are still bound by to them by a single aim—the construction of a constitution."[58]

Maklakov later recalled that the Kadet party "was created to fight *against autocracy*."[59] This helps explain its behavior in the State Duma from 1906 to 1917. For many of its members, the autocracy, not the revolutionaries, was the real enemy. Miliukov considered it vitally important that liberals not lose contact with the left; becoming too close to the government would discredit them in the eyes of the people, he feared.[60] The results of the 1906 Duma elections encouraged the Kadets in their oppositionist stance. The party won 185 out of 478 seats, making it the largest party in the Duma.[61] Kadets concluded that they had earned the right to govern, and once the Duma convened, they demanded the acceptance of their entire program. This included legislation to guarantee equal rights for all citizens, a government responsible to the Duma, introduction of the four-tail suffrage, a political amnesty, and abolition of the death penalty.[62] The focus was on political rather than social or economic change, reflecting the Kadets' belief that political reform must come first. Many of their proposals were unacceptable to the government (particularly the amnesty and abolition of the death penalty). The Kadets, however, felt that they were on the cusp of seizing power and felt no need to compromise. They were also subject to strong pressure from the left, as they lacked a parliamentary majority and were dependent on support from more radical parties in the Duma.[63]

Persuaded that the government and the Duma could not work together, Nicholas II dissolved the Duma in July 1906. Members of the Kadet party decamped to Vyborg in Finland, where they issued a manifesto calling on the Russian people to refuse to pay taxes or serve in the military. The Russian people ignored the appeal, and the attempt to incite rebellion failed.

In the meantime, Nicholas II dismissed the prime minister, Ivan Goremykin (1839–1917), replacing him with Pyotr Stolypin. The appointment did not win the liberals' approval. The Kadets' fourth party congress, held in September 1906, passed a resolution declaring that "the Government of P. A. Stolypin is a government of such violence and arbitrariness as has not been experienced in the darkest epochs of unlimited autocracy. . . . Any support of the anticonstitutional ministry, whatever form it might take, is an act aimed against the Russian people."[64] In January 1907, Stolypin held out an olive branch to the Kadets. The party had never been legally registered. Stolypin offered to legalize it if it publicly denounced revolutionary violence. Miliukov refused.[65] "We believed," said Maklakov, "that condemning political murders would mean allowing the authorities to believe that they were right."[66] Stolypin was "the minister of field courts martial," wrote Tyrkova-Williams in her diary. Making a deal with him to denounce violence would be like taking "thirty pieces of silver," she said.[67]

Liberal parties did less well in elections to the Second Duma than to the first, in large part because the socialists chose to participate. In a speech to the Duma in March 1907 Stolypin laid out his program of reform—a program that Viktor Leontovitsch describes as "one of the most significant advances for liberalism in Russian history."[68] The program included laws to guarantee freedom of speech, assembly, press, association, and religion; a reform of local self-government; abolition of the system of estates (peasants, nobles, etc.); police reform; an extension of the system of *zemstva* into the Baltic region and Poland; workers' insurance; compulsory education for all; and radical land reform designed to promote the private ownership of land by peasants.[69]

This was a remarkably liberal program, but the liberals in the Duma refused to support it. The Kadets introduced a bill in the Duma demanding the abolition of the field courts martial. Deputies such as Vasily Maklakov and Sergei Bulgakov argued that revolutionary violence was a product of government violence. If the latter came to an end, so would the former.[70] It did not take long for Stolypin to realize that the Second Duma would be no more acceptable to the government than the first, and in June 1907 it was dissolved.

From this moment on, Russian liberalism went into a period of political decline. The Third Duma was dominated by centrist and conservative forces. Membership of liberal parties, including the Kadets, fell.[71] In response to their weakened position, liberals adopted a much less confrontational line during the Third Duma. From 1912 onward, however, a number of events combined to push them once more into an oppositional stance. One was the killing by the army of some 270 striking gold miners in Siberia in April 1912, in what became known as the Lena Goldfields Massacre. Another was the trial in 1913 of a Russian Jew, Menahem Beilis (1874–1934), who was accused of murdering a boy for the purpose of a blood ritual. Beilis was eventually acquitted, but the trial highlighted the antisemitism of the authorities.

The outbreak of war in 1914 postponed outright conflict between the liberals and the state. The Kadet party's central committee issued a statement saying that "our first duty is to preserve the unity and integrity of the country . . . let us postpone our domestic disputes, let us not offer our adversary the slightest pretext for relying on the disagreements that divide us."[72]

This conciliatory stance did not last long. By early 1915, Russian liberals were losing patience with a government that they regarded as incapable of running an effective war effort. Businessmen associated with the Progressive Party complained of the government's policy of trying to purchase weapons abroad, arguing that it ought to be relying more on domestic industry.[73] Rumors of treason began to circulate widely, with fingers pointed at the defense minister Vladimir Sukhomlinov (1848–1926) and even at the empress (who was German by birth). Military defeats engendered a sense of panic that in turn induced many liberals to move once again into open opposition to the state. As a member of the Kadet party's central committee, Prince Dmitry Shakhovskoi (1861–1939), declared in June 1915, "The time when the government bore all responsibility is now over; now it is time to give real power to the people and to the public. It is time for the people to take the war into its own hands."[74]

Liberals' belief in the need for a change of government was shared by many politicians of a more conservative disposition. In summer 1915, the Kadets, the Progressives, the Octobrists, and the conservative Nationalist party united to form what they called the "Progressive Bloc," whose members controlled a majority in the State Duma. The bloc's main demand was a government "composed of individuals who enjoy the confidence of the country."[75] This phrasing implied the creation of a new government enjoying the support of the liberals, but fell short of previous liberal demands for a government accountable to the Duma. Even this compromise formula was, however, was too much for Nicholas II, who instead of meeting the bloc's demands prorogued the Duma in September 1915.

Left-leaning liberals took the emperor's move as proof that cooperation with the state was impossible.[76] In February 1916, when the Kadet party met for its sixth congress, many of its members pressed for a change of policy. "We must not hesitate at open conflict with the government," said one of the leading members of the party's left wing, Mikhail Mandelshtam (1866–1939). Miliukov succeeded in holding back the radicals at the February congress and persuaded the party to continue its policy of pressuring the state through the Duma and the Progressive Bloc. Facing further demands for a more militant policy at the Kadet party conference in October 1916, he told delegates: "In its struggle with this upheaval, the government will find itself in a vacuum. . . . At the last moment, it will reach out to us and then it will be our task not to destroy the government, which would only aid anarchy, but to instil a completely different content, that is, to build a genuine constitutional order. . . . To support anarchy in the name of the struggle with the government would be to risk all the political conquests we have made since 1905."[77]

Miliukov's appeal temporarily won over Kadet delegates, but the Progressive Bloc then collapsed when the Progressive Party walked out in protest at its supposedly conciliatory line. By now, the mood in the Kadet party was decidedly belligerent, as displayed in a speech to the State Duma at the start of November 1916 by one of the party's more moderate members, Vasily Maklakov. He said: "I ask, why does Russia stick to this government which is destroying Russia? . . . It is not an accident, it is the regime, this cursed, old regime that has outlived its time but is still alive, that is the basic cause of everything. . . . We must say to the authorities, it's either us or them. Our life together is impossible."[78]

Even more inflammatory was a speech by Miliukov, in which the Kadet leader attacked the authorities, repeating over and over the question "Is this stupidity or is it treason?" Miliukov left no doubt in listeners' minds that he thought that the answer was treason. Copies of the speech circulated widely throughout Russia.[79] The claim that the government was guilty of treason was entirely baseless, but many Russians believed it to be true.

Treason was now in the air. In November 1916, the head of the Union of Towns and Zemstva, Prince Georgy Lvov (1861–1925), proposed that the emperor be overthrown and replaced by Alexander III's cousin Grand Duke Nikolai Nikolaevich (1856–1929). Lvov dispatched the mayor of Tiflis, Aleksandr Khatisov (1874–1945), to visit the grand duke (who was viceroy of the Caucasus) to obtain his approval. The grand duke turned down the proposal and the conspirators gave up their plan.[80] Having accused the government of treason, by the end of 1916 liberal leaders had become guilty of it themselves.

Social-Economic Liberalism

One of the most significant economic developments of the period was the agrarian reform undertaken by Pyotr Stolypin. In November 1905, the government abolished the redemption payments imposed in 1861 at the time of the emancipation of the serfs. Next, a decree of October 1906 abolished the commune's ability to subject its members to forced labor, as well as its ability to prevent them from leaving the commune.[81]

The centerpiece of Stolypin's agrarian reforms followed, in the form of a decree of November 1906 that gave peasants the right to consolidate their scattered strips of land into a single plot that would be the personal property of the head of the household.[82] In a speech to the Duma in May 1907, Stolypin laid out the logic of his agrarian reform. He attacked the idea of expropriating state and noble land to redistribute to the peasants on the grounds that there was insufficient redistributable land to satisfy peasant demand.[83] Stolypin also denounced socialist plans to nationalize land, arguing that "no one would ever improve it, or put his labor into it. . . . The incentive to labor, that prudence which makes people work, would be scrapped."[84] He added: "The Government wants above all to promote and enhance peasant land ownership. It wants to see the peasant earning well and eating well. . . . But for this it is necessary to give opportunity to the capable, industrious peasant. . . . He must be given the chance to consolidate the fruits of his labor and consider them his inalienable property."[85]

As Stephen Williams notes, Stolypin's reforms were "a case of genuine liberalization from above."[86] Stolypin expanded the personal rights of the peasantry and reinforced the principle of private property. However, as Shuichi Kojima notes, "Defending the [Stolypin] reforms was a sort of taboo among Russian intellectuals at that time. . . . The reforms had little support even among liberal intellectuals."[87]

One exception was the economist Boris Brutskus, who argued that private farming of the sort encouraged by Stolypin had numerous advantages. Among other things, private farmers had a much greater incentive to work hard than did members of a commune.[88] Brutskus's free market inclinations were, however, rather unusual for the time, and liberals as a whole fiercely resisted Stolypin's reform.[89]

Indeed, it was the Kadet party's refusal to support the reform that was the major reason for the collapse of the Second Duma. Kadets rejected Stolypin's reform on the conservative grounds that it imposed a foreign form of land ownership alien to Russian traditions. Duma deputy Andrei Shingarev (1869–1918) denounced Stolypin's proposals as an attempt "to destroy the concept of family property with the help of revolutionary legislation."[90] Kadets accused Stolypin of helping rich peasants at the expense of poor ones and feared that his reforms would create divisions in the countryside that would inflame revolutionary tensions.[91]

The Kadet agrarian program called for the expropriation of state, monastic, and large noble estates, with compensation amounting to "5% of the average lease price of the last five years according to local lease conditions for a long term tenancy."[92] The expropriated land would be put in a national land fund, from which it would be leased to peasants in accordance with local forms of landownership. This meant that the land would belong to the state, not the peasants, and for the most part would be transferred to the control of communes rather than individuals.[93]

This policy reflected the Kadet party's belief that the primary cause of peasant poverty was a shortage of land.[94] It also rested on tactical considerations—the promise to expropriate and redistribute land was seen as a way of winning the support of the peasants.[95] Leon Petrazycki defended expropriation as compatible with liberal values, saying that "the juridical question of property rights not only should not be of decisive significance but is entirely irrelevant . . . the inviolability of property is not absolute but is wholly compatible with fairly compensated expropriation if the social goals of the state interest demand it."[96] Likewise, Pavel Novgorodtsev wrote that "adherents of the old dogma that derives from the principle of holy and inviolable property see this presentation of the problem [i.e., the expropriation of land] as a perversion of the idea of law. But the legal consciousness of our time places the rights of the human person above property rights and, in the name of this law, in the name of human dignity, in the name of freedom, rejects the idea that property is inviolable, and replaces it with the principle of public-legal regulation of acquired rights with necessary compensation for their owners in the case of alienation."[97]

Novgorodtsev's logic reflected the influence of Vladimir Solovyov's idea of a right to a dignified existence. Novgorodtsev explained further:

> Securing the right to a dignified human existence has in mind people who are suffering from economic dependency, from a lack of means, from unfortunate circumstances. . . . The use of freedom can be completely paralyzed by a lack of means. The task and essence of law is the protection of personal freedom, but to achieve this goal one must care for the material conditions of freedom, without which freedom can remain an empty word. . . . Thus, in the name of protecting freedom the law should be concerned with its material conditions; in the name of personal dignity, it must be concerned with defending the right to a dignified human existence.[98]

In practice, said Novgorodtsev, this meant that the state should pass legislation to protect workers, for instance regulating sanitary conditions in the workplace, providing insurance for illness and old age, legalizing trade unions, and establishing agencies to mediate disputes between employers and employees.[99]

Novgorodtsev was a great admirer of British prime minister Herbert Asquith (1852–1928), whose Liberal Party government at the start of the twentieth century exemplified the New Liberalism mentioned in chapter 1.[100] Novgorodtsev rejected socialism as utopian, but also recognized that by highlighting the evils of the existing economic system, socialism had had an important influence on liberal thought. "The Party of People's Freedom [an alternative name for the Kadets], like contemporary democratic liberalism in general, derives from socialism," he wrote.[101]

Others agreed. "Democratic politics derives from precepts that demand that everyone be guaranteed the fruit of their labor . . . that everyone be guaranteed the conditions of human existence," wrote Kadet central committee member Sergei Kotliarevsky (1873–1939).[102] Miliukov declared that "we are unalterable enemies of bureaucratic centralization and the Manchester school . . . our party most resembles those Western groupings of the intelligentsia known as 'social reformers.'"[103] Another Kadet, Nikolai Iordansky (1870–1933), similarly wrote that "from its very beginning, the KD [Kadet] party has declared itself an uncompromising opponent of old Manchesterian liberalism. The guiding idea of the party involves the recognition that *without state intervention, without the implementation of just social reforms, it will also be impossible to realise those goals that are the essence of liberalism.*"[104]

In general, Russian liberals favored a mixed market economy—that is to say that they insisted that industry should remain in private hands, but also believed that the state had an important role in regulating economic affairs, supporting the development of key sectors (such as transport), and providing social welfare.[105] Liberals hoped that by promoting the last of these, they might persuade working-class Russians to join their cause. To this end, the Kadet party's program promised to introduce government health insurance, an eight-hour working day, and legislation providing for the right to strike and to organize trade unions.[106] Later, however, the party rowed back a bit on the eight-hour working day, calling for it to be introduced gradually.[107]

William Rosenberg comments that the Kadets' appeals to the working class were framed in the party's understanding of the need for an "above class" approach to politics and therefore addressed them not as workers but as citizens sharing common interests with other classes.[108] This approach found almost no favor among workers, who almost universally preferred socialist parties.[109] Likewise, the Kadets' agrarian program "did not go far enough for the majority of peasants," almost none of whom backed the party.[110] Liberals' efforts to reach out to the peasants and workers were almost entirely in vain.

With the establishment of the State Duma in 1906, liberalism moved from local government to parliamentary politics. While there were some in the liberal camp who urged that it should rethink its confrontational approach toward the imperial state, radical voices won the day. Liberal politicians regarded the state as their main enemy and were perpetually looking over their shoulders to the left, fearing that if they adopted a more conciliatory line they would hemorrhage support to more radical groups.

In the process, Russian liberals overestimated their own political power, and underestimated Stolypin's ability to restore order in the country without their help. Their dislike of Stolypin also led them to exaggerate what they had in common with the left, while their refusal to condemn revolutionary terrorism deprived them of any chance of collaborating with the authorities. Meanwhile, their agrarian policies were an odd mixture of conservatism (maintaining the commune and the household as the basic units of rural society) and radicalism (forcible expropriation and redistribution of land), without in any obvious way being liberal. At least on the agrarian issue, the state was actually more liberal than the liberals.

Leaning left was an understandable response to the arbitrariness of the imperial regime, but it brought the liberals no benefits. Liberal policies were sufficiently radical to preclude cooperation with the state but insufficiently radical to win adherents among the masses. Support for the Kadets and other liberal parties among workers and peasants remained negligible.

The military setbacks suffered by the Russian army in the First World War proved to be the final blow to relations between Russian liberals and the imperial state. By late 1916 the Russian army's situation was actually not too bad. It had recovered from the disasters of summer 1915 and won some significant victories against the Austrians and Ottomans in 1916. These successes did not, however, prevent liberals from falling prey to conspiracy theories about treason in high places. That and their belief that they could manage the war effort better than the government induced them to break the political peace and agitate against the state in the midst of war. In so doing, they sowed the seeds of their own destruction.

CHAPTER 6

Revolution and Civil War

On March 8, 1917, workers in Petrograd marked International Women's Day by protesting against food shortages. The following day, the protests became even larger, with political demands appearing alongside economic ones. Ordered to disperse the crowds, troops of the Petrograd garrison mutinied and defected to the side of the protestors. Having lost control of the army in the capital, the government resigned.

The crisis in Petrograd presented Russian liberals with a choice: remain loyal to the emperor in the hope of suppressing what had now become a revolution, or attempt to take the lead in the revolutionary movement in order to steer it in a direction they considered desirable. Already convinced of the need for a change of government, they chose the second option,

On March 12, 1917, the State Duma formed the Provisional Committee that declared itself to be the new government. Two prominent Duma members, Aleksandr Guchkov and Vasily Shulgin (1878–1976), visited Nicholas II and persuaded him to abdicate in favor of his brother Grand Duke Mikhail Aleksandrovich (1878–1918). At the urging of members of the new government, Mikhail refused to accept the crown, and 300 years of Romanov rule in Russia came to an end.

The Provisional Committee of the Duma became the basis for the new Provisional Government that was supposed to govern Russia until such time as a constituent assembly could be convened. Liberals dominated the Provisional

Government. Its head was the chief of the Union of Towns and Zemstva, Prince Georgy Lvov, and Pavel Miliukov took the position of foreign minister. Other liberals in prominent positions included the Kadet party's Nikolai Nekrasov (1879–1940) and Andrei Shingarev (ministers of transport and agriculture, respectively; Shingarev later became finance minister), and the Progressive Party's Aleksandr Konovalov (1875–1949), who took the post of minister of trade and industry. The one woman in the government was Sofia Panina, who took the position of deputy minister of state welfare and then of deputy minister of education.

The liberals' first experience of power proved to be a disastrous failure and forced them to readdress many of their core beliefs. Following the revolution, numerous centrifugal forces were pulling Russia apart. Non-Russian nationalities, such as Ukrainians, Georgians, and Armenians, demanded political autonomy; soldiers questioned the orders of their officers; peasants sought the redistribution of noble-owned land; and industrial workers demanded an eight-hour working day and better wages and working conditions.[1] To press their demands, they formed numerous committees—soldiers' committees in the army, factory committees in industrial workplaces; and peasant committees in the countryside. At a higher level, delegates from the soldiers, workers and peasants created councils (soviets) to represent them. These soviets soon challenged the authority of the Provisional Government.

The Provisional Government, factory owners, and landlords all proved unwilling to meet the masses' demands. Factory owners considered the demands for shorter hours and better wages and conditions to be economically unrealistic and refused to make significant concessions. Workers responded by going on strike; there was a threefold increase in the number of industrial strikes between March and June 1917 alone. Factory committees in some instances went further and attempted to oust management and take control of factories themselves. Management responded with lockouts.[2]

In the army, soldiers deserted or refused to do more than the minimum required to defend their positions. In July 1917, the Russian army undertook an offensive against German and Austro-Hungarian forces in the Galicia region of Western Ukraine. The offensive failed dismally after many units disobeyed orders to advance. Meanwhile, in the countryside peasants seized wood, livestock, equipment, and land from noble landowners.[3] Inflation spiraled and tax revenues dried up. Russia faced economic collapse.

Socialists pressed for radical solutions: end the war, give autonomy to minority nationalities, nationalize industry, and immediately transfer land from nobles to peasants. The most radical socialist party, the Bolsheviks, led by Vladimir Lenin (1870–1924), also called for the overthrow of the Provisional Government and the establishment of the "dictatorship of the proletariat." Liberals moved in the opposite direction: the war was to be prosecuted to the bitter end, nationalist and separatist demands were to be resisted, discipline was to be restored in the army and industry, and the state was to defend private property. Decisions concerning Russia's future government were to be postponed until the Constituent Assembly could meet. As 1917 wore on, liberals increasingly lost their faith in democracy and favored the establishment of a military dictatorship.

The Provisional Government faced multiple political crises. The first took place in April 1917, when thousands of demonstrators came out on the streets of Petrograd to complain of a note sent by the Provisional Government to Russia's allies promising to pursue the war as long as necessary. Miliukov resigned as foreign minister, and the government sought to broaden its popular support by bringing in members of the more moderate socialist parties.

This did little to help. In July 1917 the Bolsheviks led massive demonstrations calling for the soviets to take power and for the war to be ended. Lvov resigned as head of the Provisional Government and was succeeded by the socialist revolutionary Aleksandr Kerensky (1881–1970). By now, many liberals had concluded that a strong hand was needed to restore order. The favored candidate to take the post of military dictator was General Lavr Kornilov (1870–1918), whom Kerensky had appointed as supreme commander of the Russian army in July 1917. Relations between Kerensky and Kornilov rapidly broke down, and in August 1917 Kerensky accused Kornilov of attempting to launch a coup d'état. Kornilov and other senior officers were arrested.

The Kornilov affair discredited the Provisional Government in the eyes of the left, who believed that the government was unable to protect the new order against counterrevolution, and in the eyes of the right, who believed that Kerensky had betrayed Kornilov. By November 1917, almost nobody could be found to defend the Provisional Government. Taking advantage of this situation, on November 7, 1917, Bolshevik-led troops arrested the Council of Ministers and installed a new government, notionally led by the soviets but in reality under the control of the Bolshevik Party.

In March 1918, the Bolshevik government made peace with Germany, Austria-Hungary, and Turkey by signing the Treaty of Brest-Litovsk, which among other things recognized the independence of Ukraine and the Baltic states. The Russian Empire split up into several parts. The Bolsheviks controlled the core of European Russia, centered on Moscow. Non-Russian nations, such as Ukraine, Georgia, and Armenia, declared independence. Meanwhile, the northern Caucasus, the Volga region, and Siberia were under the control of anti-Bolshevik armed formations led by former imperial military officers. These formations—known as the White armies—attracted the support of many Russian liberals.

The first White army to come into being was the Volunteer Army, founded in December 1917 in southern Russia. This provided the nucleus of what was later designated the Armed Forces of Southern Russia, led by General Anton Denikin (1872–1947), who created a special council to advise him on political matters. Members of the Kadet party dominated this council.

Counterrevolutionary forces also took control of large areas of eastern Russia. After seizing power, the Bolsheviks permitted elections to the promised Constituent Assembly to take place. The assembly met in Petrograd on January 18, 1918, but after just a few hours of debates the Bolsheviks closed it down. Some members of the assembly decamped to the city of Samara on the Volga River, 1,000 kilometers east of Moscow, where they formed an alternative government known as Komuch (Committee of Members of the Constituent Assembly). Meanwhile, a provisional Siberian government was created further to the east. In September 1918, Komuch and the Siberian government merged to form the Provisional All-Russian Government, also known as the Directory. This did not last long, as in November 1918 it was overthrown in a coup led by Admiral Aleksandr Kolchak (1874–1920), who then established himself as military dictator in the areas controlled by the White armies in eastern Russia. In this role, he was supported by a cabinet of ministers, many of whom were members of the Kadet party.

Throughout 1919, civil war raged across Russia. Kolchak's forces initially made some progress, but were then thrown back by the Bolsheviks, who had succeeded in organizing an effective army of their own. The Bolsheviks pursued Kolchak east across Siberia until they captured and killed him in February 1920. Meanwhile, General Denikin's Armed Forces of Southern Russia succeeded in advancing as far as the city of Orel, 370 kilometers south of Moscow, before they were driven back. Discredited by his defeat, Denikin handed over command of his army to General Pyotr Wrangel (1878–1928), who managed to hold out in Crimea for about a year, until in November 1920 a Bolshevik offensive forced him to evacuate his forces from Russia. The civil war was over, and Russia was under Bolshevik control.

Cultural Liberalism

As the previous chapter indicated, Russian liberalism took a nationalistic and imperialistic turn after 1905. The events of 1917 reinforced this. In 1918, Pyotr

Struve (who in 1920 became General Wrangel's foreign minister) wrote that "the vital cause of our time and of future generations must be constructed under the flag and in the name of the *nation* . . . all the tasks of our future . . . combine and unite in one thing: education of individuals and the masses in the national spirit."[4]

In the early months of the Provisional Government, Miliukov took a particularly bellicose line as foreign minister. In a pamphlet entitled "Why and for What Are We Fighting?," Miliukov stated that Russia was fighting the First World War for a "firm and enduring peace," to which end Russia needed to seize control of the Dardanelles Straits connecting the Black and Mediterranean seas. This, Miliukov said, was "completely necessary" for "reasons of defense and economic development."[5] This attitude played a major role in his forced resignation a month later.

Many liberals' opposition to the imperial state over the previous three years had derived from their perception that the state was incapable of managing the war effort efficiently. For them, the revolution represented an opportunity not to end the war but rather to prosecute it more vigorously. Thus, at a congress of the Kadet party at the end of March 1917, Fyodor Rodichev pronounced to applause that "we endorse this slogan: we will not accept peace at any price; we will embrace peace only in the full glory of victory."[6]

Liberals believed that, as well as an external enemy, there was an internal one, in the form of separatists, most notably those in Ukraine. In March 1917, following Nicholas II's abdication, Ukrainian activists formed a council, the Rada, that asserted the right to govern Ukraine, albeit still as part of the Russian Empire. When the question of Ukrainian autonomy was raised at the Kadet party congress in late March 1917, the Moscow Kadet Mikhail Mandelshtam declared to applause that "at the current time, any sort of dual power is impermissible."[7] The eighth Kadet party congress in May 1917 heard a report from Fyodor Kokoshkin that rejected federalism and national autonomy on the grounds that they would "Balkanize" Russia.[8] It then passed a resolution in favor of giving the *zemstva* "provincial autonomy" but rejecting autonomy for larger, national units.

In June 1917, the Ukrainian Rada unilaterally declared Ukrainian autonomy within the Russian Empire. The Provisional Government sent a delegation to negotiate with the Rada. The delegation promised that the demand for autonomy would be met, but only after the Constituent Assembly had convened. Even this compromise was too much for many members of the government. Three Kadet ministers resigned in protest.[9] Their party remained committed to the idea of a unitary state. National autonomy would inevitably lead to separation and the destruction of the country, they believed. As Ivan Petrunkevich put it, "It's just one step from Russia's division to its utter defeat."[10] At its ninth congress in July 1917 the Kadet party once again rejected the idea of national autonomy.[11]

Denikin's army marched under the slogan "Russia, One and Indivisible," a slogan endorsed by the Kadet party at a congress in Denikin's capital, Ekaterinodar, in October 1918.[12] Several Kadets—Nikolai Astrov (1868–1934), Sofia Panina, Vasily Stepanov (1873–1920), and Konstantin Sokolov (1882–1927)—joined Denikin's special council, in which capacity they "were resolutely opposed to any concessions to the nationalities and regional governments, even in the darkest hour of the VA [Volunteer Army]."[13] Anna Procyk concludes that "during the civil war no other party, whether conservative or socialist, defended the principle of Russia's unity and indivisibility as steadfastly and consistently as the People's Freedom Party [the Kadets], and no other political group opposed federation as unflinchingly as the liberals on Denikin's council."[14]

One Kadet who urged a different policy was Vasily Maklakov, who in late 1917 had become the Provisional Government's ambassador to France. Maklakov wrote to Stepanov, Astrov, and Panina that the Whites lacked the strength to fight both the Bolsheviks and Russia's minority nations, and that they should therefore come to terms with the latter in order to be able to defeat the former. Once the Bolsheviks had been crushed, the minority nationalities would see the advantages of union with Russia and return to the fold, Maklakov said.[15] His Kadet colleagues wrote back that his idea was "a democratic platitude not recognizing any other [method of] state formation other than self-determination, expression of will, agreement, etc. Unfortunately, state processes up to now have not conformed to these beautiful principles, and there is hardly any hope that they will ever conform to them in reality." The only way of uniting Russia, they said, was by military force.[16]

The most Denikin's Kadet advisers were willing to grant non-Russian nationalities was some degree of cultural autonomy. The intransigence on nationality issues reflected their conviction that Russian citizens of all kinds should rise above narrow group interests—be those of nationality, class, or party—and think only in terms of the interests of Russia as a whole. The Kadets imagined themselves to embody this principle of statist, "above-party," "above-class" politics. Russia's problems, they felt, derived from the fact that both the masses and political leaders lacked a proper sense of statehood (gosudarstvennost').[17] As Ariadna Tyrkova-Williams complained, "neither individual workers nor collective labour organizations took heed of the nation's interests and merely supported their own professional advantage."[18]

Prior to the revolution, the Kadets had supported universal suffrage. The experience of revolution and civil war convinced many of them that they had been wrong, and that the Russian people were an uncultured mob, to be feared, not empowered. "The people are possessed by a bestial fear, and a bestial rage and malice," said the Kadet Viktor Pepeliaev (1885–1920), who chaired Kolchak's council of ministers.[19] The revolution, wrote Tyrkova-Williams, was "a cruel object lesson demonstrating that a life of complete liberty, unfettered by any compulsory system, may only be possible to man after he attains the highest degree of culture."[20] She added: "Instead of a new perfect, free order there was a return to old primitive forms of cave dwellers, when *homini hominus lupus est*, when each strove to snatch the utmost he could get for himself, sacrificing nothing for the community. All the moral foundations erected at such hard cost by generations were smashed like brittle glass beneath the blows of the soulless theory of economic materialism. Liberty, unfettered by law or by a habit of self-discipline, unbridled the masses."[21]

"Tragically for the liberals," writes William Rosenberg, "their perspectives in the context of revolutionary democracy still meant a deep suspicion of the *narod* [the people] . . . with attitudes about 'uplifting the people,' with visions of ordinary citizens as 'utterly unreliable, ignorant people.'"[22] The experience of revolution and civil war dissolved liberals' democratic pretensions. As Tyrkova-Williams wrote: "Propriety Russia [i.e., property-owning Russians] had accumulated far more knowledge and understanding of statesmanship than the masses of the people. Men who have passed through a university or secondary school training can more easily realise the necessity of a strict State system and general submission to laws, however irksome, than those who have never learned to lift their eyes from the narrow groove into which they have been born."[23]

Political Liberalism

The story of Russian political liberalism in this era is one of a rapid shift from an idealistic belief in the virtues of democracy to an embrace of military dictatorship. Once the enemy of authoritarianism, Russian liberals became its most ardent promoter.

Following Nicholas II's abdication, the Provisional Government chose as its head Prince Lvov, a man who had earned the confidence of many liberals due to his work in the *zemstva*. The new government then had to decide what to do about the monarchy. Believing that public opinion would not support the maintenance of the Romanov dynasty, all the members of the Provisional Government except for Miliukov and Guchkov agreed that Grand Duke Mikhail Aleksandrovich should not accept the crown. At a meeting with him

on March 16, 1917, they persuaded him to turn it down.[24] Soon afterward, the
Kadet party amended its program to support a democratic republic rather
than, as before, a constitutional monarchy.[25]

Order in imperial Russia had depended in large part on obedience to, and
fear of, ancient institutions. The Provisional Government set about dismantling these with great rapidity. Regional governors and deputy governors across
the country were dismissed without replacements. The secret police and the
Corps of Gendarmes were abolished. Prisoners were released en masse. A joint
proclamation of the Provisional Government and the Petrograd Soviet at the
start of March 1917 granted all Russian citizens an array of civil and political
rights: "freedom of speech, assembly, religion; the right to unionize; the abolition of all restrictions based on class, religion, and nationality; and universal
suffrage."[26] Initially, the Provisional Government took the position that demands that women receive the vote were "premature," but following a dem-
onstration for women's rights in late March 1917, it conceded that universal
suffrage would include women. This resulted in a law of July 20, 1917, that
made Russia the first country in Europe to give women equal voting rights in
national elections.[27]

The dismantling of the old institutions of state and the granting of new
rights reflected liberals' utopian mood. In April 1917, in the midst of the protests that brought down Miliukov, Tyrkova-Williams reminded him that "all
governments have classical methods of ruling." Miliukov replied: "It's better
that I lose power than resort to such methods."[28] An article in the liberal newspaper *Rech'* (Speech) celebrated Bolshevik leader Vladimir Lenin's return to
Russia in April 1917, despite Lenin's calls for the Provisional Government's
overthrow. "It is not only natural but most desirable that the leaders of our
leftist parties . . . should hasten home . . . their arrival in Russia may be welcomed," said the newspaper.[29] This idealism did not last long.

Liberal intellectuals viewed the revolution as an opportunity to pursue the
war more effectively, but workers and peasants viewed it largely as an opportunity to achieve social and economic justice.[30] Liberals adopted the philosophy
of "nonpredetermination" (*nepredreshenstvo*), the idea that important policy issues should not be predetermined by the Provisional Government (and later in
the civil war by the White armies), but rather should wait until the Constituent
Assembly could be called. Nonpredetermination reflected liberals' beliefs that
war was not a suitable time for sweeping institutional change and that the Provisional Government, having never been elected, lacked the democratic legitimacy to impose such change. The policy also reflected a dislike of many of the
demands being made by the Russian people. The argument that these demands

could only be addressed by the Constituent Assembly was perhaps a convenient excuse for not doing things that liberals did not actually want to do.

Soon after taking power, the Provisional Government set up a commission to prepare for the Constituent Assembly. The commission suggested the creation of a republic with strong presidential power, and proposed that the assembly elect a provisional president with a one-year mandate who would have almost absolute authority.[31] In principle, the Constituent Assembly could have been summoned fairly quickly. In practice, many liberals regarded it as something that should be left until the war had been successfully concluded. In the meantime, they demanded that party and class interests be put aside for the good of the state. In effect, they insisted that the masses accept their rule and rein in their demands.

As it became clear that the majority of the Russian population had no intention of deferring to them, liberals began increasingly to speak in terms of the need to strengthen the state and restore order.[32] Thus the newspaper *Svobodnyi Narod* (Free people) wrote that "Russian people now thirst for authority and a *gosudarstvennaia* [statist] organization of life. They instinctively feel that only a statesmanlike government [*gosudarstvennaia vlast'*] and a strong army can save the country from an ignominious historical death."[33]

In summer 1917, senior Kadets began to establish close links with groups of army officers and Cossacks. Addressing the Congress of Army and Navy Officers, Fyodor Rodichev told those assembled, "There is a banner under which each citizen must stand in readiness to sacrifice all, even his life—the Holy Banner of the Defense of the Motherland."[34] When Kornilov became supreme commander of the Russian army in July 1917, many Kadets, including Rodichev, supported his demands for a restoration of the death penalty and for restrictions on the activities of the soldiers' committees that had been set up in the army after the revolution.[35] Belief in the need for a military dictatorship was growing. The Bolshevik seizure of power in November 1917 validated this belief in the eyes of many liberals.

Immediately after the Bolshevik coup, the Kadet central committee called on the Russian people not to recognize the new government.[36] The Kadets, though, were in disarray. Soon after seizing power, the Bolsheviks banned the party, and it thereafter had to operate underground. The Bolsheviks also arrested some of its most senior members. Two of those arrested, Andrei Shingarev and Fyodor Kokoshkin, were subsequently murdered. A third, Sofia Panina, was tried and convicted for alleged embezzlement of state funds (she had refused to hand over money of the education ministry to the Bolshevik government).

In the face of these repressions, some liberals lost faith in peaceful means of struggle. Tyrkova-Williams wrote in November 1917, "I can neither write nor speak about the Constituent Assembly. I don't believe in it. No parliament can put Russia back on track."[37] Meanwhile, Miliukov escaped to the Don region of southern Russia, where he undertook negotiations with the Don Cossacks and wrote the initial declaration of aims of the Volunteer Army.[38] For the most part, though, before turning to armed resistance, liberals first looked to the promised Constituent Assembly for salvation, hoping that it would bring an end to Bolshevik rule. Outside of Moscow and St. Petersburg, however, the Kadet party performed poorly in the elections to the Constituent Assembly.[39] The Bolsheviks' dissolution of the assembly on January 19, 1918, then made it clear that the time for normal politics was over.

The Kadet central committee recognized this reality at a meeting in January 1918. At this, Novgorodtsev asked his colleagues which they valued more: democracy or liberalism. If it was the latter, he said, they should be prepared to abandon the former and support a military dictatorship that could restore order, after which their liberal program could be enacted.[40] After a long debate, Novgorodtsev won the argument; the committee resolved to support a dictatorship.[41]

Thereafter, the focus of liberal action shifted to Russia's periphery, as liberals left Moscow and Petrograd to join the White armies. Some went south to link up with Denikin, whose special council contained many Kadets. Some of these, such as Astrov and Panina, argued that Denikin ought to seek popular support by making a declaration promising sweeping political and economic reform.[42] They were outvoted by others who followed the doctrine of non-predetermination and believed that political and economic matters should be postponed until after the war. The special council declared that the White movement's goal was a "united Russia" under a "free government," with the watchwords "law," "order," and "national honor." Specifics were ignored, deemed to be "matters for the future."[43]

A second group of liberals joined the army of General Nikolai Iudenich (1862–1933) in the Baltic region. Among these was the Kadet Anton Kartashev (1875–1960), who had served in the Provisional Government as a minister with responsibility for religious affairs. At a meeting of the Russian community in the city of Reval (modern-day Tallinn) in June 1919, Kartashev noted that "we are no longer the Kadets who once let power slip from our hands; now we will be able to be cruel."[44] Kartashev defended the Kadets' decision to ally with conservative army officers. "It was either to accept them as they were or to cowardly abandon the White struggle," he said. "We should either reject the principle of armed frontline battle . . . or accept it with all its cruel and dictatorial inconveniences."[45]

Other Kadets headed east. They lent their support to the provisional Siberian government and Komuch, and then after those two merged, the Directory.

Many hoped that the Directory would establish a broad coalition of anti-Bolshevik forces.[46] Before long, however, members of the Kadet party lost faith in the Directory, believing it to be incapable of providing firm leadership.

Under the influence of Viktor Pepeliaev, who arrived in Siberia in August 1918, eastern Kadets moved in the direction of military dictatorship. Speaking to a conference of Kadets in Omsk in November 1918, Pepeliaev told delegates that "the party must declare that it not only isn't afraid of dictatorship but in the current circumstances considers it necessary."[47] The Kadets threw their support behind Kolchak's overthrow of the Directory the same month. Subsequently, Kadets, including Pepeliaev, Nikolai Ustrialov (1890–1937), and Georgy Telberg (1881–1954) took a leading role in Kolchak's government.

In summer 1919, a series of military defeats sent Kolchak's army reeling eastward in retreat. Some liberals urged a change in policy and recommended that the White government broaden its political support. They persuaded Kolchak to convene a *zemstvo* congress that would have the authority to provide the admiral with advice. This led to protests from the Kadet party's eastern central committee, which declared that "the Party of People's Freedom [the Kadet party] opposes the idea of a legislative or consultative organ, for this will weaken, not strengthen, the dictatorship."[48] The contrast with Kadets' pre-revolutionary political demands is striking.

By mid-1919, the Kadet party was firmly committed to dictatorship. Novgorodtsev said in May 1919, "If nothing remains of our democratism, then that is an excellent thing, since what is needed now is dictatorship, a force for creating authority."[49] Democracy was by now discredited in the eyes of some liberals. In November 1919, the Kadet party met in Kharkov for what was to be the last congress it would ever hold on Russian soil. In November 1917 Tyrkova-Williams had written, "Bayonets, machine guns, and bombs are the weapons of brigands."[50] Now, she told her colleagues: "To have calm, you need machine guns."[51] She added: "We must support the army first, and place democratic programs in the background. We must create a ruling class, and not a dictatorship of the majority. The universal hegemony of Western democracy is a fraud, which politicians have foisted upon us."[52]

Social-Economic Liberalism

Following the revolution of March 1917, the Provisional Government's deputy minister of trade and industry, Vasily Stepanov, laid out the principles of the new regime's economic policy. The government, he said, should not change "the existing economic system into a socialist one, either now or immediately after the war." He added that, "the strong development of our productive forces is inconceivable without attracting foreign capital," although state intervention was necessary "to regulate the main branches of the economy," such as military industry and natural resource extraction.[53]

The new government faced a growing economic crisis. Workers' committees sprang up in many factories and demanded a shorter working day and better pay and conditions. Eventually, these committees also sought to take control of management. Russian businessmen resisted these demands. The Moscow Committee for Commerce and Industry, for instance, rejected the eight-hour working day, saying that "at the present time, when it is essential to conduct the war to a victorious end, everything should lead, not to a diminution of work production, but to an increase."[54]

The Provisional Government agreed with the Moscow committee. Stepanov's superior in the Ministry of Trade and Industry, Aleksandr Konovalov, was willing to work with the factory committees to a limited extent, in the hope that they would facilitate the production and delivery of vital goods, but he resisted calls from the left to give the committees control over management.[55] He also rejected government regulation of wages and prices, arguing that factory owners would shut their factories down rather than submit to state control.[56]

In May 1917, Stepanov replaced Konovalov as minister of trade and industry, but government policy remained much the same. As William Rosenberg notes, Stepanov "urged a series of measures designed both to end worker radicalism and reverse the disruption of industry. At their core was a demand that the government take a firm stand against socialism." This reflected "rapidly growing anti-labor sentiment in Kadet circles."[57] Overall, the Provisional Government wished to minimize disruption to the existing economic system. The focus was on maintaining war production in the short term. Difficult issues of long-term economic and social significance were to be postponed until the summoning of the Constituent Assembly.

This attitude applied to agriculture as much to industry. In March 1917, the agriculture minister Andrei Shingarev announced the introduction of a national grain monopoly, to which peasants were obliged to sell their grain at a fixed rate. He also ordered the creation of local food supply committees. But Shingaryov was adamant that issues of land ownership should not be addressed while the war continued. In an appeal to Russian peasants in May 1917, he said that "the property and land of the landlords, like all other possessions, is the people's property that only an all-national Constituent Assembly has the right to dispose of. Until that time, all unauthorized seizures of land, livestock, and equipment, and all cutting down of other people's forests, are an illegal and unjust plundering of the people's wealth and deprive other perhaps far more needy people of their share."[58]

Some on the left of the Kadet party, such as Dmitry Shakhovskoi and Nikolai Nekrasov, urged a change in policy, arguing that the party's conservatism was alienating it from the workers and peasants and that the Kadets should make more radical promises of social and economic reform.[59] The party rejected this argument. Novgorodtsev told the Kadets' ninth party congress in July 1917 that the party should refuse to join any government committed to introducing socialist programs. The congress resolved that the economy should be based on "free initiative."[60]

William Rosenberg concludes that "had [the Kadets] been more willing in the spring [of 1917] to respond positively to . . . social demands . . . moderation and liberal democracy might well have had a chance to survive."[61] Whereas many historians of the period before 1917 have accused the Kadets of being too radical, for Rosenberg the problem is the opposite—they were not radical enough. In practice, though, it is hard to see how the Kadets and other liberal groups could have responded to the demands of workers and peasants in 1917 without becoming fully fledged socialists. At any rate, revolution and civil war forced them to show their colors: for all their prerevolutionary radicalism, Russian liberals were firmly dedicated to the principle of private enterprise.

They continued to oppose demands for radical social and economic reform during the civil war. Kadets in Kolchak's government resisted strongly when the admiral suggested expanding peasant property rights. They insisted that the issue be left to a future constituent assembly.[62] Similarly a Kadet-dominated commission established by Denikin to consider a land reform program issued a report that argued that for "political reasons" any redistribution of land should be postponed for at least three years.[63] It has often been said that the White generals lost the civil war because of their refusal to consider reforms that might have won them popular support. This, though, was as much due to the liberal politicians who advised them as to the generals themselves.

In a letter to Ivan Petrunkevich in December 1918, Miliukov expressed what had become a common point of view among Russian liberals, asking, "Who can help it . . . that some groups of our population live not in the twentieth, not even in the eighteenth, but in the thirteenth and fourteenth centuries?"[64] If prior to 1917, many liberals believed that the granting of political and civil liberties would solve Russia's most pressing problems, after 1917 they had no such ideas. On the contrary, they came to believe that freedom and the Russian popular culture were incompatible. A responsible popular culture, in their eyes, was one that stood above the narrow interests of nation, class, or party.

The chaos of revolution and civil war convinced liberals that outside of their own ranks, this culture was absent.

Russian liberals responded to this revelation by becoming determined proponents of national unity, enthusiastic supporters of military dictatorship, and resolute defenders of private property. Many turned 180 degrees and became advocates of the sort of dictatorial order they had previously opposed. As they did so, some, especially those on the right of the Kadet party, began to reconsider their attitude to the old imperial regime. A prime example was Ariadna Tyrkova-Williams. "'Left' despotism, with the red banner of Socialism waving over it, proved incomparably harsher and more perfidious than the old regime," she wrote.[65] Pyotr Struve agreed: "At the current moment, when we live under the power of the Soviet bureaucracy and under the heel of the red guard, we are beginning to understand what a cultural role the bureaucracy and police of the overthrown monarchy played."[66] One of Pavel Novgorodtsev's pupils, the philosopher Ivan Ilyin (1883-1954), provided a suitable epitaph for imperial Russian liberals. He wrote: "Only when a truly complete unfreedom arrived—absolute and deadly—only then did we understand how free we had been in imperial Russia and what we had lost."[67]

CHAPTER 7

Emigration

In November 1920, the last major military force still fighting the Bolsheviks evacuated its base in Crimea and took ships across the Black Sea to Constantinople. Although scattered fighting continued for some months in parts of Russia, this retreat marked the effective end of the Russian Civil War. With this, liberalism disappeared in Russia for several decades, both as an ideology and as an organized political movement. Nevertheless, its history continued abroad.

A million or so Russians fled the country after the revolution, forming a community known as "Russia Abroad."[1] The largest group consisted of White army veterans, but there were also many intellectuals and activists from across the political spectrum. Some of these escaped Russia during the civil war. Others left in 1922, when the Soviet regime deported around 200 of the country's leading thinkers, including some of Russia's most prominent philosophers and economists, such as Nikolai Berdiaev, Semyon Frank, Boris Brutskus, and Nikolai Zvorykin (1853–1939).[2]

The story of émigré liberalism has two main threads. The first is the fate of the Kadet party in exile; the second the intellectual legacy of émigré philosophers and economists. The former is largely a story of infighting and fruitless efforts to forge alliances with other émigré groups. By late 1920, Kadets had organized émigré branches of their party. Before long, however, they were at each other's throats. Some sought to renew the armed struggle against Bolshevism. Others turned their backs on the White armies and sought a new direction. In the process, the Kadet party split into three. The center failed to form any lasting organization. The right coalesced around a National Committee created in 1924 that sought to unify liberal and conservative émigrés in a common front, an effort that culminated in the Émigré Congress held in Paris in April 1926. Meanwhile, the left gravitated toward an alliance with émigré socialists in the form of the Republican-Democratic Union (Respublikansko-Demokraticheskoe Ob"edinenie, RDO) established by Miliukov in 1924.

The experiences of revolution, civil war, and exile induced a "profound disillusionment with humanity" among Russian liberals, many of whom "lost their faith in the West as a model for Russia's future."[3] The Bolshevik victory in Russia, the Great Depression, and the rise of dictatorial regimes in countries such as Italy and Germany seriously undermined the positivist view of history as marching inexorably toward liberal democracy. Indeed, democracy seemed incapable of defending liberty against the threats of communism and fascism. Personal freedom remained the core of liberal philosophers' belief system, but many abandoned liberalism as previously understood and argued that in order to have meaning and be sustainable, freedom had to serve a higher truth, which for the most part they identified with Christianity. Émigrés also questioned the suitability of democracy as the mode of government best suited to defending freedom. Their history may therefore be seen as an abandonment of classical liberalism in favor of a form of liberal authoritarianism, or alternatively liberal conservatism.

Émigrés made original contributions to Russian thought that were to influence future generations, including Soviet dissidents. For instance, in an introduction to a 1976 collection of dissident essays, the authors, Pavel Litvinov (b. 1940), Mikhail Meerson-Aksyonov (b. 1944), and Boris Shragin (1926–1990), described themselves as "liberal democrats" and cited as their inspirations the émigrés Nikolai Berdiaev, Sergei Bulgakov, Aleksandr Izgoev (1872–1935), Pavel Miliukov, Pyotr Struve, Georgy Fedotov (1886–1951), and Semyon Frank.[4] Subsequently, the collapse of the Soviet Union sparked a great scholarly interest in Russia Abroad. The history of émigré liberalism is an essential part of the history of Russian liberalism as a whole.

Cultural Liberalism

In a 1935 article, the émigré religious historian Georgy Fedotov commented that the Russian emigration consisted of three groups: the military, the political, and the cultural. The last of these, Fedotov argued, was the "primary" element in the struggle for Russia's liberation.[5] For Fedotov and others like him, the negative consequences of the revolution were rooted in the spiritual failings of the Russian people—its undeveloped legal consciousness, lack of patriotism, and loss of religious faith. It followed that the path to Russia's resurrection lay not through military or political action but through culture. As the journal *Put'* (The way) put it in 1925, "The best part of the Russian emigration lies above all in the field of spiritual culture and religious life. . . . The political task is for the émigrés secondary and subject to the spiritual task."[6]

Roughly speaking, liberal thought in emigration followed three tracks. Those who had been on the idealist side of the prerevolutionary idealist-positivist divide argued that politics and economics needed to be based on Christian principles. In exile, some of these swung leftward toward a version of Christian socialism. A second group, meanwhile, went in the opposite direction and became more conservative. And third, those who had been on the positivist side of the prerevolutionary divide, such as Miliukov, scorned mystical thinking entirely.

The idealists included some of the contributors to the prerevolutionary volumes *Problems of Idealism* and *Vekhi*, such as Nikolai Berdiaev, Pavel Novgorodtsev, and Semyon Frank. Lesley Chamberlain remarks that "in truth, Berdyaev, Semyon Frank and others around them were always liberals."[7] That said, their story in exile may be seen as one of disenchantment with classical liberalism and a corresponding turn toward Christianity.

Berdiaev and others who wrote for the émigré journal *Novyi Grad* (New Town), such as Fedotov and Fyodor Stepun (1884–1965), became known as "postrevolutionaries," propounding a philosophy that has been described as a "synthesis, convergence, of liberalism and socialism."[8] By contrast, Novgorodtsev, Frank, and others such as Pyotr Struve swung rightward toward a synthesis of liberalism and conservatism. Both groups attacked classical liberalism for lacking a basis in higher values and being unable to defend the freedom to which it was theoretically dedicated.

Berdiaev has been variously labeled a socialist, a Christian socialist, a conservative, "a defender of aristocracy and conservatism," "one of the last and best representatives of classical Slavophilism," a liberal, a liberal conservative, and a Christian humanist.[9] Late in life, he referred to his belief system as "personalist socialism."[10] The multiplicity of labels attests to the changes in Berdiaev's thinking over the years and to the difficulty of fitting him within any neat categories. Insofar as Berdiaev was "liberal," it was because he placed the person and personal freedom at the center of his philosophy. He wrote: "Every human personality . . . bearing as it does within itself the image of the highest existence, cannot be a means to any end whatsoever. It has in itself a right not only to life . . . but also a right to possess the universal content of life. . . . Qualitatively distinct and unequal personalities are not only in a profound sense equal before God, but they are equal before society, to which no right belongs to discriminate among personalities on the basis of privilege."[11]

While this expresses a classically liberal idea, Berdiaev was highly critical of contemporary liberalism. He felt that it was driven solely by the pragmatic purpose of avoiding social conflict by tolerating diverse individual aims in life. True freedom, he believed, was something more than this; it involved freeing people from the inner constraints that inhibited them from serving a higher, Christian, purpose.[12] Berdiaev accused liberalism of being concerned with the means of achieving freedom without regard for what he saw as freedom's essence, which was spiritual in nature.[13] True freedom, according to Berdiaev, was an inner freedom that enabled one to resist "enslaving necessity."[14] "One must first possess it in oneself and it must be discovered from within," he wrote.[15]

The key to this inner freedom was Christianity. "Christianity demands toleration for the inner experience and spiritual development of the human soul, because freedom is part of the Christian faith, and because Christianity is the religion of freedom," wrote Berdiaev.[16] He concluded, "Communism . . . has destroyed the freedom of the spirit and denies personality. . . . Only in Christ's Church will deliverance from this destructive tyranny . . . be found."[17]

The connection between liberty and Christianity was a common theme among the postrevolutionaries. Stepun claimed that "freedom cannot be only the negative freedom of individual liberation, but must be the positive freedom of serving the truth," specifically the truth revealed by Christianity.[18] According to Stepun, freedom, truth, and personhood were mutually dependent concepts. He wrote: "In isolation from the truth, freedom becomes arbitrariness, anarchy, and the struggle of all against all; in isolation from personhood it turns into passive obedience. . . . In isolation from truth and personhood there is no freedom, just as there is no truth and personhood without freedom."[19]

Stepun edited *Novyi Grad* along with Georgy Fedotov, who has been described as a proponent of "Christian liberalism."[20] Fedotov believed that the emigration's task was to preserve prerevolutionary culture and to develop it further.[21] But for Fedotov, a strong culture could not be based on pure materialism. "Postrevolutionary Russia—the Russia of tractors and cannon—cannot be a country with a great culture," he said.[22] The source of salvation would be the Orthodox Church. Fedotov wrote: "In the Church, shrunken, imprisoned in a dark, underground dungeon, there are preserved vast, unprecedented spiritual forces. They await their actualization. . . . The churchification of culture—that is our Christian utopia which we oppose to all other possible contemporary utopias. All other utopias will be realized in it."[23]

Fedotov blamed the triumph of Bolshevism on Russia's "abandonment of Europe's high humanistic traditions."[24] This was in part the fault of the imperial autocracy but also of Russian liberals who had been more concerned with destroying the old system than with building something positive of their own. Russian liberalism, Fedotov complained, "has long been fed on journeys abroad, on superficial rapture at the wonders of Western civilization, accompanied by a total inability to link its enlightening ideals with the forces propelling Russian life."[25] Liberals lacked roots in their own country's history, he said. The result, he concluded, was "the illness of antinationalism. . . . Russia itself became an object of hatred."[26]

The postrevolutionaries were not alone in looking to Christianity. A similar trend emerges in the émigré writings of Pavel Novgorodtsev, who swung in a conservative direction after 1917. Novgorodtsev noted that "naïve and immature political thought usually supposes that it is enough just to overthrow the old order and proclaim freedom of life, electoral rights and the constituent power of the people, and democracy will come into being all by itself."[27] Reality was very different, he said. To create a stable democratic order, there "must be a people that has matured to govern itself, knowing its own rights and respecting other peoples'."[28] This was only possible, Novgorodtsev argued, if democracy was guided by a "Higher Will," by which he meant religion. He wrote: "In the absence of absolute spiritual foundations, everything tends to a struggle of forces, a struggle between the majority and the minority, and eventually class struggle. . . . The whole world is living through a crisis of legal consciousness. And the most important and fundamental thing in this crisis is a crisis of non-belief, a crisis of culture, torn from religion, a crisis of the state, which has become disconnected from the church."[29]

Another idealist who swung to the right following the revolution was Semyon Frank. In the early 1900s Frank had been a "passionate advocate of constitutional government."[30] In exile, however, he attacked liberalism for "the absence in it of any independent or positive social outlook."[31] He complained that "in Russian liberalism, belief in the value of spiritual principles such as nation, state, law and freedom remains philosophically unexplained and lacking in religious inspiration."[32]

Yet another figure who moved to the right was Pyotr Struve. "The revolution has ruptured the old ties that united the Russian people—national, state, and religious. . . . Thus all the tasks of our future come together and are united in one thing: the raising of individuals and the masses in the national spirit," he wrote.[33] In contrast to the postrevolutionaries, though, Struve remained committed to political and military struggle against the Bolsheviks. This put him in conflict with Miliukov, who rejected Struve's nationalism as well as the religious orientation of the postrevolutionaries. Natalia Iokhina notes that "as a positivist and an opponent of any type of metaphysics, Miliukov accused the postrevolutionaries of disrespecting facts, and of rejecting material principles in favor of spiritual ones, positivism in favor of metaphysics, and politics in favor of morality."[34] In a letter to socialist émigré Ekaterina Kuskova (1869–1958), Miliukov complained, "You've already become caught up with the Ilyins, Berdiaevs, and Karsavins, and other participants in the 'national cause' and proponents of the 'national spirit.' I can't be in their company. Why we need a nationalistic ideology for the sake of 'pathos and life,' I don't know. I know only that I've fought against this my whole life."[35]

For solutions to Russia's problems Miliukov looked to politics rather than to cultural and spiritual resurrection. This can be seen in his approach to issues of nationalism. He remained a believer in the unity of the Russian empire and hoped that eventually the nations that had split off from it would return. "Geography and history speak to this union," he said. "Geography and history have created over the centuries that old Russian complex, which only now has collapsed during the revolution."[36] However, in practical terms, the national self-consciousness of the minorities of the former empire was a fact that had to be recognized, and consequently, "Our republic must be 'federative.' . . . We have no other way of restoring the links of the separate parts with the former metropole."[37]

In line with this, the program of Miliukov's Republican-Democratic Union called for Russia to become a federal republic. By contrast, Miliukov's opponents on the right of the Kadet party stuck to the prerevolutionary policy of maintaining a unitary state and granting minority nationalities only cultural autonomy.[38] The founding congress of the Russian National Committee in 1921 heard a report from journalist Iuly Semyonov (1873–1947), a former Kadet party city councillor in the Georgian capital Tiflis. Semyonov argued that there was no turning back to the situation before the revolution and that it would therefore be necessary to grant some form of self-government to minority nations. Semyonov's position would later find expression in a resolution of the 1926 Émigré Congress, at which he gave one of the keynote speeches. The congress resolved that "the Provisional power . . . must guarantee . . . to all nationalities that populate Russia . . . the possibility of free development of their national cultural life."[39]

Speaking to the congress, Semyonov remarked that "the power of the communist party, which is called Soviet power, is not a Russian power . . . the desire of 'Soviet power' to artificially present itself as a national Russian government is self-deceit and deceit."[40] Semyonov continued: "What is now called Russia Abroad is an internal spiritual unity of the entire Russian emigration that rejects

the Communist International, [and is] convinced of the impossibility of any evolution of communist power in Russia, and that Russia's liberation from Soviet
power is possible only by means of its destruction."[41]

Through his reference to "evolution," Semyonov took aim at Miliukov and
other former colleagues in the Kadet party who argued that communism
would evolve in a democratic direction and that émigrés should abandon
thoughts of renewing the armed struggle against it. The issues of the Soviet
Union's evolution and the continuation of the armed struggle would prove
deeply divisive among émigré liberals. In time, they tore the Kadets apart.

Political Liberalism

As long as the civil war continued, most Kadets supported the White armies.
The evacuation of Crimea in November 1920 changed the political dynamic.
In a speech to members of the Kadet party in Paris in December 1920, Miliukov declared that the struggle against Bolshevism could "not continue in its
old forms."[42] Miliukov blamed the Whites' military defeat on a failure to resolve the issue of land ownership in a manner supported by the peasants, a
narrow-minded nationalities policy, and the predominance of military person-
nel in the White movement.[43] New tactics were required, he concluded.[44]

What this meant, said Miliukov, was first that the political leadership of the
anti-Bolshevik struggle should be removed from the hands of the generals. Second, the émigrés should abandon nonpredetermination. And third, efforts
should be made to politically unite "the left flank of the emigration" by means
of an alliance between the Kadets and émigré socialists.[45]

Miliukov's call for new tactics infuriated his fellow Kadets. The Constantinople branch of the party passed a resolution saying that the armed struggle
must continue, that the remnants of the army evacuated from Crimea should
be preserved, and that émigré social forces should rally behind the army's
leader, General Wrangel.[46] The Berlin Kadets also denounced Miliukov's position and issued a declaration that "Russia's revival cannot be accomplished
by the forces of 'left democracy' alone."[47]

Miliukov reiterated his position at a meeting of the Kadet central committee in Paris in May 1921, but met with fierce opposition. Ariadna Tyrkova-
Williams denounced Miliukov's suggestion that the party cooperate with
socialists. "The socialist revolution . . . has shown that socialism is cultural, economic and political reaction," she said.[48] Meanwhile Prince Pavel Dolgorukov
(1866–1927) argued that "a military dictatorship is necessary."[49] The committee rejected Miliukov's new tactics by a vote of ten to six.[50]

Following the central committee meeting, Kadets on the right of the party held a national unity congress in Paris along with former Octobrists and a few socialists, notably the journalist Vladimir Burtsev (1862–1942). Congress delegates applauded mentions of the White armies and sent a message of support to Wrangel.[51] They then elected a National Committee as a permanent body to represent their views. Anton Kartashev, the former Kadet minister for religious affairs in the Provisional Government, became its chairman. Thereafter the National Committee acted as the arm of the right wing of the Kadet party.

In July 1921, Kadets met in Paris in a final effort to avoid a split. After Miliukov's new tactics were again rejected, he and his supporters walked out and formed a new organization, "the Paris Democratic Group of the Party of People's Freedom."[52] Centrist-minded Kadets also formed their own group. Officially, the Kadet party staggered on for a little longer, but in practice it had split into three factions: center, left, and right.

The center was the weakest of the three. The centrists stuck to the civil war era policy of nonpredetermination, saying that the final form of government should be determined by a future constituent assembly. Prior to the summoning of such an assembly, power was to be held by a transitional dictatorship. The centrists held negotiations with Miliukov to try to reconcile their differences, but talks broke down over their respective attitudes toward socialism and private property as well as the name of any unity organization. The centrists wanted to call the organization the "Russian National Democrats," but Miliukov rejected the word "national," as he felt that public opinion associated it with the reactionary right.[53]

Miliukov's position reflected his desire to avoid anything that might derail his proposed alliance with émigré socialists. However, negotiations to create such an alliance were not particularly fruitful. In September 1922 a congress of left Kadets, socialist revolutionaries, and members of the Popular Socialist Party failed to reach agreement.[54] Miliukov next sought an alliance with the socialist party Krestianskaia Rossiia (Peasant Russia), with whom in December 1923 he formed a Republican-Democratic bloc.[55] This in due course morphed into the RDO, a loose coalition of left-minded émigrés, which at its peak had about 200 members in branches across Europe.[56]

Miliukov listed the RDO's tasks as being: continued struggle against Soviet power, establishment of contacts with democratic forces in the Soviet Union, and participation in the struggle for power within the Soviet Union.[57] These last two tasks reflected Miliukov's belief that the revolution had released democratic impulses in the Russian people which would promote a process of democratic evolution within the Soviet Union. Meanwhile, the introduction in Soviet Russia in 1921 of a new economic policy that restored some elements of private enterprise encouraged Miliukov's belief that the Soviet Union would evolve in a more positive direction.

Observing power struggles within the Soviet Communist Party, Miliukov claimed that moderate elements in the party were fighting back against the "doctrinaire Kremlin fanatics."[58] He argued that émigrés should help to facilitate the moderates' victory by adopting policies that would reassure the Soviet population that they need not fear a restoration of the old order. To this end, the RDO proclaimed itself to be a republican organization. Miliukov wrote: "Proclamation of a monarchy in Russia would be in principle a proclamation of the *old* monarchy, accompanied by the return of the old regime. . . . We must extract from Russia's troubles that which can be considered a positive result, and the main thing achieved by the revolution is this: the supremacy of the people. That is why we are republicans."[59]

Right Kadets never shared Miliukov's belief that the Soviet Union was capable of democratic evolution. In any case, they had also developed serious doubts about the benefits of democracy. The experience of the Provisional Government, as well as of democratic governments in interwar Europe, convinced many that democracy was liable to collapse into totalitarianism. Right Kadets' preference was for a constitutional monarchy, most likely preceded by a transitional dictatorship. From 1923 onward, many on the conservative end of the Russian emigration turned to the former supreme commander of the Russian army, Grand Duke Nikolai Nikolaevich, seeing in him a leader capable of uniting the emigration. Right Kadets joined them, and in May 1924 the National Committee passed a resolution in support of the grand duke.[60]

The National Committee's leader Anton Kartashev told Tyrkova-Williams, "For me, being a Kadet could never be a 'worldview'! My conscience was only in a bloc with it."[61] An acquaintance noted that "he is for military dictatorship. . . . He is an intelligent man, but a democrat by mistake, that is, actually, not a democrat at all."[62] Kartashev and the National Committee gave their support to the idea of the Émigré Congress, designed to create a single body to unite the center and right of the Russian emigration under the grand duke's leadership.

The National Committee played an active role in organizing the congress. When it finally convened in Paris in April 1926, key roles went to two former Kadets: Pyotr Struve and Ivan Aleksinsky (1871–1945), the latter of whom had represented the Kadet party in the First Duma.[63] The two men became congress president and vice-president, respectively. Other right Kadets such as Iulii Semyonov attended as delegates. So too did large numbers of representatives of conservative and monarchist organizations. The congress therefore brought the right Kadets into alliance with many of their former enemies.

Despite its conservative majority, the congress passed a series of resolutions that have been described as "often liberal and realistic."[64] Richard Pipes notes that these resolutions "were drafted in a tolerant and liberal spirit, in which there was no trace of either revanchism or restoration."[65] Nevertheless, the right Kadets' efforts to seek unity with émigré conservatives failed. The congress ended in disarray when the resolution to create a unity committee failed to receive the required majority, resulting in the subsequent creation of not one, but two, such committees. Further efforts to unite the right proved equally fruitless.

Discussing the Émigré Congress, Serguei Glebov argues that "the supraparty, national unity propagated by Kartashev, Struve and others suspiciously resembled the language of early Italian fascism. . . . Kartashev in particular sought to forge an ideology that would include his perceptions of the spirit of . . . the army as the kernel of the nation."[66] As democratic governments fell across Europe and dictatorial regimes took their place, some former liberals began to look to fascism as an ally against communism. In a 1933 speech Struve noted that liberty and democracy were not the same, and that nondemocratic regimes often proved better at defending liberty than democratic ones.[67] Struve initially welcomed Hitler's rise to power in Germany, before changing his mind and denouncing him. But, as Pipes comments, until 1938 he "was prepared . . . to give Hitler the benefit of the doubt."[68]

Struve is often described as a liberal conservative. So is Frank, whose philosophy involved a belief in strong, centralized state power, combined with the rule of law and respect for personal freedom. "A person's essence lies in his freedom, and human society is unthinkable without freedom," he wrote.[69] To Frank, though, freedom did not mean the right to do whatever one chose. "Freedom," he wrote, "is the obligation and right of the person to serve divine truth."[70] He said: "The individualistic idea that the individual has a right to a . . . definite area of freedom . . . an idea that is based on the false notion of the 'innate' rights of man, must be rejected as incompatible with the supreme principle of *service*, which alone can justify the idea of individual freedom."[71]

It was not just the émigré right that combined a belief in the importance of personal freedom with a skeptical view of liberal democracy. Similar ideas could be found among the postrevolutionaries. Fedotov, for instance, claimed that democracies had proven incapable of defending themselves. "Democracy is too good for our cruel times," he said.[72] He predicted "the inevitability of dictatorship" after the collapse of communism, commenting that "democracy is possible now in Russia only through the methods of dictatorship," due to the lack of "intellectual growth of the popular consciousness."[73] To avoid fascism, it was essential that "this future dictatorship have a democratic content. This means that its task should be to bring the people toward democracy. . . . The democratic character of the dictatorship consists in the fact that its goal (like a Roman legal dictatorship) is to make itself unnecessary."[74]

Fedotov argued that freedom was something that developed along with culture.[75] It followed that political freedom should belong first to the more culturally advanced members of society. Freedom for everybody all at once ended up destroying freedom. Fedotov explained, "Freedom is at root always aristocratic."[76] Elections should be based "not on programs but on the personal qualities of candidates," he wrote, for which reason candidates should stand as individuals and not as members of parties and should be selected not on a geographic basis but through their place of work, where people knew them and their personal qualities.[77]

Fedotov's postrevolutionary colleague Stepun agreed that the postcommunist order in Russia was much more likely to be "a dictatorship rather than a democracy of the old type." He continued: "I am personally convinced that without such a fascist-ization of democratic consciousness and democratic principles it will be impossible to defend real freedom in the economic and spiritual sense in our fascist-ized world."[78] Stepun was not supporting fascism. Instead, he spoke of "the need to fascist-ize democracy in order to overcome fascism."[79] Fascists, said Stepun, had correctly identified the fact that liberalism failed to connect freedom to any higher truth, but they were mistaken in how they tried to overcome this problem. He wrote: "Fascism is unacceptable not because . . . it restricts the political rights of its citizens . . . but because of its hatred of freedom and of the spiritual nature of man. . . . Its biggest mistake is that it doesn't understand that it is impossible to build a state without also building a personality who to some degree thinks differently, without giving that personality the chance . . . to govern and realize itself."[80] Consequently, Stepun concluded, "Our task is to do all we can so that the Bolsheviks are replaced not by national fascism but by a new democratic order which, despite its inevitable authoritarian firmness, will be genuinely philanthropic."[81]

Social-Economic Liberalism

Émigré economists devoted considerable attention to the issue of the agrarian economy. Many of them, such as Nikolai Zvorykin, regarded the peasant commune as the main cause of Russia's prerevolutionary economic difficulties. Their preferred form of agricultural unit was the family farm, which was seen as more efficient than both the peasant commune and large-scale capitalist agro-industries due to the personal interest that family farmers had in the success of their operations.[82]

Like Zvorykin, Vladimir Kosinsky (1864–1938) believed that family farms were the most efficient. However, he also argued that the development of new agricultural technologies created opportunities for large agricultural enterprises. Kosinsky predicted that the future of agriculture lay in a mixture of the two types of farming. Most farms would be family-owned and run, but these would exist side by side with a highly mechanized capitalist agricultural sector.[83]

While the economists addressed the issue of land ownership from an economic perspective, émigré Kadets considered its political aspect. In theory most supported private land ownership, but some believed that this might prove unpopular with the peasantry. They favored solutions in which the state distributed land to peasants for their use and regulated the market to prevent land from becoming concentrated in the hands of a few.[84] Due to his desire for an alliance with émigré socialists, Miliukov refused to commit to private land ownership, saying that while it would be better if the RDO platform supported the idea, "this is prevented by the unresolved argument among us."[85]

The RDO platform was deliberately vague on the matter, glossing over differences among its liberal and socialist members as to whether land should be peasants' "property" (*sobstvennost'*) or merely in their "possession" (*vladenie*). It avoided the use of either word, speaking only of "a decisive struggle against all efforts to take land from those who currently hold it."[86] Rejecting the arguments of those who sought an unregulated land market, Miliukov wrote: "As I've already said, it is impossible to return to this position of old 'Manchesterism.' The modern state has already spread its sphere of influence so far that the position of pure state noninterference in private affairs must be considered obsolete. Recognition of the *principle* of state regulation of certain private affairs . . . is unavoidable in any democratic program. . . . Nowadays the state is an important factor in cultural and social justice."[87]

Miliukov and the RDO proposed a mixed economy. The RDO platform called for "the revival of the country's productive forces on the basis of free economic activity."[88] Miliukov noted that "it is impossible to raise economic activity, to strengthen the productivity of labor, and to give labor an impulse, without private property."[89] He qualified this, however, by saying that "we are not talking about recognizing private property . . . as an unlimited right to make use of something. On the contrary, private property may be limited and . . . in fact is limited in all law-based democratic countries."[90]

The move to a regulated market economy implied the denationalization of Soviet industry. That raised the question of how this was to be done. The issue proved quite divisive. In February 1921, members of the Kadet party in Constantinople held a debate concerning a draft resolution on the issue of property. The draft said that property taken in the revolution would not be restored to its previous owners. Some complained that the resolution condoned "theft" and demanded that it be amended to apply only to "moveable" property.[91] Some objected even to the amended article, but others defended it as politically essential. As one of those present said: "In three years of Bolshevism there has been such a redistribution of moveable property by means of sales, exchanges, and so on, that without a doubt the majority of the population does not want to see the old rights of property restored."[92]

Similar thinking determined Miliukov's position on the issue of property restoration. In theory, he favored restoring nationalized enterprises to their former owners on condition that they immediately resumed production. In practice, he refused to include this idea in the RDO program, commenting that the proposal to return property to its former owners was politically "dangerous." "One must bear in mind the impression that it will produce," he wrote.[93]

Among those who favored the denationalization of Soviet industry was Fedotov, whose economic thinking was more liberal than that of some other postrevolutionaries, notably Berdiaev, who was resolutely anticapitalist.[94] Fedotov argued in favor of economic freedom. "Bolshevik dictatorship is above all a social, i.e., economic, dictatorship. . . . The first, perhaps only thing that the Russian people pines for is economic liberation," he wrote.[95]

Economic liberation was relatively "simple," Fedotov claimed. The "renewal of property and of freedom of labor and capital . . . [will] quickly raise the level of wellbeing," he said.[96] This renewal would involve the denationalization of state industry, but Fedotov urged some caution: national interests needed to be taken into consideration and the "state should get rid of only what it can't manage itself."[97] Care also needed to be taken to ensure that the process of denationalization did not lead to Russian industry falling into the hands of foreign capital.

Fedotov argued that "even the crudest capitalist exploitation guarantees workers a higher standard of living than does communism."[98] That did not mean, however, that capitalism was without its faults. "The era of economic liberalism has gone forever," he wrote. "Nowhere is the rule of competition or the freedom of the market accepted entirely."[99] Having abolished communism, the state would need to protect workers' rights, wrote Fedotov. "It would be good if it were to prove possible to preserve Bolshevik labor laws. Liberated Russia must show its mutinous son that he is not an outcast."[100]

If Fedotov sought a middle way between capitalism and socialism, Pyotr Struve was less equivocal. He remarked that economic success and economic equality were mutually incompatible.[101] In Struve's eyes, the former should take priority over the latter. He argued that economic success rested on three principles: private property, economic freedom, and the market.[102] In a 1933 lecture, Struve stated that the heart of liberalism was the defense of human rights, the most fundamental of which was economic freedom, whose foundation was private property.[103] In this way, Struve, a onetime Marxist who in 1898 had written the first manifesto of the forerunner of the Communist Party, the Russian Social Democratic Labor Party, had by 1933 come to the conclusion that the most important human right was the right to private property.

The cause of economic freedom found its foremost spokesman in the person of Boris Brutskus. In emigration, Brutskus influenced the Austrian economist Friedrich von Hayek, who would later become famous as an inspiration for the neoliberal turn in Western economic thought in the 1980s and 1990s. Hayek wrote a preface to Brutskus's book *Economic Planning in the Soviet Union*, which has been seen as a precursor of Hayek's own denunciation of socialism, *The Road to Serfdom*. Insofar as the Hayekian view of economics influenced free market reforms in Russia in the early 1990s, Brutskus's ideas were to have a powerful, albeit indirect, influence on Russian history.[104]

In opposition to Marx's labor theory of value, which argues that value is a product of the amount of labor expended on producing something, Brutskus argued that value is a product of social need, as reflected in prices. As he wrote: "At the root of the value phenomenon lie subjective valuations; these are summed up and crystalized in the market price, which reflects the intensity of social need for commodities. . . . By means of the market prices, capitalist society provides all productive organizations with powerful directives, and it compels them to regulate their expenditure in accordance with these prices."[105]

According to Brutskus, to replace the guidance provided by prices the socialist state would have to resort to a huge bureaucratic apparatus dedicated to collecting statistics about the population. But this apparatus would never be able to determine the subjective tastes of millions of distinct individuals. Thus, concluded Brutskus, "the socialist state is not in a position, even with the help of all its scientific theory and immense statistical apparatus, to measure the needs of its citizens . . . for this reason it is unable to provide production with the guidance which it needs."[106]

Lacking proper information, investment decisions in a socialist economy were divorced from economic realities, Brutskus claimed. The result was a considerable waste of resources.[107] Brutskus further argued that innovation was bound to stagnate under communism. Socialism suppressed the "profit motive," Brutskus wrote, and so, "If . . . socialist organization succeeded in assuming stable forms it would be distinguished by immense indolence and conservatism. It would offer nothing which could be compared to the unceasing movement of economic life under capitalism."[108]

Surveying the first Soviet five-year plan (1928–1932), Brutskus commented that the Soviets had destroyed the "spontaneous regulators of economic life," with extremely negative consequences.[109] According to Brutskus, the experience showed that "it would be completely wrong to think that any sort of stable compromise can be found between communism and capitalism. Between capitalism, whose basis is a legal order, and communism, in the sense of revolutionary socialism, whose base is a dictatorial regime, no stable compromise can be concluded. . . . In order for Russia to escape from the dead end into which it has fallen, communism must be finally overcome and all traces of it eliminated from national life."[110]

If one is looking for liberalism in the sense generally understood in the West today, outside the work of economists one will largely search in vain in the interwar Russian emigration. Elements of liberalism were combined with elements of other modes of thought as thinkers sought a third way between capitalist liberal democracy, on the one hand, and communist or fascist dictatorship, on the other.

By the late 1920s, liberalism had ceased to exist as an organized political movement in the Russian emigration. Their movement in tatters, émigré liberals were left with little to do but engage in historical debates about what had gone wrong. Particularly notable were the writings of Vasily Maklakov, who from 1929 onward wrote a series of articles for the journal *Sovremennye Zapiski* (Contemporary notes) in which he surveyed the history of the liberal movement from the mid-nineteenth century through to the revolution.

Maklakov pinned the blame for the revolution on liberals who, he said, had not in truth been liberals but radicals. Liberals, said Maklakov, were those "who recognized the need to fundamentally reform Russia in the direction of what in Europe is called liberal," but who wanted to do this "not by means of forced catastrophes and leaps, not by destroying the old, but by natural development and improvement, in other words by what is called 'evolution.'"[111] Unfortunately, said Maklakov, the Kadet party had proven itself to be a "radical party . . . a party of abstract principles" with a "doctrinaire program."[112] It had adopted policy positions that were revolutionary in nature, such as the four-tailed franchise. "Everybody understands that you can't go to university without having first completed middle school," said Maklakov. "It's exactly the same with a country, that having not passed through political school has not been educated for complete freedom."[113]

The Kadets should have cooperated with the imperial government for the good of the country, Maklakov argued. Instead, they had adopted a position of "chronic opposition," in which "any simple truce with the authorities was considered treason."[114] "Society became used to viewing the authorities only as an evil and its ideology strove to weaken this evil, to paralyze the authorities, to subordinate them to what was called 'the will of the people.'"[115] The ultimate result of this "irresponsible opposition," said Maklakov, was the destruction of all authority in Russia.[116]

Miliukov denied that liberals shared any responsibility for the revolution. In response to Maklakov, he argued that the radical elements of the Kadet program were not incompatible with liberalism. "Liberalism is undoubtedly indebted to socialism for a whole series of new ideas introduced into the programs of liberal parties without in the process depriving liberalism of its progressive character," he said.[117] Besides, Miliukov wrote, the blame for liberals' radicalization "falls on the autocracy," adding that, "the actions of the autocracy justified the positions of the leftists and led to a revolutionary outcome."[118] "The autocracy left no other path to a constitutional monarchy than the revolutionary one," he concluded.[119]

Late in his life, Miliukov accepted that his expectations concerning the Soviet Union's democratic evolution had been mistaken. "How naïve we were in all our hopes," he remarked. "Now it's hard to understand how we missed the symptoms showing that the course of development was moving . . . toward the physical destruction of all those in the party who might oppose Stalin."[120]

If liberalism fared badly in exile, it fared even worse in the Soviet Union. Miraculously, though, pockets of liberalism survived. After the death of Soviet leader Joseph Stalin (1878–1953), liberalism reemerged from hiding.

CHAPTER 8

Soviet Liberalism

Following its victory in the Russian Civil War, Vladimir Lenin's Bolshevik Party, later renamed the Communist Party of the Soviet Union (CPSU), set about transforming the territories under its control. Under Lenin's successor, Joseph Stalin, the Union of Soviet Socialist Republics (as it was known from 1922) replaced the free market economy with a state-controlled, centrally planned system, and clamped down firmly on any manifestations of political dissent. Russian liberalism appeared to be dead.

From the mid-1950s, however, a form of Soviet liberalism began to emerge. Most Soviet intellectuals believed in communism in principle. At the same time, many were aware that the realities of Soviet life did not match official propaganda and sought to construct a more humane form of socialism. A key moment was the twentieth congress of the CPSU in 1956, when the then Soviet leader Nikita Khrushchev (1894–1971) delivered a speech denouncing Stalin. A period of relative freedom of thought and expression known as the "Thaw" then followed.

The Thaw raised the hopes of Soviet intellectuals, but these hopes were dashed after Khrushchev was ousted as Soviet leader in 1964 and replaced by Leonid Brezhnev (1906–1982).[1] In spring 1968—known as the Prague Spring—the communist authorities in Czechoslovakia embarked on a series of reforms designed to liberalize Czechoslovak society. As Robert English comments, "Soviet liberals were absolutely galvanized by the Prague Spring. . . . When it seemed to be succeeding, liberals were ecstatic."² The Soviet authorities took note, and in August 1968 ordered the Soviet army to occupy Czechoslovakia, depose the communist party leadership, and impose a new one. The hopes of would-be Soviet reformers were crushed. "Czechoslovakia shook me up," said Aleksandr Yakovlev (1923–2005), who would later act as adviser to the USSR's last leader, Mikhail Gorbachev (1931–2022).³

Roughly speaking, one can identify three groups of Soviet intellectuals who sought to change their society in a more liberal direction. The first worked within the communist system, including in the CPSU itself. Heirs of the "enlightened bureaucrats" of the imperial era, they proposed cautious reforms while not challenging the fundamentals of the system itself. In some cases they enjoyed the protection of senior officials. In the mid-1960s, the future head of the CPSU, Iury Andropov (1914–1984), employed a group of such "systemic liberals" as consultants on foreign affairs.⁴ Many of Andropov's consultants would go on to play leading roles in Gorbachev's government.

The second group also worked within the system, and consisted of intellectuals at academic journals, universities, and research institutes, as well as at scientific cities such as Akademgorodok in Siberia.⁵ These intellectuals noted deficiencies in Soviet economic and social life, but like the enlightened bureaucrats kept their criticisms within the boundaries set by the authorities.

The third group, the dissidents, went further. They published and distributed their works underground, a form of publishing known as *samizdat* (self-publishing). Dissidents paid particular attention to human rights issues, and in 1968 they began producing the *Chronicle of Current Events*, which collected information about abuses of human rights in the USSR.

The most prominent Soviet dissident was the physicist Andrei Sakharov (1921–1989), who in 1970, along with Valery Chalidze (1938–2018) and Andrei Tverdokhlebov (1940–2011), formed the Human Rights Committee in Moscow to highlight Soviet human rights abuses.⁶ The signing of the Helsinki Final Act in 1975 provided further impetus to the dissident human rights movement. Designed to regulate interstate relations in Europe, the act contained various provisions guaranteeing human rights. In 1976, a group of Moscow dissidents under the leadership of physicist Iury Orlov (1924–2020) founded the Group to Assist the Implementation of the Helsinki Agreements in the USSR. The group's aim was to monitor Soviet violations of the act's human rights guarantees. Similar Helsinki Watch groups appeared in Soviet Ukraine, Lithuania, Georgia, and Armenia.⁷

The in-system reformers are said to have numbered "perhaps in the hundreds," and the dissidents somewhere between several hundred and 2–3,000.⁸ Vasily Zharkov argues that Soviet liberalism was a phenomenon of the former rather than the latter, being the purview of people "wearing ties . . . graduates of MGU [Moskovskii Gosudarstvennyi Universitet (Moscow State University)] and MGIMO [Moskovskii Gosudarstvennyi Institut Mezhdunarodnykh Otnoshenii (Moscow State Institute for International Affairs)], working in the [CPSU] Central Committee and other nomenklatura structures."[9]

Dissidents tended to think in terms of humane socialism and a "return to Leninist norms."[10] They rarely referred to themselves as liberals.[11] Nevertheless, some historians are willing to call them "liberal" because of the importance they attached to human rights and the rule of law. "Liberalism was the major intellectual force of the entire dissident movement," claims Mikhail Epstein in a 2019 study of late Soviet philosophy.[12] Emma Gilligan comments that the dissident Sergei Kovalyov (1930–2021), who edited the *Chronicle of Current Events*, personified "the tradition of classical liberalism as founded in Western cultures—respect for individual rights and political liberty."[13] She notes, however, that Kovalyov "maintained that his understanding of liberalism was informed more by his own experiences than through formal study of liberal theory."[14] Soviet liberalism was not a copy of its Western counterpart. Rather it was very much a "Soviet" liberalism, shaped by the experiences of Soviet life.

Cultural Liberalism

In the first years of their rule, the Soviet authorities hoped that revolution would spread rapidly to the rest of Europe. Before long, it became clear that these hopes were in vain. From the mid-1920s onward, the Soviet state to a large degree turned its back on the Western world, and travel to and from the West was highly restricted. After 1945, the Cold War institutionalized the distinction between liberal democratic Western Europe and communist Eastern Europe. Through organizations such as the North Atlantic Treaty Organization (NATO) and the Warsaw Pact, Russia and the West became institutionally separate places.

As time went on, a small, but intellectually significant element of the Soviet elite sought to overcome this division between East and West and return Russia to "Western civilization." According to Robert English, the period from the early 1960s onward witnessed "the rise of a global, 'Westernizing' identity among a liberal policy-academic elite" in the Soviet Union.[15] These Soviet Westernizers were concentrated in academic research institutes such as the Institute of World Economy and International Relations (Institut Mirovoi Ekonomiki i Mezhdunarodnykh Otnoshenii, IMEMO) and on the staff of journals such as *Problemy mira i sotsializma* (Problems of peace and socialism;

published in English as the *World Marxist Review*). English comments that these Westernizers "did not just posit an end to conflict with the West or the desirability of cooperation with the liberal international community. [They] argued that the USSR was, or should be, a *member* of that community."[16]

Soviet intellectuals who worked for *Problemy mira i sotzializma* included the philosopher Merab Mamardashvili (1930–1990) and several members of the Soviet "enlightened bureaucracy" who would later serve as advisers to the Soviet Union's last leader, Mikhail Gorbachev, such as Georgy Arbatov (1923–2010), Georgy Shakhnazarov (1924–2001), and Anatoly Chernyaev (1921–2017). Arbatov said that the journal "helped build an intellectual bridge from the Twentieth Party Congress to *perestroika*."[17] According to Chernyaev, "It was a totally non-Soviet environment. . . . We were exposed to a huge amount of information on the outside world. And from all that, the idea of imperialist aggression, that the West posed a real threat to the Soviet Union, it instantly disappeared."[18]

Another source of new thinking was MGU, where in the early 1950s Mikhail Gorbachev befriended Czechoslovak student Zdenek Mlynar (1930–1997), who later became one of the ideological architects of the Prague Spring. In 1952, graduate students at MGU formed a philosophical discussion group known as the Moscow Methodological Circle. Among the members were Mamardashvili, Georgy Shchedrovitsky (1928–1994) and Vladimir Lefebvre (1936–2020), as well as the future dissident Aleksandr Zinoviev (1922–2006).[19] Not a member of the circle, but a friend of some of its members, was another philosophy student at MGU, Raisa Titarenko (1932–1999), who in 1953 married Gorbachev.

According to Mikhail Epstein, "Mamardashvili's influence cannot be overstated. . . . The theme of his reflection was philosophy itself, which he regarded as a moral imperative to question the identity of all values. . . . In later years, he was regarded as an outsider, a challenger of established positions of every kind."[20] Mamardashvili avoided politics, but his insistence on questioning authority inevitably meant that he posed a challenge to communist dogma.

For Mamardashvili, Europe was not a geographic entity but an idea embodied in values such as freedom, the rule of law, and self-determination.[21] Becoming European required continuous self-improvement: "At one point this problem had already begun to be solved, but we were derailed and became feral. Now if we really want to save or take part in saving civilization on earth, if we want to go back to our European house and have a right to talk about it as its defenders, we ourselves have to first become civilized—more civilized, or simply civilized people; in other words, to jump to a new track altogether."[22]

Mamardashvili's comments reflected a common view among Westernizers, namely that the West constituted the center of "civilization" and that the Soviet Union needed to return to it. Mamardashvili described the problem in the following manner: "Speaking directly and succinctly, this state is simply monstrous—but, apparently, it couldn't have been otherwise. The people who jumped out of history and life (I have in mind all peoples within Russia's territory) could not have been avoided being sick as a result. . . . It is obvious that we are dealing with a disorganized, lost, feral consciousness."[23]

Mamardashvili's comment about jumping "out of history" reflected a deterministic view of the world in which history marched in a single direction. The revolution, he thought, had diverted the Soviet Union onto the wrong course, which therefore needed correcting if the Soviet people was to return to the European path of "civilization."

Another member of the Moscow Methodological Circle, Aleksandr Zinoviev, became well known for his critique of *homo sovieticus*, the "Soviet man." According to Zinoviev, the characteristics of *homo sovieticus* included "poor workmanship, laziness, deception, disinclination to work."[24] "Communist society is not a moral society just as it is not a society under the rule of law. Moral norms do not actually operate there. The point is not that they have been broken, it is simply that there aren't any," he claimed.[25]

Such criticisms were common in dissident circles. The Soviet people had "the psychology of a slave," wrote one *samizdat* author.[26] "Behind us are decades of shameful servility," said another, Boris Shragin.[27] "This is a sick society," wrote Sergei Kovalyov.[28] The Soviet people had no understanding of freedom and human rights, claimed Andrei Amalrik (1938–1980), adding that "it is hard to tell whether . . . the bulk of our people possess any kind of moral criteria—such as 'honorable' or 'dishonorable,' 'good' and 'bad,' 'right' and 'wrong.' . . . I have formed the impression, which may be wrong, that our people do not have any such criteria—or hardly any."[29]

Many dissidents were engineers or scientists—so-called ITRs (*inzhenerno-tekhnicheskie rabotniki*, engineering-technical workers). Others hailed from the "creative classes"—writers, artists, and so on. Nearly all were intellectuals.[30] Mark Lipovetsky speculates that "it was ITR discourse that in fact shaped *the cultural mainstream of late Soviet and post-Soviet liberalism*."[31] Specifically, "Enlightenment zeal, based on a belief in progress and supported by the power of reason, science, and technologies (including political ones), placed the sharers of the ITR discourse in double opposition: to the state and the 'people,' to the absurdity of the regime, on the one hand, and to the idiocy of the 'uneducated masses,' on the other."[32]

On the basis of interviews with dissidents, Theodore Friedgut concluded in 1975 that "there appears to be no attempt [by dissidents] to proselytize among the Soviet masses. . . . The most prominent reason cited . . . was the total lack of community of values between the democrats, who are virtually all in the intelligentsia, and the working people."[33] Dissidents contrasted them-selves with the masses. "Around us is a spiritless, dull mass that has forgotten conscience and is lacking in knowledge. . . . Therefore, it is necessary that . . . we [the intelligentsia] not only preserve moral purity . . . but also develop our culture," wrote Shragin.[34]

According to Shragin, the intelligentsia had "shown that it alone is capable of becoming an active force of spiritual, and then also social, transformation."[35] The most famous exponent of this theme was Grigory Pomerants (1918–2013). In an article entitled "The Man from Nowhere," he wrote that "the urban and rural proletariat has replaced the people in political life, but not in society's spiritual life . . . one cannot expect anything from the worker in this regard. . . . Everything that's called proletarian is in spiritual terms no different from the rest of the urbanized mass. It's simply its lowest layer, without any providen-tial perspectives."[36]

The solution to the country's cultural deficiencies, according to Pomerants, lay in the intelligentsia. "When the intelligentsia is free, the path to freedom is open. Where the intelligentsia is enslaved, all are enslaved," he said, adding that "those engaged in creative intellectual labor are the chosen people of the twentieth century."[37]

The intelligentsia's role was to act as an example for the whole nation. For dissidents, one of the great failings of Soviet society was the way it forced everybody to practice deceit on a regular basis. By protesting Soviet abuses of power, dissidents imagined that they were fighting back against this. As Shra-gin put it, "We will set culture against the regime's lack of culture."[38]

For some dissidents, this cultural purpose had a religious element. Philip Boobbyer notes that "a kind of Christian liberalism was not unusual in dissi-dent circles."[39] Father Aleksandr Men (1935–1990), whose parish lay just out-side Moscow, acquired a large following among the capital's intelligentsia. Men's mother was a Ukrainian Jew who converted to Russian Orthodoxy and was active in the underground "catacomb" church that operated outside the purview of the Soviet state and the official hierarchy of the Russian Ortho-dox Church. Men is said to have "represented the spiritual voice of a demo-cratic, nonauthoritarian Christianity."[40] He taught that "the very essence of Christian faith" was "the limitless value of human individuality."[41]

Men identified two major strands in world religion—one creative, the other static and repressive.[42] The former required freedom and "openness to the world," including dialogue with other faiths.[43] According to Men, "There is no single answer."[44] Pluralism, he argued, "is an important precondition for the vitality of Christianity. And perhaps it was providential that Christianity was split into different tendencies, because without this it would probably have been something uniform and forced. It is as if, knowing people's tendency to intolerance, God divided them so that each person in their place, in their own garden could bring forth their own fruit."[45]

Although Men limited himself to religious matters, his praise of pluralism had obvious political overtones, and it brought him into conflict with Russian nationalists. Late in his life he noted, "I understand that every culture, every nation, must to a certain degree love its own identity, but now this has got to the point where we love ourselves and no one and nothing else."[46]

This highlights the fact that Soviet liberal intellectuals had an enemy other than the Soviet state, namely Russian nationalists who expressed the sentiment that Russia had a unique civilizational destiny. This viewpoint clashed firmly with the liberal belief that the Soviet Union was part of Europe.

Perhaps the best-known exponent of Russian nationalism was the author Aleksandr Solzhenitsyn (1918–2008). Fellow dissidents generally held Solzhenitsyn in great respect, but his nationalist views did create some controversy among them. Sakharov, for instance, wrote: "I also find myself far from Solzhenitsyn's views on the role of Marxism as an allegedly 'Western' and anti-religious teaching which perverted a healthy Russian course of development. In general I cannot comprehend this very separation of ideas into Russian and Western."[47] Pomerants similarly attacked *pochvennichestvo* ("native soil"-ism), a form of nationalist ideology often associated with the nineteenth-century writer Fyodor Dostoevsky. According to Pomerants, *"zapadnichestvo* [Westernism] offers the chance to move into a new apartment, but *pochvennichestvo* responds emotionally. . . . I like the old one, I'm used to it, and I don't know that I'll get used to the new one! *Zapadnichestvo* offers a 'capital house with a thousand-year contract' . . . and *pochvennichestvo* irrationally turns it down."[48]

According to a *samizdat* article written under the pseudonym of V. Gorsky, "Overcoming the national-messianic temptation is Russia's first and foremost task. Russia will not be able to rid itself of despotism until it rejects the idea of national greatness."[49] Gorsky continued: "One thing is certain. The collapse of the Soviet empire will not be humiliating or unnatural for Russia. . . . Freed from the yearnings of occupation and coercion, it will confront its true problems: the building of a free democratic society, religious renaissance, and the creation of a national culture."[50]

Political Liberalism

Marxist theory valued class interests over individual rights, thus justifying the "dictatorship of the proletariat." Communist thinking also gave a higher priority to economic and social rights than to civil and political rights. That said, communism and liberalism had some common values.[51] Successive Soviet constitutions promised significant personal rights to Soviet citizens, while the Soviet Union played a leading role in drafting a series of international human rights conventions. The Soviet authorities regularly ignored these legal documents. Nevertheless, the fact that they notionally guaranteed the rights in question provided an opportunity for dissidents to campaign for them, and to argue that they were doing no more than demanding that the Soviet state respect its own laws. Human rights and the rule of law became centerpieces of dissident discourse.

In 1918, the first constitution of the Russian Socialist Federative Soviet Republic (RSFSR) stated that the republic was "guided by the interests of the working class as a whole" (Article 23). It stipulated that the right to vote belonged only to soldiers, sailors, and those who earned their living through "productive and socially useful labor" (Article 64), excluding private traders, those who lived off rent or unearned income, monks and priests, and former policemen (Article 65).[52]

The 1936 constitution of the USSR was very different, granting rights to all citizens, regardless of class background. This reflected a belief that the class enemy had been defeated, as well as an understanding that expanded rights for Soviet citizens could be a useful tool for the state in combating what the Soviet leadership regarded as an unresponsive bureaucracy.[53] To this end, writes Samantha Lomb, "the Constitutional Drafting Commission consulted multiple 'bourgeois,' i.e. Western, constitutions, and ensconced many of the ideals of universal suffrage, popular participation, and the responsiveness of the state to its constituents. . . . The collected materials of the Constitutional Commission contain election laws from England, Belgium, Germany, Norway, Czechoslovakia, and Switzerland, copies of the 'Declaration of the Rights of Man and of the Citizen' (1789), and various Western (bourgeois) constitutions."[54]

The 1936 constitution granted legal equality to "all citizens of the USSR, regardless of nationality or race" (Articles 122 and 123). It also provided citizens with a large set of social, economic, and civil rights, including the right to work, to leisure, to material security in old age, and to education (Articles 118, 119, 120, and 121). The constitution enshrined civil rights, such as freedom of speech, freedom of the press, and freedom of assembly and meetings (Article 125), but these rights were to be applied "in accordance with the interests of the workers and with the purpose of strengthening the socialist order."[55] This provided a loophole that allowed the Soviet state to ignore these rights when they failed to suit its purposes.

The next version of the Soviet constitution, enacted in 1977, contained very similar provisions concerning rights. The most notable amendments in the

1977 constitution concerned the role of the CPSU. Article 6 defined the party as "the leading and guiding force of Soviet society." It also required that "all party organizations act within the framework of the Constitution of the USSR."[56] On the one hand, this reinforced the party's leadership role. On the other hand, it also theoretically subjected the party to the law.

In addition, Article 4 of the 1977 constitution required that "the Soviet state and all its organs act on the basis of socialist legality. . . . State and social organizations . . . are obliged to observe the Constitution of the USSR and Soviet laws." Meanwhile, Article 58 stated that "citizens of the USSR have the right to compensation for loss brought about by illegal acts by state and social organizations."[57] While largely declarative, the gradual shift away from the dictatorship of the proletariat toward the rule of law was not unimportant. As Geoffrey Hosking argues, "Strangely enough, it may be that . . . the first germ of civil society was contained in the Stalin Constitution of 1936."[58] No less important, adds Hosking, was the fact that the Soviet Union publicly committed itself to guarantee human rights via several international treaties and conventions.[59]

The first of these was the 1948 Universal Declaration of Human Rights (UDHR), which the Soviet Union helped to draft.[60] During negotiations over the document, disagreements arose between the Western and Soviet sides. The former wanted the UDHR to focus on civil and political rights; the latter insisted on the inclusion of social and economic rights.[61] The West wanted the declaration to focus on individual rights; the Soviets put more emphasis on collective rights.[62] Soviet diplomats achieved some success. In particular, they managed to have included in Article 2 of the UDHR words prohibiting discrimination on the grounds of "race, color, sex, language, religion, political or other opinion, national or social origin, property, birth or other status."[63] The Soviet Union thereby made an important contribution to international human rights law.[64]

The differences between the West and the Soviets over the relative importance of civil and political rights, on the one hand, and social and economic rights, on the other, led to the enactment in 1966 of two extra conventions, both of which the Soviet Union signed and ratified: the International Covenant on Civil and Political Rights and the International Covenant on Economic, Social and Cultural Rights.[65] Even more significant was the 1975 Helsinki Final Act. This enshrined ten principles of interstate relations among European countries: sovereign equality, refraining from the threat or use of force, inviolability of frontiers, territorial integrity of states, peaceful settlement of disputes, nonintervention in internal affairs, respect for human rights, equal rights and self-determination of peoples, cooperation among states, and fulfillment in good faith of obligations under international law.[66] From the Soviet point of view, the key elements were those involving the inviolability of frontiers and noninterference in the internal affairs of other states. The Soviets accepted the inclusion of the clauses on human rights as a necessary price for the achievement of their objectives.[67] The result was a statement in the Helsinki Final Act that "the participating States will respect human rights and fundamental freedoms, including the freedom of thought, conscience, religion or belief, for all without distinction as to race, sex, language or religion. They will promote and encourage the effective exercise of civil, political, economic, social, cultural and other rights and freedoms all of which derive from the inherent dignity of the human person and are essential for his free and full development."[68]

The Soviet ratification of multiple international human rights treaties did not go unnoticed by elements of the Soviet intelligentsia. They seized on the treaties as opportunities to press the Soviet state to do what it had promised. As the dissident Pavel Litvinov wrote: "In a strange way, by pronouncing . . . the spirit of freedom and rights, Soviet official ideology made it possible for them to be resurrected in the Soviet human rights movement. . . . The human rights movement, by drawing attention to the lack of correspondence between the regime's behavior and the constitution, Soviet law, and also the series of international convention and pacts on human rights that the Soviet Union has signed . . . revealed a powerful lever for social transformation—the law."[69]

Dissident Valery Chalidze noted that "the movement's credo can be expressed in an old adage: A bad law is better than no law at all. We did not admire Soviet law. . . . But we tried to take it seriously, and we reminded the authorities that it was important to observe their own laws."[70] The generally recognized initiator of this strategy was the mathematician Aleksandr Yesenin-Volpin (1924–2016). On December 5, 1965, Soviet Constitution Day, Yesenin-Volpin organized one of the first protests in the USSR, in Pushkin Square in Moscow. Demonstrators unveiled banners saying "Respect the Soviet constitution."[71] Another dissident, Liudmila Alekseeva (1927–2018), described Yesenin-Volpin's logic as follows: "He would explain to anyone who cared to listen a simple but unfamiliar idea . . . all laws ought to be understood in exactly the way they are written . . . and the government ought to respect those laws to the letter. . . . What would happen if citizens acted on the assumption that they have rights . . . if everyone did it, the state would have to become less oppressive."[72]

Some dissidents rejected Yesenin-Volpin's approach as too accommodating to the Soviet regime. Rather than accepting Soviet law in the manner of the "legalists," the "politicals" sought its destruction. Dissident Valeria Novodvorskaya (1950–2014) remarked that "it always seemed to me that it had to be 'one or the other.' Either them or us. Either freedom or slavery."[73] This was a minority view.

Most dissidents accepted Yesenin-Volpin's strategy. Andrei Amalrik noted that while the dissident movement contained adherents of numerous ideologies, "all its supporters assume at least one common aim: the rule of law."[74]

Chalidze commented that "when we said we were not struggling against the authorities, but simply demanding that they respect their own laws, we were also sincere."[75] Dissidents did not want to overthrow the Soviet government, he claimed: "The only projections for Russian society after the overthrow of the regime that I have seen have been primitive, even ludicrous. . . . Perhaps I reject the idea of destroying the current regime simply because I prefer reform to revolution."[76]

This emphasis on the law leads Serguei Oushakine to argue that dissidence owed little to Western influences, but was instead a "strategy of identification with the dominant symbolic regime—a strategy of mimetic reproduction of already existing rhetorical tools."[77] Because dissidents did not denounce communism per se, but rather called for it to abide by its own principles, they were incapable of drawing up an alternative model for Soviet society: "the dissidents' discursive dependence on the regime prevented them from being the regime's reformers," claims Oushakine.[78]

This may go a bit too far, but it is noticeable that dissidents often rejected the idea that they were involved in politics.[79] Chalidze wrote that "the Russian Human Rights Movement does not fit any slot in the Western political spectrum, simply because it is not a political movement."[80] Similarly, Litvinov remarked that "it seems to me to be extremely important to underline the *nonpolitical* character of this movement, which defends the right to express any opinion, even an antidemocratic one."[81]

Consequently, concrete proposals for political reform were rare in dissident discourse.[82] In 1970, Andrei Sakharov, Valentin Turchin (1931–2010) and Roy Medvedev (b. 1925) wrote the "Letter to the Leaders of the Party and the Government" that is said to have "made the call for democratization mainstream in the political dissident movement."[83] But even this was moderate in its demands, accepting the leading role of the CPSU in Soviet society and limiting itself to calls for the gradual introduction of elections with more than one candidate.[84] Turchin specifically rejected the idea of a multiparty system, saying that "voting does not solve problems."[85] In his 1974 essay "Progress, Coexistence, and Intellectual Freedom," Sakharov wrote that "the author, incidentally, is not one of those who consider the multiparty system to be an essential stage in the development of the socialist system . . . but he assumes that in some cases a multiparty system may be an inevitable consequence of the course of events when a Communist Party refuses for one reason or another to rule by the scientific democratic method required by history."[86]

Sakharov's position evolved over time. As he noted, initially "I called my-self a socialist, but now I have modified my beliefs . . . I would no longer label myself a socialist. I am not a Marxist-Leninist, a Communist. I would call my-self a liberal."[87] By 1976, Sakharov's book *My Country and the World* showed that his position had become more radical, since it lists "a multiparty system" as one of the reforms necessary in the Soviet Union.[88] "I consider the path of democratic development to be the only favorable one for any country," he wrote.[89] Sakharov was also a forthright exponent of human rights, stating that "only by having *all* his rights is a person free."[90] He wrote: "The basic aim of the state is the protection and safeguarding of the basic rights of its citizens. . . . The happiness of the people is safeguarded, in particular, by their freedom of work, freedom of consumption, freedom in their private lives, and in their ed-ucation, their cultural and social activities, freedom of opinion and of con-science, and freedom of exchange of information, and of movement."[91]

In promoting human rights, dissidents rejected the Soviet view that social and economic rights took precedence over civil and political ones. Turchin re-marked that "in the history of Western civilization, social-economic rights were won (to the degree that they are won) after and as a result of the recog-nition of civil rights. The modern explosion in industrial and scientific devel-opment cannot be separated from the Western idea of personal freedom."[92] Similarly, Litvinov wrote that "the preference for social-economic rights over civil and political rights destroys the idea of human rights as such."[93] Litvinov did not, however, reject economic and social rights. "There is no reason to speak of the primacy of one set of rights over another," he wrote.[94]

Social-Economic Liberalism

Following their seizure of power in late 1917, the Bolsheviks resorted to the policy of "war communism." This involved the nationalization of industry and the forcible requisitioning of agricultural produce. War communism proved useful in mobilizing resources to meet the demands of the civil war, but it came at a heavy price: agricultural and industrial production plummeted. Once the civil war ended, it was clear that a change in direction was necessary. The result was the New Economic Policy (NEP) of 1921. This may be seen as the first ef-fort at economic liberalization in Soviet history. While the state retained con-trol of major industries, the NEP legalized small-scale private enterprise. In this way, it moved the Soviet economy a little in the direction of the market.

Liberal economic thought managed to survive for some years in Russia fol-lowing the revolution and civil war. An example was the journal *Ekonomist*, which was published until 1922, when it was closed down by the Bolshevik government. Among the contributors to *Ekonomist* was Lev Litoshenko (1886–1943), who was highly critical of war communism and supportive of Stolypin's prerevolutionary land reforms.[95] He commented that "individual and collective ownership of land imply totally different social psychologies," adding that collective ownership suppressed "individual initiative and responsibility."[96] Litoshenko argued that the revolution had reversed the economic progress made in the final years of the imperial regime by interrupting the spread of individual land ownership started by Stolypin. The condition of the Russian peasant had been set back fifty years, he assessed.[97]

In the brief period of the NEP, the Bolshevik state tolerated Litoshenko's views. But in the late 1920s, the Soviet state abandoned the NEP and liberal economic thinking became unacceptable to those in power. In 1930, Litoshenko was arrested. In 1943, he died in a Soviet labor camp.

The results of the NEP were never very satisfactory and within a few years the Soviet state choose to change direction, deciding in the late 1920s to collectivize agriculture and to embark on a policy of rapid industrialization by means of centralized allocation of resources. Private enterprise was largely abolished, prices and production targets were henceforth set by state authorities, and the centrally planned economy replaced the market.

Until Stalin's death, the tenets of the Soviet economic system remained unchallengeable. From the mid-1960s, however, new economic thinking began to emerge. In 1965 Soviet prime minister Aleksei Kosygin (1904–1980) introduced a package of reforms that relaxed central controls, gave state-owned enterprises greater autonomy, and permitted them to retain some of the profits they generated. One of the architects of the reforms, Soviet economist Yevsei Liberman (1897–1981), noted that excessive central control hampered initiative. He wrote that the aim of the reforms was "to give the enterprises themselves a material stake in the better utilization of their assets and in providing the best possible service to their consumers. To do this the enterprises obviously had to be relieved of the excessive number of planned targets and their work had to be judged, first by how they fulfilled the contracts for deliveries of commodities, and if they did this, secondly by their profit level. . . . Profit is used as the chief index of, and incentive to, efficiency of production."[98]

Despite early promise, Kosygin's reforms soon ran out of steam. By the early 1970s the Soviet government had abandoned them. Nevertheless, they left a lasting intellectual legacy in the form of ideas of market socialism, in which state ownership was to be combined with market mechanisms for regulating production—such as freeing prices and allowing enterprises to determine what they produced and to keep and reinvest their profits.

One area in which communist doctrine was challenged was in analyses of economic development in Third World countries. The initial view was that such countries should follow the Soviet model: nationalize industry, collectivize agriculture, and isolate themselves from the capitalist international division of labor. Before long, however, observant Soviet economists noticed that countries who adopted this model ended up in trouble. As a result, they began to question the universality of the Soviet experience.[99] In a 1970 article in the journal *Narody Azii i Afriki* (Peoples of Asia and Africa), R. N. Andreasian and L. N. Vinogradova commented that "in some countries, where planning derives from ideas of extreme forced industrialization, not reinforced by objective possibilities, one expects an overexertion of effort, the construction of unprofitable enterprises, and . . . in the final analysis, general national crisis."[100]

In another article in *Narody Azii i Afriki*, published in 1974, Anatoly Dinkevich (1923–2011) argued that "models of economic development . . . cannot be identical for all developing countries," and that growth could "be accomplished in many ways."[101] Whereas Soviet doctrine called on countries to limit their trade with capitalist states, Dinkevich pointed out that "a diversified structure coincides with participation in the international division of labor."[102] Protectionism had negative consequences, he wrote. These included "outdated, uncompetitive ineffective factories with high costs of production, and with low productivity of labor and poor quality. This in turn lowers the competitiveness of exports, the value of currency, and the rate of growth."[103]

Writers such as Dinkevich were careful to limit their recommendations to developing countries. Nevertheless, by casting doubt on the universality of the Soviet model, they laid the ground for doubting whether the model suited the Soviet Union too. In a notable example, Nikolai Shmelyov (b. 1936) echoed Dinkevich's argument in favor of greater participation in international trade, but applied it to the Soviet Union, writing that it was "impossible to study the international economy seriously without concluding that our country must become a real participant in it."[104] From the early 1970s, Shmelyov was arguing that the Soviet state should abandon its monopoly on foreign trade and give enterprises the freedom to trade directly with foreign customers and suppliers. This would require a shift to world market prices, which in turn would mean the abandonment of price controls.[105] The state rejected Shmelyov's proposals.

Other important figures were Abel Aganbegyan (b. 1932) and Tatyana Zaslavskaya (1927–2013) of the Novosibirsk Institute of Economics and Industrial Organization, which became "a key center of reformist economic and socioeconomic research."[106] Aganbegyan and Zaslavskaya became leading proponents of market socialism, laying out the case in favor in a report that described the state of the Soviet economy as "deeply disturbing." The authors argued that "the fault lay in Stalinist methods, and solutions were to be found in enterprise autonomy, rational prices, and other marketizing steps."[107]

While the concept of market socialism challenged elements of communist economist dogma, it carefully avoided attacking that orthodoxy's most fundamental element—state ownership of the means of production. Much the same could be said of the economic thinking of Soviet dissidents. By and large dissidents did not pay much attention to economic issues, but when they did they tended to believe that socialism had certain advantages over Western capitalism. Andrei Amalrik commented that Soviet "believers in 'liberal ideology' ultimately envisage a transition to a Western kind of democratic society, which would, however, retain the principle of public or government ownership of the means of production."[108] Benjamin Nathans concludes that dissidents were mostly "content to leave the planned socialist economy undisturbed . . . one rarely finds criticism of collective ownership within the corpus of dissident writing."[109]

There were some exceptions. Aleksandr Zinoviev dismissed the Soviet economic system as less efficient than that of the capitalist West. "Centralized government," he wrote, "causes a lack of initiative, wastefulness, senseless loss of assets, a brake on productivity and many other phenomena which are well known and enable us to affirm that the Communist countries cannot 'pursue and overtake' the leading capitalist countries."[110] Meanwhile, Iury Orlov argued that communist economics had a negative impact on the morals of the Soviet people. According to Orlov, the right to employment, guaranteed by the Soviet constitution, "in practice means that the citizen is freed of responsibility for the results of his labor."[111] Orlov continued: "Deprived of the possibility of raising his living standard by means of such honorable methods as strikes, demonstrations, public protests, and so on, [the worker] gives himself the right to work worse, and sometimes a lot worse, than he could do."[112] A centrally planned economy, wrote Orlov, "is incapable of adopting new technical and scientific achievements in a sufficiently successful manner."[113]

Orlov's alternative to communism fell short, however, of free market capitalism. Any new economic program, he argued, would have to take into account "the growing revulsion towards private property." Although restrictions on private enterprise should be abolished, he argued also that there should be no right to inherit property and that the right to property should exclude those who "exploit hired laborers."[114]

In his 1968 essay "Progress, Coexistence, and Intellectual Freedom," Sakharov wrote that "the prospects of socialism now depend on whether socialism can be made attractive . . . compared with the egotistical ideas of private ownership and the glorification of capital."[115] Socialism and capitalism should "merge," he argued, which meant "not only wide social reforms in the capitalist countries, but also substantial changes in the structure of ownership [in the capitalist world], with a greater role played by government and cooperative ownership," resulting eventually in the "convergence" of the two systems.[116]

By the mid-1970s, however, Sakharov had abandoned all talk of socialism's alleged benefits and instead concentrated on what he saw as the negative aspects of the Soviet economic system. In a 1973 interview, he remarked that "our extreme state socialism has led to the elimination of private initiative in areas in which it would be most effective."[117] In 1976, he went further, writing in his book *My Country and the World* that the following reforms were necessary: "*One.* Broadening the reform of 1965 . . . full autonomy for plants, factories, etc. *Two.* Partial denationalization of all types of economic and societal activity, excluding heavy industry, major transportation, and communications. Partial denationalization is especially critical in the area of services (repair shops, hotels, restaurants, etc.), in retail trade, and in educational and medical care. In agriculture, we must have partial decollectivization and government encouragement of the private sector."[118]

The partial nature of Sakharov's proposed denationalization and decollectivization meant that this was far from being a call for a complete liberalization of the Soviet economy. By the standards of the time, however, it was extremely radical. It would take the rest of the Soviet intelligentsia nearly fifteen years to catch up with Sakharov's way of thinking.

Underlying Soviet liberalism was a sense that the Soviet Union had lost its moral way. Stalin's policies had diverted the country from the natural path of historical development and in the process had corrupted public morals. The liberal intelligentsia set itself the task of addressing this problem.

The moral focus of Soviet liberalism meant that it did not offer well-developed programs of economic or political change. Few challenged the leading role of the CPSU in Soviet society. Likewise, while some economists questioned communist theory, most accepted the core elements of the Soviet economic model. The aspiration was socialism with a human face, not Western-style free markets and liberal democracy.

Nevertheless, would-be reformers' thinking contained strong liberal elements. Both in-system reformers and dissidents tended to have a deterministic view of history, believing that it moved in a single direction—toward "civilization," exemplified by Western Europe. Liberals rejected both communist ideas of the preeminence of the class struggle and conservative ideas of a separate Russian path of development. At the same time, they promoted human rights and the rule of law. Vladislav Zubok concludes that "the birth of a human rights movement . . . was a milestone in the transformation of left-leaning cultural activities into a *liberal* opposition."[119] Somewhat paradoxically, this transformation was made possible by the regime itself, which through the constitution and international human rights conventions had committed itself to respect and promote human rights.

Beneath the surface the Soviet Union was a more intellectually diverse society than is often imagined. Liberal ideas acquired a hold on important figures within the CPSU. In 1985, Gorbachev's rise to power gave these figures an opportunity to put their ideas into action. The results were dramatic.

CHAPTER 9

Perestroika

In February 1985, Soviet leader Konstantin Chernenko (1911–1985) died, aged seventy-three. Chernenko was the third elderly head of the CPSU to die in as many years. Seeking somebody more dynamic, the CPSU turned to the relatively youthful fifty-four-year-old Mikhail Gorbachev. In March 1985 Gorbachev assumed the leadership of the party and thus of the Soviet Union.

On one hand, Gorbachev was a "true believer" in communism but, on the other hand, he was convinced that the Soviet Union had taken a wrong path.[1] His foreign policy adviser Anatoly Chernyaev noted that his reforms were based "on the notion of the enlightening, propagandistic influence of the Party."[2] Indeed, Gorbachev stressed that his policies were to be judged by "socialist standards."[3]

The problems Gorbachev faced were severe. The Soviet economy was slowing, the country was mired in a war in Afghanistan, and in 1986 the Chernobyl nuclear accident dealt a humiliating blow to Soviet prestige. In response, Gorbachev embarked on a series of unprecedented reforms known as *perestroika* (restructuring) that he described as "an urgent necessity" because "the country was verging on crisis."[4]

Perestroika touched every aspect of Soviet society. An associated policy, *glasnost'* (openness), reduced, and eventually abolished, censorship.[5] At Gorbachev's behest, the CPSU congress in June 1988 resolved that the Soviet Union should be a "state under the rule of law" (*pravovoe gosudarstvo*) and declared that "the law is paramount in all spheres of society's life."[6] Gorbachev abolished the Communist Party's "leading role" in Soviet society, permitted the establishment of rival political parties, and created a new elected parliament—the Congress of People's Deputies. Perestroika also had an international dimension, as Gorbachev accepted the collapse of communist rule in Eastern Europe. Overall, perestroika constituted a far-reaching and rapid process of liberalization.

Designed to solve the country's problems, perestroika instead accentuated them. Economic production declined and separatist movements agitated in various parts of the country. In an effort to stop the country's collapse, in August 1991 a group of senior officials arrested Gorbachev and announced the transfer of power to the State Emergency Committee. The coup proved to be short-lived and within a few days Gorbachev was back in his office. However, the incident thoroughly destroyed what remained of the old system's legitimacy. A few months later, the constituent republics of the USSR went their own ways, forming fifteen independent countries. On December 26, 1995, the USSR ceased to exist.

Two distinct processes were visible during perestroika. The first was a policy of liberalization from above. The second was a bottom-up process driven by members of the Soviet intelligentsia. Tipping-point theories suggest that when small changes reach a certain threshold—a moment of critical mass or "no return"—large change occurs suddenly and dramatically.[7] In the Soviet Union, such a tipping point was reached sometime around early 1990. Prior to then, most Soviet intellectuals believed that it was possible to create a more humane socialist system. But from early 1990, in a relatively short space of time, they switched en masse to an anticommunist position and adopted liberal ideas of multiparty democracy and free markets.[8]

A number of factors caused this sudden change. One was perestroika's failure to solve the Soviet Union's economic problems. Another was the collapse of communism in Eastern Europe in 1989. Another was access to new ideas through "the cascade of new publications and information during the period of Gorbachev's *glasnost'*," particularly articles in the so-called thick journals, such as *Novyi Mir* (New world).[9] Such articles included revelations about Soviet history and contemporary life, as well as the works of prerevolutionary and émigré philosophers.[10] These were more important than dissident literature, which was "not widely used" in liberal circles.[11] Western ideas, particularly those of neoliberal economists, also found their way into the Soviet Union, but not until quite late in the perestroika era.

As the attitudes of Soviet intellectuals shifted, so did their political loyalties. Initially they supported Gorbachev, but they then transferred their support to his main political rival, Boris Yeltsin (1931–2007). In 1991 Yeltsin was elected president of the RSFSR, the largest of the component republics of the USSR. In this position, Yeltsin set about undermining Gorbachev's authority. Gorbachev found that he had unleashed forces he could not control and had laid the ground for the collapse of the country he governed.

Cultural Liberalism

Gorbachev spoke of "Europe 'from the Atlantic to the Urals,'" and wrote that "Europe is our common home."[12] This vision of a common European home did not imply that the Soviet Union would abandon communism. Rather, the communist and capitalist parts of Europe would retain their distinct systems but coexist peacefully and cooperate in solving collective problems.[13] As Gorbachev put it, "the human race has entered a stage where we are all dependent on each other."[14] The desire to end the division of Europe also derived from a perception that Western Europe was the home of "civilization," from which the Soviet Union had been unnaturally separated. The historian Leonid Batkin (1932–2016) expressed this view in a 1988 article, writing that "we too are the 'West' . . . to the extent that we managed or have not managed to get rid of what Lenin liked to call Russian 'barbarism.' . . . [The West] is the general definition of the economic, scientific-technical and structural-democratic level without which it is impossible for any really modern society . . . to exist."[15]

At the start of the twentieth century, Russia had had the chance to become Western, said Batkin, but "from the middle of the 1920s, and quite fatally in the 1930s, we completely rejected this vector."[16] As a result, he concluded, "We have dropped out of world history. . . . We must in our own way and in accordance with our own historical peculiarities and ideals return to the highroad of modern civilization."[17]

The idea of returning to civilization had important foreign policy implications. After the Second World War much of Eastern Europe fell under the sway of communist governments. For Gorbachev and his advisers, mending the division of Europe and returning to "civilization" was impossible as long as the Soviet Union remained an imperial power. Gorbachev therefore made it clear to the peoples of Eastern Europe that he would not intervene if they chose to depose their communist governments. This they proceeded to do, beginning with Poland in early 1989, followed in quick succession the same year by Hungary, Czechoslovakia, East Germany, and finally in December 1989, Romania.

The concept of a return to Western civilization put liberals in opposition to conservatives who stressed Russia's distinct nature. In the late 1980s, the Soviet

Union consisted of fifteen union republics, each named after the largest eth-nonational group within it.[18] Perestroika opened the way to the expression of secessionist sentiment in various of these republics, most notably the Baltic states—Estonia, Latvia, and Lithuania—as well as Georgia. Similar national sentiments emerged in Russia. Many Russians felt that Russia was financially subsidizing the other republics and that the Soviet Union discriminated against them. This led to a belief that Russia might be better off outside the USSR.

Aware of this, some liberals felt it necessary to take up the Russian national cause lest the political initiative pass to others.[19] In October 1989 activists cre-ated the Popular Front of the RSFSR. This demanded "the establishment of the political, territorial and cultural sovereignty of the republic, the restoration to the Russian Federation of full statehood."[20] The Popular Front soon folded but the moment was indicative of growing pressure in liberal circles for Russia to become more autonomous or even entirely independent. Chernyaev recorded in his memoirs that in early 1990 "I was reading Vladimir Solovyov's *The Rus-sian Question*, thinking and reflecting. Maybe the USSR's nationalities problem could be solved by letting them all go, even Ukraine. It's true that Russia would cease to be a great power for some time. But we'd live through it. And we'd win back that status through the rebirth of Russia itself."[21]

In spring 1990, elections were held to the RSFSR Congress of People's Dep-uties, which in turn elected a new Russian Supreme Soviet. This appointed Yeltsin as its chairman. Yeltsin and his supporters then sought to transfer power from the central Soviet government to the Russian government. To this end, the Russian Congress of People's Deputies passed the "Declaration of State Sovereignty," which announced "the superiority of the Constitution of the RS-FSR and the laws of the RSFSR on the whole territory of the RSFSR."[22] From this moment on, many Soviet liberals turned into Russian liberals, promoting the interests of Russia at the expense of the Soviet Union.

Even if liberals did not actively seek the Soviet Union's destruction, by 1991 they were unwilling to make an effort to preserve it.[23] In January 1991, Rus-sian troops opened fire on protestors in the Lithuanian capital Vilnius, killing fourteen people. Chernyaev wrote a letter of resignation to Gorbachev, al-though he never delivered it. He wrote, "You started the process of returning the country to the path of world civilization, but the process has been stalled by your own maxim of 'one and indivisible.' You've told me and the others many times that the Russian people would never permit the destruction of the empire. But now Yeltsin is impudently doing just that—in the name of Rus-sia! And very few Russians are protesting."[24]

Chernyaev's evocation and rejection of the White armies' slogan "One and Indivisible" was striking. In contrast to the Kadet party, by 1991 some late

Soviet liberals had adopted a form of Russian nationalism that sought to jettison the empire in favor of a smaller, more purely Russian core.

By 1991, Gorbachev had decided that concessions were necessary to save the union and he negotiated a new union treaty with the leaders of the union republics. This would have substantially decentralized authority in the USSR. Nevertheless, the umbrella group Democratic Russia, which included most of the liberal organizations in the RSFSR, campaigned against the treaty when it was presented to the public in a referendum in March 1991.[25] The logic was simple: if the treaty had been approved, it would have secured Gorbachev's position as Soviet leader. Preventing this was more important than keeping the Soviet Union together. When given a choice of advancing their political goals or saving the union, those who backed Yeltsin in his struggle against Gorbachev opted firmly for the former.

Political Liberalism

Gorbachev and his advisers sought to revitalize the Soviet system by allowing for greater competition in the political process. When this failed to produce the desired results, Gorbachev set about dismantling the institutions of the state and replacing them with new ones that he hoped would be more malleable to his will. Fatally weakened by Gorbachev, the Soviet state then collapsed from blows inflicted by the popular forces unleashed by perestroika.

Perhaps the most radical of Gorbachev's advisers was Aleksandr Yakovlev, whom Gorbachev had appointed to the CPSU politburo with responsibility for ideology. Yakovlev initially believed that the Soviet system could be successfully reformed.[26] In December 1985 he sent Gorbachev a memorandum in which he wrote, "The problem is not economics. . . . The crux is in the political system." He proposed "a change in the relationship between party and state power," including: "internal party democracy," a new "relationship between the legislative and executive branches," a "permanent parliamentary apparatus" (the USSR Supreme Soviet met only occasionally for short sessions), multicandidate elections, "exhaustive *glasnost'*," "real independence of the judiciary," and "real guarantees of securing the rights of the individual."[27]

Yakovlev stated that "I was inspired by the idea of law as the embodiment of civilization. . . . With the advent of *glasnost'* . . . my basic message was that . . . a democratic government was the appropriate form for the state, and that this should all be implemented as soon as possible."[28] Gorbachev shared Yakovlev's belief in the rule of law, saying that "democracy cannot exist and develop without the rule of law."[29] But in Gorbachev's eyes, *glasnost'* was meant to improve the system, not replace it. It was an appeal to society to expose deficiencies so that the authorities could then make the necessary corrections. Gorbachev rejected Yakovlev's proposals as premature.

In the spirit of the constructive criticism Gorbachev proposed, from early 1987 Soviet intellectuals organized themselves into informal discussion groups. These included the Perestroika Club, the Committee for Trust Between the East and West, and Moscow Tribune.[30] At first, these sought to cooperate with the government, presenting it with proposals for reform.[31] As such, they mostly remained loyal to the Soviet system.

One exception was the Democratic Union, founded in 1988 as the first opposition party in the Soviet Union.[32] The union focused its efforts on unsanctioned street demonstrations and called for the creation of a multiparty system, a new constitution, and the withdrawal of Soviet troops from Eastern Europe.[33] Its most famous member was Valeria Novodvorskaya, who expressed the organization's uncompromising anticommunism by saying that she lived in a country "so terrible that if the atomic bomb was dropped on it and killed us but at the same time killed the system, this would be a desirable outcome."[34] The Democratic Union believed that civil disobedience would foster a new civic consciousness in Soviet citizens. Union members were said to have "exhibited a singular talent for attracting the blows of police clubs and landing in jail," leading to complaints that the union "seemed more a fringe group of martyrs than a real opposition."[35]

By late 1988, it had become clear that perestroika had failed to improve the country's economy. Gorbachev concluded that the reason was that conservative elements within the CPSU were obstructing reform. To eliminate this opposition, he decided to create a new center of power outside the party. This took the form of a new two-tier Soviet parliament. The lower tier was the Congress of People's Deputies, that was to meet on only an occasional basis. The upper tier was a new Supreme Soviet, elected by the Congress of People's Deputies from among its own members. The Supreme Soviet would be the USSR's permanent legislature.

Elections to the Congress were competitive, but one-third of the seats were guaranteed to members of social organizations such as the CPSU and official trade unions, and the complex method of nominating candidates for the other seats ensured the dominance of Communist Party members. Still, the elections did produce shocks, as some senior party officials were defeated. With the support of "voters' clubs" that nominated and campaigned for candidates, a considerable number of liberal intellectuals won election to the Congress.

Once the Congress of People's Deputies convened in May 1989, liberal-minded deputies formed a faction within it known as the Interregional Group

of Deputies.³⁶ In September 1989, the group produced a program for the transformation of the USSR into a liberal democracy. It proposed a new constitution; a clear separation of the powers of the executive, legislature, and judiciary;
the abolition of Article 6 of the Soviet Constitution that enshrined the CP-
SU's "leading role" in Soviet society; "demonopolization" of the economy; le-
galization of private property; and freedom of the press and of assembly.³⁷

Sakharov said, "The Interregional Group of Deputies is neither an opposition nor a faction. . . . It is a group of active supporters of *perestroika.*"³⁸ Over
time, though, members of the group moved to a more oppositional position.
Shortly before his death in December 1989, Sakharov wrote that Soviet leaders were "leading the country to catastrophe. . . . The only path, the only evolutionary path possible is a radicalization of *perestroika.*"³⁹

As the situation in the Soviet Union worsened, Gorbachev decided to remove power from the CPSU. At his behest, the Congress amended Article 6
of the Soviet Constitution to remove reference to the CPSU's leading role and
to permit the existence of other political parties. However, Gorbachev's new
institutions were unable to restore order or rescue the ailing economy. During 1990, Gorbachev seemed to start having doubts as to the direction of his
policy and swung back and forth between reform and reaction in a desperate
attempt to hold together his collapsing country. As he did so, he lost the support of many liberal intellectuals who had previously backed perestroika.

Glasnost' led to more and more revelations in the Soviet press about dark
episodes in the Soviet Union's past. Meanwhile, fear that conservatives might
depose Gorbachev led many members of the intelligentsia to conclude that
the only way to guarantee the liberties gained during perestroika was to destroy the communist system entirely. Events in Eastern Europe made this seem
feasible: the unthinkable—the collapse of communism—had suddenly become
thinkable. The result was a rapid radicalization of opinion from early 1990
onward.

Wishing to move faster than Gorbachev was willing, liberal intellectuals
turned to Boris Yeltsin for leadership. A former head of the Communist Party
in the city of Sverdlovsk (Ekaterinburg), Yeltsin was appointed to run the Moscow party in 1985 but soon fell out with Gorbachev. In October 1987 Yeltsin
resigned from the CPSU politburo, giving a tempestuous speech in which he
attacked Yegor Ligachev (1920–2021), who after Gorbachev was considered
the most important man in the party. The speech made Yeltsin a hero in liberal circles, and before long Yeltsin attached himself to the liberal cause.

In 1990 Yeltsin and his allies switched their focus from the Soviet Union to
the RSFSR, where elections were held in March to the Russian Congress of
People's Deputies as well as to local councils. The elections proved to be a big

success for liberal forces, with candidates from the electoral alliance Democratic Russia sweeping the board in Moscow and Leningrad.

As 1990 progressed, informal liberal groups in the Soviet Union began to coalesce into political parties. The most significant were the Democratic Party of Russia (DPR), the Republican Party of Russia (RPR), and the Social Democratic Party of Russia (SDPR). The DPR sought to unite liberal forces into a disciplined party that would be able to challenge the CPSU. This approach alienated many intellectuals for whom the idea of party discipline was too reminiscent of the Communist Party, and who preferred the more loosely structured RPR or SDPR.[40] The former was established by former members of the CPSU; in contrast, most of the latter's members had never been in the party. Ideologically, little distinguished the three groups, all of which supported a multiparty democratic system and a transition towards market capitalism.[41]

In an effort to unite liberal political forces, in October 1990 groups from across the country came together to form a loose coalition, named Democratic Russia (not to be confused with the electoral bloc from the Russian elections earlier in the year). This threw its support behind Yeltsin, backing his efforts to create a directly elected presidency.[42] The educated classes dominated Democratic Russia. A survey of its second congress in November 1991 showed that 20 percent of delegates were ITRs, 20 percent were academics or "education workers," 8 percent "entrepreneurs," 6 percent full-time politicians, and 5 percent from the "creative classes." Only 7.6 percent were workers, and none were collective farmers.[43]

The loose nature of Democratic Russia reflected the tendency of late Soviet liberals toward "hyperdemocracy."[44] Apart from the DPR, liberal organizations had a collective leadership structure with multiple co-chairs.[45] Peter Duncan notes that "the difficulty of the democrats was that they were much better at creating new structures within the democratic movement than they were at taking control and making real decisions to improve peoples' lives."[46] Examples were the Moscow and Leningrad city councils, in both of which liberal democratic groups won majorities in spring 1990. Before long, the liberal mayors of both cities—Gavriil Popov (b. 1936) and Anatoly Sobchak (1937–2000)—became frustrated with the quarrels of their council members and demanded the transfer of powers from the councils to the mayors. "The executive leader should have the decisive voice in administration, not the soviet," said Popov.[47]

By mid-1990, liberal intellectuals had moved en masse from a belief in reformed socialism to support for a multiparty, democratic system. At the same time, although they called themselves "democrats," many liberals demonstrated a utilitarian attitude toward democracy, which they often viewed as a means of destroying the existing system rather than an end in itself.[48] As Guillaume Sauvé puts it, for liberals "democracy did not reside at all in a certain mode of exercising power but rather in the political victory of the leaders who incarnated this ideal."[49] Alexander Lukin cites a study of Russian democrats undertaken in the early 1990s, which concluded that "'democrats' saw their aim as replacing the abnormal, unnatural, and immoral totalitarian society with democracy, which they saw as normal, natural, and moral. The specific programme of bringing about democratic society was not carefully thought out by them, since they believed that the mere destruction of unnatural totalitarianism would allow natural democracy to develop by itself. . . . Finally . . . the authors [of the study] . . . discovered a tendency to approve authoritarian methods, which, according to some respondents, were more effective in rapidly toppling totalitarianism and promoting reforms and democracy."[50]

Indeed, late Soviet liberals occasionally supported a form of liberal authoritarianism. In a 1989 article in *Novyi Mir*, political scientist Andranik Migranian (b. 1949) argued that the transition process from totalitarianism to democracy was immensely complex and until such time as a civil society had been created, "it is extremely important that a firm authoritarian regime be maintained in the political sphere."[51] Migranian concluded that "we cannot make a transition to a multiparty system without cataclysms and catastrophes, since to attempt such a transition in a country that lacks an adequate political culture and a clear consensus among the various social, national, religious, cultural and other interests . . . could lead to the collapse and disintegration of the existing political system and its replacement with an even more oppressive, totalitarian dictatorship."[52]

Migranian reiterated his views in an interview with liberal sociologist Igor Kliamkin (b. 1941), published under the title "Do We Need an Iron Hand?" Both men viewed history as developing toward a free market and liberal democracy, but if the process was to be successfully completed it had to follow a given pattern. Civil society had always come first, democracy second, Migranian claimed. Civil society, however, was lacking in the Soviet Union. Consequently, a period of transitional authoritarianism was necessary in order to move from Soviet totalitarianism to liberal democracy. "Yes, at present I am for a dictatorship, for a dictator," said Migranian.[53]

Kliamkin agreed. Historically, just as civil society preceded democracy, so did the market, he said: "Absolute regimes created national markets."[54] "If we pretend that economic and political reforms advance in parallel, we know nothing (or don't want to know) about the entirety of world history," said Kliamkin.[55]

The publication of Migranian's and Kliamkin's discussion caused considerable controversy in liberal circles. Batkin described their views as "atrocious."[56] Most members of the liberal intelligentsia remained committed to democratization as the best protection against any reversal of perestroika.[57] However, during 1990 and 1991 the attraction of the authoritarian approach grew.

Intellectuals' suspicion that the masses were reactionary played a role in this. Particularly influential was the sociologist Iury Levada (1930–2006), who became famous for his attempt to provide a scientific foundation for the concept of *homo sovieticus*, the "Soviet man." On the basis of a survey of 2,700 Soviet citizens in the late 1980s, Levada drew up a list of characteristics of *homo sovieticus*, according to which, "the Soviet man was (a) simple and simplified (in a sense of being obedient to authorities . . . not trying to stick out, not trying to be different from others), (b) isolated, (c) lacking choice, (d) mobilized, (e) hostage to the group, and (f) hierarchical. Furthermore, the fundamental features of *homo sovieticus* included a sense of exceptionalism, state paternalist orientations, and imperial character."[58]

Democracy, by giving power to the unenlightened *homo sovieticus*, threatened reform. Novodvorskaya put it in the bluntest terms, saying that democracy "is too much of a good thing. . . . Freedom of speech, press, rallies, and gatherings—this is sacred. But everything else—later. After the victory of the middle class, the class of owners, after the victory over the reds."[59]

Economists were particularly inclined to such thinking. Aware that market reform would cause considerable suffering, they feared that the population would rapidly turn against it. A strong government was needed to resist popular pressure to stop reform. In 1990 the Association of Social-Economic Sciences in Leningrad, headed by the future deputy prime minister of Russia Anatoly Chubais (b. 1955), issued a report noting that

> the current scale of the democratic movement significantly exceeds the extent to which democratic ideas and values have been disseminated in the mass consciousness. . . . Under the influence of the difficulties brought about by reform the majority of these movements . . . will move toward populism. . . . The biggest problem for democrats . . . is the need to express the necessity during reforms of the government's antidemocratic measures (such as banning strikes, control of information, etc.). . . . There is a fundamental contradiction between the aims of reform (the forming of a democratic economy and society) and the means of their achievement, including measures of an antidemocratic nature.[60]

The model for liberal authoritarianism was Chilean dictator General Augusto Pinochet (1943–2006), whom some admired for having combined free market reforms with authoritarian political leadership.[61] In April 1991, a group of Russian economists visited Chile to investigate the free market reforms undertaken under Pinochet.[62] Among the group was Alfred Koch (b. 1961), who later became deputy prime minister responsible for privatization. Koch remarked that

> a strong hand, when it's really strong, that's harmonious; it's a dictatorship in its complete, mature form. Pinochet didn't try to pass himself off as a democrat, which he was not. He knew they needed to build a liberal economy, and he built it; he knew they need to stifle the opposition, and he stifled it, just as he was supposed to do. . . . Chile 1973. Total collapse. The economy just stopped. The country was bankrupt. Politically, a dead end. Then, like in a bad movie, fast forward on the calendar, twenty years later. . . . What better example do we need to see that we must act and not just gab about reforms?[63]

By 1991 the top choice for Russian dictator was Boris Yeltsin. In March 1991, the Russian Congress of People's Deputies granted Yeltsin the right to rule by decree. In a referendum held the same month, the Russian people approved the idea of creating an elected presidency. A presidential election was held in June 1991, which Yeltsin convincingly won. Next, following the short-lived coup against Gorbachev in August 1991, Yeltsin set about enacting a series of authoritarian measures: banning the Communist Party, postponing all local elections (opinion polls suggested that many former CPSU officials were likely to win office), and assuming the right to appoint regional governors.[64] Liberal authoritarianism had found its man.

Social-Economic Liberalism

Tatyana Zaslavskaya and Larisa Piyasheva (1947–2003) took the lead in promoting the two main approaches to economic reform: market socialism and neoliberal free market economics, respectively. In the end it was Piyasheva's free market line that won the day.

In a 1983 report, Zaslavskaya noted "a noticeable decline in the rate of growth of the economy of the USSR."[65] Previously, she said, the Soviet economy had grown by increasing inputs.[66] This was no longer possible, and future progress depended upon raising workers' productivity. This required that workers be given "a sufficiently wide margin of freedom," while the economy as a whole needed "far more active use of 'automatic' regulators in balancing production, linked to the development of market relations."[67]

Zaslavskaya commented that the fundamental problem in Soviet society was that the economic system deprived people of incentives. To overcome this, she argued, "we must have economic pluralism—not just state ownership, but also cooperative and individual ownership."[68] Zaslavskaya's model still restricted private ownership to cooperatives and individuals, ruling out larger-scale private enterprise. It did not envisage full free market capitalism.

Another notable supporter of market socialism was Nikolai Shmelyov. In 1987 Shmelyov published an article in the journal *Novyi Mir* in which he argued that economic progress was possible "only on the basis of 'self-financing socialism' [*khozraschetnyi sotsializm*], through the development of the market." This in turn required price reform, and "the expansion of the individual and cooperative sectors."[69] "Competition is the objective condition without which no economic system can flourish," Shmelyov wrote.[70]

Shmelyov later acquired a reputation as a heartless proponent of pure economic logic, due to his statement that "everything that is economically inefficient is immoral and everything that is economically efficient is moral."[71] In reality, he tempered his economic utilitarianism with moral considerations, calling for "market socialism," in which "there will be a large state sector, but most of its enterprises will have to function within the market."[72] Shmelyov envisaged the economy as having a mix of state-owned enterprises, cooperatives, and "small family enterprises," but rejected large-scale private firms. "Some of our economists think we should allow private firms to hire ten to twenty workers, but I personally don't know where to set the limit. A thousand people working for one person is clearly immoral," he wrote.[73]

Market socialism appealed to Gorbachev. The Soviet leader came to power convinced that the Soviet system was performing poorly, but he remained committed to socialism as an economic model.[74] Retaining state ownership of the means of production but improving its efficiency by giving enterprises greater freedom was a policy that offered hope of progress while not challenging fundamental socialist assumptions.

In 1987, the Soviet government made a limited effort to put the concept of market socialism into practice with the new Law on Enterprises.[75] Under the new law, once they had fulfilled their state quota, enterprises were free to trade the remainder of what they produced with other enterprises. They could also keep their profits, "albeit under high taxation."[76] The law also introduced an element of democracy into state-owned businesses, giving workers the right to elect managers, foremen, and team leaders.[77]

For the most part, Soviet economists accepted the move toward market socialism. One exception was Piyasheva, who was perhaps the first person in the Soviet Union to declare herself a fully fledged free market liberal. She wrote that "my views are based on the theories of the Chicago school, and I believe that all attempts to find a 'third way' [between socialism and capitalism] are headed for a dead end."[78] Journalist Igor Svinarenko (b. 1957) described her views as follows: "Piyasheva talked a lot about the invisible hand. . . . I couldn't at all understand what kind of mechanism it was. But she kept on and on about this hand, which would immediately bring order everywhere, and that everyone would begin living a happy and rich life. I asked Piyasheva then, how could happiness just suddenly appear—after all, don't needs and troubles always intensify at the start of any new capitalist period? She explained that problems occurred if you didn't start out building the system correctly, but that if you did it right, there wouldn't be any problems."[79]

In a 1987 article entitled "Where Are the Pies Fluffier?" Piyasheva (writing under the pseudonym A. Popkova) argued that "socialism . . . is by its essence incompatible with the market."[80] There was no "third way," she said. "Either the plan or the market. Either directives or competition."[81] "Look at developing countries through the lens of 'plan or market,'" Piyasheva wrote, "and you will see how rapidly those who chose the market are catching up, and how hungry they are where the market is treated with suspicion. . . . The more market, the fluffier the pies."[82]

Together with her husband, Boris Pinsker (1947–2021), Piyasheva contended that "the idea that private property always and everywhere leads to injustice and immorality is a mistake, both in fact and in theory."[83] Citing Hayek and Milton Friedman (1912–2006), Pinsker and Piyasheva claimed that inflation is political in nature: it results from governments spending more in order to satisfy voters. As the USSR democratized, pressure to spend would increase, especially from workers in state-owned industries, who would demand subsidies from the state. The lesson was that democracy was incompatible with nationalized industries.[84]

Following the 1987 Law on Enterprises, in 1988 the Soviet government made a tentative step toward a market system by passing laws permitting the establishment of cooperatives and allowing workers to lease state enterprises in which they worked.[85] But Soviet officials did not yet have in mind a capitalist economy. Yakovlev commented that "when we speak of the market we don't mean what the West means by this idea—unlimited competition, the creation of prices on the free market, unemployment, and other negative social consequences."[86] Similarly, one of Gorbachev's main economic advisers, Abel Aganbegyan, wrote in 1988 that "when we speak of the radical nature of the reform of economic management, we should emphasize that we do not intend to abandon any of the real attainments of socialism. . . . The new economic mechanism will be based on the dominance of socialist, especially public, ownership, on a planned economic development."[87]

Such thinking persisted for some time. By late 1989, however, it became clear that the government's economic reforms had failed. In fact, the laws of

1987 and 1988 possibly made the Soviet Union's situation worse. Mixing the planned economy with elements of the market undermined the advantages of the former without bringing many of the benefits of the latter. Workplace democracy led to "a significant slackening of workplace discipline," as well as to inflationary pressures, as managers responded by becoming "more permissive" and raising wages.[88] By late 1989, "only 11 percent of 989 consumer goods monitored by an economic research organization were readily obtainable. Almost entirely absent from stores were televisions, refrigerators, washing machines, most household cleaning products, furniture of all sorts, electric irons, razor blades, perfumes and cosmetics, school notebooks and pencils."[89]

The growing crisis led to a turnaround in economic thinking. In mid-1989 deputy prime minister Leonid Abalkin (1930–2011) established the State Commission on Economic Reform that included a number of reform-minded economists such as Grigory Yavlinsky (b. 1952) and Yevgeny Yasin (b. 1934). In October 1989, the commission issued a report offering three alternative approaches to reform: one conservative, one radical, and one "moderate-radical." The last of these would become the basis of what become known as the "500 Days" plan, which envisaged that the Soviet Union would transition to a market economy over a period of 500 days. The first step would be to establish the institutional bases of a market economy, by privatizing small businesses, dismantling monopolies, and passing laws on private property.[90] Next, prices were to be gradually deregulated. By the end of the 500 days, 70 percent of industrial enterprises and 80–90 percent of other businesses were to have been privatized.[91]

Gorbachev initially welcomed the plan, but soon got cold feet.[92] The 500 Days met heavy resistance from ministers, the Communist Party, and the Supreme Soviet. Abalkin and prime minister Nikolai Ryzhkov (b. 1929) proposed a much more gradual transition program. Gorbachev asked Aganbegyan to combine elements of this program and of the 500 Days.[93] This proved an impossible task, and economic reform halted.

As the government dithered, economic thinking in the USSR took on a new tone. In 1990, Gavriil Popov wrote an introduction to the ideas of Milton Friedman in the journal *Voprosy Ekonomiki*, while *Novyi Mir* published a translation of part of Hayek's *The Road to Serfdom*.[94] Meanwhile, the shock therapy introduced in Poland in 1989 by the first postcommunist Polish finance minister, Leszek Balcerowicz (b. 1947), provided a model. More and more economists joined Piyasheva in demanding a rapid transition to a market economy. The prevailing view now became that free markets were "natural" in a way that communist planning was not.[95] It followed that the USSR should return to the "natural road of historical development."[96]

The question that then arose was how to manage the transition to the market. In a 1991 article entitled "Problems of Making the Transition to a Market Economy," Yevgeny Yasin proposed the "far-reaching destatization of the economy" through the transformation of the majority of state enterprises into joint-stock companies and through the freeing of prices.[97] The latter would inevitably cause a "a high rate of inflation."[98] A prime issue in the transition to a market was how to deal with this inflationary pressure.

Yasin proposed three options. The first was to liberalize prices gradually. This could keep inflation low and prevent a major fall in production but would not solve the problem of shortages of consumer goods. The second option was "shock therapy": the state would free all prices immediately and control inflation through a tight monetary policy (for instance, by eliminating state subsidies to industry). This would cause a massive fall in production but would have the advantage that "it would be possible to emerge from the crisis in the shortest possible time." The third option involved a rapid liberalization of prices accompanied by a loose monetary policy, designed to save businesses from bankruptcy. This would keep unemployment low but would come with a "high probability of hyperinflation."[99] In Yasin's eyes, the second option was preferable, but was possible only if the government enjoyed substantial political support. To this end, he proposed that the reforms should win the backing of the public by making "the majority of workers owners. Not formal co-owners of state property, but actual owners of their home, apartment, and what is especially important, of the means of production. . . . Therefore, when addressing the tasks of destatization, part of the value of productive capital represented in stocks and bonds should be presented to workers under preferential conditions."[100]

Anatoly Sobchak also proposed a plan for a transition to the free market. The first step, he wrote, had to be a "period of economic stabilization" to limit inflation. This would involve a drastic "curb of government spending."[101] Next should come "measures to create the market infrastructure," including the creation of labor and capital markets as well as "numerous small and midsize enterprises."[102] The third step, which would last eighteen months to two years, would involve breaking up monopolies and privatizing state-owned enterprises.[103]

In cooperation with American academic Graham Allison (b. 1940), Yavlinsky prepared a more detailed plan in 1991. This involved six steps: (1) "stabilization of the macroeconomy, which means sharply reducing governmental budget deficits"; (2) "liberalization of prices so that market forces of supply and demand determine prices, production, and consumption"; (3) creation of legal protection for property rights; (4) "privatization . . . of most state enterprises, and the demonopolization of large state industries"; (5) opening the economy to international trade and foreign investment; and (6) limiting the state's involvement in the economy to "creating the legal economic framework of a market in which private citizens and private enterprises play the decisive role."[104]

In making these proposals, Soviet economists made no attempt to hide what Chubais described as their "extremely negative consequences," such as "mass unemployment and a high probability of strikes."[105] Yasin noted that "opponents of a market economy in our country . . . claim that our market will initially be so uncivilized that it is not known whether it is worthwhile subjecting it to all these tribulations. Unfortunately, there is a measure of truth to this."[106]

Yasin and others argued that there was no other choice. As Allison and Yavlinsky put it, "Success requires that leaders understand that transformation means the death of the old system and the birth of an entirely new system. . . . Radical economic reform offers the only viable alternative."[107]

Perestroika's aim was not to create a free market liberal democracy but to strengthen and revitalize Soviet communism. It failed. Perestroika radicalized public opinion, leading to ever greater demands from national minorities, liberal intellectuals, and other dissatisfied groups. The intelligentsia lost its faith in the possibility of reforming socialism and turned toward the belief that the entire communist system had to be dismantled. In 1990 this process reached a tipping point, after which liberal intellectuals swung suddenly and dramatically in the direction of Russian sovereignty, multiparty elections, and a free market economy.

In so doing, Soviet liberals broke decisively with their past.[108] At the same time, it has been claimed that Soviet intellectuals to some extent retained a communist outlook—that is to say, they transferred the absolute certainty of Marxism-Leninism into an equally absolute certainty of the correctness of Western models. Joachim Zweynert claims that free market ideas were interpreted in a way that "clearly reflected intellectual traditions inherited from the socialist past, namely utopianism."[109] "This liberalism," says Zweynert, "was deeply influenced by the very ideology it opposed. The Russian liberals were just as convinced bearers of an absolute truth, and in the end their liberalism was no less utopian than the vulgarised Marxism of their opponents. . . . What was not changed . . . was the notion of history as a purposeful process. The Soviet *telos* was replaced by a liberal *telos*."[110]

The struggle to defeat the system and ensure the transition to a new order took precedence over democratic procedure and was held to justify antidemocratic measures in the name of democracy. The effects of all this would become clear once the Soviet Union collapsed in December 1991 and a new independent Russian Federation came into being.

CHAPTER 10

Russian Liberalism under Yeltsin

Following the collapse of the Soviet Union in December 1991, the newly independent Russian Federation, under the leadership of Boris Yeltsin, embarked on a program of radical liberal economic reform, known as "shock therapy." This aimed to transform the Soviet system into a free market economy in the shortest possible time. The state surrendered its control over prices and foreign trade, removed restrictions on private business, and privatized the majority of state-owned enterprises.

The pace of the reforms reflected both the perceived urgency of the situation and Yeltsin's own temperament. The Russian president was not theoretically inclined. His memoirs are almost entirely devoid of any sort of philosophical ruminations. They reveal no specific ideological commitment.[1] Biographer Timothy Colton notes, "Yeltsin was eclectic—if not to say platitudinous—about his societal models. He considered himself free to cherry pick, without worrying about coherence in the abstract."[2] He acted, writes Colton, "out of intuition more than a panoramic master plan."[3] Specifically, his intuition told him that the old system was broken and that it was necessary to act decisively.

The results were dramatic. Yeltsin's government laid the foundations of a market economy, but the price was high. Between 1992 and 1996, Russian gross domestic product (GDP) fell by 40 percent, industrial production by 50 percent, and real wages by 26 percent.[4] Corruption, crime, alcoholism, drug use, suicide, and other social problems dramatically worsened. Life expectancy plummeted.

And in August 1998 the Russian currency, the ruble, crashed in value, aggravating the economic crisis.

Elements of Russian society soon turned against the reforms and demanded that they be slowed down or halted. Yeltsin's policies met growing resistance in the Russian parliament. To eliminate opposition, in October 1993 Yeltsin sent the army to bombard the parliament's building, the "White House," and forced the legislature into submission. A referendum was then held that endorsed a new constitution for the Russian Federation that concentrated authority in the president's hands.

This was not the only violent event of the 1990s. The collapse of the Soviet Union encouraged various regions of Russia to seek more autonomy from Moscow. Under the leadership of former Soviet general Dzhokhar Dudayev (1944–1996), the republic of Chechnya in the northern Caucasus attempted to secede from the Russian Federation. To prevent this, in December 1994 the Russian army launched an attack on the Chechen capital Grozny, sparking a war that saw the Chechens inflict a number of humiliating defeats on the Russians. In August 1996 the Russians and the Chechens agreed to a ceasefire, but this did not last long, and in summer 1999 war broke out again.

The most notable liberal politicians of the era were Yegor Gaidar (1956–2009), Anatoly Chubais, and Grigory Yavlinsky. Gaidar served as deputy and later acting prime minister until December 1992, and then again as deputy prime minister from September 1993 to January 1994. Chubais led Russia's privatization program and also ran Yeltsin's reelection campaign in 1996. By contrast, Yavlinsky, who headed the liberal Yabloko party, remained in opposition.

In a short time, Russia's liberal reformers transformed their country. In the eyes of most Russians, however, their failures far outweighed their successes. Rightly or wrongly, liberal rule in the 1990s helped to discredit liberalism in the eyes of the Russian population. Liberalism's triumph proved to be the cause of its own demise.

Cultural Liberalism

Olga Malinova comments that Gaidar and his colleagues "were probably the most radical Westernizers in Russian history. They argued for a drastic change of the existing social order to become 'like the West,'" a task that was to be achieved by "the assimilation of the ready-made products of Western civilization."[5] Pyotr Aven (b. 1955), who served as minister of foreign economic relations from 1991 to 1992, stated that "there are no special countries. All countries from the point of view of an economist are the same."[6] The exemplar of the universal path of development was the West, and the idea that Russia should "return to civilization," in other words, to Europe, or the West more generally, was dominant. Thus, Yavlinsky said that "Russia has to answer a three-hundred-year-old question of whether it wants to turn to Europe. My answer is that Russia belongs to Europe. . . . I would like Russia to be a normal country in a civilized way as part of Europe."[7] Likewise, Gaidar said that the objective was to "enter the commonwealth of civilized nations."[8] He wrote: "An important result of the changes of recent years is Russia's return to the modern world. . . . Before World War I the Russian intellectual and business elite was part of a Eurocentric world. The ties were broken in subsequent decades. . . . Over the last few years, we have started our return to the world."[9]

Gaidar divided the world up into "Eastern" and "Western" societies. In Eastern societies, he claimed, there was no "true private ownership" as "ownership and government authority are joined at the hip," a characteristic that doomed such societies to "backwardness and . . . poverty."[10] Western countries, by contrast, enjoyed true property rights and were more successful. Communism, said Gaidar, fitted firmly within the Eastern tradition, but "Russia today has a unique opportunity to change her entire historical orientation . . . to become a republic in the Western sense of that term."[11]

The sudden turn to Russian nationalism in the perestroika era served to transfer power from Gorbachev to Yeltsin. At the same time, a perception that most of the other republics in the Soviet Union were not prepared to embark on radical economic reform persuaded Gaidar and others that Russia would be better off going its own way. However, once nationalism had served the purpose of breaking free from the Soviet Union, Russian liberals dropped it as rapidly as they had adopted it.

Overwhelmingly, liberal politicians and intellectuals opposed the war in Chechnya. Some viewed it as a reason to withdraw all support for Yeltsin's government; others continued to be willing to work with the government in order to advance economic reform. The result was considerable tension within the liberal camp.

In private, Gaidar was strongly opposed to the war but in public he at first tried to steer a middle course of neither supporting nor opposing it.[12] Other liberals were more forthright. Yavlinsky called the war "a genuine, inexcusable crime."[13] He added, "It is clear that the Chechens will secede from Russia if they can, but I regard this 'price' (if one wants to use such a term) as one that we should be prepared to pay for the crime which we committed."[14]

Possibly the most outspoken critic of the war was former dissident Sergei Kovalyov, whom Yeltsin had appointed as head of the Presidential Commission on Human Rights. Kovalyov called the Chechen war an "act of terrorism" by the Russian government.[15] Visiting Grozny while it was under attack by the Russian army, Kovalyov found himself holed up in the bunker of Chechen leader Dzhokhar Dudayev, from where he was said to have encouraged surrounded Russian soldiers to surrender to the Chechens. Kovalyov's opponents accused him of treason. Kovalyov replied by saying on TV that "patriotism is the last refuge of the scoundrel."[16]

Although the war was unpopular, Chechen terrorism meant that if there was one thing the Russian public hated even more than the war it was the Chechen rebels. As Gaidar wrote, "not many people liked the idea of a war, but they didn't like Dudayev's regime either."[17] By appearing to take Dudayev's side, liberals like Kovalyov severely damaged their public image. As Malinova notes, opposition to the Chechen war "saddled liberals with the reputation of an 'antinational' political force."[18]

Liberals' handling of foreign affairs exacerbated the problem. In the early 1990s, Russian foreign policy followed a pro-Western line under foreign minister Andrei Kozyrev (b. 1951). In 1992, Yeltsin and US president George H. W. Bush signed the "Charter of Russian-American Partnership and Friendship."[19] In 1994, Russia joined NATO's Partnership for Peace Program; in 1996 it sent troops to join the NATO mission in Bosnia; and in 1997 it signed the NATO-Russia Founding Act that set up a permanent joint committee as a forum for cooperation between the two parties.

Russian hopes that their country would be embraced by the West were soon dashed. In 1997, NATO invited several Eastern Europe countries to become alliance members, an act that even some Russian liberals considered threatening. Yavlinsky wrote, "Talk that this is a different NATO, a NATO that is no longer a military alliance, is ridiculous. It is like saying that the hulking thing advancing toward your garden is not a tank because it is painted pink, carries flowers, and plays cheerful music. It does not matter how you dress it up; a pink tank is still a tank."[20]

Even more damaging to Russian-Western relations was NATO's bombardment of Yugoslavia in 1999 to defend the population of the province of Kosovo. Russia had friendly relations with Yugoslavia and regarded NATO's action as a grievous breach of international law. Journalist Dmitry Sokolov-Mitrich (b. 1975) explained how the war shattered many Russians' belief in the West as the center of "civilization": "In 1990 we voted for 'Yabloko' democrats, went to the White House barricades on the side of democratic forces . . . and listened to the [liberal] Echo of Moscow radio. Our first journalistic articles always mentioned the 'civilized world' and we firmly believed that it was really civilized. . . . The first serious blow to our pro-Western orientation in life was

Kosovo. It was a shock; our rose-colored glasses were shattered into pieces. . . . Worldviews turned 180 degrees."[21]

Some liberals responded by abandoning their pro-Western orientation. Others hung on, cementing their growing reputation as an antinational force. To many Russians, the foreign policy pursued by Kozyrev became evidence of liberals betraying Russian interests to hostile foreign powers. Anatol Lieven comments that many Russian liberals exhibited "a blind adulation of everything western and [a tendency] to identify unconditionally with US policies. In terms of public image, this made them look like western lackeys."[22] Arguably, this image was unfair. Due to Russia's economic plight, Kozyrev had a weak hand when dealing with Western states. Still, even he insisted that "Russia is doomed to be a great power . . . it can only be an equal partner, not a junior one."[23] Nevertheless, in politics perceptions can be more important than realities, and as Lieven points out, there was a widespread perception among the Russian public that the liberals in Yeltsin's government had sold out Russia's interests to the West. It is a perception that lingers to this day.

Political Liberalism

Yeltsin stated that "the political system had to be overturned, not just changed. . . . What was needed was a kamikaze crew that would step in the line of fire and forge ahead, however strong the general discontent might be."[24] To this end he appointed a government led by youthful intellectuals with little political or administrative experience. Technocrats rather than politicians, they displayed little interest in selling their policies to the public.[25] Gaidar himself admitted that "the intelligentsia . . . was by its very nature alien to organizing political activity."[26]

Post-Soviet Russia lacked a clear division of powers between the president and the parliament, the latter of which consisted of the Congress of People's Deputies, which met only occasionally, and a smaller, permanent Supreme Soviet elected by the Congress from among its own members. In October 1991, the Congress granted Yeltsin emergency powers to enact economic reform by means of decree.[27] However, parliament retained control of certain levers of power, such as the central bank. Before long, many parliamentarians, under the leadership of the speaker of the Supreme Soviet, Ruslan Khasbulatov (b. 1942), began to have doubts about shock therapy and sought to claw back the emergency powers they had granted to Yeltsin.

In December 1992, the Congress of People's Deputies won a significant victory over Yeltsin, forcing him to replace Gaidar as acting prime minister with the head of the state gas company Gazprom, Viktor Chernomyrdin (1938–2010). This, however, did not resolve the dispute between the two parties, and by early 1993 the president and the parliament were at loggerheads. At a meeting of the Congress of People's Deputies in March 1993, Yeltsin demanded the consolidation of power in the hands of the executive, including control of the central bank.[28] The Congress refused.

In March 1993, the two sides agreed to a compromise: a referendum would be held asking the Russian people four questions: whether they supported the president; whether they supported his economic reforms; whether they favored early parliamentary elections; and whether they favored an early presidential election. In the subsequent vote, 60 percent voted yes to the first question, 54 percent to the second, and 60 percent to the third, but only 49 percent to the fourth (an early presidential election) with 51 percent against. Yeltsin and his supporters interpreted the result as giving him the right to rule by himself. Aleksandr Yakovlev wrote a memo to Yeltsin telling him that "the will of a majority of voters, expressed through the referendum, must be held . . . to be superior . . . to the will of a majority in any of the representative bodies . . . the president is entitled to reject any acts of the Supreme Soviet or the Congress of People's Deputies aimed at stopping the reforms."[29]

Yeltsin perhaps imagined that at this point the parliament would back down. Instead, opposition to Yeltsin's government grew ever stronger. Witnessing the parliament's resistance to Yeltsin, many liberal intellectuals argued that it represented the forces of communist and fascist reaction and urged Yeltsin to take action against it. In September 1993, a delegation of Russian writers visited Yeltsin in the Kremlin. One of them, Andrei Nuikin (1931–2017), told the president: "We urge you, Boris Nikolaevich, not to become obsessed solely with constitutional matters in the search for a legitimate solution. After all, your opponents are past masters at bogging down any problems in endless coordination-and-agreement meetings. . . . It seems that the very idea of giving top priority to legitimacy has been skillfully imposed on us by those who themselves spit on it."[30]

Yeltsin took the advice. On September 21, 1993, he issued a decree dissolving the parliament, transferring control of the central bank to his authority, and ordering elections to a new parliament, the State Duma. Yeltsin's decree went far beyond his constitutional authority. The Supreme Soviet responded by impeaching him. On October 3, 1993, the political crisis turned violent when a crowd of parliamentary supporters attempted to storm the central TV station. Yeltsin ordered the army to attack the White House and on October 4 army tanks shelled the Supreme Soviet, forcing it into submission.

Most liberals fully backed Yeltsin's actions. Sergei Kovalyov, for instance, said that "there is no doubt that the victory of Khasbulatov and his supporters . . . would have meant the end of democracy, the end of parliamentarism and the final result, the end of freedom in Russia."[31] While acknowledging that Yeltsin had violated the constitution, Kovalyov argued that this was not important. "What is constitutionalism—following the bad letter of a bad law or the fundamental principles of constitutionalism?" he asked.[32] Even more passionate was former dissident Valeria Novodvorskaya. She wrote:

On the night of October 4 . . . we had a choice: to kill or to die. We preferred to kill and even found moral satisfaction in it. . . . And if during the night they had given tanks to us, democrats and humanists . . . nobody would have hesitated. The "White House" wouldn't have survived till morning, not even ruins would have remained of it. . . . We are not dealing with people, with equal opponents, but with some evil black fog. . . . To deal with it, we need bullets. . . . I know that 20 percent of my fellow citizens regularly vote for communists, fascists, Zhirinovsky, and simple filth . . . and I am completely prepared to get rid of every fifth person. . . . I am no longer afraid of Pinochet. I am prepared to use any methods to win this civil war.[33]

The attack on the parliament was only the first step. Liberals demanded further action. On October 5, 1993, the newspaper *Izvestia* (News) published a letter by forty-two leading intellectuals urging Yeltsin to dissolve the Communist Party, various nationalist organizations, associated media outlets, all local councils (soviets), and the Constitutional Court.[34] Yeltsin obliged his liberal supporters, issuing a decree dissolving all regional and municipal soviets. As Gaidar noted, after the attack on the Supreme Soviet, "It immediately became clear that the first casualty was democracy itself. On the morning of October 3, President Yeltsin was still only one of many players on the Russian scene. . . . On the morning of October 5, all the power in the country was in his hands. We had leapt from the gelatinous *dvoevlastie* [dual power] into a de facto authoritarian regime."[35]

Few liberals expressed much regret. Too much democracy had proven to be a bad thing, they felt. As Sergei Chuprinin (b. 1947) put it in an article entitled "Notes of a Russian liberal," "experience with universal and overhasty introduction [of democracy] in Russia has driven almost everyone to think it may first be necessary to cultivate the soil a bit."[36] Anatoly Chubais commented that "democracy in Russia played a very malicious joke on the process not just of economic, but also political reform. . . . Legislative organs were elected at all levels. After which, these elected organs consistently, determinedly, often maliciously fought against democracy and the reforms. . . . Authoritarian rule, or . . . 'a strong hand plus the market' is undoubtedly technically much more attractive."[37]

Citing the example of General Franco in Spain and Syngman Rhee in South Korea, one of Chubais's assistants, Dmitry Travin (b. 1961), wrote: "History teaches us that most radical economic reforms, if not all, are implemented not by democratic rulers, but by autocrats. . . . If we pull through these reforms successfully, then we can also, after some time, speak about democratization."[38] As Anatol Lieven commented, such views reflected the "contempt on the part of the educated classes of Moscow and St Petersburg for ordinary Russians, who were dubbed *Homo Sovieticus* and treated as an inferior species whose loathsome culture was preventing the liberal elites from taking their rightful place among the 'civilised' nations of the west. . . . I vividly remember one Russian liberal journalist state his desire to fire machine guns into crowds of elderly Russians who joined communist demonstrations to protest about the collapse of their pensions."[39]

Yeltsin's next step to consolidate power consisted of drawing up a new constitution. In December 1993 this was ratified by a referendum.[40] The constitution's drafters sought to combine lofty principles with their desire to centralize authority. The result was a document that was, on the one hand, very liberal but, on the other hand, decidedly autocratic, in the sense that it concentrated power in the hands of a single individual.

The "liberal" part of the constitution is chapter 2, entitled "Rights and Freedoms of the Person and Citizen." This guarantees rights to citizens in accordance with "universally recognized principles and norms of international law," and lays out a long list of specific rights, including the equality of all persons, "the right to freedom and personal immunity," "freedom of ideas and speech," a ban on censorship, the "right to association," and "the right of private property."[41]

The autocratic elements of the constitution are to be found in those articles laying out the power of the president. He or she appoints the prime minister and subordinate ministers, the head of the central bank, and the members of the security council. While the lower house of parliament, the State Duma, can reject the president's nominee for prime minister, if it does so three times, the president can dissolve parliament and call new elections, providing a strong incentive for the Duma not to oppose the president's choice. The president also has the right of legislative initiative and the power to issue decrees.[42] The balance of power between the executive and legislative branches is tilted firmly toward the former. As one of Gaidar's assistants, Vladimir Mau (b. 1959), put it, the new constitution "was designed to minimize the populist influence on economic decision making . . . strengthening the power of the executive branch."[43]

The first elections to the new parliament, the State Duma, took place in December 1993. The largest number of votes went to the nationalist Liberal Democratic Party of Russia (LDPR), led by Vladimir Zhirinovsky (1946–2022). Liberal parties performed respectably, receiving about a third of the vote, but this was split between several groups, weakening their overall influence.

Divisions in the liberal camp were in part a product of Yeltsin's refusal to create a party of his own, on the grounds that he represented the people as a whole and not any particular group. It also reflected the technocratic tendencies of those around him, who made little effort to sell their policies to the public or to create political organizations to do so.[44] Liberals fractured into a large number of competing groups.

The main liberal grouping in the perestroika era—Democratic Russia—was a loose coalition whose only unifying force was its opposition to communist rule. Once the collapse of the Soviet Union deprived it of that unifying element, the movement fell apart as different members took different positions on whether to support Yeltsin's government.

Liberal parties formed in the late Soviet era met much the same fate and new ones emerged to replace them. Roughly speaking, these can be divided into two main types: progovernment parties marked by their commitment to economic liberalism and antigovernment parties supporting a form of "social liberalism," in other words a more moderate form of economic reform.[45] Another division was between "statist liberals," who favored the concentration of power in the hands of the executive, and "rule-of-law liberals," who tended to be more focused on constitutional procedure and human rights.[46] Economic and statist liberalism tended to overlap, with those favoring more radical economic reform also tending to support a powerful executive.[47]

Statist economic liberalism initially had no party of its own. In belated recognition of the need for such an organization, in 1993 Gaidar created a coalition of progovernment forces known as Russia's Choice. In September 1994, Russia's Choice was converted into a formal party, Russia's Democratic Choice (RDC), which in 1999 was then subsumed within another new party, the Union of Right Forces (URF).

The most successful representative of social liberalism was Yavlinsky's Yabloko, founded in 1993. Efforts to unite RDC and Yabloko failed. In 1996, Gaidar offered to support Yavlinsky for president if RDC and Yabloko united. Yavlinsky refused the offer, declaring that Yabloko would not cooperate with RDC "under any circumstances."[48] Personal relations between Yavlinsky, Gaidar, and Chubais were very poor. In 1999, Chubais repeatedly called Yavlinsky a "traitor" because of his opposition to the Second Chechen War, while Yavlinsky accused Chubais of lying and of manifesting an "extreme form of Bolshevism."[49]

Yavlinsky also felt that cooperation with those who had worked in Yeltsin's government would weaken rather than strengthen Yabloko. "My sense of the matter," he wrote, "is that such a bloc would have suffered . . . total defeat . . . and we would have wound up with no democrats at all in the Duma."[50] Yavlinsky refused to join the government, and Yabloko acquired a reputation for being so concerned with maintaining its moral purity that it rejected any opportunity to work with the authorities.[51] Yabloko in effect admitted this, saying in its 1999 program: "We are not in politics to gain power at any cost. . . . People accuse us for wanting to wear 'white gloves' and say we don't want to get our hands dirty. We reply: we are ready to shovel dirt but not sit in the dirt."[52]

Divisions within the liberal camp were ideological as well as personal. While the RDC was committed to the most rapid possible economic transformation, Yabloko rejected the economic policy pursued by Yeltsin's government. Yabloko also regarded the political structure created under Yeltsin as deeply undemocratic. In an examination of the 1995 State Duma elections, M. Stephen Fish wrote that "Yavlinsky clearly regarded other liberal parties as his main competitors. . . . [His aim] was to emerge unequivocally as the leading figure in the liberal camp, *not* to maximise the size of the vote accruing to liberal parties as a whole."[53]

Fish also observed that "Russia's liberals have often exhibited an almost scornful condescension in their attitudes toward ordinary citizens. Liberal politicians . . . have consistently shown far more interest in educating and edifying voters than in listening to them."[54] David White echoes this, saying that Yabloko's "electoral programmes have never been specifically designed with the intention of catching the mood of the Russian voter."[55] The party's attitude was shown in its membership system prior to 2001, whereby "prospective members were required to serve a six to twelve month probationary period as a 'candidate member' before being considered for full membership. . . . During this period the probationary member was expected to prove himself/herself through participation in the association's activities." Explaining this system, a senior party official said that if the party took everyone who wanted to join, it would "make it possible for stupid people to take over and our intellectual capacity will be dissolved in their stupidity. So we cannot make our party a mass party."[56]

Internal divisions, unwillingness to appeal to a mass audience, and the economic and social crisis enveloping Russia in the mid-1990s combined to inflict a severe defeat on the liberal camp when elections were again held for the Duma in 1995. Yabloko received just under 7 percent of the vote, while all other liberal parties failed to surmount the 5 percent hurdle required to win seats under the country's proportional electoral system. The biggest winner in the election was the Communist Party of the Russian Federation (CPRF), the successor to the Communist Party of the Soviet Union, which received 22 percent of the vote. This communist revival posed a serious threat to Yeltsin. Presidential elections were due in June 1996 and opinion polls put Yeltsin behind CPRF leader Gennady Zyuganov (b. 1944). What followed was possibly the most corrupt election in Russian history.

By this time, the structure of power in Russia had shifted in a dramatic way. Economic reform unfolded in a way that concentrated financial capital in the hands of a small number of people, the so-called oligarchs, the most notable of whom were Vladimir Potanin (b. 1961), Boris Berezovsky (1946–2013), Vladimir Gusinsky (b. 1952), and Mikhail Khodorkovsky (b. 1963). These men acquired enormous wealth in a very short time, in large part by exploiting connections with government. Khodorkovsky, for instance, made his initial fortune by acting as an intermediary disbursing money from central to local government and taking a "hefty cut" along the way.[57]

What made men like Gusinsky and Berezovsky oligarchs rather than mere billionaires was that they used their newfound money to acquire political power. One way of doing this was by subsidizing political parties. Gusinsky's MOST Corporation, for instance, funded Yabloko.[58] Another was by cultivating connections with the president. Berezovsky built a close relationship with Yeltsin's daughter, Tatyana Dyachenko (b. 1960), allegedly buying her a $4 million mansion in the south of France.[59] Berezovsky acquired the rights to sell Yeltsin's memoirs abroad and then regularly transferred thousands of dollars in cash to Yeltsin, claiming that the money came from sales of the book.[60]

Most importantly, the oligarchs gained control of important elements of the Russian media. Particularly valuable were Gusinsky's MOST Media, which included the NTV television station, and ORT, the most watched television station in Russia, in which Berezovsky acquired a major interest. Former deputy prime minister Alfred Koch wrote that "Goose [Gusinsky] and Birch [Berezovsky] had a strong influence on Yeltsin. It wasn't total. . . . But in tandem with the media, in tandem with all the wire-tapping, it worked. Those men truly ran the country."[61] These media assets would prove particularly useful during the 1996 presidential campaign. According to independent researchers, Yeltsin received 54 percent of all election coverage, whereas Zyuganov received only 18 percent. Moreover, the coverage of Yeltsin was overwhelmingly positive, whereas that of Zyuganov was almost all negative.[62]

Anatoly Chubais, who ran Yeltsin's election campaign, exercised strong control over media stories and "introduced the practice of regular meetings with the chief editors of leading newspapers . . . [at which he] gave out guidelines for media coverage of government activities."[63] At one such meeting, he allegedly told an editor to do as he was told or "bones will break."[64] Oleg Poptsov, head of the State Television and Radio Company, said "the government is now ours, but it behaves like the previous [Soviet] one. There's no difference in the way such meetings are conducted. The Party Central Committee used to summon a larger group, whereas now a narrower group is called in. But the methods are the same."[65]

Russian electoral law limited spending by presidential candidates to $2.9 million. Yeltsin's campaign spent at least $100 million, and probably substantially more.[66] Peter Reddaway and Dmitri Glinski assess that the 1996 presidential election "was marked by spectacular violations of the law on behalf of the incumbent."[67] The electoral manipulation worked. Yeltsin was reelected.

Yeltsin's second term in office began optimistically, with the president bringing a number of prominent liberals into the government. The most notable was Boris Nemtsov (1959–2015), who had acquired a reputation as a dynamic reformer as governor of the Nizhny Novgorod region and who in 1997 was appointed as deputy prime minister.[68] But the optimism did not last long. The oligarchs fell out with one another, and with the government, as they quarreled over the division of the privatization spoils. A series of corruption scandals, the collapse of the ruble in 1998, and the domination of the Duma by opposition forces eventually obliged Yeltsin to change his government, replacing Chernomyrdin as prime minister with Evgeny Primakov (1929–2015). There then followed something similar to the "ministerial leapfrog" that characterized the final two years of the imperial regime, with prime ministers and ministers being replaced in rapid succession, until in summer 1999 Yeltsin settled on Vladimir Putin as prime minister. On December 31, 1999, Yeltsin resigned, designating Putin to replace him.

Social-Economic Liberalism

By the end of 1991, the Russian economy was in a dire state. Production had fallen substantially in the previous year and there were severe shortages of basic goods in the shops. The Yeltsin government decided that radical action was required to address the economic crisis. The result was "shock therapy."

The Soviet economy was highly centralized. Enterprises were state-owned and production targets and prices were set by the government. Shock therapy sought to replace the communist system with a free market economy in the shortest possible time. It had two main elements. First, prices would be freed, so that enterprises could charge whatever they wanted. The resultant inflation would be held in check by a tight monetary policy, including slashing government expenditure. Second, state-owned enterprises would be privatized. In the logic of shock therapy, the faster this was done the better, both for economic reasons—doing one part of the therapy but not another would produce harmful contradictions—and for political reasons—the hardship caused by shock therapy would result in opposition to further reform, and it made sense to do as much as possible while public opinion still tolerated it.

The form shock therapy took owed much to the circumstances of the time. The collapse of the Soviet Union coincided with a moment in history when free market and monetarist ideas were ascendant in the West, as exemplified by the governments of Ronald Reagan (1911–2004) and Margaret Thatcher (1925–2013) in the 1980s. Had the Soviet Union collapsed at some other time, reformers might have adopted a different model. As it was, the Reaganite/Thatcherite model seemed to represent the most up-to-date Western thinking. Russia's liberal reformers considered it to represent universal economic law, and the idea that Russia might have some specific characteristics that rendered it unsuitable was dismissed. "We proceeded from the fundamental laws of economic behavior of *homo sapiens*," said Gaidar, "And it turned out that these laws work in Russia, with our specific character, as well as they work in Argentina, Korea, the Czech Republic, Slovakia or Australia."[69]

Gaidar and others displayed considerable naïveté about the likely consequences of their reforms. Nemtsov admitted: "I believed that our main job then was to kill communism. If we managed that, we thought that we would live like the Americans, maybe in six months, perhaps nine months. . . . We thought things would work out in a short time."[70]

The need for radical reform was widely recognized, but there was disagreement as to the sequencing, given that everything could not be done all at once. Gaidar opted to start by liberalizing prices. On January 2, 1992, prices for the vast majority of goods and services were freed, although price controls were retained in some instances, such as energy (oil, gas, and electricity). Gaidar argued that the longer the government waited to free prices, the greater the subsequent inflation was likely to be.[71] "Let us first replace empty store shelves with rapidly rising prices, then let us halt their rise," he wrote.[72] Later he justified his decision, saying, "We were approaching a very severe crisis in the supply of grain and bread to the big cities. . . . In this situation, any discussion of taking a gradual approach to Russian economic reform would have been meaningless."[73]

The second step in Gaidar's plans was to cut state subsidies to enterprises and individuals. Underlying this was the monetarist conception that inflation is a product of an excess money supply and that the only way to reduce it is to reduce the supply, which requires policies such as lowering spending, increasing taxes, and imposing high interest rates. Gaidar slashed military spending, lowered state subsidies, reduced capital investment, cut spending on social services, and introduced a value added tax of 28 percent.[74]

In another step, on January 29, 1992, Yeltsin issued a decree removing all restrictions on private trade, declaring that "enterprises and private citizens may sell things . . . in any place of their convenience."[75] The result was the appearance of huge numbers of people on the streets of Russian cities selling whatever they could get their hands on. The unregulated street trade provided enormous opportunities for organized crime, prompting municipal authorities to attempt to regulate it by requiring vendors to obtain licenses. This in turn generated widespread corruption, as officials demanded bribes in return for licenses or for refusing licenses to competitors.[76]

The government retained price controls on key commodities such as oil, gas, and timber, keeping the domestic prices for these goods well below those of world markets. Due to fear that Russia would run short of vital supplies if export controls were removed, the government also restricted exports of many of the same products. Entrepreneurs whose connections to officialdom gave them the ability to buy these goods from state enterprises at the artificially low domestic price, and also to obtain export permits, could then sell the goods abroad at the much higher world market price, generating huge profits.[77]

Economic liberalization thus resulted in a massive growth in corruption, as well as the rapid accumulation of enormous wealth by a handful of well-connected individuals. To defenders of shock therapy, these negative consequences were a product not of excessively radical reform, but rather a failure to go all the way. It was argued that had the government eliminated all price and export controls, the opportunities for corruption noted above would not have arisen. The problem, therefore, was that the reform was not radical enough.[78]

Reformers also blamed the director of the central bank, Viktor Gerashchenko (b. 1937), for undermining the government's efforts to limit the money supply. In order to prevent state enterprises from going out of business, Gerashchenko continued to provide them with cheap credit. This fueled spiraling inflation, which in 1992 reached 2,650 percent per annum.[79] Given that controlling the money supply was a key element of shock therapy, the government's failure to do so has led its supporters to claim that, as Gaidar said, "There was no real 'shock therapy' in 1992," and this was the cause of Russia's economic crisis.[80]

Not everyone in the liberal camp accepted this logic. Yavlinsky rejected the monetarist concept that inflation was a consequence of excessive money supply. The "neoliberal-monetarist doctrine" did not fit Russia's circumstances, he wrote, because it "assumes the presence of a functioning market economy. . . . The special feature of the economies of the countries in the former socialist camp are such that standard monetarist methods yield different results there than they do in a developed market economy."[81] According to Yavlinsky, freeing prices in a highly monopolized economy, with few small businesses and a lack of property rights and other free market institutions, was a recipe for inflation.[82]

The problem with shock therapy, claimed Yavlinsky, was that "instead of liberating the economy from the monopolies, the shock therapists liberated the monopolies, which went ahead and charged whatever prices they wanted when prices were freed in early 1992."[83] "Earlier, Moscow fixed prices; now the monopolist does it," he added.[84] According to Yavlinsky, the government should have demonopolized and privatized before freeing prices.

When privatization happened, it proved to be just as controversial as price liberalization. While the principle of privatization was widely accepted, the exact way to do it was hotly debated. The most radical proposal was a scheme to speedily privatize Moscow's retail sector by giving enterprises to their workers.[85] However, the scheme was abandoned after a few months in the face of complaints that worker management was inefficient and that enterprise directors had engaged in asset stripping or had illegally sold the privatized businesses and pocketed the profits.[86]

At the national level, privatization was the responsibility of Chubais, who issued every Russian citizen a voucher with a notional value of 10,000 rubles. This could either be sold or be used to buy shares in a state-owned enterprise when it was put on the market. Chubais initially opposed vouchers, as they failed to generate revenue for the state or to provide investment income for the privatized enterprises. Eventually, though, Chubais accepted vouchers as a means of generating public support for privatization and overcoming opposition in the Supreme Soviet.[87] Chubais said, "From an economic point of view, voucher privatization . . . was not the best way to achieve privatization. . . . It was the only way to make it doable."[88]

The government's privatization law allowed for enterprises to sold be off in a number of different ways according to their size. In a concession to managers and trade unions, the government allowed workers to obtain 25 percent of the shares of their enterprise free of charge as nonvoting shares, with an additional 10 percent of voting shares at a reduced price, or to buy 51 percent of the shares at full price, half of which could be paid for with vouchers. A third option allowed managers to buy 20 percent of shares if the workers agreed.[89] The result of these concessions to workers and managers was that a large percentage of enterprises ended up under the control of their directors, who often bought up the vouchers of their workers.[90] Told that voucher privatization had led to enormous corruption, Chubais responded, "They are stealing absolutely everything and it is impossible to stop them. But let them steal and take their property. They will then become owners and decent administrators of the property."[91] The priority was getting rid of state property as fast as possible; what sort of system was created was of secondary importance, as it was assumed that any problems would be self-correcting.

Voucher privatization transferred tens of thousands of state enterprises into private hands within a couple of years. By 1995, however, the priorities of the Russian government had changed. In the face of a large budget deficit, generating revenue became more important. The result was perhaps the most scandalous affair of the Yeltsin era—the "loans for shares" scheme.

The Russian state had retained control of a number of valuable enterprises in the energy and communications sectors, but the State Duma had passed legislation prohibiting the government from privatizing these. Loans-for-shares bypassed this prohibition by making the enterprises in question collateral for one-year loans given to the state by select individuals. If the state failed to repay the loans at the end of the year, the lenders would have the right to auction the businesses to the highest bidder, keeping 30 percent of the profit for themselves.[92]

All involved knew from the start that the state had no intention of repaying the loans. Furthermore, when the year was up the auctions were rigged in such a way as to enable the lenders to sell the enterprises to themselves at rock-bottom prices. In the case of the energy company Surgutneftgaz, the auction was held in the remote Siberian city of Surgut, whose airport was mysteriously closed on the day of the auction, preventing unwanted bidders from attending. In other cases, bids from competitors were disqualified for alleged technical violations.[93] The result was that select lenders were able to obtain control of twelve of Russia's most valuable companies at well below market price. Before long, the companies' value would be many times what they had paid for them. For instance, Mikhail Khodorkovsky gained control of the oil company Yukos for $300 million, but within a couple of years it would be valued at several billion dollars.

Loans-for-shares has its supporters. Daniel Treisman argues that those who benefited from the scheme took a considerable risk, as the companies they acquired had large debts. Moreover, the new owners proved to be very competent managers, greatly improving the efficiency of their companies.[94] In the eyes of critics, however, "Russia was robbed in broad daylight," with valuable assets being handed over to a handful of rich men for a fraction of their true value.[95]

It would appear that Chubais initially rejected the scheme as insider dealing, but eventually accepted it because he saw it as a way of raising money.[96] He said, "the dilemma was simple: Either we will not sell state shares at all, or we will sell them via the controversial shares scheme, which would bring real money to the Russian budget."[97] But his reasoning was political as well as economic. He added: "I strongly believe that the only way to prevent [the Communist leader] Zyuganov from becoming president was to create big private business in Russia. Their [the oligarchs'] mentality differed from Soviet-style management. . . . They fought for improving economic efficiency. . . . That is the economic side of the story. At the same time, they became powerful and wanted to use their power according to their understanding of the political situation. The presidential election of June 1996 raised the question of Yeltsin or Zyuganov, and they [the oligarchs who bankrolled Yeltsin's election] definitely said Yeltsin."[98]

Chubais's statement supports a commonly accepted interpretation of loans-for-shares as a quid pro quo: the oligarchs would profit and in return would back Yeltsin for president.[99] As Gaidar said, "The loans-for-shares created a political pact. They helped to ensure that Zyuganov did not come to the Kremlin."[100] Seen this way, loans-for-shares played a key role in the corruption of the Russian political system.

Loans-for-shares was not the final scandal of the era. In 1997, for instance, Alfred Koch resigned as deputy prime minister following revelations that he had been paid tens of thousands of dollars as an advance for a book. In the eyes of some, the advance was a poorly camouflaged bribe, something that Koch denied. Regardless of the truth, scandals like this cemented the perception that there was high-level corruption among the liberal officials in Yeltsin's government.

Koch had been part of a team that Yeltsin assembled after his 1996 victory. The most prominent member of this team was Nemtsov, who soon ran into trouble due to his plans for social security, which he hoped to drastically cut. Especially unpopular was a proposed pension reform, which envisioned raising the retirement age for men to seventy, even though average male life expectancy had plummeted to fifty-eight years.[101] Nemtsov's insensitive statement that "Russia must enter the 21st century with only young people" did not help.[102]

Soviet citizens' utility bills had been highly subsidized by the state, which covered some 70 percent of the cost of water, gas, and heating. These subsidies continued into the post-Soviet era, and Nemtsov proposed eliminating them in order to help balance the state budget.[103] This proved immensely unpopular among a Russian population that was already struggling financially.[104] In face of mounting opposition, Nemtsov had to abandon his plans, and shortly after Yeltsin's dismissal of Chernomyrdin's government, he resigned. With this, the period of economic reform under Yeltsin largely came to an end.

Russian liberals of the Yeltsin era owed little if anything to their forebears.[105] In the many writings of Gaidar, for instance, one will search in vain for any influence from prerevolutionary Russian liberalism.[106] The liberals who governed Russia in the 1990s prioritized free market economic reform at the expense of democratic procedure and the rule of law, even resorting to force to eliminate opposition. Consequently, they are often portrayed as heirs of the Soviet Union more than of prerevolutionary or émigré Russian liberalism, earning them the pejorative title "Market Bolsheviks."

Nevertheless, one can observe some features common to the liberalism of the 1990s and that of the past. The first and most obvious is the combination in both cases of Westernism and historical determinism, with liberalism being associated with a desire to align Russia with Western civilization. A second similarity was their elite nature. In the early 1990s, liberalism briefly enjoyed broad popular support, but this support soon faded away, leaving liberalism, as before, as the ideology of a narrow section of the educated classes. The liberals who pushed through shock therapy and privatization were intellectuals who displayed little interest in talking to and winning the support of the public at large. They exhibited what has been called "an almost scornful condescension in the attitudes towards ordinary citizens."[107]

Where the liberals in Yeltsin's government more obviously differed from their predecessors was in their "ends justify the means" and "greed is good" mentality. Gaidar said, "The struggle to realize the goals that have been set . . . dictates the harsh logic of the deeds."[108] And Koch argued that "'socialism with a human face' and 'capitalism without greed' are equally utopian dreams." One could not have the good sides of capitalism without the bad sides, he said.[109] This reflected another aspect of Yeltsin-era liberalism—its neglect of what one might call the "losers" of economic restructuring, as manifested for instance in Nemtsov's proposed social security reforms. However logical they were from the point of view of balancing the state budget, they ignored the poverty that most Russians had to endure in the 1990s. Economic reform was presented as an opportunity for all to get rich. The fact that most were instead impoverished was largely ignored. Thus Gaidar said in 1993: "Of course, prices are high and there are enormous problems with corruption and instability. . . . But in everyday life the improvements are obvious. There are opportunities in this enormous economy that were previously nonexistent. . . . It is a rapidly changing world, a world of opportunities!"[110]

Gaidar was not entirely wrong. Russians in the 1990s enjoyed unprecedented political, civil, and economic freedoms. In less than a decade, the liberals of the era succeeded in turning one of the most centralized, state-controlled economic systems in the world into a market economy, albeit an imperfect one. Tens of thousands of enterprises were privatized. Domestic and international trade became much freer. And after the chaos of 1992–1993, Yeltsin succeeded in creating a new political order that has proven to be remarkably stable. This included a new constitution that greatly expanded Russians' rights.

Defenders of Yeltsin and his government point out that the situation they inherited at the end of 1991 was dire and that drastic measures were required.[111] William Tompson argues that "it is difficult to see how a reforming government at the beginning of 1992 could have pursued a radically different strategy."[112] It is perhaps unrealistic to blame the reformers for all the negative consequences of their policies. Many of them were possibly unavoidable given the circumstances of the time. That said, in their determination to act with the utmost speed, Yeltsin and his team created a corrupt, undemocratic, and inefficient system.[113] They showed little concern about inequality and created an unhealthy symbiosis between wealth and political connections that continues to bedevil Russia to this day.

Opinions of Yeltsin vary considerably. In the West, there is an inclination to look on his time in office as a period of liberalization that contrasts sharply with the era that followed. Yeltsin's Western supporters highlight the relative freedoms that Russians enjoyed under his presidency and on occasion have showered Yeltsin himself with praise. Herbert Ellison, for instance, writes that "Russia and the other former Soviet republics had every reason to be grateful to the main leader of one of the most ambitious, progressive, and successful political transformations in modern history. . . . Yeltsin's words and deeds amply justify calling him 'Russian liberator.'"[114] Likewise, Timothy Colton claims that "for what he wrought . . . [Yeltsin] belongs with the instigators of a global trend away from authoritarianism and statism and toward democratic politics and market-based economics. As a democratizer, he is in the company of Nelson Mandela, Lech Wałesa, Mikhail Gorbachev, and Václav Havel."[115] By contrast, Yeltsin has few supporters any more in Russia. Lilia Shevtsova expresses a common viewpoint, writing: "It was Yeltsin who handed over power to his favourites and enabled cliques to help themselves to state property. It was Yeltsin who adopted (and even edited) the authoritarian constitution that created the framework for the 'electoral monarchy.' It was Yeltsin who, by failing to cope with the deepening crisis and paralysis of power, provoked among Russians the longing for order and an 'iron hand.' . . . Putin has merely followed the path laid out by his predecessor."[116]

Russian public perceptions of the 1990s are almost entirely negative.[117] These negative views have thoroughly discredited liberalism as a political force, with liberals being seen as corrupt, antipatriotic, antidemocratic, and contemptuous of the views and interests of ordinary people. Although moderate liberals, such as Yavlinsky and his Yabloko party, opposed shock therapy and other policies of the Yeltsin government, they too have suffered, as the public seems to make little distinction between liberals of different sorts. The fact that oligarchs like Berezovsky and Khodorkovsky portrayed themselves as liberals and democrats further undermined both concepts, as many Russians came to the conclusion that if that was what liberals and democrats were like, they wanted nothing to do with either. As Leonid Batkin lamented in a play on the Russian word for "dung"—*dermo*—"it is our fault and no one else's if the word 'democrats' is now used either in quotation marks or accompanied by a 'so-called' or simply in the injurious form 'dermocrat.'"[118]

CHAPTER 11

Russian Liberalism under Putin

A single figure has dominated the past twenty years of Russian history—Vladimir Putin, who served as president from 2000 to 2008 and then prime minister from 2008 to 2012, while Dmitry Medvedev (b. 1965) was president. In 2012 Putin once again became president, a post he still occupies at the time of writing. In 2000, liberalism was still a powerful political force in Russia. Twenty years later, it has been almost extinguished.

When Putin was first elected, Russia was in disarray. The economy had yet to recover from the travails of the 1990s. Crime was rampant. Life expectancy had fallen significantly. Many of Russia's regions ran themselves largely independently from Moscow, and in late 1999, war broke out again in Chechnya. Over the next ten years, under Putin, the war in Chechnya eventually ended in a Russian victory, and the economic reforms of the 1990s began to show some benefits. A sharp rise in the global price of oil filled the government's coffers, producing an economic boom that lasted nearly a decade. Putin restored Moscow's control over the regions, and purged the oligarchs, including imprisoning billionaire Mikhail Khodorkovsky. Putin's popularity soared as order and prosperity returned.

Political scientists have given the modern Russian political system many names, such as "managed democracy" and "soft authoritarianism," reflecting its mixture of liberal democratic and illiberal nondemocratic features. Richard Sakwa calls it "a hybrid of democratic and authoritarian impulses and governing practices," with a "dual state, in which two systems of rule run in parallel, the 'administrative regime' and the 'constitutional state.'"[1] The former acts in an arbitrary manner, according to its own rules, while the latter follows the letter of the constitution.

Elena Chebankova describes the ideological system of Putin's Russia as "paradigmatic pluralism, which assumes the existence and dialogue between varying paradigms of socio-political thinking."[2] This model sees Putin as a "centrist," who has acted as an "arbiter" between the different ideological groupings in Russian society. All these groupings, including liberalism, have been allowed some say in the running of the state but none has been allowed to dominate.[3]

While there is something to this model, over time the role allowed to liberalism has diminished until by now it has been almost eliminated. A turning point was Putin's return to the presidency in 2012. Many had viewed Medvedev's election as president in 2008 as an opportunity for Russia to go back to the liberal path. These hopes proved largely unjustified. Allegations of electoral fraud in the December 2011 State Duma elections impelled thousands of people to take to the streets in protest. The demonstrations continued into 2012, with several tens of thousands turning out in Moscow in February and March 2012 to demonstrate against Putin's return to the presidency. The protest movement fizzled out, however, having failed to galvanize the Russian population as a whole.

The 2012 protests marked a decisive break between Putin and Russian liberals. As legal methods of political struggle became increasingly difficult, leadership of the liberal movement began to shift toward those willing to engage in street protests, such as Boris Nemtsov and Aleksei Navalny (b. 1976), the second of whom came to prominence due to his social media activities exposing official corruption. In February 2015, Nemtsov was murdered in Moscow. In August 2020, Navalny became violently ill while on a flight in Siberia. Taken to Germany for treatment, he was diagnosed as having been poisoned. An investigation by independent researchers pointed the finger of blame at agents of the Russian Federal Security Service. In January 2021, Navalny returned to Moscow and was arrested and imprisoned. The authorities' tolerance for opposition seemed to have become exhausted.

Meanwhile, relations between Russia and the West had significantly worsened. A number of events were responsible, including further expansion eastward by NATO, the Anglo-American invasion of Iraq in 2003, and NATO's bombing of Libya in 2011. Particularly important was a revolution that took place in Ukraine in February 2014, resulting in the overthrow of the Ukrainian government. Shortly after the Ukrainian revolution, Russia took control of the Crimean peninsula and annexed it. This act proved to be enormously popular in Russia, but provoked the wrath of the West, which responded by levying economic sanctions against Russia.

Further sanctions followed, responding to a variety of issues, such as human rights violations in Russia, alleged Russian interference in the 2016 US presidential election, and Russian support for a rebellion that broke out in the eastern Ukrainian region of Donbass in spring 2014. With fighting in Donbass still raging, at the start of 2022 Putin demanded that NATO cease all further expansion eastward. After this demand was rejected, in February 2022 Russian forces invaded Ukraine, causing Western countries to almost entirely cut off relations with Russia. The results of Putin's Ukrainian gamble remain to be determined.

Cultural Liberalism

According to Elena Chebankova, modern Russian liberalism divides into two main types: "pluralistic moderate and monistic radical." The first "admits that life can flourish in differing forms that should be taken into account, while the other defends the Eurocentric political path toward freedom."[4] The difference is in large part cultural. The pluralists argue that Russian liberalism must align with Russian history and traditions, and the monists instead adopt a full-throated Westernism.

An example of the former is historian Aleksei Kara-Murza who at one time served as a member of the coordinating committee of the liberal party URF. Kara-Murza argues for a synthesis of classical European liberalism and national tradition, saying that "The experience of successful liberal modernization in Western European countries shows that liberal traditions are . . . nationally colored."[5] In Russia's case, he writes, "Russian society and Russian liberals need to consider the religious culture in Russia—which has deep Christian roots—in implanting the liberal project of political culture based on national traditions. Otherwise, radical liberalism, which denies the religion and values of national culture, will assume an approach similar to the Bolshevik dictatorship and scientific atheism."[6]

Liberals of this sort are relatively rare. Aleksandr Tsipko (b. 1941) argues that Russia's tragedy is that those who value Russia's traditions don't value freedom, whereas those who value freedom don't value tradition. "It is precisely because we don't have a single political force that wants to unite the values of European humanism with our national values that we have ended up in our current ideological dead end," he writes.[7]

Monist Westernism is the prevailing current of thought in contemporary Russian liberalism, with most self-defined liberals sharing "an open and even explicit western orientation."[8] Mikhail Khodorkovsky declares: "We are Europeans! We built and defended this civilization and have no less right to it than the French, German, British, Australians, Canadians or Americans. For centuries we marched shoulder to shoulder, and we know: we need them, and they us."[9] Grigory Yavlinsky remarks that the West is the "core of the contemporary world economy," and urges Russia to join that core.[10] "Russia is still the West. If we're not on board the 'Western boat,' we lose our identity, turning into just a tempting territory with an abundance of natural resources," he says.[11] This viewpoint found expression in the 2012 Yabloko election manifesto, which declared: "In light of its historical fate, cultural traditions, and geography, Russia is a European country. Its future is indivisibly connected with Europe. The Russian nation's potential can be revealed only through a creative assimilation of the values of European civilization."[12]

For journalist Dmitry Gubin (b. 1964), "The greatest achievements of Russian culture happened only when it was open to the West and learnt from the West."[13] And according to writer Iulia Latynina (b. 1966), "Russian culture became great . . . when it became part of Western culture. . . . If Peter I had not made Russia part of the European world, there would have been no Tolstoy or Turgenev. There would have been no Russian empire, so beloved by our patriots. It simply wouldn't have existed."[14]

Liberal attitudes to the West are not entirely uncritical. Yavlinsky, for instance, complains that Western foreign policy has been marked by "public hubris and arrogance . . . the readiness to overlook inconvenient facts, lies, torture in secret prisons, and the financial crimes of 'our' politicians."[15] Meanwhile, in a 2011 article, Latynina berated Europe for having adopted concepts of social justice, multiculturalism, and state regulation of the economy, in the process supposedly abandoning the classical liberal principles that had made it great.[16]

For Latynina, the West's problems "began when the left began to dominate in the mass media, universities and elections of the Greater West," and spread various narratives that she finds objectionable. These include the "anticolonial narrative," according to which "every historical loser was a victim and every victor a criminal"; the "feminist narrative," according to which "white sexist men are the oppressors of women"; and the "narrative against slavery," according to which "every white person is systemically racist." These "absurd" narratives, says Latynina, constitute "a new totalitarianism disguised as humanism. It's a struggle for the rights of the poor and of losers, so that not a single rich and successful person remains."[17]

The Black Lives Matter (BLM) protests in America in 2020 also drew Latynina's wrath, largely on the grounds that the protestors looted private property. Other Russian liberals were equally hostile to BLM. For instance, journalist Oleg Kashin (b. 1980) caused a scandal after he posted a picture of Martin Luther King surrounded by stolen shoeboxes with the caption "Martin Looter King."[18] And journalist Konstantin Eggert (b. 1964) resigned from the British think-tank Chatham House after it gave an award to a BLM leader. In his letter of resignation, he noted: "I was born in the Soviet Union. My family members suffered imprisonment and death at the hands of a regime that espoused many of the traits that BLM displays directly or by implication: contempt for the rights of those they do not agree with, for freedom of speech and inquiry . . . people with my historical experience know the totalitarian ethic when they see it. Today I do."[19]

A particularly striking attack on this supposed "totalitarian ethic" appeared in a 2021 article by theater director Konstantin Bogomolov (b. 1975) in the liberal newspaper *Novaia Gazeta* (New newspaper). In this, Bogomolov expresses his hatred of modern Western "woke" culture. "The contemporary Western world is turning into a new ethical Reich with its own ideology," he writes, "the Nazis have been replaced by an equally aggressive mix of queer activists, fem-fanatics and eco-psychopaths, who similarly thirst for the total transformation of the world."[20] Bogomolov continues:

> In the 1990s, Russia strived toward Europe. . . . [But] Europe has become an abandoned and looted cherry orchard. . . . Russia is far from being the Europe it was striving for. But it obviously doesn't want to join the new European panopticon. . . . We find ourselves in the tail of mad train, steaming to a Hieronymous Bosch–style hell, where we will be met by multicultural gender-neutral devils. We simply have to unhitch the wagon, cross ourselves and start building our own world. To build anew our old, good Europe, the Europe of which we dreamed, the Europe we have lost, the Europe of the healthy.[21]

Bogomolov's article evoked a generally negative response, and his views cannot be said to be representative of liberals as a whole. Nevertheless, Jan Surman and Ella Rossman describe the article as reflecting a "moral panic" among liberal intellectuals concerning the "new ethics" that involve "discussions about minorities and their rights . . . inclusivity and affirmative action."[22] Objecting to these new ethics, "the liberal opposition espouses positions which one knows from [the] European right or American republicans," placing it "in solidarity with . . . even the sworn propagandists of the Putin regime."[23] Surman and Rossman comment that "while there are groups prone to espouse these agendas [the 'new ethics'], the main opposition sees them rather with scepticism and instead of engaging with them on the intellectual level, hyperbolizes and caricaturizes [them]. . . . The dissidents of the Soviet past identified with the West, seeing it as the opposite of everything bad that [the] USSR embodied. Today, many of them . . . want to rebuild their own West, in which there will be no protests against sexual harassment or BLM movement . . . the West is still an important figure, but it is even more imaginary than before.[24]

A common theme in Russian liberal attacks on Western identity politics and "cancel culture" is that they are reminiscent of Soviet communism. As Latynina puts it, "Specialists on gender, race, and so on explain to corporations that they must have courses on 'white fragility' and diversity consultants, just as in the USSR every factory had its party cell." Identity politics, she says, is a "destructive cult," led by "commissars of diversity, gender and race."[25] Viktor Shenderovich (b. 1958) likewise claims that "cancel culture" is reminiscent of Bolshevik attempts to level society down to the lowest level rather than raise people up. Underneath it, he says, lies "not the ethic of the enlightener but the fervor of the revolutionary and the thirst for revenge."[26]

Rossen Djagalov argues that such talk is a reaction to the antiracist and anticolonial rhetoric employed by the Soviet Union. Liberals see complaints that Western society is racist as a continuation of communist propaganda, and so feel a need to reject them.[27] Another factor is that liberal historical determinism lends itself to a belief in a "civilizational hierarchy," at the top of which lies the West and beneath which lie other cultures.[28] As a close associate of Aleksei Navalny, Vladimir Ashurkov (b. 1972), puts it: "What is closer to me is the theory of the progressive development of mankind, according to which—from the point of view of social evolution—society can be on different levels of civilization. . . . The gradual transformation of non-Europeans into Europeans is a big, difficult, and painful process but . . . there is no alternative."[29]

For some Russian liberals, "Europe" is White and Christian. Journalist Oleg Kashin, for instance, states: "We look like a white European Christian people, we act like a white European Christian people, we possess all the signs of white European Christian people, but for some reason are afraid of saying out loud that we are a white European Christian people."[30] Some liberals therefore oppose large-scale immigration into Russia from the Muslim countries of Central Asia, which "damages Russia's efforts to integrate into Europe," in the words of the Coordinating Council of the Opposition, set up during the 2012 protests.[31]

The most famous proponent of this point of view is Aleksei Navalny. Believing that to be successful, liberalism needed to be aligned with Russian ethnonationalism, in 2006 Navalny created the Russian National Liberation

Movement (NAROD, the Russian word meaning "people"), which said that the state's goal should be "to stop the processes of the degradation of Russian civilization, and to create the conditions for the preservation and development of the Russian people, its culture, its language, its historical territory."[32] To this end NAROD demanded a "sensible" immigration policy, saying that "those who come to our home but do not want to respect our laws and traditions must be thrown out."[33] Navalny supported the "introduction of a visa regime with the countries of Central Asia," and campaigned on the slogan "Stop Feeding the Caucasus," complaining about the aid provided by Moscow to the Muslim republics of the Caucasus region.[34] Navalny accused Muslim immigrants of being responsible for a high percentage of crimes and stated that "I do not see any contradiction in being liberal and speaking at the same time about illegal immigration and ethnic criminality."[35]

Explanations of Navalny's stance differ. Some view him simply as an "opportunist."[36] Marlene Laruelle remarks that Navalny is "a doer, not a thinker. His goals are eminently political: the broader the support, the better."[37] According to this line of thought, Navalny's nationalist turn merely reflected a belief that these views might be popular. In the late 2010s, he dropped them after they became a political liability.

Others see Navalny as having endeavored to create a "benign nationalism" that would "outflank and expose belligerent nationalism."[38] According to this view, Navalny's engagement with nationalist groups was an effort to moderate their views. Navalny's assistant Leonid Volkov (b. 1980) claims that "he believes that if you don't talk to the kind of people who attend these [nationalist] marches, they will all become skinheads. But, if you talk to them, you may be able to convince them that their real enemy is Putin."[39] This explanation does not fit easily with some of the inflammatory statements made by Navalny in the late 2000s and early 2010s.[40] Laruelle notes that "Navalny refrains from criticizing other nationalist movements—even when skinheads commit unlawful racist crimes. . . . Navalny also defended Aleksandr Belov and Dmitriy Demushkin, the latter who is a notorious neo-Nazi, both of whom stand accused of inciting racial hatred."[41]

Navalny's attempt to meld liberalism and Russian ethnonationalism has some supporters. Kashin, for instance, echoes the complaint that Central Asian migrants commit a disproportionate number of crimes and states that "the Russian people are always in the position of a second-grade person hiding under the counter."[42] In a 2021 article in *Novaia Gazeta* Vladimir Pastukhov (b. 1963) argued that Putin's success derived from the fact that he is in tune with the "historically insoluble 'cultural substrate'" of the Russian masses, whereas "the intelligentsia prefers to ignore the Russian cultural archetype, presenting Russian society as an 'undeveloped' version of European society, in need of correction."[43] Liberals could achieve success only if they abandoned this idea, said Pastukhov: "It is possible to be a nationalist and even an imperialist . . . and also to think about democracy, a law-based state, and observing international treaties. . . . But for now, the majority of the regime's opponents consider nationalism and liberalism, and likewise patriotism and devotion to democracy, to be incompatible."[44]

As the last sentence above reveals, the appeal to nationalism has limited support within the liberal opposition, most of which continues to consider it as anathema. The Yabloko 2012 program noted: "We are a party of Russian [rossiiskikh] patriots. But not the type that puts the state above the person, who summons the country into isolation and nationalist madness. Nationalism in all its manifestations, but especially ethnic nationalism, is hostile to Russia, as it ignites national divisions and the destruction of the international peace on which the integrity of our country depends."[45]

In line with this sentiment, many Russian liberals state a preference for patriotism over nationalism, but stress that theirs is a "true" patriotism, which they contrast with the "false," "imperial" patriotism of the state.[46] This "true" patriotism is demonstrated "by a critical attitude to the state and a consequent defense of individual citizens against the state's infringements of their rights and freedoms."[47] Sergei Medvedev (b. 1966), a professor at Moscow's Higher School of Economics, writes: "genuine patriotism means freedom."[48] "Putin thinks that patriotism is about fighting. I think patriotism is when people like living in their country and are not scared of each other," says Novaia Gazeta's editor Dmitry Muratov (b. 1961).[49]

In practice, a "critical attitude to the state" often appears to the public not as patriotism but the opposite. Tatyana Felgengauer (b. 1985) of the now-banned liberal Ekho Moskvy (Echo of Moscow) radio station notes that "the average Russian does not like Radio Echo of Moscow. They constantly blame us: claiming that we are the Echo of the US State Department, that we are not patriots, that we have sold ourselves to the Americans, that we are against Russia."[50] However unwarranted such complaints may be, they reflect the reality that liberals are widely viewed as unpatriotic, a perception that is necessarily harmful to their political prospects.

In 2014, the clash between popular patriotism and the attitudes of the liberal intelligentsia came to a head following the annexation of Crimea. Whereas the vast majority of the Russian people celebrated Crimea's "return" to Russia, most Russian liberals condemned it wholeheartedly.

For Igor Kliamkin, the 2014 Ukrainian revolution was "an effort to join European civilization," and as such exactly the kind of civilizational turning point that Russian liberals hoped to see in their own country.[51] Opposition to the revolution, and to the subsequent annexation of Crimea and uprising in Donbass, were regarded as anti-European, and thus negative, phenomena. As Yavlinsky put it, "The country [Russia] has adopted an anti-European course."[52] "The main consequence of the current policy toward Ukraine is the strengthening of Russia's course as a non-European country," Yavlinsky said.[53]

In March 2014 Yabloko issued a declaration denouncing "Vladimir Putin's aggressive, neoimperialist course" and stating that the annexation of Crimea demonstrated the government's hatred of the West.[54] Sergei Mitrokhin (b. 1963), president of Yabloko from 2008 to 2015, declared that "the use of military force to annex parts of Ukraine contradicts the UN Charter, the norms of international law, and the Russian constitution."[55] A member of Yabloko's political committee, Boris Vishnevsky (b. 1955), referred to Crimea as "stolen," while another, Aleksandr Gnezdilov (b. 1986), called the annexation an "Anschluss."[56] Similarly, former world chess champion Gary Kasparov (b. 1963) compared the Crimean events to the Nazi annexation of Sudetenland.[57]

What to do in response to Crimea and the war in Donbass proved a difficult question for liberals. Kasparov urged NATO to send weapons to Ukraine to help it fight the Donbass rebels, while Nemtsov "called for Ukraine to wall off the breakaway regions in the Donbass," and said that, "The sooner Ukraine understands that the so-called 'DNR' [the breakaway Donetsk People's Republic] is its Gaza Strip, the better."[58] Others condemned the annexation of Crimea while also recognizing that it was a fait accompli. An example of the latter is Navalny, who said, "Even though Crimea was seized in gross violation of all international norms, it is now part of the Russian Federation—these are the realities. . . . Crimea will remain part of Russia and will never be Ukrainian in the foreseeable future."[59]

Yabloko's position was somewhat confusing. The party's 2016 election platform stated firmly: "We support Ukraine's territorial inviolability. We consider that Crimea belongs to Ukraine, and that its annexation is illegal and must be reversed." But it left open the possibility of Crimea remaining Russian by calling for the issue to be settled by means of an international conference made up of representatives of the Crimean population, Russia, Ukraine, the European Union, and other interested countries.[60] This slight compromise has not hidden the fact that Yabloko strongly opposed the annexation of Crimea, a position that was highly unpopular.[61]

The surge in support for Vladimir Putin that followed the annexation of Crimea forced many liberals to face the enormous gulf that separated them from the public. As the Christian humanist poet Olga Sedakova (b. 1949) put it: "The feeling of complete mental derangement arose at the moment of all this story about Crimea. Until then, there remained some illusions. That on the one hand there were the authorities, and on the other hand the people. . . . But during and after the Crimean epic we saw that the authorities' actions fully corresponded to the aspirations of the people. . . . Indeed, the great majority of the people truly support the authorities. . . . It was, of course, a difficult revelation."[62]

This revelation led some to conclude that Russia's problems went far beyond Putin and lay in the psychological failings of the Russian people, that allegedly "can be explained, at least partially, by the Freudian inferiority complex concept, as a form of psychological compensation."[63] Sergei Medvedev, for instance, argues that the public celebrations over Crimea demonstrated an "inferiority complex" and the "morals of slaves," in other words "the slave's hatred of everything that looks to him like freedom."[64]

Such thinking reflects what has been called the "Two Russias" theory.[65] In this, the mass of the people are viewed as "zombified" by state-controlled mass media, and they are contrasted with "the informed intelligentsia," which has the role of "spreading real understanding among those groups of the population who are ready to listen."[66] As Nemtsov described it, "The Russian people, for the most part, are divided into two uneven groups. One part is the descendants of serfs, people with a slavish consciousness. There are very many of them and their leader is V. V. Putin. The other (smaller) part is born free, proud and independent. It does not have a leader but needs one."[67]

The Two Russias theory reflects contemporary Russian liberalism's social base, which rests largely on the so-called creative class, defined as "a strange unity of software engineers, intellectuals, scholars/scientists, architects, designers, university professors, people of art—in a word, those selling the product of their creative activity."[68] The values and priorities of this class are far removed from those of the rest of the population. After Western states imposed sanctions against Russia following the annexation of Crimea, the Russian government introduced countersanctions that included banning the import of certain luxury Western goods, including European cheeses. Liberals were indignant. Sergei Medvedev complained: "Among the losses of recent years—the free press, fair elections, an independent court—what has hurt especially hard has been the disappearance of good cheese . . . a piece of brie, a bottle of Italian chianti and a warm baguette . . . drew him [the Russian] close to Western values and were acts of social modernization. . . . Striking against cheese was equivalent to a strike against the quasi-Western idea of normality."[69]

Similarly, in a 2015 article, Masha Gessen (b. 1967) lamented the loss of Western cheeses in Russia but found consolation in the fact that they could still be purchased at the Caviar House and Prunier Seafood Bar in a departure lounge at London's Heathrow airport. She wrote:

> "It's my first time in Europe after all that's happened," the journalist and filmmaker Inna Denisova, a critic of the annexation of Crimea, wrote on her Facebook page in February. "And it's exceedingly emotional. And of course it's not seeing the historic churches and museums that has made me so emotional—it's seeing cheese at the supermarket. My little Gorgonzola. My little mozzarella. My little Gruyère, chèvre and Brie. I held them all in my arms—I didn't even want to share them with the shopping cart—and headed for the cash register." There, Ms. Denisova wrote, she started crying.[70]

The liberal intelligentsia is well aware of the social gulf separating it from the bulk of the Russian population. Irina Prokhorova (b. 1956), editor of the liberal journal *Novoe Literaturnoe Obozrenie* (New literary review), remarks that "I often go to conferences and meetings and one thing always strikes me: the enormous snobbery of intellectuals and their adhesion to stereotypes. . . . Somewhat simplified, the stereotypes are the following: our society is talentless and incapable of anything; nobody listens or values us intellectuals; and consequently, the situation is completely hopeless."[71]

Examples of such stereotypes abound. "The Russian form of slavery has been fixed at the mental level, in the soul," wrote Nemtsov.[72] "Why do the people vote for the authorities?" asked Valeria Novodvorskaya, answering, "The psychology of beggars. . . . And if this people dies out, then, quite honestly, to hell with it."[73] For Sergei Medvedev, the Russian "mass consciousness" is "embittered, alienated and provincial," "undeveloped," "archaic and superstitious."[74] Former diplomat Andrei Kovalyov (b. 1953) states that "Russia is sick. Its illness is complex and psychosomatic in character. This presents itself, among other ways, as manic-depressive psychosis accompanied by acute megalomania, persecution complex, and kleptomania, all compounded by dystrophy."[75] And Dmitry Gubin writes: "Alas I don't love the Russian people. . . . If the main instrument of survival in the West is a struggle for one's rights, for the Russian population it is conformism, opportunism, and doublethink. . . . If the people were given their freedom, they'd turn America into atomic ash, restore the death penalty and imprison all the liberasts and anyone who simply has any brains."[76]

Sedakova argues that the causes of the people's "mental derangement" can be found in Russian religious thought, in particular "an inability to distinguish between good and evil."[77] Whereas the West has a "simple" understanding of good and evil, seeing the two as distinct, the Russian concept is more "complex" and may even be described as a "friendship with evil," she says.[78] Inclined to "love the prisoner, pity the criminal, and show mercy to the fallen," Russians refuse to admit the existence of absolute good or absolute evil, resulting in "moral relativism" and toleration of repressive government.[79]

Others blame the trauma of seventy years of communist rule. Andrei Kovalyov remarks that "the communist regime brainwashed an inert people. . . . Sadomasochistic perversions became the norm of life in Russia."[80] Such arguments fit well with the concept of *homo sovieticus*, an idea kept alive by sociologist Lev Gudkov (b. 1946), who states that "the main obstacle for Russia's modernization is the type of soviet or post-soviet man (*homo sovieticus*)—his basic social distrust, his experience of adaptation to violence—that makes him incapable of understanding more complex moral/ethical views and relationships, which, in turn, makes the institutionalization of new social forms of interaction impossible."[81]

The thesis that that the alleged psychological deficiencies derive from the communist legacy leads to the conclusion that more must be done to decommunize Russian society. Sedakova comments that in the 1990s, "many opportunities were missed. The first of these, in my opinion, was finally ridding ourselves of the Soviet past. . . . If the past had been called by its proper name—criminal—the problems of the time of troubles would perhaps have been endured differently."[82] "What is needed is nothing less than a cultural or, rather, moral revolution," she concludes.[83] Sergei Medvedev argues that "the cancerous tumor of Stalinism . . . must be cut out from all organs of state control; the crimes of the past should be reflected in our history books, in declarations by our political leaders, decisions of the courts, national memorials and labor camp museums."[84] Likewise, Yabloko's 2016 election program stated that "overcoming Stalinism and Bolshevism in Russia must be accomplished as deeply and responsibly as de-Nazification after the Second World War." The program continued: "The Bolshevik dictatorship stopped the natural historical development of our country, and for many decades tore Russia from the general European path of civilizational development. . . . A complex of measures should be implemented to eradicate the Stalinist-Bolshevik system of state government. . . . We should pursue a consistent policy of cleansing towns, streets and squares of the names of state leaders, organizers, and active participants in terror. . . . The old names, laid down during the centuries of Russian history, should be restored."[85]

Similarly, the liberal People's Freedom Party (PARNAS), set up in 2010 by former members of the URF, declares: "Russia must free itself from immortalizing the memory of the executioners of many peoples and from the symbols of the communist regime. . . . The historic names of streets and towns should be restored, or new ones given. Any propaganda of the communist regime, its leaders and symbols should be prohibited by law."[86]

The envisaged decommunization is difficult, because many Russians see the Soviet past as including enormous achievements as well as enormous crimes. A particular source of pride is the Soviet victory in the Second World War. In recent years, celebrations of Victory Day (May 9) have become increasingly popular, with many Russians wearing the orange and black ribbon of the St. George's medal. The government has coopted this and other symbols, turning Victory Day into a means of legitimizing the state. Consequently, many liberals have turned against it. Sergei Medvedev, for instance, writes that "over the years . . . I realized that 9 May had ceased to exist as a national holiday [for me]," especially because of the St. George ribbon and "the cult surrounding it, poured out in a flood of banality and jingoism."[87] Kashin also denounces the "cult" of Victory Day, writing: "Once it gets rid of Putin . . . Russia will be forced to say goodbye to the St. George ribbon and to 'Thank you, grandad' and military songs and the old soldiers' blouses. By playing with historical legitimacy, today's Kremlin guarantees that in the future we will revise all the sacred objects which seem incontestable today."[88]

In some cases, liberals' efforts to disassociate themselves from the Soviet victory in the Second World War has taken them so far as to defend Russians who collaborated with the Nazis. Film director Grigory Amnuel (b. 1957), for instance, has defended members of the Lokot Republic, a collaborationist autonomous zone established in central Russia under German supervision during the war.[89] Similarly, Nikita Sokolov (b. 1957), deputy director of the Yeltsin Center in Ekaterinburg, "pressed for the rehabilitation of General Andrey Vlasov," a Soviet officer who following his capture by the Germans established a collaborationist anti-Soviet Russian army.[90] Vlasov was also the subject of a sympathetic book by the former mayor of Moscow, Gavriil Popov. Popov wrote: "I was not at the trial that called you, Andrei Andreevich [Vlasov], a traitor. But I was in that hall of the Grand Kremlin Palace, where thousands of people's deputies of the USSR . . . squealed, screamed, raged—condemning Andrei Dmitrievich Sakharov, who was standing on the rostrum, as a traitor. There I finally realized that there are situations when, only by becoming a traitor in the eyes of the ruling class and the part of the masses manipulated by it, is it possible to remain a true, real Citizen and Patriot."[91]

The logic here appears to be that since the Soviet victory over the Nazis plays such an important role in perpetuating positive views of the Soviet era, and since such positive views are said to be the greatest stumbling block to

Russia's cultural advancement, it is necessary to delegitimize the victory, which in turn leads to sympathy for Nazi collaborators. It must be noted that the number of people expressing such sympathy is few, but the fact that they include some prominent personalities has allowed political opponents to seize on their statements and use them to denounce liberals as a whole as "Vlaso-vites," in other words as Nazi-sympathizing traitors. Liberals' opposition to the annexation of Crimea has had a similar effect. As a member of Yabloko's political committee, Anatoly Rodionov (b. 1948), told his colleagues during a party debate on the subject of Crimea: "Russian society has said 'No, Crimea is ours, and Yabloko is not ours.' You understand, this is what has happened. We shouldn't fool ourselves. We have crossed a red line separating society's understanding . . . from society's hostility. . . . I think there's been a sort of ethical glitch. We've taken the enemy's side."[92]

Whether liberals' attitude to the February 2022 invasion of Ukraine will similarly put them in conflict with the mass of the Russian people remains to be seen, but at present it seems likely. Several months after the invasion, opinion polls showed Putin's rating at a near all-time high, and in a September 2022 survey 72 percent of respondents expressed support for the war in Ukraine.[93] By contrast, many liberal intellectuals vehemently denounced the invasion. Dmitry Muratov, editor of *Novaia Gazeta*, called it "madness."[94] Writing in the online version of the same newspaper, a group of independent liberal journalists declared in an article that was subsequently removed from the internet: "Pain, anger, and shame—these are three words that express our attitude to what has happened. . . . We wish firmness and strength to the people of Ukraine as they resist aggression."[95]

In line with this sentiment, some members of Russia's liberal opposition have urged the West to take action to ensure Russia's military defeat. For instance, the Free Russia Forum, an organization that meets regularly in Lithuania and unites some of the more radical elements of Russia's exiled intelligentsia, issued a statement in September 2022 saying:

> The Free Russia Forum calls on the countries of the Free World to stand firm and stop trying to find a compromise with the Putin regime or "let him get out the situation keeping a face." The Putin regime is the existential enemy of modern civilization. It is possible to eliminate the threat emanating from it only by defeating its war machine and liquidating the regime itself. . . . Today we decide what our world will be like. We must not allow the establishment of a "Putin-style new world order." One has to be willing to pay the price for it. We call for the maximum expansion of military assistance to Ukraine in all its forms.[96]

Defeatism of this sort is a luxury reserved for those in exile. The expression of similar sentiments within Russia itself would be liable to lead to arrest and imprisonment. This is true even of statements that merely oppose the war, without calling for Russia's defeat. Legislation that prohibits the dissemination of "false information" about the armed forces of the Russian Federation has been used to silence critics of the war. An example is TV journalist Marina Ovsyannikova (b. 1978), who was fined and placed under house arrest after she held up a sign in the middle of a news broadcast saying "Stop the war, don't believe the propaganda, they are lying to you here."[97]

Such protests have, however, been rare. The primary form of resistance to the war has been emigration, with tens of thousands of Russians leaving the country in two waves—the first in February 2022, following the start of the war, and the second in September 2022, following the declaration of a partial mobilization. In liberals' eyes, Russia's future looks bleak. As Iulia Latynina declared: "Whatever Ukraine's losses, Russia's will be worse. Everything will fall into the abyss: the ruble, wages, the future. . . . The world is being divided into the free world, where there is an economy, technology, and science, and places like Iran and Russia, where there is only the official ideology of struggle against enemies. . . . What part of Ukraine remains free depends on the Ukrainians. But for Russia, I fear, it's all over. And for a very long time."[98]

Political Liberalism

Putin's first government, in the early 2000s, contained a large number of liberal ministers, especially in positions related to economics. Examples include Mikhail Kasyanov (b. 1957), who was prime minister from 2000 to 2004, and Andrei Illarionov (b. 1961), who served as economic adviser to Putin from 2000 to 2005. Over time, the number of so-called systemic liberals has declined. These who remain include: Aleksei Kudrin (b. 1960), who was finance minister from 2000 to 2011, and has been head of the Accounts Chamber since 2018; Sergei Kirienko (b. 1962), who was briefly prime minister under Yeltsin in 1998 and is currently Putin's first deputy chief of staff; Elvira Nabiullina (b. 1963), the head of the Russian Central Bank; Ella Pamfilova (b. 1953), who served as commissioner of human rights before becoming head of the Central Electoral Commission; and Herman Gref (b. 1964), the head of the state-owned bank Sberbank, who declares "I am a liberal, and I am not ashamed to recognize myself as a liberal. I am an absolute liberal in the economy."[99] Riccardo Mario Cucciolla notes that "the system liberals are technically competent, and more open to integration with the global economy and adoption of international rules. Nevertheless, they are cogs in the state machine and will not promote regime change or rapid democratization in Russia."[100]

The issue of whether to cooperate with the state has proven a difficult one for liberals under Putin, and their attitudes have varied. In a 2002 interview, Boris Nemtsov noted that many in the URF wanted to work with the government but he argued against it on the grounds that it would have a negative impact on the party's support.[101] Yabloko was initially ready to work with Putin, adopting the concept of "constructive opposition." In September 2003 Yavlinsky said that the party was "prepared and willing to cooperate in areas where there is mutual understanding between us."[102] Similarly in March 2008, he told party members: "We must engage in dialogue with the authoritarian government in all acceptable political forms."[103] Since then, however, Yabloko's position has hardened, and in 2020 Yavlinsky remarked that "the democratic opposition should not take on the role of adviser or consultant to the authorities."[104] To many in the liberal opposition, the Russian state is anathema. "Cooperation with the authorities is simply dishonorable," says Sedakova.[105]

The liberal opposition is, however, deeply fragmented. At the start of Putin's rule there were two main liberal parties—the URF and Yabloko. Together, the two parties won some 14 percent of the vote in the December 1999 Duma elections. However, in the next elections, in 2003, both parties failed to cross the 5 percent threshold required to secure seats in that half of the chamber elected via party lists. Half the seats in the Duma are assigned via party list and half elected directly. Since 2003, if one excludes the New People party in 2021 (see Conclusion), liberals have entirely failed to win any of the party list seats, and just a handful have been elected directly (in 2021, for instance, just two liberals were directly elected—Boris Titov [b. 1960] of the Party of Growth and Rifat Shaykhutdinov [b. 1963] of Civic Platform).

One reason for the liberals' electoral defeats has been loss of access to the mass media. This was a by-product of Putin's decision during his first term to eliminate the political power of the oligarchs. A first step in this direction involved the issuing of an arrest warrant for Vladimir Gusinsky on charges of money laundering, in response to which Gusinsky left the country. The state then took over control of Gusinsky's MOST media company, including the NTV television station, which had often taken a broadly liberal, antigovernment line. Another oligarch, Boris Berezovsky, also went into exile and sold his share in Russia's top TV channel ORT to billionaire Roman Abramovich (b. 1966), who in turn sold it to the Russian state.

The next target was Mikhail Khodorkovsky and his company, Yukos. The latter had used its money to buy political influence, funding the URF, Yabloko, and the Communist Party. In return for Yukos funding, Yabloko included three of the company's officials in its party list for the 2003 State Duma elections. Yavlinsky remarked, "That was Yukos's condition for funding our party. We accept that condition and we believe that this open policy is right."[106]

Yukos also resorted to even more unsavory methods. In the early 2000s, Aleksei Kudrin and Herman Gref sought to increase taxes on the resource extraction industry. The independent media outlet *Meduza* records that,

> according to Gref, major oil companies were not happy with the proposal. He says, "a representative of the company Yukos" approached him on the night before the new law was to be discussed by the Duma and told him that they'd made an agreement with all the deputies. As a result, the ministers were given a choice: they could either not take the proposal to parliament, or they could "be taken out [feet first]," after which the company would demand their resignation from Putin "due to professional incompetence." Gref called Kudrin and found out that he'd also been visited and threatened. . . . In the end, the legislation failed miserably.[107]

Following the assault on the oligarchs' power, liberals' access to the mass media, especially television, declined significantly. In addition, liberal political parties have had considerable difficulties in registering candidates for elections, with local electoral commissions regularly rejecting attempts to register candidates on what many consider to be dubious grounds.[108] Meanwhile, since 2012, media outlets and nongovernmental organizations (NGOs) have been obliged to register as "foreign agents" if they receive any foreign funding. Most dramatically, in 2021, Russia's best-known human rights organization, Memorial, was forced to shut down after alleged breaches of the law on foreign agents. Other opposition organizations, such as Navalny's Anti-Corruption Foundation and Khodorkovsky's Open Russia, have also been banned on the grounds of being "undesirable" or "extremist."

A few liberal media outlets and political parties have continued to operate. Until February 2022, the primary liberal media outlets were the newspaper *Novaia Gazeta*, the online TV station Dozhd (Rain), and the radio station Ekho Moskvy.[109] In 2021, *Novaia Gazeta*'s editor Dmitry Muratov was awarded the Nobel Peace Prize. The prize's website notes that Muratov is "a leading advocate for democracy and freedom of expression in Russia" and that under his leadership "*Novaia Gazeta* has criticized the Russian authorities for corruption, electoral fraud and human rights violations."[110] Following the invasion of Ukraine, both Dozhd and Ekho Moskvy were banned, and *Novaia Gazeta* chose to cease publication due to the restrictions placed on it, although it has since restarted publication in Latvia.

With limited access to traditional media, opposition groups have made considerable use of the internet and social media, which until the February 2022 invasion of Ukraine were relatively free of censorship. Navalny has been particularly active on social media, using YouTube to post videos exposing official corruption, and mobilizing protests via platforms such as Twitter, Instagram, TikTok, and Telegram.[111] In part, this strategy is a matter of necessity, but it also reflects a deep faith in the transformative power of modern information technologies. In line with this, in the early 2010s Navalny's assistant Leonid Volkov promoted the concept of "cloud democracy." According to Volkov and coauthor Fyodor Krasheninnikov (b. 1976), cloud democracy is an "ideology of direct, digital democracy," with "large potential for the transformation of the fundamental system of relations in society."[112] They wrote: "There is a real technological alternative [to representative democracy]. . . . We see the possibility that any citizen can take part in direct electronic democracy; the practice of mouse-clicking in political computer games half an hour on Saturdays and Sundays can become part of our everyday life, and totally change our societal life."[113] As they had to admit, however, they could "not precisely determine" how this would work in practice.[114]

The decline of the liberal media in Russia points to the weakness of liberal civil society in the country. Russia does have a vast number of voluntary associations, including trade unions, environmental groups, charitable organizations, church groups, and others. During Putin's first two terms as president (2000–2008), "the number of non-governmental organizations expanded from 100,000 to more than 600,000, with at least another 600,000 active unofficially. . . . More than ten million Russians are involved in some form [of] organized volunteer activity."[115] But while civil society in the form of citizens organizing themselves independently of the state is thriving, organizations devoted to the promotion of liberal causes (human rights, democracy, and so on) are doing less well.

Under Putin, the Russian state has sought simultaneously to encourage and to coopt civil society. In June 2001, Putin met representatives of civil society organizations and proposed a dialogue between them and the government. The result was the convening of a civic forum of about 5,000 civil society representatives in November 2001.[116] Some human rights activists, such as former dissidents Sergei Kovalyov and Liudmila Alekseeva, chose to attend the forum.[117] Others, however, refused to participate, with one critic, scientist Leonid Radzikhovsky (b. 1953), denouncing it as "a profanation."[118]

Liberal civil society views its role as including criticizing the state and holding it to account. Organizations that expose official abuses of human rights, and that seek to bring those responsible to justice by means of the courts, are a case in point. A much larger part of civil society, however, is either entirely apolitical or supportive of the state, and sees it role as working with it to achieve common goals. Charities, for instance, cooperate with local authorities in order to carry out their work effectively, and therefore tend to eschew confrontational politics.

Putin's strategy has been to undermine the organizations that are critical while encouraging those that are quiescent. As Kirsti Stuvøy notes, "the state encourages those elements of civil society that it considers helpful to its mission of establishing a civil society that collaborates . . . supporting 'harmless' or pro-government civil society organisations while suppressing or obstructing others."[119] Stuvøy continues: "The Russian government [has] emphasized the role of civil society in the modernization of Russia and, in 2010, introduced presidential grants and other funding opportunities for civil society. The state concern with civil society development also led to the initiation of consultative bodies, among them the so-called 'public chambers' comprising civil society representatives whose role is to provide a public point of view in the policy process . . . [the] aim [is] to ensure civil society is heard. . . . Thus, the Russian state nurtures a specific form of institutionalized civil society."[120]

But whereas Moscow encourages civil society as a whole, it has imposed severe restrictions on those civil society groups that directly challenge it, making it harder and harder for them to operate. Particularly important in this regard was the 2012 legislation obliging organizations that received foreign funding to register as "foreign agents." In general, Russian NGOs have difficulty raising money from domestic sources, and liberal civil society has tended to rely heavily on Western funding as well as Western training. Increasing political tensions between Russia and the West have led the Russian state to view such Western-financed organizations as a fifth column aimed at inspiring a revolution. The preferences of Western donors have to some degree played into this narrative. Stuvøy divides Russian NGOs into the "principled," who condemn state policies and urge the West to pressure Russia to change its ways, and the "pragmatists," who work with the state to achieve their missions.[121] The European Union (EU), Stuvøy notes, quite specifically targets its support at "non-pro-regime" NGOs (i.e., "principled" ones) while not providing any support to the "pragmatists." This reinforces the impression that the EU's aid is fundamentally political in nature, and raises the question of whether foreign funding of this sort may have been counterproductive.[122]

Alfred Evans complains that the product of Putin's policy is not a true civil society but rather a "quasi-civil society."[123] Others argue that even this quasi-civil society retains a fair degree of agency, although it does not always act for what one might deem liberal purposes. For instance, the war between Russia and Ukraine that started in February 2022 has prompted the creation of a large number of citizen-led groups dedicated to providing support to Russian soldiers. Meanwhile, war correspondents and military bloggers (some of whom have hundreds of thousands of followers on the Telegram social media app) have been scathing in their criticisms of the Russian state. It is notable, however, that their criticisms are directed not at the war itself (which they support) but at the state's incompetent handling of it, and they argue not that the war should be ended but that it should be prosecuted more vigorously.[124] They also tend to be not merely illiberal but also forcefully antiliberal, regarding their country's liberals as something akin to traitors. In Russia's case, the idea that civic institutions help to build a liberal order has not been validated.

The difficulties faced by liberal civil society are mirrored in the travails of liberal political parties, none of which have performed well in the Putin years. The primary liberal political party throughout this period has been Yabloko. Its 2012 program outlined its principles in the following terms: "Human dignity and respect for the person and the family are the unshakeable foundation of the social-political and state order in Russia. . . . It is necessary to create a democratic alternative to the regime. . . . The main thing is a really working system of regular and inevitable transfer of power, a principled rejection of populism, nationalism and force, and the guarantee of citizens' practical participation in running the country."[125]

Yabloko is not the political force it once was. In the 2021 election, it received only about 1 percent of the vote. The party nevertheless remains active. The same is not true for the URF, which disbanded in 2008. Systemic liberals within it formed a new party—Right Cause—sometimes described as "Kremlin friendly."[126] Meanwhile, opposition liberals from URF created a new organization known as Solidarity. A loose coalition of antigovernment forces, Solidarity focused largely on street protests.[127] In December 2010 Nemtsov and others formed PARNAS. The Justice Ministry refused to register PARNAS, as a result of which it merged with the Republican Party of Russia (RPR) to form RPR-PARNAS.[128] The party has not been a success. In 2015, PARNAS agreed on a joint platform with Navalny for the 2015 municipal elections and 2016 Duma elections.[129] However, the group was able to register candidates in only one region—Kostroma—where it gathered a mere 2 percent of the vote. The coalition collapsed soon afterward, following the leak of a sex tape involving PARNAS leader Mikhail Kasyanov.[130] PARNAS did not compete in the 2021 Duma elections.

Various other liberal parties have appeared over the years. These include Civic Platform, founded in 2012 by businessman Mikhail Prokhorov (b. 1965), and the Party of Growth, led by the presidential commissioner for entrepreneurs' rights, Boris Titov. The Party of Growth describes itself as representing the interests of business and states that its values are "sacred rights of property; the supremacy of law that ensures human freedom; a market economy and laissez-faire as the basis for the economic existence of society."[131] The party won 0.5 percent of the vote in the 2021 Duma election.

All attempts to unify the liberal opposition have failed. Differences over tactics and ideology play a part. So do personal animosities. In 2002, oligarch Boris Berezovsky sought to create his own liberal political party and issued a "manifesto of Russian liberalism" in *Nezavisimaia Gazeta* (Independent newspaper). This took a somewhat libertarian position, arguing that "the authorities objectively must limit their citizens' activities, but these limitations should be minimal, aiming to increase the possibilities for the self-realization of the person."[132] Others in the liberal camp did not appreciate Berezovsky's efforts. Nemtsov declared: "Telling voters that they should vote for Boris Abramovich Berezovsky is like suggesting that they soap the rope and hang themselves right there in the voting booth."[133]

Nemtsov was equally critical of Yabloko. "Yabloko is not a reformist group. . . . It is a party of the impoverished intelligentsia, just as the Communists are the party of poor people. . . . We are closer to Yabloko on political issues, but we disagree with them on their stupid economic policies."[134] Explaining why the URF and Yabloko had failed to unite, Nemtsov pointed the finger of blame firmly at Yavlinsky. "The answer is obvious to me: personal ambitions," he wrote.[135]

Yavlinsky in turn complained that the URF "positioned themselves not as a right-liberal party that defends human rights but as a party that defends, in words anyway, the principles of private property. A party that defends private property but does not defend human rights is a party that traditionally falls into the category of totalitarian and profascist."[136] Yavlinsky has used similar language about Navalny, writing: "Navalny's political direction is populism and nationalism. If the mob follows Navalny, the country can expect fascism."[137] In return, Navalny has sharply criticized Yabloko. The party's candidates, he told an interviewer, were "unpleasant people."[138]

The divisions among liberals reflect differences of opinion over tactics, stemming from different understandings of what is wrong with Russia. For more radical liberals, Russia's fundamental problem is that the state has been usurped by a small and corrupt elite. Leonid Gozman (b. 1950), writing with Swedish economist Anders Åslund (b. 1952), comments that "Russia's main problem at present is that the state has been captured by a small group of top officials."[139] As described in the previous section, others see the fundamental issue as being the defective psychology of the masses. For others still, Russia's difficulties lie in the economic-political system created under Yeltsin. As Yavlinsky puts it: "In the process of the reforms of the 1990s . . . a system was created on the basis of the merging of property and power that doesn't allow the existence of an independent judiciary, independent media, a real parliament, and honest elections. Without a categorical separation of property and business from power . . . the struggle against corruption is impossible."[140]

Those who view the state as being usurped by a small elite think that the solution is to throw that elite out of power. Khodorkovsky writes that "revolution in Russia is inevitable. . . . Wanting revolution is in general unnatural . . . but now it's too late; it is necessary, like a surgeon needs a knife."[141] What will come after the revolution is not clear. In this regard, it is notable that Navalny has often been criticized for failing to produce a detailed political platform.[142] His movement is characterized by activism—opposing and overthrowing the existing authorities are its raisons d'être.

Since radical liberals are focused on overthrowing the government, they are often willing to make common cause with nonliberals who share the same goal. For instance, Solidarity allied with the National Bolshevik Party, despite its fascist iconography, on the grounds that "my enemy's enemy is my friend." Kasparov said, "Eduard Limonov's National Bolshevik Party . . . wasn't as scary as the name sounds by the 2000s but was still more than enough to scare off the respectable liberal opposition, but they were willing to march against Putin for free speech and fair elections, and that was all that mattered to me."[143]

Similar logic lay behind a tactical voting scheme known as "smart voting" promoted by Navalny during the 2021 Duma election. This identified the candidates who were most likely to defeat those of the pro-Putin United Russia (UR) party and urged voters to cast their ballots for those candidates. In the majority of constituencies, the party most likely to defeat UR was the CPRF. For the most part, therefore, voting "smart" meant voting communist. Only in a few cases did smart voting recommend liberal candidates, such as those of Yabloko.

Despite this, some liberals lent it their support. Economist Sergei Guriev (b. 1971) remarked that "voting in accordance with the recommendations of 'smart voting' is the most effective blow against the Russian authorities—even if they are people who support Stalin or are open homophobes and racists." Fellow economist Konstantin Sonin (b. 1972) stated, "I believe that it's possible to vote for a Stalinist and for a pedophile, for whoever. Because, I say, it's a means of screaming out." And Iulia Latynina argued: "Smart voting shows you not how to vote for decent people but how to most effectively express your distrust in the authorities. And yes, in the conditions created by the authorities that can sometimes mean voting for vampires."[144]

Yabloko rejects the tactics of the radical opposition. Its 2016 program stated that "the social order and political regime cannot be changed in an instant.

We must do everything to achieve changes . . . in an evolutionary manner. . . . We are against any attempt to decide political problems by forceful or bloody means. We are against revolution and radicalism of any sort."[145] A resolution by the party's political committee in October 2021 similarly stated that "calls to 'smash the regime' . . . lead only to an increase in the number of arrests, thousands of court cases, social disillusionment, . . . and as a result, to the strengthening of Putin's system. . . . It is completely obvious to us that in Russia you can't change power and its course from the streets."[146]

Along the same lines, Yabloko's former president Sergei Mitrokhin says that "the revolutionary scenario is unacceptable for Russia because Russia is the biggest country in the world, with the longest borders, and large ethnic and confessional diversity. . . . Any revolution could lead to our country's disintegration."[147] Likewise, Yavlinsky objected to the street protests that followed Navalny's arrest at the start of 2021, saying: "The main result of this protest activity is a growth in the number of people arrested and of political prisoners. . . . Yet another cycle of street actions is the path to even greater disillusionment."[148]

Many liberals also objected to the smart voting scheme. Dmitry Muratov complained that telling him to vote for communists was telling him to vote "for Stalin."[149] And Yabloko's political committee denounced smart voting as "extremely dangerous. . . . Communists in contemporary Russia are not opponents but close allies of the aggressive-repressive authorities. . . . They fully share Putin's imperial, revanchist foreign policy line as well as a neo-Stalinist internal policy line."[150]

Differences also exist regarding the ideal form of the Russian state. Liberal authoritarianism has retained some supporters, an example being Latynina, who argues that "it's not enough to be a dictatorship, it's necessary to be a good dictatorship, like in Singapore or Chile and not like in the Philippines or Haiti."[151] Similarly, Vladimir Pastukhov writes, "Before occupying oneself with modernization, industrialization, liberalization, democratization, and God knows what else, society needs to rid itself of criminal tutelage, to throw off the mafia yoke oppressing all productive forces." "The path to democracy lies through dictatorship," he says.[152]

This is very much a minority view. The overwhelming majority of contemporary Russian liberals take the view that "democratization is inevitable and necessary for our country."[153] A consensus has emerged in recent years in favor of replacing the presidential system created in 1993 with a parliamentary one.[154] For instance, Igor Kliamkin, who in the late 1980s had been a supporter of a "strong hand," now declares that "for a long time I have considered that the supremacy of law cannot be guaranteed in conditions of a constitutional presidential monopoly of power, like in Russia. . . . Without constitutional reform and a real division of power into independent branches, it will be impossible to move toward a law-based state."[155] Likewise, Khodorkovsky writes that "Russia has no alternative to democracy. . . . The best way of achieving it is moving to a parliamentary democracy."[156] And Vladimir Inozemtsev (b. 1968) opines: "The only way to deal with the current situation is to dismantle it completely—to make Russia a parliamentary instead of a presidential republic; to restore federalism in its true form and delegate powers to regional and local authorities."[157]

Liberal political parties share this view. PARNAS states: "We support a parliamentary state, in which the government is formed by the parliament and is responsible to it."[158] And Yabloko declares that "fundamental political reform is necessary, changing the balance between the executive, the president, and the parliament in favor of the latter," so that the government would be responsible to the parliament not to the president.[159] The party's program says that the first step in reforming the country needs to be the creation of "a government enjoying the confidence of the people," after which a constitutional assembly should be summoned with the aim of "creating a law-based and social state, limiting the executive branch of government, and separating the state from business."[160]

The rule of law, including the creation of a truly independent judiciary, remains another liberal demand. The record of the Russian state in this regard is mixed. On the one hand, politically motivated trials such as those of Khodorkovsky and Navalny have highlighted a lack of independence of the courts. On the other hand, the past twenty years have witnessed a number of liberal judicial reforms. During Putin's first term in office these included the introduction of jury trials and of a system of justices of the peace (JP) and arbitration courts. Nicolai Petro notes that "during Putin's second term, courts struck down compensation limits for government negligence, strengthened the rights of defendants to exculpatory evidence, provided clearer guidelines on secrecy, and ruled that compensation must be paid to persons who are arrested without merit. Closed judicial proceedings and pretrial detention centers have been all but eliminated, privacy protections for individuals expanded, and 24,000 free legal aid centers created."[161]

Kathryn Hendley comments that the JP courts "have benefited litigants by making courts more accessible."[162] The number of cases heard by the arbitration courts, mainly tax disputes, has increased dramatically, which "indicates that citizens are becoming less tentative about suing the state." The courts tend to judge in favor of the petitioner, meaning that citizens generally win when they challenge the authorities. As Hendley says, this "contradict[s] the common wisdom that [the courts] are in the pocket of the state."[163] "The institutional progress cannot be dismissed as mere window dressing," she remarks. "After all, the vast majority of the millions of cases heard each year within the Russian judicial system are resolved on the basis of the law on the books, as interpreted by the judge, and without any interference from political authorities."[164]

Liberalization has also occurred in the area of criminal law, following the introduction of a new criminal code that came into effect in 2002, that required the police "to obtain warrants for investigative activities that previously could be carried out without judicial supervision. The code also limits the circumstances under which the accused may be kept in pretrial detention."[165] Further amendments to the criminal code in 2012 reduced punishments for minor offences and replaced imprisonment with fines or community work.[166] A study of criminal justice legislation from August 2014 to August 2016 found that most draft laws "proposed strengthening of criminal liability," but that laws on criminal procedure for the most part "expand[ed] the procedural guarantees of the rights of suspects, the accused, persons on trial, and victims."[167] The overall effect of these reforms has been a dramatic decrease in the Russian prison population, which has shrunk by 50 percent over the past twenty years, although it remains high by European standards.[168]

As access to the courts has become easier, liberal NGOs have made increasing use of them. Mary McAuley remarks that law became "the key instrument" for promoting human rights under Putin.[169] She notes that between 2003 and 2011, the Committee Against Torture "won 77 cases against police officers for torture," and the NGO Public Verdict "won 60 cases."[170] Igor Kalyapin of the NGO Nizhny Novgorod Human Rights comments, "I am continually amazed by the fact that the cornerstone or, more properly, the basic instrument with which we work is the courts. . . . About 70 percent of our claims are granted by the court."[171] The issue of the rule of law illustrates the complexity of modern Russia, in which liberalizing measures have taken place alongside the consolidation of methods of arbitrary government. Hendley concludes: "The contemporary Russian legal system is best conceptualized as a dual system, under which mundane cases are handled in accordance with the prevailing law, but under which the outcomes of cases that attract the attention of those in power can be manipulated to serve their interests. To put it more simply, justice is possible and maybe even probable, but cannot be guaranteed."[172]

Social-Economic Liberalism

Putin began his time in office with a reputation as an economic liberal. Writing in 2004, liberal politician Vladimir Ryzhkov (b. 1966) described the president as "a staunch fan of the market economy," who "vehemently rejects such communist tenets as state planning, economic self-isolation, and opposition to the market and private property."[173] Indeed, Putin's first government introduced a series of important reforms. These included the introduction of a flat income tax rate of 13 percent, a reduction in corporate tax rates, a new labor code, a new land code that "allowed land to be sold for the first time," the breaking up of the state electricity monopoly UES, and reductions in the number of business activities requiring licenses.[174]

Thereafter, liberalization stalled. A key moment was 2005, when the government attempted to monetize social benefits. In the Soviet Union, certain social groups, such as pensioners and war veterans, were entitled to a number of benefits, such as free use of public transportation and subsidized housing. In 2005 the government proposed to replace these benefits with cash grants.[175] The result was large-scale protests. In response, Putin offered concessions, such as increasing pensions and providing more money to regional governments. Proposed pension reform was postponed.[176]

Following the global financial crash of 2008, the Russian government made a final effort to liberalize the economy, announcing a plan to privatize state assets worth $30 billion between 2011 and 2013. In an article entitled "Our Economic Tasks," Putin declared his intention to substantially cut the state sector, saying that "privatization will have not a financial but a structural character," with the aim of increasing competition.[177] In practice, the pace of privatization remained slow, in part due to lobbying by managers of state companies, and the state raised only 21 percent of the amount of money planned.[178]

Putin's rhetoric has remained largely promarket. In December 2015 he declared that "freedom for development in the economic and social spheres, for public initiatives, is the best possible response both to any external restrictions and to our domestic problems."[179] In January 2016 he denounced communist economic planning, saying that despite its achievements it ultimately led to "economic collapse."[180] And in a speech on April 21, 2021, Putin rejected the idea of imposing price controls in response to the COVID-19 pandemic. He said: "We are now facing price hikes that are undercutting peoples' incomes . . . but we cannot rely solely on targeted and essentially directive measures. We remember potential outcomes. Back in the late 1980s and the 1990s in the Soviet Union, they resulted in empty shelves. . . . The government's goal is to create conditions that . . . thanks to market mechanisms . . . guarantee the predictability of prices and quality replenishment of the domestic market."[181]

There has been a significant disconnect between the liberal tone of Putin's economic rhetoric and the actual direction taken under his leadership. The share of the economy controlled by the state has doubled in the past twenty years.[182] Putin has bet on state-funded national infrastructure projects as the primary tool to stimulate economic growth, while Western sanctions have forced the Russian government to take a more active role in the economy. This has led to criticism from one of the most prominent remaining "systemic" liberals, the head of the Accounts Chamber, Aleksei Kudrin, who has argued that Russia should seek to improve its relations with the West, as on its own it lacks the technological and financial resources it needs for rapid economic growth.[183] According to Kudrin's Center for Strategic Research, "the conflict [between Russia and the United States] . . . is causing a serious shortfall in economic benefits."[184] Kudrin has also expressed doubt about the state-financed national projects that have been the center of Putin's recent economic policy. "National projects will not produce the desired results," he said.[185]

In 2017, Kudrin presented Putin with a plan for Russia's economic development. The main idea was that state funds should be focused on the development of human capital. To this end, Kudrin proposed reducing the amount spent on defense and transferring funds into education and health care.[186] Later, commenting on the economic effects of the COVID-19 pandemic, Kudrin remarked that public-sector companies were "less flexible" than private ones and "highly dependent on the bureaucratic machine." He argued for further privatization. "The financial benefits of privatization cannot be denied," he said.[187] The government has not, however, accepted Kudrin's proposals.[188]

While some economic liberals like Kudrin decided to remain in the system after Putin came to power, most have preferred to be in opposition. As in the 1990s, they can be divided roughly into two groups—those who support radical free market liberalism and those who favor a form of "social" liberalism.

Over time, the ranks of the latter have grown, in large part in acknowledgment of the unpopularity of the former. Kasparov, for instance, remarks that "those like me who favor free markets and an open, Western-leaning society, learned to accept the need for the social and economic stability programs touted by the left."[189] Navalny appears to have learned the same lesson. Having originally been a "market fundamentalist," by 2018 he was being described as someone who "straddles left and right, advocating conventionally pro-business economic policy, including tax cuts and reduced regulation, while also supporting a higher minimum wage and signaling openness to a universal basic income."[190]

Mikhail Khodorkovsky has similarly argued for a shift in policy away from radical free market principles. In a 2004 article, he declared that "Russian liberals . . . turned a blind eye to social realities when they conducted sweeping privatization, ignoring the negative consequences. . . . The stoic fighters for liberalism, who were prepared to die for their ideals, were superseded by effete bohemians who did not even attempt to conceal their indifference towards the fate of ordinary people, the silent masses. . . . Where was big business all this time? Standing shoulder to shoulder with the liberal rulers. We were accomplices in their misdeeds and lies."[191]

According to Khodorkovsky, "Russia must say goodbye to the dream of 'a small state.'"[192] He advocates for social supports to be maintained or raised.[193] "It's utopian to imagine that one can come to power by democratic means by proposing a right wing, even extreme right, partly libertarian agenda, advertising the charms of a 'small state' and the potential of the 'free market,'" he says.[194]

Khodorkovsky's position brings him somewhere close to the Yabloko party, which remains an advocate of social liberalism. The party declares that "not only the rich and strong, but also the poor and weak, have a right to freedom. The latter must have the chance to receive it. This is what distinguishes contemporary—social—liberalism from its radical nineteenth century version. . . . Our orientation is a society of equal opportunities based on the principles of social justice and the social solidarity of the strong and the weak."[195]

To this end, Yabloko proposes "guaranteeing private property . . . creating favorable conditions for investment . . . [an] active struggle with monopolism . . . [the] creation of a reliable system of obligatory state insurance . . . [a] struggle against poverty . . . and raising wages," and notes that it is necessary to create a "postindustrial economy," which requires major investments in education, science, and technology.[196]

Yavlinsky argues that Russia has a system of "peripheral capitalism," characterized by "the absence of self-sufficiency and integral mechanisms for growth in the Russian economy and the high degree of dependence of Russia's economy and business on the nucleus of modern capitalism."[197] He writes: "In the 1990s, a peripheral capitalist system was created in Russia. This is a system that cannot exist on its own, but only as an appendage to a group of leading, better developed nations to supply them with raw materials. . . . Now this peripheral system has cut itself off from the center, thinking that it can survive on its own. So what will happen to the system now? It will wither because it is no longer connected to its core. . . . Our economy fell victim to our foreign policy."[198]

Yabloko's social liberalism has not helped it gather political support. It would appear that many Russians do not distinguish between social liberals and liberals of a more radical free market variety. Until 2008, the main political vehicle of the latter was the URF, whose 2001 political program stated: "Rights and individual freedoms have no point or value where people are deprived of the possibility of securing themselves and their families by means of honest labor and profitable entrepreneurship on the basis of private property, where the institute of private property is not socially recognized and respected, where property is not protected by law. . . . The liberal response to this challenge consists of affirming property rights as sacred and inviolable."[199]

The URF has been described as having been "geared to orthodox 19th century liberalism, which denies the state any role in the economy and lacks a defined social aspect to its goals."[200] With the URF's collapse in 2008, the free market cause has lacked a strong advocate, although both PARNAS and the Party of Growth continue to promote it. The latter uses the slogan "Capitalism Is for Everyone"—the idea being that creating more opportunities for private enterprise will ultimately benefit everybody.[201]

The popularity of radical free market views has declined, even among liberals. Nevertheless, a few continue to espouse them. A notable example is Latynina, who particularly objects to state-funded welfare systems. She writes: "Social justice means that if you have an unemployed drug addict with five children, she will live in a comfortable residence, because you can't let the children suffer, but if you work and have a wife and family . . . the state will take half of what you earn in order to give it to the unemployed drug addict. . . . In my opinion, it's unjust to steal from those who work to give their money to those who do nothing."[202]

Nemtsov was equally suspicious of social welfare programs. He opposed government policies to counter Russia's falling birth rate by providing financial benefits to families with children. "Russia is dying," he wrote, but

> the demographic projects of the authorities will solve nothing. They are giving out 250,000 rubles for the birth of a second child. . . . The fact is that the main beneficiaries . . . will be drunks and the lumpen part of society. This is a huge sum of money for them. The new allowance will also resonate in Muslim regions of Russia, where everyone has lots of kids even without extra money. And so, despite their superficial attractiveness, the authorities' attempts to solve the demographic problem will lead to the alcohol-ization and Islamization of Russia. . . . Instead of building Russia for the hearty and sober, we are building a Russia of drunks and idlers.[203]

Nemtsov's references to Islamization reflects the concern some liberals feel about Russia's Muslim minority, a minority that has become larger under Putin due to immigration from Central Asia. In the 2010s, about ten million immigrants arrived in Russia, mostly coming from other countries of the former Soviet Union to meet Russia's demand for cheap labor.[204] The Russian state has pursued contradictory objectives, flipping back and forth as it has responded to the lobbying efforts of various groups, including business and the security agencies. The government has tried to attract foreign workers by making it easier for them to legally register as residents, but has also thrown up barriers preventing them from doing so.[205] In this way, state policy has managed to be simultaneously liberal and illiberal.

Reactions among liberals have varied. Some such as Navalny have adopted a firm anti-immigration line. Others recognize the economic need for immigration but argue that it needs to be better regulated. In general, though, the issue is not a high priority. Nor do liberals pay a lot of attention to other matters that might fit within the general categories of multiculturalism and identity politics, including gender equality.

Elena Chebankova identifies two main trends in Russian feminism: first, "feminists of equality," who "search for ways to include women within the extant structure of power relations" and who "propose to adopt a gender-blind androgynous society, in which biological differences have no relevance in the course of social, political, and economic affairs"; and second, "feminists of difference," who "claim that there are cases in which differential treatment of the sexes is legitimate and even desirable."[206] Chebankova considers the former to be the more "liberal" of the two, and notes that "feminists of equality usually focus on women's position in business and power institutions," whereas feminists of difference "usually focus on women of lower-income groups."[207] Neither has much political influence.[208] Jan Surman and Ella Rossman note that relations between feminist groups and many liberal oppositionists are poor, to the extent that "feminist groups . . . are . . . dissidents among dissidents," and that "in some regions, local opposition leaders have such a negative attitude towards feminism that according to one of the feminists from Kazan (Tatarstan), the opposition becomes even more of a problem for activists than conservative (i.e. fundamentalist religious) groups."[209]

Gender issues are notably absent from most liberal parties' discourse. An exception is Yabloko, whose 2016 platform contained a section on "gender equality." This said that it was necessary, among other things, "to guarantee the conditions for women's real participation in the activities of state organs and social organizations . . . [for] women's competitiveness in the labor market by teaching them new professions, entrepreneurial activity, overcoming women workers' relative lack of qualifications, overcoming the imbalance in what men and women are paid for labor . . . [and] organizing and developing social services that allow parents to combine the fulfillment of their parental duties with work and social activities."[210]

The Russian government's record on women's rights has been mixed. It was criticized for a 2016 law decriminalizing domestic violence that does not cause seriously bodily harm, but there have been some liberalizing measures promoting women's rights. The Soviets had prohibited women from doing a large number of jobs considered to be potentially harmful to their health. In March 2020, the Labor Ministry reduced the number of such jobs from 456 to 100. Employment still closed to women includes "hazardous chemical handling, diving, mining, welding, firefighting, and working as aviation mechanics." In response to the change, the NGO Anti-Discrimination Center declared that "abolishing the bans on a number of very important and popular professions for women is undoubtedly a positive step, but it is not enough. Our goal is to abolish all discriminatory articles in labor codes and these lists of prohibited professions and types of work for women."[211]

Just as liberals have paid little attention to women's rights, they have also shown little concern for sexual orientation rights, and when they have addressed them, their attitudes have varied. Navalny, for instance, originally opposed same-sex marriage but now supports it.[212] Sergei Medvedev argues that "Russia desperately needs an injection of tolerance in order to defend and publicize the rights of sexual minorities."[213] And Oleg Kashin remarks that "any new president . . . will be forced to start with the rehabilitation of gays. . . . The most savage law is the law concerning the struggle with homosexual propaganda, which . . . legalizes a completely fascist discrimination of a whole category of the country's citizens."[214] Support for minority rights tends to be voiced in terms of economic utility; supporters argue that America has come to lead the world in modern intellectually based industries precisely because of its embrace of multiculturalism.[215] Sergei Medvedev writes: "In post-industrial society an atmosphere that is multinational and tolerant and allows for sexual freedom encourages the flowering of entrepreneurism, innovation and creativity. . . . All the major centers of creating value . . . are marked out by their multiculturalism . . . broadmindedness, and acceptance of variety in ethnicity, race, religion and sexual orientation. . . . In our interdependent world, questions of sex, gender, race and tolerance are no longer matters of ethics or identity, but to do with the economy and the survival of the country in global competition."[216]

Over the past twenty years, support for liberal political parties has steadily declined, while the state has exerted ever more pressure on civil society and the media. "The prospects for liberalism in contemporary Russia are miserable," wrote political scientist Valery Solovey (b. 1960) in 2019.[217] Since then, they have only gotten worse. The February 2022 invasion of Ukraine dealt Russian liberalism a further blow. Russian liberals' dream of a "return to Europe" appears to have been shattered, at least for now.

There are numerous reasons for liberalism's troubles. The first is the public's association of liberalism with the economic and social travails of the

1990s.[218] The second is government repression. As David White says, "The fact that the liberal parties failed to revive their fortunes after 2003 is due, in part, to regime machinations. . . . The liberals are no longer a force in Russian politics because the Kremlin did not want them to be a force."[219] A third reason is the political conflict between Russia and the West. This has weakened the appeal of liberal Westernism while also allowing the authorities to paint liberals as unpatriotic. And fourth, liberals themselves have adopted policies that have alienated them from the general public. According to one survey, the words most associated with liberalism in Russian eyes are: "West, transition, chaos, oligarchs, foreign, unpatriotic, nonconformists, artists, and no respect for Russia's values, traditions and history."[220] Olga Malinova remarks that "the main problem of post-Soviet 'liberalism' is that it doesn't speak in a language comprehensible to fellow citizens." It is, she says, the "ideology of a minority" that is "at best indifferent and at worst hostile to the majority. . . . This clearly expressed antipopulism . . . meets a completely natural reaction from the audience."[221]

The current eclipse of liberalism as a political movement does not necessarily mean that Russians reject liberal values. It has often been argued that Russians dislike liberals while not disliking liberalism. Solovey, for instance, states that: "The main values and ideas of political liberalism—such as checks and balances, an independent judiciary, competitive elections, a multiparty system, civil rights and liberties, and the like—are valued highly by Russians. . . . Russians appear to reject the forms of liberalism while endorsing its political and economic content."[222]

Opinion polls partly bear this out, although only partly. Surveys on democratic values indicate that two-thirds of Russians consider law and order and just courts to be very important. Fifty-two percent consider free elections very important; 42 percent, freedom of speech; 36 percent, an independent press; 30 percent, minority rights; and 26 percent, political opposition.[223] This indicates some support for liberal principles, although the lack of interest in political opposition suggests some limitations to this support. This conclusion is backed up by a 2017 survey, in which Russians stated that the things that most concerned them were their health, their family, their personal security, and social infrastructure, such as roads, shops, and health care. Only 8 percent deemed "participation in social and political life" to be important.[224]

Surveys suggest a preference for a paternalistic state and a rejection of radical free market ideas. In a 2020 poll, 60 percent of respondents supported the idea that the state had a duty to provide citizens with what they need for a dignified life; 49 percent supported the statement that "Our people always need a 'strong hand'"; 31 percent embraced the idea that the state should merely "establish the rules of the game;" and only 7 percent agreed that "the state should interfere in the life and economic activity of citizens as little as possible."[225] In a 2021 survey, 49 percent said that they preferred the "Soviet system as it was until the 1990s," 18 percent the "current system," and only 16 percent "democracy according to the model of Western countries." As regards economic models, 67 percent favored "a system based on state planning and distribution" and only 24 percent a system "founded on private property and market relations."[226] And as far as minority rights are concerned, a 2020 poll concluded that in recent years Russians had become more tolerant of sexual minorities but less tolerant of religious sects. Young Russians were in general more tolerant than older ones.[227]

This last point raises the possibility that Russia may become more liberal as the current younger generation grows up. The evidence for this is somewhat mixed. A 2020 poll of 1,500 Russians aged fourteen to twenty-nine asked them to identify the values that were most important to them. The top response (78 percent) was human rights, followed by security (57 percent), employment (52 percent), economic welfare of citizens (37 percent), equality (31 percent), and democracy (18 percent). However, young Russians' understanding of human rights had a socialist tint to it, with the rights to life and medical care coming top, followed by the right to a fair trial, right to social security, right to education, and the right to free speech, in that order. Of those surveyed, only 12 percent declared themselves "liberals," with 28 percent considering themselves "social democrats" and 16 percent "nationalists." Meanwhile, 58 percent disagreed with the statement that "Russia is a European country," and 80 percent responded that it would be a "bad" thing if a homosexual individual or couple moved into their neighborhood.[228] It would appear that liberalism has its limits even among youth.

None of this means that liberalism in Russia is doomed. The invasion of Ukraine has introduced a new element of uncertainty into Russian politics. It is not entirely impossible that the Ukrainian war could unleash processes that again bring about revolutionary change and allow for a liberal revival. But it could also lead to a further consolidation of authoritarian rule. The most one can say is that the Putin era has not been kind to Russian liberalism, and at the time of writing it is in a very parlous state.

Conclusion

Despite efforts by contemporary Russian historians to depict a distinctive Russian version of liberalism with deep roots in the country's history, it is hard to see a strong connection between the liberalism before and since the Soviet period. Unlike their conservative counterparts, modern Russian liberals do not draw obviously on the philosophical heritage of either the imperial era or the Russian emigration. Still, one can observe certain commonalities across the eras that can help characterize Russian liberalism and explain its apparent failure as a political movement.

The first is its narrow social base. The 1993 State Duma elections marked the all-time peak of liberalism's popularity, with liberal parties winning about a third of the vote between them. For a very short period, liberalism enjoyed wide popular support. This proved to be a blip. Both before and after, liberalism failed to establish deep roots in the Russian population. As the surveys cited at the end of the last chapter show, Russians have some sympathy for liberal principles, but they value other things, such as social stability, more highly, and have tended to reject liberals even when they do not reject liberalism.

One can say, therefore, that one of Russian liberalism's fundamental problems is that it has failed to dispel the impression that it is a movement of intellectuals whose attitudes are far removed from those of ordinary people. This was true of the prerevolutionary Kadet party, which was known as a "party of professors," just as it is true today, when liberals are sometimes disparagingly referred to as *kreakly* (*kreativnye klassy*, creative classes).

In return, the language liberals have used to describe the Russian people has often been contemptuous, as shown by modern discussions of the alleged psychological failings of *homo sovieticus*. Liberals have had a somewhat paradoxical relationship with democracy. They have repeatedly demanded the expansion of civil and political liberties, but they have also on occasion displayed authoritarian tendencies when faced with the reality that giving power to the people can lead to undesired outcomes.

Liberals' relationship with the state has been equally paradoxical. On the one hand, there has been a strong statist trend within Russian liberalism and a desire to avoid revolutionary turmoil. On the other hand, hatred of the state's repressive policies has sometimes induced liberals to throw in their lot with the revolutionaries. The Russian state has rarely made life easy for liberals. In imperial times, state repression took the form of censorship and restrictions on the activities of civil society; in Soviet times, it took even harsher forms—exile, imprisonment, or execution; and in the Putin era it has involved an ever-growing pressure that has squeezed liberals to the margins of political life. Many liberals have concluded that the state is their country's primary problem and that it must be weakened by all means possible. Consequently, Russian liberalism has sometimes taken on a radical tinge, which has even included wishing for Russia's defeat in war, as in 1904–1905 and as also in some circles today.

This has created the impression that liberals lack patriotic feeling, a feeling that is connected to another important feature of Russian liberalism—its pronounced Westernism. Russian liberalism has long contained a strong element of historical determinism. This has led Russian liberals to view history as marching inexorably toward the model of Western liberal democracy, from which "is" liberals have derived the "ought" that Russia should move in the same direction. In recent decades, the demand that Russia "return to European civilization" has been a centerpiece of Russian liberal doctrine.

Russian liberals' overt Westernism has proven to be a political liability. As political tensions between Russia and the West have escalated during the past twenty years, the Russian state has had considerable success in portraying liberals as a traitorous fifth column taking the West's side against Russia. Liberals' response that it is patriotic to oppose a state that is leading the country to ruin has largely fallen on deaf ears. In particular, liberals' rejection of the annexation of Crimea put them in direct opposition to the bulk of the Russian people and severely dented their political prospects.

International trends pose significant problems for Russian liberalism if it continues to associate closely with the West. Actions such as the 2003 Anglo-American invasion of Iraq have deprived the West of some of its moral authority. Meanwhile, the balance of world power is shifting to the East. The rise of China, in particular, poses a challenge to the historical determinist model that sees Western liberal democracy and capitalism as the "End of History," toward which all other countries, including Russia, must inevitably march. The allure of the West may not be quite what it was and this threatens one of Russian liberalism's most important intellectual foundations.

None of this means that liberalism in Russia is doomed. It is not impossible that economic stress due to the Ukrainian war or some other unexpected event could provoke mass protests that topple the government and pave the way for a liberal revival. At present, though, this looks rather unlikely. Having experienced regime change twice in the past century, Russians are perhaps understandably wary of undergoing it again, and they show little interest in political protest.

This may change, but in this regard a comparison with 1917 is useful. In 1917, there was an enthusiasm for revolution in Russia that is almost entirely absent today. Furthermore, liberals were able to take power following the Nicholas II's abdication in March 1917 because they had a powerful presence within the Russian parliament, where they had formed a coalition with moderate conservatives. There was also a strong liberal civil society, elements of which had established good relations with the military high command. This is not the case today. Moreover, after taking power in 1917, liberals soon lost it, in large part due to the fact that they lacked strong roots in the Russian population. Power shifted to organizations that did have such roots and who were able to speak to people in a language they understood. In this regard, liberals are even worse placed than they were 100 years ago. As in 1917 so too today, there are reasons to doubt that the beneficiaries of regime collapse in Russia would be liberals.

Bottom-up liberalization requires some organizational base. At present this is lacking, with the older liberal parties, notably Yabloko, having no realistic prospects of future success. The only semiliberal group to have significant parliamentary representation is the party New People, which in 2021 won just over 5 percent of the national vote. The party's founder, Alexei Nechaev (b. 1966), says, "We aren't liberals [but] democratic values are close to us."[1] The decision to eschew the liberal label may reflect an understanding of its unpopularity more than a rejection of liberal values. The party program calls for the decentralization of power, "political diversity . . . and competition," and "freeing entrepreneurs" from the pressure of the state.[2] But the party specifically states that it aims to work within the political system not to overthrow it. It also avoids overt Westernism and emphasizes that its focus is on local affairs. In this way it stays within the boundaries of what the central authorities will tolerate. Given this, it possibly represents a mechanism through which liberalism can regain a small foothold in Russian politics. It remains to be seen, though, what will become of it.

Overall, the prospects of liberalization driven from the bottom up seem slim. Historically, reform in Russia has rarely come that way. Rather, it has been driven from the top down. In particular, liberal reforms have largely been the product of what are known as "enlightened bureaucrats." They have promoted change not so much out of respect for liberal ideas as out of a recognition that the state would benefit from some degree of liberalization. This was the case during the Great Reforms of the 1860s and in the era of perestroika in the 1980s. In both instances, change came from within the system.

Modern-day equivalents of the enlightened bureaucrats of the past do exist, and a handful still retain relatively high office, particularly in the economic sphere. Their numbers, however, have shriveled over the past twenty years. At present, it is hard to see them being able to amass the influence required to successfully promote a reform agenda. Defeat in war could perhaps change this calculus and provide the necessary impetus for reform, as in the aftermath of the Crimean War. If the country's elites decide that drastic liberalization is the only way of preserving their own privileges, of saving the state from collapse, or of preventing revolution, then change is possible.

There is, however, a crucial difference between the situation today and in previous eras of reform. In the 1860s, Russia was at peace. Similarly, perestroika coincided with a period of improved international relations—indeed, Gorbachev and his advisers brought the Cold War to an end precisely because they believed that peace was a prerequisite of successful reform. Today, by contrast, Russia is at war. Moreover, there is little to no chance of Russia's relations with the West improving significantly in the foreseeable future. Among other reasons, the conditions set by the West for the normalization of relations include demands that no Russian government, of any political hue, could probably ever satisfy (the return of Crimea to Ukraine being the most obvious example). It could be that the invasion of Ukraine marked a historical turning point at which Russia and the West separated themselves from each other once and for all. There may be no turning back—or at least not for a very, very long time.

Consequently, Russia's elites at present seem to have little option but to rally round the flag (even in 1917 they defected not because they were opposed to Russia's war with Germany but because they felt that the emperor was losing it and that they could fight it better without him). In the context of prolonged East-West tensions, it is as hard to visualize liberalization from the top down as from the bottom up. Russian liberalism has been defeated before and yet come back to life. The same may happen again, but as in the twentieth century the wait may be long.

NOTES

Introduction

1. Adrian Pabst, "Liberalism," in *Handbook on the Economics of Reciprocity and Social Enterprise*, ed. Luigno Bruni and Stefano Zamagni (Cheltenham: Edward Elgar, 2013), 217. Duncan Bell, "What Is Liberalism?" *Political Theory* 42, no. 6 (2014): 689.

2. Lionel Barber and Henry Foy, "Vladimir Putin Says Liberalism Has 'Become Obsolete,'" *Financial Times*, June 27, 2019, https://www.ft.com/content/670039ec-98f3-11e9-9573-ee5cbb98ed36.

3. Daniel Field, "Kavelin and Russian Liberalism," *Slavic Review* 32, no. 1 (1973): 59.

4. V. A. Gutorov, "Rossiiskii liberalizm v politiko-kul'turnom izmerenii: Opyt svravnitel'nogo teoreticheskogo i istoricheskogo analiza" (part 2), *Politeks* 13, no. 2 (2017): 7, 18.

5. Jeremy Waldron, "Theoretical Foundations of Liberalism," *Philosophical Quarterly* 37, no. 147 (1987): 128. Vanessa Rampton, *Liberal Ideas in Tsarist Russia: From Catherine the Great to the Russian Revolution* (Cambridge: Cambridge University Press), 185.

6. E. E. Grishnova, "Politicheskii liberalizm v Rossii: Uroki istorii," *Sotsialno-politicheskie nauki* 3 (2016): 63.

7. For instance, Pabst, "Liberalism," 217. B. N. Karipov, "Sushchnost' i osnovnye cherty russkogo liberal'nogo klassicheskogo diskursa," *Vestnik Moskovskogo Universiteta* 12, no. 2 (2008): 89.

8. Raymond Geuss, "Liberalism and Its Discontents," *Political Theory* 30, no. 3 (2002): 321.

9. Michael Freeden, *Liberalism: A Very Short History* (Oxford: Oxford University Press, 2015), 20–21.

10. For a summary of the tenets of classical liberalism, see Eamonn Butler, *Classical Liberalism: A Primer* (London: Institute of Economic Affairs, 2015).

11. Nikolai Chernyshevsky, "[On Liberalism]," in *A Documentary History of Russian Thought: From the Enlightenment to Marxism*, ed. William Leatherbarrow and D. C. Offord (Ann Arbor, MI: Ardis, 1987), 204.

12. Freeden, *Liberalism*, 13.

13. Freeden, *Liberalism*, 76.

14. Michael Freeden, *The New Liberalism: An Ideology of Social Reform* (Oxford: Clarendon Press, 1986).

15. Freeden, *Liberalism*, 34–35.

16. Charles Taylor, "The Politics of Recognition," in *Multiculturalism: Examining the Politics of Recognition*, ed. Amy Gutmann (Princeton, NJ: Princeton University Press, 1994), 39.

17. Edmund Fawcett, *Liberalism: The Life of an Idea* (Princeton, NJ: Princeton University Press, 2018), 12.

18. Rostislav Kapeliushnikov, "Rossiiskii liberalizm: Byt' ili ne byt'?" *Colta*, July 16, 2019, https://www.colta.ru/articles/specials/21886-rossiyskiy-liberalizm-byt-ili-ne-byt.

19. General surveys of the topic include: Victor Leontovitsch, *The History of Liberalism in Russia* (Pittsburgh, PA: University of Pittsburgh Press, 2012); George Fischer, *Russian Liberalism: From Gentry to Intelligentsia* (Cambridge, MA: Harvard University Press, 1958); Susanna Rabow-Edling, *Liberalism in Pre-Revolutionary Russia: State, Nation, and Empire* (Abingdon: Routledge, 2019); Rampton, *Liberal Ideas*.

20. Biographies include: Julia Berest, *The Emergence of Russian Liberalism: Alexander Kunitsyn in Context, 1783–1840* (New York: Palgrave, 2011); Gary M. Hamburg, *Boris Chicherin and Early Russian Liberalism, 1828–1866* (Stanford, CA: Stanford University Press, 1992); Priscilla Reynolds Roosevelt, *Apostle of Russian Liberalism: Timofei Granovsky* (Newtonville, MA: Oriental Research Partners, 1986); Richard Pipes, *Struve: Liberal on the Left, 1870–1905* (Cambridge, MA: Harvard University Press, 1970); Pipes, *Struve: Liberal on the Right, 1905–1944* (Cambridge, MA: Harvard University Press, 1980); Thomas Riha, *A Russian-European: Paul Miliukov in Russian Politics* (Notre Dame, IN: University of Notre Dame Press, 1969); Adele Lindenmeyr, *Citizen Countess: Sofia Panina and the Fate of Revolutionary Russia* (Madison: University of Wisconsin Press, 2019); Stephen F. Williams, *The Reformer: How One Liberal Fought to Preempt the Russian Revolution* (New York: Encounter, 2017). Studies of individual aspects of thought include: Andrzej Walicki, *Legal Philosophies of Russian Liberalism* (Oxford: Oxford University Press, 1987); Daniel Beer, *Renovating Russia: The Human Sciences and the Fate of Liberal Modernity, 1880–1930* (Ithaca, NY: Cornell University Press, 2008). Works on liberal parties include: Shmuel Galai, *The Liberation Movement in Russia, 1900–1905* (New York: Cambridge University Press, 1973); Galai, "The Kadets in the Second Duma," *Revolutionary Russia* 23, no. 1 (2010): 1–28; Ingeborg Fleischhauer, "The Agrarian Program of the Russian Constitutional Democrats," *Cahiers du monde russe et soviétique* 20, no. 2 (1979): 173–201.

21. For instance, Randall A. Poole, ed., *Problems of Idealism: Essays in Russian Social Philosophy* (New Haven, CT: Yale University Press, 2005), and B. N. Chicherin, *Liberty, Equality, and the Market: Essays* (New Haven, CT: Yale University Press, 1998).

22. The most notable example for the Civil War period is William Rosenberg, *Liberals in the Russian Revolution: The Constitutional Democratic Party, 1917–1921* (Princeton, NJ: Princeton University Press, 1974). Writings on liberal émigrés include: Serguei Glebov, "'Congresses of Russia Abroad' in the 1920s and the Politics of Émigré Nationalism: A Liberal Survival," *Ab Imperio* 2000, no. 3 (2000): 159–85; Shuichi Kojima, "Exiled Russian Economists and the USSR: Brutzkus and Prokopovich," in *Economics in Russia: Studies in Intellectual History*, ed. Joachim Zweynert (London: Routledge, 2008), 123–40; and John Howard Wilhelm, "The Soviet Economic Failure: Brutzkus Revisited," *Europe-Asia Studies* 45, no. 2 (1993): 343–57.

23. Exceptions include: Robert D. English, *Russia and the Idea of the West: Gorbachev, Intellectuals, and the End of the Cold War* (New York: Columbia University Press, 2000); Guillaume Sauvé, *Subir la victoire: Essor et chute de l'intelligentsia libérale en Russie (1987–1993)* (Montreal: Les Presses de l'Université de Montréal, 2019); Mark Lipovetsky, "The Poetics of ITR Discourse in the 1960s and Today," *Ab Imperio* 2013, no. 1 (2013): 109–39; Benjamin Nathans, "Coming to Terms with Late Soviet Liberalism," *Ab Imperio* 2013, no. 1 (2013): 175–82; Nathans, "Human Rights Defenders within Soviet Politics,"

in *Dimensions and Challenges of Russian Liberalism: Historical Drama and New Prospects*, ed. Riccardo Mario Cucciolla (Cham: Springer, 2019), 87–96.

24. An exception is Elena Chebankova, "Contemporary Russian Liberalism," *Post-Soviet Affairs* 30, no. 5 (2014): 341–69.

25. For an analysis of the Russian historiography of Russian liberalism, see S. M. Smagina, "Rossiiskii liberalizm nachala XX veka: Teoriia i praktika. Istoriograficheskie siuzhety," *Gumanitarnye i iuridicheskie issledovaniia* 94, no. 47 (2014): 36–43. See also Konstantin Shneider and David C. Fisher, "Was There an 'Early Russian Liberalism?' Perspectives from Russian and Anglo-American Historiography," *Kritika: Explorations in Russian and Eurasian History* 7, no. 4 (2006): 825–41.

26. Valentin Shelokhaev, *Liberal'naia model' pereustroistva Rossii* (Moscow: Rosspen, 1996); Shelokhaev, "Russian Liberalism as a Historiographical and Historico-Philosophical Problem," *Russian Studies in History* 37, no. 3 (1998): 7–31; Shelokhaev, ed., *Rossiiskii liberalizm: Itogi i perspektivy izucheniia. "X Muromtsevskie chteniia"* (Orel: Orlik, 2018); Aleksei Kara-Murza, "Nekotorye voprosy genezisa i typologii russkogo liberalizma," *Istoriia filosofii* 21, no. 2 (2016): 69–76; Kara-Murza, *Svoboda i poriadok: Iz istorii russkoi politicheskoi mysli xix–xx vv.* (Moscow: Moskovskaia shkola politicheskikh issledovanii, 2009); and Kara-Murza, ed., *Rossiiskii liberalizm: Idei i liudi* (Moscow: Fond "Liberal'naia missiia" 2007).

27. S. A. Aleksandrov, *Lider rossiiskikh kadetov P. N. Miliukov v emigratsii* (Moscow: AIRO-XX, 1996); Natal'ia Viktorovna Antonenko, "Emigrantskie liberal'nye konseptsii resheniia natsional'nogo voprosa v Rossii," *Vestnik TGU* 93, no. 1 (2011): 259–63; Vladimir Kara-Murza, "Andrei Dmitrievich Sakharov," in Kara-Murza, *Rossiiskii liberalizm*, 887–95.

1. Defining Russian Liberalism

1. Randall A. Poole, "Editor's Introduction: Philosophy and Politics in the Russian Liberation Movement," in Poole, *Problems of Idealism*, 4.

2. Adam Gopnik, *A Thousand Small Sanities: The Moral Adventure of Liberalism* (New York: Basic, 2019), 14.

3. M. Steven Fish, "The Predicament of Russian Liberalism: Evidence from the December 1995 Parliamentary Elections," *Europe-Asia Studies* 49, no. 2 (1997): 211.

4. John Gray, *Liberalism* (Minneapolis: University of Minnesota Press, 1986), x.

5. Fawcett, *Liberalism*, 2–3.

6. Freeden, *Liberalism*, 15.

7. Grishnova, "Politicheskii liberalizm," 64.

8. A. I. Solov'ev, "Liberalizm: Logika istorii i problemy sovremennogo diskursa," *Problemnyi analiz i gosudarstvenno upravlencheskoe proektirovanie* 5 (2010): 68.

9. Leontovitsch, *History of Liberalism*, 1; and Aleksei Kara-Murza, "O natsional'nykh variantakh liberalizma i russkoi modeli v chastnosti," in Shelokhaev, *Rossiiskii liberalizm*, 50–51. For a dissenting viewpoint, see Waldron, "Theoretical Foundations," 131.

10. Freeden, *Liberalism*, 58.

11. Isaiah Berlin, "Two Concepts of Liberty," in *Liberty* (Oxford: Oxford University Press, 2002), 170.

12. Berlin, "Two Concepts," 181.

13. Ben Colburn, *Autonomy and Liberalism* (New York: Routledge, 2010), 2.

14. H. J. McCloskey, "Liberalism," *Philosophy* 49, no. 187 (1974): 14.

15. McCloskey, "Liberalism," 14.

16. Waldron, "Theoretical Foundations," 129.

17. Bell, "What is Liberalism?" 684.

18. Paul Kelly, *Liberalism* (Cambridge: Polity, 2005), 9.

19. Kelly, *Liberalism*, 7.

20. Friedrich von Hayek, *The Constitution of Liberty: The Definitive Edition* (Chicago: University of Chicago Press, 2011), 150.

21. John Gray, *Black Mass: Apocalyptic Religion and the Death of Utopia* (Toronto: Doubleday Canada, 2007), 76.

22. Pabst, "Liberalism," 223.

23. Gopnik, *Thousand Small Sanities*, 45.

24. E. M. Spirova, "Konservatizm vs liberalizm," *Vek globalizatsii* 9 (2016): 14. See also Pierre Manent, "The Greatness and Misery of Liberalism," *Modern Age* (Summer 2010): 181.

25. Leontovitsch, *History of Liberalism*, 13–14. For a similar viewpoint, see Gopnik, *Thousand Small Sanities*, 40.

26. Gray, *Liberalism*, 62.

27. Shelokhaev, "Russian Liberalism," 24.

28. For instance, Manent, "Greatness and Misery," 176; Fawcett, *Liberalism*, 11; Randall A. Poole, "Nineteenth-Century Russian Liberalism: Ideals and Realities," *Kritika: Explorations in Russian and Eurasian History* 16, no. 1 (2015): 157–58; Smagina, "Rossiiskii liberalizm," 36.

29. Nancy L. Rosenblum, "Civil Societies, Liberalism and the Moral Uses of Pluralism," *Social Research* 61, no. 3 (1994): 543.

30. Elena Chebankova, "Competing Ideologies of Russia's Civil Society," *Europe-Asia Studies* 67, no. 2 (2015): 244.

31. Paul Bunyan, "Re-Conceptualizing Civil Society: Towards a Radical Understanding," *Voluntas* 25, no. 2 (2014): 541.

32. Rosenblum, "Civil Societies," 541.

33. Rosenblum, "Civil Societies," 542.

34. For discussions of this issue, see Poole, "Nineteenth-Century Russian Liberalism," 158–59; Karipov, "Sushchnost' i osnovnye cherty," 92–93; Chebankova, "Contemporary Russian Liberalism," 350–51.

35. Alexey Kara-Murza and Olga Zhukova, "The Political Philosophy of Russian Liberalism," in Cucciolla, *Dimensions and Challenges*, 33. See also S. P. Zolotarev and T. N. Zolotareva, "Vozniknovenie i razvitie liberalizma v Rossii," *Nauchnye Vedomosti* 45, no. 3 (2018): 573–80.

36. For instance, Lidiia Novikova and Irina Sizemskaia, "Ideinye istoki russkogo liberalizma," *Obshchestvennye Nauki i Sovremennost'* 3 (1993): 126.

37. Karipov, "Sushchnost' i osnovnye cherty," 93.

38. Berest, *Emergence of Russian Liberalism*, 3.

39. Rabow-Edling, *Liberalism in Pre-Revolutionary Russia*, 9, 87.

40. Field, "Kavelin and Russian Liberalism," 60; Grishnova, "Politicheskii liberalizm," 65.

41. Rampton, *Liberal Ideas*, 1, 38.

42. Shelokhaev, "Russian Liberalism," 20; Zolotarev and Zolotareva, "Vozniknove-nie," 576; and A. A. Zharikov, "Zashchita idei pravoporiadka predstaviteliami liberal'noi filosofii prava v dorevolutsionnoi Rossii," *Mezhdunarodnyi Nauchno-Issledovatel'skii Zhurnal 53*, no. 11 (2016): 84.

43. Andrei Medushevskii, "Byt' liberalom v Rossii: o svobodnom obraze myshleniia i ego kritikakh," in Shelokhaev, *Rossiiskii liberalizm*, 52–53.

44. Charles E. Timberlake, "Introduction: The Concept of Liberalism in Russia," in *Essays on Russian Liberalism*, ed. Charles E. Timberlake (Columbia: University of Missouri Press, 1972), 6–7; Rampton, *Liberal Ideas*, 3–4; Grishnova, "Politicheskii liberalizm," 66.

45. Gray, *Liberalism*, xi.

46. Freeden, *Liberalism*, 37–39.

47. Freeden, *Liberalism*, 3.

48. Bell, "What is Liberalism?" 689–90. Emphasis in the original.

49. Leontovitsch, *History of Liberalism*, 14.

50. Leontovitsch, *History of Liberalism*, 56-63.

51. Leontovitsch says that the Octobrists were the party of liberalism and the Kadets the party of radicalism. Leontovitsch, *History of Liberalism*, 294.

52. Aileen Kelly, "'What Is Real Is Rational:' The Political Philosophy of B. N. Chicherin," *Cahiers du monde russe et soviétique 18*, no. 3 (1977): 195–222.

53. Aileen Kelly, "Byl' li Gertsen liberalom?" *Gor'kii Media* 6 (2002), https://magazines.gorky.media/nlo/2002/6/byl-li-gerczen-liberalom.html.

54. Field, "Kavelin and Russian Liberalism," 59–78.

55. For instance, Kara-Murza, "Nekotorye voprosy," 70–71. Also Elizabeth Kristofovich Zelensky, "*Bud' gotov razvedchik delu chestnomu* / 'Be Prepared, Scout, for Honorable Deeds': Russian Scouting as a School for Liberalism," *Russian History* 41 (2014): 242, 242n2; Novikova and Sizemskaia, "Ideinye istoki," 124; and Zolotarev and Zolotareva, "Vozniknovenie," 579. The importance of the person as the focus of prerevolutionary Russian liberalism is also noted by Western historians, for instance William G. Rosenberg, "Representing Workers and the Liberal Narrative of Modernity," *Slavic Review 55*, no. 2 (1996): 247. For a discussion of how prerevolutionary thinkers defined *lichnost'*, see Derek Offord, "*Lichnost'*: Notions of Individual Identity," in *Constructing Russian Identity in the Age of Revolution, 1881–1940*, ed. Catriona Kelly and David Shepherd (Oxford: Oxford University Press, 1998), 13–25.

56. V. V. Shelokhaev, "Liberalizm v Rossii: Perspektivy izucheniia," in Shelokhaev, *Rossiiskii liberalizm*, 1920. This view is shared by many Western historians. See for instance, Gary M. Hamburg and Randall A. Poole, "Introduction: The Humanist Tradition in Russian Philosophy," in *A History of Russian Philosophy, 1830–1930: Faith, Reason, and the Defense of Human Dignity*, ed. Gary M. Hamburg and Randall A. Poole (Cambridge: Cambridge University Press, 2010), 4.

57. Novikova and Sizemskaia, "Ideinye istoki," 127.

58. Kara-Murza, *Rossiiskii liberalizm*.

59. Rampton, *Liberal Ideas*, 85.

60. Grishnova, "Politicheskii liberalizm," 65.

61. Shelokhaev, "Russian Liberalism," 14. Theodore H. von Laue, "The Prospects of Liberal Democracy in Tsarist Russia," in Timberlake, *Essays on Russian Liberalism*, 170.

62. Peter Enticott, *The Russian Liberals and the Revolution of 1905* (London: Routledge, 2016), 179. Leontovitsch, *History of Liberalism*, 2.

63. Solov'ev, "Liberalizm," 80.

64. Shelokhaev, "Liberalizm v Rossii," 22–23.

65. Cited in Shneider and Fisher, "Was There an 'Early Russian Liberalism'?," 832.

66. Rampton, *Liberal Ideas*, 4.

67. Alfred J. Rieber, "Interest-Group Politics in the Era of the Great Reforms," in *Russia's Great Reforms, 1855–1881*, ed. Ben Eklof, John Bushnell, and Larissa Zakharova (Bloomington: Indiana University Press, 1994), 63.

68. Smagina, "Rossiiskii liberalizm," 38

69. Greg Gaut, "A Practical Unity: Vladimir Solov'ev and Russian Liberalism," *Canadian Slavonic Papers* 42, no. 3 (2000): 300.

70. Shelokhaev, "Russian Liberalism," 16; Grishnova, "Politicheskii liberalizm," 65.

71. Paul Milyoukov, *Russia and Its Crisis* (Chicago: University of Chicago Press, 1906), 226. Emphases in the original.

72. Lipovetsky, "Poetics of ITR Discourse," 109–39.

73. Gutorov, "Rossiiskii liberalizm" (part 2), 11.

74. Galai, *Liberation Movement*, 120–21.

75. Milyoukov, *Russia and its Crisis*, 34.

76. Rabow-Edling, *Liberalism in Pre-Revolutionary Russia*, 123.

77. Gutorov, "Rossiiskii liberalizm" (part 1), 6.

78. Marcia A. Weigle, "Political Liberalism in Postcommunist Russia," *Review of Politics* 58, no. 3 (1996): 478.

79. For instance, Lindenmeyr, *Citizen Countess*, 122,

80. Poole, "Nineteenth-Century Russian Liberalism," 170. See also Grishnova, "Politicheskii liberalizm," 66.

81. Shelokhaev, *Rossiiskii liberalizm*, 21; N. A. Baranov, "Liberal'no-konservativnyi sintez v Rossii: Istoriia i perspektivy," *Problemnyi analiz i gosudarstvenno-upravlencheskoe proektirovanie* 5 (2010): 94.

82. Shelokhaev, "Russian Liberalism," 22.

83. Walicki, *Legal Philosophies*, 1.

84. Walicki, *Legal Philosophies*, 3, 402.

85. Marc Raeff, "Some Reflections on Russian Liberalism," *Russian Review* 18, no. 3 (1959): 223.

86. Shuichi Kojima, "Russian Liberal Versions of Agricultural Development at the Beginning of the Twentieth Century: Litoshenko and Brutzkus," *Oeconomia* 4, no 1 (2014): 55.

87. Fish, "Predicament of Russian Liberalism," 211.

88. Riccardo Mario Cucciolla, "Introduction: The Many Dimensions of Russian Liberalism," in Cucciolla, *Dimensions and Challenges*, xxiii.

2. Early Russian Liberalism

1. V. F. Ivanov, *Russkaia intelligentsia i masonstvo: Ot Petra I do nashikh dnei* (Moscow: Moskva, 1997), 185.

2. Zolotarev and Zolotareva, "Vozniknovenie i razvitie," 579.

3. Andrzej Walicki, *The Flow of Ideas: Russian Thought from the Enlightenment to the Religious-Philosophical Renaissance* (Frankfurt: Peter Lang, 2015), 45.

4. Walicki, *Flow of Ideas*, 84.

5. Walicki, *Flow of Ideas*, 84.

6. Rabow-Edling, *Liberalism in Pre-Revolutionary Russia*, 6–7.

7. Alexander Gerschenkron, "The Problem of Economic Development in Russia Intellectual History of the Nineteenth Century," in *Continuity and Change in Russian and Soviet Thought*, ed. Ernest J. Simmons (New York: Russell and Russell, 1955), 17.

8. Marc Raeff, *The Decembrist Movement* (Eaglewood Cliffs, NJ: Prentice-Hall, 1966), 46.

9. Raeff, *Decembrist Movement*, 50–51.

10. Raeff, *Decembrist Movement*, 57.

11. Nikita Mikhailovich Muravev, "A Project for a Constitution (Extracts)," in Leatherbarrow and Offord, *Documentary History of Russian Thought*, 42. See also Raeff, *Decembrist Movement*, 104.

12. Raeff, *Decembrist Movement*, 134–36.

13. Pavel Ivanovich Pestel, "Russian Law (Extracts)," in Leatherbarrow and Offord, *Documentary History of Russian Thought*, 137.

14. Roosevelt, *Apostle*, 43.

15. Roosevelt, *Apostle*, 43.

16. Alexander Polunov, *Russia in the Nineteenth Century: Autocracy, Reform, and Social Change, 1814–1914* (Armonk, NY: M. E. Sharpe, 2005), 59.

17. Walicki, *Flow of Ideas*, 235.

18. Leontovitsch, *History of Liberalism in Russia*, 141.

19. Randall A. Poole, "Religious Toleration, Freedom of Conscience, and Russian Liberalism," *Kritika: Explorations in Russian and Eurasian History* 13, no. 3 (2012): 621. See also A. V. Gorlov, "Dva 'vzgliada' russkogo liberala XIX veka: K. D. Kavelin o razvitii instituta sobstvennosti v Rossii," *Vestnik Gosudarstvennogo i Munitsipal'nogo Upravleniia* 3 (2012): 39–49; and R. A. Arslanov, "Istoriia rossiiskogo gosudarstva v kontseptsii K. D. Kavelina," *Vestnik RUDN* 1 (2007): 37–47.

20. Konstantin Dmitrievich Kavelin, "Vzgliad na iuridicheskii byt drevnei Rossii," in *Nash umstvennyi stroi: Stat'i po filosofii russkoi istorii i kul'tury* (Moscow: Pravda, 1989), 22.

21. Kavelin, "Vzgliad na iuridicheskii byt," 22–23.

22. Kavelin, "Vzgliad na iuridicheskii byt," 13.

23. Kavelin, "Vzgliad na iuridicheskii byt," 66.

24. Walicki, *Flow of Ideas*, 45; Karipov, "Sushchnost' i osnovnye cherty," 93–94; Novikova and Sizemskaia, "Ideinye istoki," 126.

25. Marc Raeff, *Michael Speransky: Statesman of Imperial Russia, 1772–1839* (The Hague: Martinus Nijhoff, 1957), 31.

26. G. M. Hamburg, *Russia's Path toward Enlightenment: Faith, Politics, and Reason, 1500–1801* (New Haven, CT: Yale University Press, 2016), 388–89.

27. Hamburg, *Russia's Path*, 389.

28. Hamburg, *Russia's Path*, 389.

29. Hamburg, *Russia's Path*, 529.

30. Walicki, *Flow of Ideas*, 55.

31. Hamburg, *Russia's Path*, 589.

32. Hamburg, *Russia's Path*, 590.

33. Hamburg, *Russia's Path*, 603.

34. Hamburg, *Russia's Path*, 620; Walicki, *Flow of Ideas*, 61.

35. Hamburg, *Russia's Path*, 628.

36. Elias L. Tartak, "The Liberal Tradition in Russia: A. Herzen and V. Soloviev," in *European Ideologies: A Survey of 20th Century Political Ideas*, ed. Feliks Gross (New York: Philosophical Library, 1948), 312.

37. Milyoukov, *Russia and Its Crisis*, 253–54.

38. Aleksandr N. Radishchev, "[On Autocracy]," in Leatherbarrow and Offord, *Documentary History of Russian Thought*, 17.

39. Hamburg, *Russia's Path*, 645, 650.

40. Marie-Pierre Rey, *Alexander I: The Tsar Who Defeated Napoleon* (DeKalb: Northern Illinois University Press, 2012), 76.

41. Rey, *Alexander I*, 100–103.

42. Rey, *Alexander I*, 105–16.

43. W. Bruce Lincoln, *In the Vanguard of Reform: Russia's Enlightened Bureaucrats, 1825–1861* (DeKalb: Northern Illinois University Press, 1982), 26–27.

44. Raeff, *Michael Speransky*, 138–40.

45. Rey, *Alexander I*, 214.

46. Raeff, *Michael Speransky*, 143–52.

47. Walicki, *Flow of Ideas*, 109.

48. Raeff, *Michael Speransky*, 156.

49. Raeff, *Michael Speransky*, 164.

50. Rey, *Alexander I*, 215.

51. John Gooding, "The Liberalism of Michael Speransky," *Slavonic and East European Review* 64, no. 3 (1986): 402. Walicki, *Flow of Ideas*, 111.

52. Rey, *Alexander I*, 314–15.

53. Rey, *Alexander I*, 316. See also Polunov, *Russia in the Nineteenth Century*, 32.

54. Berest, *Emergence of Russian Liberalism*, 42.

55. Berest, *Emergence of Russian Liberalism*, 50.

56. Berest, *Emergence of Russian Liberalism*, 78.

57. Berest, *Emergence of Russian Liberalism*, 147.

58. Berest, *Emergence of Russian Liberalism*, 148.

59. Berest, *Emergence of Russian Liberalism*, 157.

60. Berest, *Emergence of Russian Liberalism*, 195.

61. Anatole G. Mazour, *The First Russian Revolution, 1825: The Decembrist Movement, Its Origins, Development, and Significance* (Stanford, CA: Stanford University Press, 1963), 97.

62. Muravev, "A Project for a Constitution," 42–50.

63. Patrick O'Meara, *The Decembrist Pavel Pestel: Russia's First Republican* (Basingstoke: Palgrave, 2003).

64. Raeff, *Decembrist Movement*, 126.

65. Pestel, "Russian Law," 52.

66. O'Meara, *Decembrist Pavel Pestel*, 156.

67. Milyoukov, *Russia and Its Crisis*, 262.

68. Walicki, *Flow of Ideas*, 52. Emphasis in the original.

69. Isaiah Berlin, *Russian Thinkers* (London: Penguin, 2008), 93.

70. Kermit E. McKenzie, "The Political Faith of Fedor Rodichev," in Timberlake, *Essays on Russian Liberalism*, 49–50.

71. Kelly, "Byl li Gertsen liberalom?"

72. Walicki, *Flow of Ideas*, 57.

73. Rampton, *Liberal Ideas*, 55.

74. Paul Robinson, *Russian Conservatism* (DeKalb: Northern Illinois University Press, 2019), 69.

75. Polunov, *Russia in the Nineteenth Century*, 63.

76. Vissarion Grigorevich Belinsky, "Letters to V. P. Botkin 1840–1841 (Extracts)," in Leatherbarrow and Offord, *Documentary History of Russian Thought*, 125.

77. Belinsky, "Letters to V. P. Botkin," 124.

78. Belinsky, "Letters to V. P. Botkin," 128–29.

79. Rabow-Edling, *Liberalism in Pre-Revolutionary Russia*, 63–64.

80. Lincoln, *In the Vanguard of Reform*, 85.

81. Novikova and Sizemskaia, "Ideinye istoki," 127.

82. Lincoln, *In the Vanguard of Reform*, 12.

83. Richard Wortman, *The Development of a Russian Legal Consciousness* (Chicago: University of Chicago Press, 1976), 42.

84. Wortman, *Development of a Russian Legal Consciousness*, 52.

85. Kojima, "Russian Liberal Visions," 56.

86. Andrey N. Medushevsky, *Russian Constitutionalism: Historical and Contemporary Development* (London: Routledge, 2006), 75–77.

87. Leontovitsch, *History of Liberalism in Russia*, 18–19.

88. Leontovitsch, *History of Liberalism in Russia*, 20–21.

89. Walicki, *Flow of Ideas*, 55.

90. Hamburg, *Russia's Path*, 595.

91. Hamburg, *Russia's Path*, 592–93.

92. Hamburg, *Russia's Path*, 594.

93. Vincent Bennett, *A History of Russian Economic Thought* (London: Routledge, 2013). 20.

94. Bennett, *History of Russian Economic Thought*, 20.

95. Leontovitsch, *History of Liberalism in Russia*, 34, 36.

96. Berest, *Emergence of Russian Liberalism*, 45, 81.

97. Berest, *Emergence of Russian Liberalism*, 90, 45.

98. Gooding, "Liberalism of Michael Speransky," 414.

99. Raeff, *Michael Speransky*, 299-304

100. Gooding, "Liberalism of Michael Speransky," 414, 428.

101. Gooding, "Liberalism of Michael Speransky," 419.

102. Raeff, *Michael Speransky*, 52–53.

103. Bennett, *History of Russian Economic Thought*, 20; Raeff, *Decembrist Movement*, 9.

104. Gerschenkron, "Problem of Economic Development," 19.

105. Raeff, *Decembrist Movement*, 148–52.

106. Raeff, *Decembrist Movement*, 18.

107. Berest, *Emergence of Russian Liberalism*, 88–90.

108. Walicki, *Flow of Ideas*, 122; Bennett, *History of Russian Economic Thought*, 25; Gerschenkron, "Problem of Economic Development," 18.

109. Lincoln, *In the Vanguard of Reform*, 91.

110. Lincoln, *In the Vanguard of Reform*, 123–24.

3. The Great Reforms

1. Field, "Kavelin and Russian Liberalism," 60.

2. Rabow-Edling, *Liberalism in Pre-Revolutionary Russia*, 86.

3. Elena Nikolaevich Zhidkova, "Vozzreniia A. D. Gradkovskogo na publichnoe pravo," *Vestnik TGU* 10, no. 114 (2012): 328.

4. Alexander Semyonov, "Russian Liberalism and the Problem of Imperial Diversity," in *Liberal Imperialism in Europe*, ed. Matthew P. Fitzpatrick (New York: Palgrave, 2012), 75.

5. Semyonov, "Russian Liberalism," 76.

6. Eugene Pyziur, "Mikhail N. Katkov: Advocate of English Liberalism in Russia, 1856–1863," *Slavonic and East European Review* 45, no. 105 (1967): 441.

7. Marc Raeff, "A Reactionary Liberal: M. N. Katkov," *Russian Review* 11, no. 3 (1952): 160; Pyziur, "Mikhail N. Katkov," 446, 454.

8. Robinson, *Russian Conservatism*, 83–84.

9. Robinson, *Russian Conservatism*, 84.

10. Boris N. Chicherin, "Contemporary Tasks of Russian Life," in Chicherin, *Liberty, Equality, and the Market*, 115.

11. Boris N. Chicherin, "Konstitutsionnyi vopros Rossii," in *Opyt russkogo liberalizma: Antologiia*, ed. M. A. Abramov (Moscow: Kanon, 1997), 55.

12. Rabow-Edling, *Liberalism in Pre-Revolutionary Russia*, 88.

13. Rabow-Edling, *Liberalism in Pre-Revolutionary Russia*, 90–92.

14. Chicherin, "Konstitutsionnyi vopros Rossii," 73.

15. Philip Boobbyer, "Russian Liberal Conservatism," in *Russian Nationalism Past and Present*, ed. Geoffrey Hosking and Robert Service (Basingstoke: Macmillan, 1998), 41.

16. Cited in Milyoukov, *Russia and Its Crisis*, 280.

17. Orlando Figes, *The Europeans: Three Lives and the Making of a Cosmopolitan Culture* (New York: Metropolitan, 2019), 239.

18. Michael Pursglove, "Introduction," in Ivan Turgenev, *Smoke* (London: Alma Classics, 2013), xv.

19. Turgenev, *Smoke*, 27.

20. Turgenev, *Smoke*, 32.

21. Pursglove, "Introduction," xvi–xvii.

22. Nina B. Khailova, "Mikhail Matveevich Stasiulevich," in Kara-Murza, *Rossiiskii liberalizm*, 308.

23. Khailova, "Mikhail Matveevich Stasiulevich," 308.

24. V. M. Khevrolina, "Russian Liberalism's Views on Foreign Policy at the End of the Nineteenth Century," *Russian Studies in History* 37, no. 3 (1998): 80.

25. Khevrolina, "Russian Liberalism's Views on Foreign Policy," 80.

26. Khevrolina, "Russian Liberalism's Views on Foreign Policy," 80–81. Anton A. Fedyashin, *Liberals under Autocracy: Modernization and Civil Society in Russia, 1866–1904* (Madison: University of Wisconsin Press, 2012), 96.

27. Fedyashin, *Liberals under Autocracy*, 13.

28. Terence Emmons, *The Russian Landed Gentry and the Peasant Emancipation of 1861* (Cambridge: Cambridge University Press, 1968), 258.

29. Polunov, *Russia in the Nineteenth Century*, 104.

30. Fedor Rodichev and J. E. S. C., "The Liberal Movement in Russia (1855–1891)," *Slavonic Review* 2, no. 4 (1923): 3.

31. Emmons, *Russian Landed Gentry*, 343–44.

32. Medushevsky, *Russian Constitutionalism*, 93–94; W. Bruce Lincoln, *The Great Reforms: Autocracy, Bureaucracy, and the Politics of Change in Imperial Russia* (DeKalb: Northern Illinois University Press, 1990), 100.

33. Lincoln, *Great Reforms*, 102.

34. Lincoln, *Great Reforms*, 102.

35. William E. Pomeranz, *Law and the Russian State: Russia's Legal Evolution from Peter the Great to Vladimir Putin* (London: Bloomsbury, 2019), 36–40.

36. Wortman, *Development of a Russian Legal Consciousness*, 269.

37. Lincoln, *Great Reforms*, 109; Wortman, *Development of a Russian Legal Consciousness*, 254.

38. Wortman, *Development of a Russian Legal Consciousness*, 257.

39. Wortman, *Development of a Russian Legal Consciousness*, 257.

40. N. A. Kotel'nitskii, "Obshchestvennaia deiatel'nost' I. I. Petrunkevicha na Chernigovshchine (1868–1879)," *Vestnik RUDN, ser. Istoriia Rossii* 4 (2010): 5–24.

41. Rodichev and J. E. S. C., "Liberal Movement in Russia," 7.

42. Charles E. Timberlake, "Ivan Il'ich Petrunkevich: Russian Liberalism in Microcosm," in Timberlake, *Essays in Russian Liberalism*, 30.

43. "Zapiska Moskovskikh liberalov gr. Loris-Melikovu, nachal'niku verkhovnoi rasporiaditel'noi komissii," in Abramov, *Opyt russkogo liberalizma*, 123.

44. "Zapiska Moskovskikh liberalov," 138.

45. Robinson, *Russian Conservatism*, 87.

46. Konstantin Dmitrievich Kavelin and Boris N. Chicherin, "Pis'mo k izdatel'iu," in Abramov, *Opyt russkogo liberalizma*, 30.

47. Kavelin and Chicherin, "Pis'mo k izdatel'iu," 26.

48. Rabow-Edling, *Liberalism in Pre-Revolutionary Russia*, 64.

49. Walicki, *Flow of Ideas*, 453.

50. Gutorov, "Rossiiskii liberalizm" (part 2), 15.

51. Konstantin Dmitrievich Kavelin, "Dvorianstvo i osvobozhdenie krest'ian," 1862, http://dugward.ru/library/kavelin/kavelin/_dvorianstvo_i_osvobojdenie.html.

52. Kavelin, "Dvorianstvo."

53. Konstantin Dmitrievich Kavelin, "Chto nam byt'?," in Abramov, *Opyt russkogo liberalizma*, 89, 92.

54. Kavelin, "Chto nam byt'?," 108.

55. O. L. Gnatiuk, "Konservativnyi ('okhranitel'nyi') liberalizm B. N. Chicherina," *Filosofskie Traditsii i Sovremennost'* 2 (2013): 25. Also, Igor Yevlampiev, "Man and Mind in the Philosophy of Boris N. Chicherin," *Studies in East European Thought* 61, no. 2/3 (2009): 120.

56. Chicherin, "Contemporary Tasks," 115.

57. Chicherin, "Contemporary Tasks," 117.

58. Chicherin, "Contemporary Tasks," 121.

59. Chicherin, "Contemporary Tasks," 133–34.

60. Chicherin, "Contemporary Tasks," 134–39.

61. B. N. Chicherin, "Razlichnye vidy liberalizma," in Abramov, *Opyt russkogo liberalizma*, 41–42.

62. Chicherin, "Razlichnye vidy liberalizma," 44–45.

63. Chicherin, "Razlichnye vidy liberalizma," 49.

64. Chicherin, "Konstitutsionnyi vopros v Rossii," 56.

65. B. N. Chicherin, "Excerpts from 'Property and the State,'" in Chicherin, *Liberty, Equality, and the Market*, 365.

66. B. N. Chicherin, "Excerpts from 'On Popular Representation,'" in Chicherin, *Liberty, Equality, and the Market*, 182.

67. Chicherin, "Excerpts from 'On Popular Representation,'" 162.

68. Chicherin, "Excerpts from 'On Popular Representation,'" 206.

69. Lincoln, *In the Vanguard of Reform*, 196.

70. Polunov, *Russia in the Nineteenth Century*, 129–30.

71. Polunov, *Russia in the Nineteenth Century*, 129–30.

72. Polunov, *Russia in the Nineteenth Century*, 134.

73. Gary M. Hamburg, "Boris Chicherin and Human Dignity in History," in Hamburg and Poole, *A History of Russian Philosophy*, 122.

74. Aleksandr Viktorich Kiriakin, "Politicheskii, ekonomicheskii i sotsial'nyi liberalizm B. N. Chicherina," *Vestnik TGU* 2, no. 2 (2015): 61.

75. B. N. Chicherin, "On Serfdom," in Chicherin, *Liberty, Equality, and the Market*, 73.

76. Chicherin, "On Serfdom," 71.

77. Chicherin, "On Serfdom," 74.

78. Walicki, *Flow of Ideas*, 238.

79. Walicki, *Legal Philosophies*, 125–28.

80. Chicherin, "On Serfdom," 102.

81. Gary M. Hamburg, "Peasant Emancipation and Russian Social Thought: The Case of Boris N. Chicherin," *Slavic Review* 50, no. 4 (1991): 896–98.

82. Robinson, *Russian Conservatism*, 94.

83. Robinson, *Russian Conservatism*, 94–95.

84. Robinson, *Russian Conservatism*, 94.

85. Gorlov, "Dva 'vzgliada' russkogo liberala," 47.

86. Gorlov, "Dva 'vzgliada' russkogo liberala," 48.

87. Gorlov, "Dva 'vzgliada' russkogo liberala," 48.

4. The Era of Counter-Reform

1. Joseph Bradley, "Associations and the Development of Civil Society in Tsarist Russia," *Social Science History* 41, no. 1 (2017): 19.

2. Mary Schaeffer Conroy, "Civil Society in Late Imperial Russia," in *Russian Civil Society: A Critical Assessment*, ed. Alfred B. Evans Jr., Laura A. Henry, and Lisa McIntosh Sundstrom (Armonk, NY: M. E. Sharpe, 2006), 11–27.

3. Bradley, "Associations," 38.

4. Rampton, *Liberal Ideas*, 65.

5. Galai, *Liberation Movement*, 126.

6. Milyoukov, *Russia and Its Crisis*, 30.

7. Riha, *Russian-European*, 78.

8. Khevrolina, "Russian Liberalism's View on Foreign Policy," 89.

9. Vladimir S. Soloviev, "Pan Mongolism," http://max.mmlc.northwestern.edu/mdenner/Demo/texts/panmongolism.html.

10. Patrick Lally Michelson, "Freedom of Conscience and the Limits of the Liberal Solovyov," *Solov'evskie issledovaniia* 1, no. 41 (2014): 37. Also, Walicki, *Flow of Ideas*, 547.

11. Vladimir Sergeyevich Solovyov, *The Justification of the Good: An Essay on Moral Philosophy* (New York: Cosimo, 2010), 1.

12. Solovyov, *Justification of the Good*, 88.

13. Paul Valliere, *Modern Russian Theology: Bukharev, Soloviev, Bulgakov: Theology in a New Key* (Grand Rapids, MI: William B. Eerdmans, 2000), 137.

14. Gaut, "Practical Unity," 295.

15. Vladimir S. Soloviev, "Morality and Politics," in Soloviev, *Politics, Law and Morality: Essays by V. S. Soloviev* (New Haven, CT: Yale University Press, 2000), 6.

16. Vladimir S. Soloviev, "Nationality from a Moral Point of View," in Soloviev, *Politics, Law, and Morality*, 53.

17. Soloviev, "Morality and Politics," 11.

18. Poole, "Editor's Introduction," 26.

19. Sergei N. Bulgakov, "Basic Problems of the Theory of Progress," in Poole, *Problems of Idealism*, 86–87.

20. Bulgakov, "Basic Problems," 105.

21. Petr B. Struve, "Toward Characterization of Our Philosophical Development," in Poole, *Problems of Idealism*, 148.

22. P. I. Novgorodtsev, "Ethical Idealism in the Philosophy of Law (On the Question of the Revival of Natural Law)," in Poole, *Problems of Idealism*, 275.

23. Novgorodtsev, "Ethical Idealism," 276.

24. Petr B. Struve, "V chem zhe istinnyi natsionalizm?," in *Na raznye temy (1893–1901 gg.): Sbornik stat'ei* (St. Petersburg: Tipografiia Doma Prizren. Malopheti. Bedn., 1902), 545.

25. Struve, "V chem zhe istinnyi natsionalizm?," 555.

26. Pipes, *Struve: Liberal on the Left*, 28; Sergei Sekirinskii, "Petr Berngardovich Struve," in Kara-Murza, *Rossiiskii liberalizm*, 454.

27. Rabow-Edling, *Liberalism in Pre-Revolutionary Russia*, 115–16.

28. Vlada V. Vostrikova, "Rossiiskie liberaly o roli gosudarstva v obshchestvennom razvitii," *Izvestiia vysshikh uchebnykh zavedenii. Povolzhskii region* 1 (2008): 23.

29. Fischer, *Russian Liberalism*, 162–63.

30. Galai, *Liberation Movement*, 195.

31. Shmuel Galai, "The Impact of War on the Russian Liberals in 1904–5," *Government and Opposition* 1, no. 1 (1965): 94.

32. Fischer, *Russian Liberalism*, 161. Also, Pipes, *Struve: Liberal on the Left*, 338–42.

33. Galai, "Impact of the War," 94–95.

34. Fischer, *Russian Liberalism*, 49.

35. Fischer, *Russian Liberalism*, 27.

36. Fischer, *Russian Liberalism*, 26.

37. Fedyashin, *Liberals under Autocracy*, 149.

38. Vladimir S. Soloviev, "Law and Morality," in Soloviev, *Politics, Law, and Morality*, 136.

39. Soloviev, "Law and Morality," 147.

40. Solovyov, *Justification of the Good*, 381.

41. Solovyov, *Justification of the Good*, 459.

42. Struve, "V chem zhe istinnyi natsionalizm?," 538.

43. Gianmaria Ajani, "Russian Liberalism and the Rule of Law: Notes from Underground," in Cucciolla, *Dimensions and Challenges*, 45.

44. Leon Petrazycki, *Law and Morality* (New Brunswick, NJ: Transaction, 2011), 112.

45. Petrazycki, *Law and Morality*, 236.

46. Petrazycki, *Law and Morality*, 98.

47. Petrazycki, *Law and Morality*, 99.

48. Walicki, *Flow of Ideas*, 734.

49. Galai, *Liberation Movement*, 25.

50. Galai, *Liberation Movement*, 26.

51. Galai, *Liberation Movement*, 52–54; Also, Terence Emmons, "The Beseda Circle, 1899–1905," *Slavic Review* 32, no. 3 (1973): 464–66.

52. Galai, *Liberation Movement*, 3.

53. For an alternative interpretation of events, see Gregory L. Freeze, "A National Liberation Movement and the Shift in Russian Liberalism, 1901–1903," *Slavic Review* 28, no. 1 (1969): 81–91.

54. Leontovitsch, *History of Liberalism in Russia*, 222.

55. Leontovitsch, *History of Liberalism in Russia*, 223–24.

56. Fischer, *Russian Liberalism*, 134.

57. Galai, *Liberation Movement*,172–75.

58. Galai, *Liberation Movement*, 189.

59. Rampton, *Liberal Ideas*, 91.

60. Rampton, *Liberal Ideas*, 33.

61. Medushevsky, *Russian Constitutionalism*, 105.

62. Leontovitsch, *History of Liberalism in Russia*, 224.

63. Pipes, *Struve: Liberal on the Left*, 326.

64. Rampton, *Liberal Ideas*, 92.

65. Galai, *Liberation Movement*, 220.

66. Fischer, *Russian Liberalism*, 172.

67. Fischer, *Russian Liberalism*, 192–94.

68. Fischer, *Russian Liberalism*, 183.

69. Leontovitsch, *History of Liberalism in Russia*, 232.

70. Pipes, *Struve: Liberal on the Left*, 374–75.

71. Rampton, *Liberal Ideas*, 95.

72. A. N. Medushevsky, "The Constitutional Projects of Russian Liberalism and Its Political Strategy," *Russian Studies in History* 37, no. 3 (1998): 51–52.

73. Medushevsky, "The Constitutional Projects of Russian Liberalism," 52–53.

74. Pipes, *Struve: Liberal on the Left*, 381–82.

75. Riha, *Russian-European*, 62.

76. Milyoukov, *Russia and Its Crisis*, 561.

77. Valerii Stepanov, "Nikolai Khristianovich Bunge," in Kara-Murza, *Rossiiskii liberalizm*, 264–74.

78. Bennett, *History of Russian Economic Thought*, 43.

79. Polunov, *Russia in the Nineteenth Century*, 179.

80. Bennett, *History of Russian Economic Thought*, 44–45.

81. Polunov, *Russia in the Nineteenth Century*, 181; Frederick C. Giffin, "The Formative Years of the Russian Factory Inspectorate," *Slavic Review* 25, no. 4 (1966): 641–42.

82. Polunov, *Russia in the Nineteenth Century*, 179.

83. Bennett, *History of Russian Economic Thought*, 45.

84. Bennett, *History of Russian Economic Thought*, 45.

85. Sekirinskii, "Petr Berngardovich Struve," 451; Wayne Dowler, "The Intelligentsia and Capitalism," in *A History of Russian Thought*, ed. William Leatherbarrow and Derek Offord (Cambridge: Cambridge University Press, 2010), 282.

86. Pipes, *Struve: Liberal on the Left*, 64.

87. Pipes, *Struve: Liberal on the Left*, 92.

88. Milyoukov, *Russia and Its Crisis*, 459.

89. Milyoukov, *Russia and Its Crisis*, 474.

90. Anton A. Fedyashin, "Humane Modernization as a Liberal Ideal: Late Imperial Russia on the Pages of the 'Herald of Europe,' 1891–1904," *The Historian* 71, no. 4 (2009): 801.

91. Fedyashin, *Liberals under Autocracy*, 171.

92. Fedyashin, *Liberals under Autocracy*, 191.

93. Fedyashin, *Liberals under Autocracy*, 150.

94. Fedyashin, *Liberals under Autocracy*, 169.

95. Robinson, *Russian Conservatism*, 110.

96. Fedyashin, *Liberals under Autocracy*, 158.

97. Fedyashin, *Liberals under Autocracy*, 192.

98. Fedyashin, *Liberals under Autocracy*, 193.

99. Fedyashin, *Liberals under Autocracy*, 140; Also, V. A. Kitaev, "The Unique Liberalism of *Vestnik Evropy* (1870–1890)," *Russian Studies in History* 46, no. 1 (2007): 49, 59.

100. Vladimir Soloviev, "The Social Question in Europe," in Soloviev, *Politics, Law, and Morality*, 32–33. See also Solovyov, *Justification of the Good*, 274–75.

101. Solovyov, *Justification of the Good*, 318, 323.

102. Solovyov, *Justification of the Good*, 325.

103. Soloviev, "Law and Morality," 169.

104. Soloviev, "Law and Morality," 179, 184.

105. Beer, *Renovating Russia*, 35–44.

106. Beer, *Renovating Russia* 57–58.

107. Beer, *Renovating Russia*, 67.

108. Beer, *Renovating Russia*, 23, 122–28.

109. Beer, *Renovating Russia*, 208–09.

110. William G. Wagner, "Family Law, the Rule of Law, and Liberalism in Late Imperial Russia," *Jahrbücher für Geschichte Osteuropas* 43, no. 4 (1995): 522.

111. Wagner, "Family Law," 526–27.

112. Wagner, "Family Law," 530.

113. Rosenberg, "Representing Workers," 251.

114. Rosenberg, "Representing Workers," 248.

115. Galai, *Liberation Movement*, 179.

116. F. A. Gaida, "Osobennosti natsional'nogo politicheskogo opyta rossiiskogo liberala nachala xx v.," in Shelokhaev, *Rossiiskii liberalizm*, 178.

5. Between Revolutions

1. Robert W. Thurston, *Liberal City, Conservative State: Moscow and Russia's Urban Crisis, 1906–1914* (Oxford: Oxford University Press, 1987), 188.

2. Shmuel Galai, "The True Nature of Octobrism," *Kritika: Explorations in Russian and Eurasian History* 5, no. 1 (2004): 137–47.

3. Galai, "True Nature of Octobrism," 144.

4. Enticott, *Russian Liberals*, 45.

5. Dittmar Dahlmann, "Liberals in the Provinces: The Kadets and the Duma Elections in Saratov, 1906–1912," in *Emerging Democracy in Late Imperial Russia: Case Studies on Local Self-Government (the Zemstvos), State Duma Elections, the Tsarist Government, and the State Council before and during World War I*, ed. Mary Schaeffer Conroy (Niwot: University Press of Colorado, 1998), 98.

6. Enticott, *Russian Liberals*, 177.

7. Enticott, *Russian Liberals*, 180.

8. Enticott, *Russian Liberals*, 180.

9. David Wartenweiler, *Civil Society and Academic Debate in Russia, 1915–1914* (Oxford: Oxford University Press, 2011), 76.

10. Wartenweiler, *Civil Society*, 78.

11. Wartenweiler, *Civil Society*, 166, 172.

12. Lindenmeyr, *Citizen Countess*, 95–100.

13. Lindenmeyr, *Citizen Countess*, 100, 135.

14. Lindenmeyr, *Citizen Countess*, 134.

15. Irina Sizemskaia and Lidiia Novikova, "Novyi liberalizm v Rossii," *Obshchestvennye nauki i sovremennost'* 5 (1993): 136.

16. Shamil' Shamkhalov, "Osobennosti ideino-politicheskikh programmnykh ustanovok kadetov," *Vlast'* 11 (2010): 84.

17. Rosenberg, "Representing Workers," 259. Emphases in original.

18. George Putnam, "P. B. Struve's View of the Russian Revolution of 1915," *Slavonic and East European Review* 45, no. 105 (1967): 465.

19. Pipes, *Struve: Liberal on the Right*, 69–70.

20. Nikolai Berdiaev, "Philosophical Verity and Intelligentsia Truth," in Berdiaev et al., *Landmarks*, 6.

21. Sergei N. Bulgakov, "Heroism and Asceticism: Reflections on the Religious Nature of the Russian Intelligentsia," in Berdiaev et al., *Landmarks*, 39.

22. Bogdan Kistiakovskii, "In Defense of Law: The Intelligentsia and Legal Consciousness," in Berdiaev et al., *Landmarks*, 91–113.

23. Semen Frank, "The Ethic of Nihilism: A Characterization of the Russian Intelligentsia's Moral Outlook," in Berdiaev et al., *Landmarks*, 141.

24. Petr B. Struve, "The Intelligentsia and Revolution," in Berdiaev et al., *Landmarks*, 127.

25. Riha, *Russian European*, 175.

26. Riha, *Russian European*, 177.

27. Petr B. Struve, "Chto zhe takoe Rossiia?" *Russkaia Mysl'*, January 1911, http://az.lib.ru/s/struwe_p_b/text_1911_chto_takoe_rossia.shtml.

28. Riha, *Russian European*, 185.

29. Liutz Khefner and A. Kaplunovskogo "'Konstitutsionno-demokraticheskaia partiia ne menee tverdo derzhitsia printsipa edinstva i nerazdel'nosti Rossii': Liberalizm i natsionalizm v rossiiskoi provintsii, 1905–1914 gg.," *Ab Imperio* 2000, no. 3 (2000): 116.

30. Shelokhaev, *Liberal'naia model'*, 76.

31. Shamil' Shamkhalov, "Sushchnostnye kharakteristiki novogo liberalizma kak ideino-politicheskoi platformy kadetov," *Vlast'* 4 (2011): 60–61.

32. Enticott, *Russian Liberals*, 153; Rabow-Edling, *Liberalism in Pre-Revolutionary Russia*, 110.

33. Shamkhalov, "Sushchnostnye kharakteristiki," 61.

34. Petr B. Struve, "Velikaia Rossiia: Iz razmyshlenii o probleme russkogo mogushchestva," *Russkaia Mysl'*, 1908, https://yabloko.ru/Themes/History/struve.htm.

35. Petr B. Struve, "Otryvki o gosudarstve," in Abramov, *Opyt russkogo liberalizma*, 269–70.

36. Williams, *The Reformer*, 263.

37. Shelokhaev, *Liberal'naia model'*, 204.

38. Shelokhaev, *Liberal'naia model'*, 203.

39. Shelokhaev, *Liberal'naia model'*, 218.

40. Shelokhaev, *Liberal'naia model'*, 218.

41. Riha, *Russian European*, 217.

42. Randall A. Poole, "Religion, War, and Revolution: E. N. Trubetskoi's Liberal Construction of Russian National Identity, 1912–20," *Kritika: Explorations in Russian and Eurasian History* 7, no. 2 (2006): 211.

43. Poole, "Religion, War, and Revolution," 214.

44. Poole, "Religion, War, and Revolution," 214.

45. For detailed discussions of the different viewpoints on this matter, see Walicki, *Legal Philosophies*, 292–402; Rampton, *Liberal Ideas*, 135–84; Vlada V. Vostrikova, "Vlast' v predstavlenii rossiiskikh liberalov nachala xx v.," *Vlast'* 1 (2010): 67–69; Vostrikova, "Gosudarstvo i pravo v teoriakh rossiiskikh liberalov nachala xx v.," *Izvestiia Vysshikh Uchebnykh Zavedenii. Povolzhskii Region* 3 (2010): 36–43; Vostrikova, "Rossiiskie liberaly o roli gosudarstva v obshchestvennom razvitii," *Izvestiia vysshikh uchebnykh zavedenii. Povolzhskii region* 1 (2008): 20–27; and Zharikov, "Zashchita idei pravoporiadka," 84–86.

46. Ajani, "Russian Liberalism and the Rule of Law," 49.

47. Walicki, *Legal Philosophies*, 367.

48. M. M. Kovalevskii, "Uchenie o lichnykh pravakh," in Abramov, *Opyt russkogo liberalizma*, 175.

49. Nina B. Khailova, "'Drug poriadka, osnovannogo na svobode i prave': M. M. Kovalevskii protiv P. A. Stolypina," in *Sergei Andreevich Muromtsev—Predsedatel' pervoi gosudarstvennoi dumy: Politik, uchenyi, pedagog* (Orel: Orlik, 2000), 213.

50. Williams, *The Reformer*, 146.

51. Donald W. Treadgold, "The Constitutional Democrats and the Russian Liberal Tradition," *American Slavic and East European Review* 10, no. 2 (1951): 92.

52. Enticott, *Russian Liberals*, 73; Riha, *Russian European*, 105.

53. Linda Harriet Edmonson, *Feminism in Russia, 1900–17* (Stanford, CA: Stanford University Press, 1984), 27–28.

54. Edmonson, *Feminism in Russia*, 44.

55. Edmonson, *Feminism in Russia*, 50.

56. Edmonson, *Feminism in Russia*, 61.

57. Enticott, *Russian Liberals*, 52; Riha, *Russian European*, 95-97.

58. Enticott, *Russian Liberals*, 57.

59. Enticott, *Russian Liberals*, 178. Emphasis in original.

60. Michael Karpovich, "Two Types of Russian Liberalism: Maklakov and Miliukov," in Simmons, *Continuity and Change*, 138.

61. Williams, *The Reformer*, 123.

62. Enticott, *Russian Liberals*, 111; E. K. Zolotukhina, "Bor'ba za prava cheloveka: Konstitutsionno-demokraticheksaia partiia i partiia demokraticheskikh reform v pervoi gosudarstvennoi dume," in *Sergei Andreevich Muromtsev*, 235–36.

63. Enticott, *Russian Liberals*, 197.

64. Riha, *Russian European*, 138.

65. Riha, *Russian European*, 140–41.

66. Andrei N. Egorov, "Kadety i P. A. Stolypin: Problema vsaimootnosheniia," in *Sergei Andreevich Muromtsev*, 205.

67. T. A. Saburova, "'Revolutsionnyi i konservativnyi liberalizm': Vospominaniia russkikh liberalov o vsaimootnosheniiakh vlasti i obshchestva v Rossii nachala xx v.," *Vestnik Omskogo universiteta: Seriia "Istoricheskie nauki"* 8, no. 4 (2015): 55.

68. Leontovitsch, *History of Liberalism in Russia*, 314.

69. Abraham Ascher, *P. A. Stolypin: The Search for Stability in Late Imperial Russia* (Stanford, CA: Stanford University Press, 2001), 186–87.

70. Galai, "Kadets in the Second Duma," 11.

71. Riha, *Russian European*, 197.

72. Raymond Pearson, *The Russian Moderates and the Crisis of Tsarism, 1914–1917* (London: Macmillan, 1977), 16.

73. Pearson, *Russian Moderates*, 31–32.

74. Oleg V. Budnitskii and Robin Ganev, "Russian Liberalism in War and Revolution," *Kritika: Explorations in Russian and Eurasian History* 5, no. 1 (2004): 155.

75. Pearson, *Russian Moderates*, 49.

76. Pearson, *Russian Moderates*, 67; Rosenberg, *Liberals in the Russian Revolution*, 41–42.

77. Pearson, *Russian Moderates*, 112–13.

78. Williams, *The Reformer*, 292–93.

79. Pearson, *Russian Moderates*, 117.

80. Paul Robinson, *Grand Duke Nikolai Nikolaevich: Supreme Commander of the Russian Army* (DeKalb: Northern Illinois University Press, 2014), 290–91.

81. Stephen F. Williams, *Liberal Reform in an Illiberal Regime: The Creation of Private Property in Russia, 1906–1915* (Stanford, CA: Hoover Institution Press, 2006), 141–42.

82. Leontovitsch, *History of Liberalism in Russia*, 167.

83. Peter Stolypin, "We Need a Great Russia," in *Readings in Russian Civilization*, vol. 2, *Imperial Russia, 1700–1917*, ed. Thomas Riha (Chicago: University of Chicago Press, 1964), 458.

84. Stolypin, "We Need a Great Russia," 459.

85. Stolypin, "We Need a Great Russia," 462.

86. Williams, *Liberal Reform*, 146.

87. Kojima, "Russian Liberal Visions," 60.

88. Kojima, "Russian Liberal Visions," 68.

89. A possible exception could be made for Struve. See Anna Klimina, "Ideas of Constructed Market in Late Imperial Russia: Constructivist Liberalism of Peter Struve (1870–1944)," *Economics Bulletin* 31, no. 3 (2011): 2041–52.

90. Leontovitsch, *History of Liberalism in Russia*, 170.

91. Egorov, "Kadety i P. A. Stolypin," 201; Khailova, "'Drug poriadka,'" 215.

92. Fleischhauer, "Agrarian Program," 182–83.

93. Fleischhauer, "Agrarian Program," 173–201.

94. Fleischhauer, "Agrarian Program," 176.

95. Rampton, *Liberal Ideas*, 108.

96. Kirill Solov'ev, "Lev Iosifovich Petrazhitskii," in Kara-Murza, *Rossiiskii liberalizm*, 686.

97. P. I. Novgorodtsev, "Pravo na dostoinoe chelovecheskoe sushchestvovanie," in P. I. Novgorodtsev and I. A. Pokrovskii, *O prave na sushchestvovanie* (St. Petersburg: Izdanie T-va M. O. Vol'f, 1911), 10–11.

98. Novgorodtsev, "Pravo na dostoinoe chelovecheskoe sushchestvovanie," 5–6.

99. Novgorodtsev, "Pravo na dostoinoe chelovecheskoe sushchestvovanie," 9, 11, 12.

100. Rampton, *Liberal Ideas*, 155–56. For a critique of Novgorodtsev's New Liberalism, see George Putnam, *Russian Alternatives to Marxism: Christian Socialism and Idealistic Liberalism in Twentieth-Century Russia* (Knoxville: University of Tennessee Press, 1977), 166.

101. P. I. Novgorodtsev, "Idealy partii narodnoi svobody i sotsializm," in Abramov, *Opyt russkogo liberalizma*, 298. For a discussion of the influence of socialism on liberal thought, see Sizemskaia and Novikova, "Novyi liberalizm," 135.

102. S. A. Kotliarevskii, "Predposylki demokratii," in Abramov, *Opyt russkogo liberalizma*, 225.

103. Riha, *Russian European*, 92.

104. Rosenberg, "Representing Workers," 261. Emphases in original.

105. Shelokhaev, *Liberal'naia model'*, 114–30.

106. Shelokhaev, *Liberal'naia model'*, 256; V. I. Sedugin, "Liberaly tsentral'noi Rossii i rabochii klass," *Izvestiia Vysshikh Uchebnykh Zavedenii. Povolzhskii Region* 3 (2008): 19–20; N. K. Volkova, "P. N. Miliukov: Istorik, politik," *Vestnik Rossiiskogo Universiteta Kooperatsii* 2 (2015): 130.

107. Rosenberg, "Representing Workers," 257–58.

108. Rosenberg, "Representing Workers," 255.

109. Sedugin, "Liberaly tsentral'noi Rossii," 22.

110. Dahlmann, "Liberals in the Provinces," 100.

6. Revolution and Civil War

1. For details of workers' and peasants' demands, see Marc Ferro, *The Russian Revolution of February 1917* (London: Routledge and Kegan Paul, 1972), 113–16, 129.

2. Ferro, *Russian Revolution*, 271.

3. Ferro, *Russian Revolution*, 279.

4. Petr B. Struve, "Istoricheskii smysl' russkoi revolutsii i natsional'nye zadachi," in *Iz glubiny: Sbornik statei o russkoi revolutskii*, ed. S. A. Askol'dov (Paris: YMCA Press, 1967), 303–4.

5. Rosenberg, *Liberals in the Russian Revolution*, 74–76.

6. Budnitskii and Ganev, "Russian Liberalism in War and Revolution," 152.

7. E. A. Tamarenkova, "Konstitutsionnye demokraty i 'ukrainsky vopros' v 1917 g.: Problemy preodoleniia kompleksov," in Shelokhaev, *Rossiiskii liberalizm*, 350.

8. Rosenberg, *Liberals in the Russian Revolution*, 126.

9. Tamarenkova, "Konstitutsionnye demokraty," 353–54.

10. Tamarenkova, "Konstitutsionnye demokraty," 355.

11. Rosenberg, *Liberals in the Russian Revolution*, 204.

12. Rosenberg, *Liberals in the Russian Revolution*, 330.

13. Procyk, *Russian Nationalism*, 82.

14. Procyk, *Russian Nationalism*, 172.

15. Procyk, *Russian Nationalism*, 102.

16. Procyk, *Russian Nationalism*, 103.

17. Rosenberg, *Liberals in the Russian Revolution*, 134.

18. Ariadna Tyrkova-Williams, *From Liberty to Brest-Litovsk: The First Year of the Russian Revolution* (London: Macmillan, 1919), 200.

19. E. V. Liubeznova, "Kadety Sibiri v poiskakh form organizatsii vlasti v pervyi god grazhdanskoi voiny," *Omskii nauchnyi vestnik* 2 (2011): 24.

20. Tyrkova-Williams, *From Liberty to Brest-Litovsk*, 202.

21. Tyrkova-Williams, *From Liberty to Brest-Litovsk*, 196

22. Rosenberg, *Liberals in the Russian Revolution*, 259.

23. Tyrkova-Williams, *From Liberty to Brest-Litovsk*, 205.

24. Williams, *The Reformer*, 321–25.

25. Shelokhaev, *Liberal'naia model'*, 67.

26. Pomeranz, *Law and the Russian State*, 69.

27. Lindenmeyr, *Citizen Countess*, 162.

28. Gaida, "Osobennosti," 180.

29. Riha, *Russian European*, 298.

30. Michael C. Hickey, "Discourses of Public Identity and Liberalism in the February Revolution: Smolensk, Spring 1917," *Russian Review* 55, no. 4 (1996): 615–37.

31. Medushevsky, *Russian Constitutionalism*, 126–28.

32. Rosenberg, *Liberals in the Russian Revolution*, 134–35.

33. Rosenberg, *Liberals in the Russian Revolution*, 173.

34. Rosenberg, *Liberals in the Russian Revolution*, 206.

35. Rosenberg, *Liberals in the Russian Revolution*," 48, 208, 222. For the examples of Evgeny Trubetskoi and Pavel Miliukov, see Poole, "Religion, War, and Revolution," 223, and Volkova, "P. N. Miliukov," 133.

36. F. A. Seleznev, "Partiia kadetov v gody grazhdanskoi voiny: Problemnye voprosy istoriografii," in Shelokhaev, *Rossiiskii liberalizm*, 145.

37. Valentin Shelokhaev, "Ariadna Vladimirovna Tyrkova," in Kara-Murza, *Rossiiskii liberalizm*, 741.

38. Rosenberg, *Liberals in the Russian Revolution*, 267–68. Budnitskii and Ganev, "Russian Liberalism in War and Revolution," 154.

39. William G. Rosenberg, "Russian Liberals and the Bolshevik Coup," *Journal of Modern History* 40, no. 3 (1968), 338.

40. Rosenberg, "Russian Liberals and the Bolshevik Coup," 345.

41. Rosenberg, "Russian Liberals and the Bolshevik Coup," 347.

42. Lindenmeyr, *Citizen Countess*, 244.

43. Rosenberg, *Liberals in the Russian Revolution*, 310.

44. Andrei N. Egorov, "'A Democrat by Mistake': Political Activity of Anton Kartashev during the Russian Civil War," *Historia Provinciae: The Journal of Regional History* 4, no. 3 (2020): 968.

45. Egorov, "Democrat by Mistake," 969.

46. Liubeznova, "Kadety Sibiri," 24.

47. Liubeznova, "Kadety Sibiri," 26.

48. Rosenberg, *Liberals in the Russian Revolution*, 416.

49. Rosenberg, *Liberals in the Russian Revolution*, 410.

50. Rosenberg, "Russian Liberals and the Bolshevik Coup," 335.

51. Budnitskii and Ganev, "Russian Liberalism in War and Revolution," 154.

52. Rosenberg, *Liberals in the Russian Revolution*, 426.

53. Shelokhaev, *Liberal'naia model'*, 132–33.

54. Ferro, *Russian Revolution*, 90-91.

55. Rosenberg, *Liberals in the Russian Revolution*, 81.

56. Rosenberg, *Liberals in the Russian Revolution* 138–40.

57. Rosenberg, *Liberals in the Russian Revolution*, 141.

58. Mikhail Karpachev, "Andrei Ivanovich Shingarev," in Kara-Murza, *Rossiiskii liberalizm*, 721.

59. Rosenberg, *Liberals in the Russian Revolution*, 91–92.

60. Rosenberg, *Liberals in the Russian Revolution*, 200–203.

61. Rosenberg, *Liberals in the Russian Revolution*, 246.

62. Rosenberg, *Liberals in the Russian Revolution*, 404.

63. Rosenberg, *Liberals in the Russian Revolution*, 424.

64. Riha, *Russian European*, 332.

65. Tyrkova-Williams, *From Liberty to Brest-Litovsk*, 368.

66. Struve, "Istoricheskii smysl' russkoi revolutsii," 291.

67. Ivan Il'in, *Nashi zadachi: Stat'i 1948–1954 gg.*, vol. 1 (Paris: Izdanie Russkogo Obshche-Voinskogo Soiuza, 1956), 129.

7. Emigration

1. For histories of Russia Abroad, see: Marc Raeff, *Russia Abroad: A Cultural History of the Russian Emigration, 1919–1939* (Oxford: Oxford University Press, 1990); Mikhail Nazarov, *Missiia russkoi emigratsii* (Stavropol: Kavkazskii krai, 1992); L. K. Shkarenkov, *Agoniia beloi emigratsii* (Moscow: Mysl', 1986); Robert H. Johnson, *New Mecca, New Babylon: Paris and the Russian Exiles, 1920–1945* (Montreal: McGill-Queen's University Press, 1988); and Robert C. Williams, *Culture in Exile: Russian Émigrés in Germany, 1881–1941* (Ithaca, NY: Cornell University Press, 1972).

2. For a history of the expulsions of 1922 and the fate of those involved, see Lesley Chamberlain, *The Philosophy Steamer: Lenin and the Exile of the Intelligentsia* (London: Atlantic, 2006).

3. Lindenmeyr, *Citizen Countess*, 257, 258.

4. Pavel Litvinov, Mikhail Meerson-Aksenov, and Boris Shragin, "Ot sostavitelei," in *Samosoznanie: Sbornik statei*, ed. Pavel Litvinov, Mikhail Meerson-Aksenov, and Boris Shragin (New York Khronika, 1976), 6–7.

5. Georgy P. Fedotov, "Zachem my zdes'?," *Sovremennye Zapiski* 48 (1935): 436.

6. W. Chapin Huntington, *The Homesick Million: Russia-out-of-Russia* (Boston: Stratford, 1933), 153–54.

7. Chamberlain, *Philosophy Steamer*, 26.

8. Natal'ia Aleksandrovna Ekhina, "Transformatsiia politicheskikh pozitsii kadetskoi intelligentsii v 1917—pervoi polovine 1930 gg.," PhD diss., Moskovskii Gosudarstvennyi Universitet, 2012, 16.

9. See, for instance, Tsoncho Tsonchev, "Person and Communion: The Political Theology of Nikolai Berdyaev," PhD diss., McGill University, 2020, 117, 199; Ekhina, "Transformatsiia," 16; Chamberlain, *Philosophy Steamer*, 26; Aleksandr S. Tsipko, "Liberal'nyi konservatizm Nikolaia Berdiaeva i Petra Struve i zadachi dekommunizatsii sovremennoi Rossii," *Tetradi po konservatizmu* 2, no. 1 (2014): 31–39.

10. Nicolas Berdyaev, *Slavery and Freedom* (New York: Charles Scribner's Sons, 1944), 17.

11. Berdyaev, *Slavery and Freedom*, 10.

12. Tsonchev, "Person and Communion," 188.

13. L. G. Berezovaia, "Interpretatsiia liberalizma v obshchestvennoi mysli russkoi emigratsii," in Shelokhaev, *Rossiiskii liberalizm*, 77.

14. Berdyaev, *Slavery and Freedom*, 59.

15. Nicolas Berdyaev, *Freedom and the Spirit* (London: Geoffrey Bles, 1948), 145.

16. Berdyaev, *Freedom and the Spirit*, 152.

17. Berdyaev, *Freedom and the Spirit*, 157.

18. F. A. Stepun, "O svobode (Demokratiia, diktatura i 'Novyi Grad')," in Abramov, *Opyt russkogo liberalizma*, 356, 367.

19. Stepun, "O svobode," 356, 358.

20. Aleksei Kara-Murza, *Svoboda i poriadok: Iz istorii russkoi politicheskoi mysli xix–xx vv.* (Moscow: Moskovskaia Shkola Politicheskikh Issledovanii, 2009), 207.

21. Fedotov, "Zachem my zdes'?," 444.

22. Georgy P. Fedotov, "Problemy budushchei Rossii," (part 1) *Sovremennye Zapiski* 46 (1931): 391.

23. Fedotov, "Problemy budushchei Rossii" (part 1), 392.

24. Kara-Murza, *Svoboda i poriadok*, 206.

25. Kara-Murza, *Svoboda i poriadok*, 207.

26. Kara-Murza, *Svoboda i poriadok*, 207.

27. V. A. Gusev, *Russkii konservatizm: Osnovnye napravleniia i etapy razvitiia* (Tver: Tverskii Gosudarstvennyi Universitet, 2001), 110.

28. Gusev, *Russkii konservatizm*, 111.

29. Gusev, *Russkii konservatizm*, 113.

30. Philip J. Swoboda, "Semen Frank's Expressive Humanism," in Hamburg and Poole, *History of Russian Philosophy*, 207.

31. Vladimir Kantor, "Semen Liudovich Frank," in Kara-Murza, *Rossiiskii liberalizm*, 857.

32. Kantor, "Semen Liudovich Frank," 857.

33. Struve, "Istoricheskii smysl'," 303–4.

34. Ekhina, "Transformatsiia," 31.

35. Letter, P. N. Miliukov to E. D. Kuskova, in *Politicheskaia istoriia russkoi emigratsii, 1920–1940 gg.: Dokumenty i materialy*, ed. A. F. Kiselev (Moscow: Gumanitarnyi Izdatel'skii Tsentr, 1999), http://www.rus-sky.com/history/library/emigration.

36. Pavel N. Miliukov, *Tri platformy Respublikansko-Demokraticheskikh Ob"edinenii (1922–24 gg.)* (Paris: Izdanie Respublikansko-demokraticheskogo ob"edineniia, 1925), 24.

37. Miliukov, *Tri platformy*, 19–20. For a discussion of Miliukov's views on the nationality issue, see Antonenko, "Emigrantskie liberal'nye kontseptsii," 259–63.

38. Valentin Shelokhaev, *Konstitutsionno-demokraticheskaia partiia v Rossii i emigratsii* (Moscow: Rosspen, 2015), 750–51.

39. Glebov, "Congresses of Russia Abroad," 180–83.

40. "Doklad I. F. Semenova," in *Rossiiskii Zarubezhnyi S"ezd 1926 Parizh: Dokumenty i materialy* (Moscow: Russkii Put', 2006), 503.

41. "Doklad I. F. Semenova," 499.

42. Pavel N. Miliukov, "Chto delat' posle Krymskoi katastrophy?" in *Protokoly Tsentral'nogo Komiteta i zagranichnykh grupp konstitutsionno-demokraticheskoi partii, 1905—seredina 1930–kh gg.* (Moscow: Rosspen, 1996), 4:76.

43. Miliukov, "Chto delat' posle Krymskoi katastrophy?" 77.

44. Miliukov, "Chto delat' posle Krymskoi katastrophy?" 78.

45. Miliukov, "Chto delat' posle Krymskoi katastrophy?" 79–82; Aleksandrov, *Lider rossiiskikh kadetov*, 29–35.

46. Shelokhaev, *Konstitutsionno-demokraticheskaia partiia*, 784.

47. Shelokhaev, *Konstitutsionno-demokraticheskaia partiia*, 797.

48. Shelokhaev, "Ariadna Vladimirovna Tyrkova," 743.

49. Shelokhaev, *Konstitutsionno-demokraticheskaia partiia*, 814–15.

50. Shelokhaev, *Konstitutsionno-demokraticheskaia partiia*, 819.

51. Shkarenkov, *Agoniia*, 34.

52. Rosenberg, *Liberals in the Russian Revolution*, 461.

53. Shelokhaev, *Konstitutsionno-demokraticheskaia partiia*, 721–22.

54. Shelokhaev, *Konstitutsionno-demokraticheskaia partiia*, 833–34.

55. Shelokhaev, *Konstitutsionno-demokraticheskaia partiia*, 835.

56. Shelokhaev, *Konstitutsionno-demokraticheskaia partiia*, 838.

57. Pavel N. Miliukov, *Emigratsiia na pereput'e* (Paris: Izdanie Respublikansko-Demokraticheskogo Ob"edineniia, 1926), 101.

58. Ekhina, "Transformatsiia," 29.

59. Miliukov, *Tri platformy*, 17, 19.

60. Shelokhaev, *Konstitutsionno-demokraticheskaia partiia*, 827.

61. Egorov, "Democrat by Mistake," 968.

62. Egorov, "Democrat by Mistake," 968.

63. For a description of Aleksinsky's life, see Kara-Murza, *Svoboba i poriadok*, 160–99.

64. Glebov, "Congresses of Russia Abroad," 169.

65. Pipes, *Struve: Liberal on the Right*, 383.

66. Glebov, "Congresses of Russia Abroad," 169.

67. Pipes, *Struve: Liberal on the Right*, 412.

68. Pipes, *Struve: Liberal on the Right* 416.

69. Kantor, "Semen Liudvigovich Frank," 858.

70. Kara-Murza, *Svoboda i poriadok*, 82.

71. Boobbyer, "Russian Liberal Conservatism," 43.

72. Georgy P. Fedotov, "Nasha demokratiia," *Novyi Grad 9* (1934): 12.

73. Fedotov, "Problemy budushchei Rossii" (part 2), 476, 477.

74. Fedotov, "Problemy budushchei Rossii" (part 2), 480.

75. Kara-Murza, *Svoboda i poriadok*, 208.

76. Kara-Murza, *Svoboda i poriadok* 210.

77. Fedotov, "Nasha demokratiia," 21–22.

78. Stepun, "O svobode," 366–67.

79. Stepun, "O svobode," 371

80. Stepun, "O svobode," 371.

81. Stepun, "O svobode," 379.

82. A. V. Berlov, "Predstaviteli liberal'noi ekonomicheskoi shkoly russkoi emigrat-sii 1920–1930-kh gg. o putiakh resheniia krest'ianskogo voprosa v Rossii v nachale xx veka," *Prostranstva i vremia* 1, no. 15 (2014): 162. Galina Vasil'evna Nintsieva, "Osnovnye techeniia ekonomicheskoi mysli russkoi emigratsii 20–50-x godov xx stoletiia," PhD diss., Kandidat ekonomicheskikh nauk, Sankt-Peterburgskii Gosudarstvennyi Universitet Ekonomiki i Finansov, 2004, 16.

83. Nintsieva, "Osnovnye techeniia," 17–18.

84. Shelokhaev, *Konstitutsionno-demokraticheskaia partiia*, 757–58.

85. Miliukov, *Tri platformy*, 38.

86. Miliukov, *Tri platformy*, 61

87. Miliukov, *Tri platformy*, 41.

88. Miliukov, *Tri platformy*, 32.

89. Miliukov, *Tri platformy*, 33.

90. Miliukov, *Tri platformy*, 34.

91. Shelokhaev, *Konstitutsionno-demokraticheskaia partiia*, 755.

92. Shelokhaev, *Konstitutsionno-demokraticheskaia partiia*, 756.

93. Shelokhaev, *Konstitutsionno-demokraticheskaia partiia*, 753.

94. Berdyaev, *Slavery and Freedom*, 211.

95. Fedotov, "Problemy budushchei Rossii" (part 1), 414.

96. Fedotov, "Problemy budushchei Rossii" (part 1), 414.

97. Fedotov, "Problemy budushchei Rossii" (part 1), 417.

98. Fedotov, "Problemy budushchei Rossii" (part 1), 420.

99. Georgy P. Fedotov, "My i oni," *Sovremennye Zapiski* 70 (1940): 224.

100. Fedotov, "Problemy budushchei Rossii" (part 1), 420.

101. Nintsieva, "Osnovnye techeniia," 10.

102. Nintsieva, "Osnovnye techeniia," 12.

103. Pipes, *Struve: Liberal on the Right*, 410.

104. For a summary of Brutskus's views, see Wilhelm, "Soviet Economic Failure."

105. Boris Brutzkus, *Economic Planning in Soviet Russia* (London: Routledge, 1935), 25–26.

106. Brutzkus, *Economic Planning*, 44.

107. Shuichi Kojima, "Exiled Russian Economists and the USSR: Brutzkus and Prokopovich," in *Economics in Russia: Studies in Intellectual History*, ed. Joachim Zweynert (London: Routledge, 2008), 127.

108. Brutzkus, *Economic Planning*, 69.

109. Boris Brutskus, "Narodnoe khoziastvo sov. Rossii, ego priroda i ego sud'by" (part 1), *Sovremennye Zapiski* 38 (1929): 430.

110. Brutskus, "Narodnoe khoziastvo sov. Rossii" (part 2), 474.

111. V. A. Maklakov, "Iz proshlogo" (part 1), *Sovremennye Zapiski* 38 (1929): 296.

112. Maklakov, "Iz proshlogo" (part 1): 300.

113. Maklakov, "Iz proshlogo" (part 1): 313.

114. Maklakov, "Iz proshlogo" (part 2), 301, 305.

115. Maklakov, "Iz proshlogo" (part 2), 306.

116. Maklakov, "Iz proshlogo" (part 3), 267.

117. Pavel N. Miliukov, "Sud nad kadetskim 'liberalizmom,'" *Sovremennye Zapiski* 41 (1930): 359.

118. Pavel N. Miliukov, "Liberalizm, radikalizm, i revolutsiia," *Sovremennye Zapiski* 47 (1935): 292, 294.

119. Miliukov, "Liberalizm, radikalizm, i revolutsiia," 306.

120. Marina Galas, "'Respublikansko-demokraticheskoe ob"edinenie' Rossiiskoi emigratsii: Organizatsiia, strategiia i taktika," *Vlast'* 6 (2008): 84.

8. Soviet Liberalism

1. Vladislav Zubok, *Zhivago's Children: The Last Russian Intelligentsia* (Cambridge, MA: Belknap Press of Harvard University Press, 2009), 131.

2. Robert David English and Ekaterina (Kate) Svyatets, "Soviet Elites and European Integration: From Stalin to Gorbachev," *European Review of History* 21, no. 2 (2014): 224–25.

3. Richard Pipes, *Alexander Yakovlev: The Man Whose Ideas Delivered Russia from Communism* (DeKalb: Northern Illinois University Press, 2015), 49.

4. Philip Boobbyer, *Conscience, Dissent and Reform in Soviet Russia* (London: Routledge, 2005), 161.

5. For a Soviet dissident's view on "opposition sentiments in scientific towns," see Boris Shragin, "Oppozitsionnye nastroeniia v nauchnykh gorodakh," *SSSR: Vnutrennie protivorechiia* 1 (1981): 100–120.

6. Andrei Sakharov, *Memoirs* (New York: Vintage, 1992), 319.

7. Daniel C. Thomas, *The Helsinki Effect: International Norms, Human Rights, and the Demise of Communism* (Princeton, NJ: Princeton University Press, 2001), 161–64, 211.

8. Thomas, *Helsinki Effect*, 2.

9. Vasilii Zharkov, "Liberaly v SSSR i RF," *Russkii Zhurnal*, April 7, 2009, http://www.russ.ru/Mirovaya-povestka/Liberaly-v-SSSR-i-RF.

10. Benjamin Nathans, "The Dictatorship of Reason: Aleksandr Vol'pin and the Idea of Rights under 'Developed Socialism'," *Slavic Review* 66, no. 4 (2007): 661.

11. For an exception, see the editors' introduction to the collection of dissident essays entitled *Samosoznanie*, in which the editors identified themselves as "liberal democrats": Litvinov, Meerson-Aksenov, and Shragin, "Ot sostavitelei," in Litvinov, Meerson-Aksenov, and Shragin, *Samosoznanie*, 5–7. Marc Raeff contests this self-identification. See Marc Raeff, "What Became of the Liberal Tradition? Comments on *Samosoznanie*," *Slavic Review* 37, no. 1 (1978): 116.

12. Mikhail Epstein, *The Phoenix of Philosophy: Russian Thought of the Late Soviet Period (1953–1991)* (New York: Bloomsbury Academic, 2019), Kobo edition, part IIIB, section 1.

13. Emma Gilligan, *Defending Human Rights in Russia: Sergei Kovalyov, Dissident and Human Rights Commissioner, 1969–2003* (London: Routledge, 2004), 2.

14. Gilligan, *Defending Human Rights*.

15. English, *Russia and the Idea of the West*, 3.

16. English, *Russia and the Idea of the West*, 5.

17. Georgi Arbatov, *The System: An Insider's Life in Soviet Politics* (New York: Times Books, 1992), 37.

18. English, *Russia and the Idea of the West*, 72.

19. Epstein, *Phoenix of Philosophy*, part II, section 4.

20. Epstein, *Phoenix of Philosophy*, part II, section 7.

21. Alisa Slaughter and Julia Sushytska, "Introduction," in *A Spy for an Unknown Country: Essays and Lectures by Merab Mamardashvili*, ed. Alisa Slaughter and Julia Sushytska (Stuttgart: Ibidem-Verlag, 2020), 17.

22. Merab Mamardashvili, "The 'Third' State," in Slaughter and Sushytska eds, *Spy for an Unknown Country*, 176.

23. Mamardashvili, "'Third' State," 165.

24. Alexander Zinoviev, *The Reality of Communism* (New York: Schocken, 1984), 109.

25. Zinoviev, *The Reality of Communism*, 234.

26. V. Gorskii, "Russian Messianism and the New National Consciousness," in *The Political, Social and Religious Thought of Russian "Samizdat": An Anthology*, ed. Michael Meerson-Aksenov and Boris Shragin (Belmont: Nordland, 1977), 386.

27. Lev Ventsov, "To Think!," in Meerson-Aksenov and Shragin, *Political, Social and Religious Thought of Russian "Samizdat"*, 158.

28. Gilligan, *Defending Human Rights*, 30.

29. Andrei Amalrik, *Will the Soviet Union Survive Until 1984?* (New York: Harper and Row, 1971), 36–37.

30. Geoffrey Hosking, *The Awakening of the Soviet Union* (London: Heinemann, 1990), 43-44.

31. Lipovetsky, "Poetics of ITR Discourse," 116.

32. Lipovetsky, "Poetics of ITR Discourse," 119.

33. Theodore Friedgut, "The Democratic Movement: Dimensions and Perspectives," in *Dissent in the USSR: Politics, Ideology, and People*, ed. Rudolf L. Tokes (Baltimore: Johns Hopkins University Press, 1975), 131.

34. Ventsov, "To Think!" 159.

35. Boris Shragin, "Toska po istorii," in Litvinov, Meerson-Aksenov, and Shragin, *Samosoznanie*, 277.

36. Grigorii Pomerants, "Chelovek niotkuda," http://www.liv.piramidin.com/publ/Pomerants_G/chelovek-niotkuda.htm.

37. Pomerants, "Chelovek niotkuda."

38. Ventsov, "To Think!" 164.

39. Boobbyer, *Conscience, Dissent and Reform*, 228.

40. Wallace L. Daniel, *Russia's Uncommon Prophet: Father Aleksandr Men and His Times* (DeKalb: Northern Illinois University Press, 2016), 2.

41. Aleksandr Men, "Christianity," http://www.alexandermen.com/Christianity.

42. Daniel, *Russia's Uncommon Prophet*, 174.

43. Daniel, *Russia's Uncommon Prophet*, 209, 215.

44. Alexander Men, "From 'On Christ and the Church'," http://alexandermen.com/On_Christ_and_the_Church.

45. Alexander Men, "Two Understandings of Christianity," http://www.alexandermen.com/Two_Understandings_of_Christianity.

46. Alexander Men, "Interview on the State of the Russian Church," http://alexandermen.com/Interview_on_the_state_of_the_Russian_Church.

47. Andrei Sakharov, "On Aleksandr Solzhenitsyn's *Letter to the Soviet Leaders*," in Meerson-Aksenov and Shragin, *Political, Social and Religious Thought*, 294.

48. Grigorii Pomerants, "Modernizatsiia nezapadnykh stran," in Litvinov, Meerson-Aksenov and Shragin, *Samosoznanie*, 218.

49. Gorskii, "Russian Messianism," 366, 386.

50. Gorskii, "Russian Messianism," 393.

51. For comments to this effect, see M. A. Abramov, "Liberalizm v SSSR," in Abramov, *Opyt russkogo liberalizma*, 441; Also, Hosking, *Awakening of the Soviet Union*, 141.

52. "Konstitutsiia (Osnovnoi zakon) Rossiiskoi Sotsialisticheskikh Federativnoi Sovetskoi Respubliki (priniata V Vserossiiskim S"ezdom Sovetov v zasedanii ot 10 ii-ula 1918 g.)," Sait Konstitutsii Rossiiskoi Federatsii, http://www.constitution.garant.ru/history/ussr-rsfsr/1918/.

53. Samantha Lomb, *Stalin's Constitution: Soviet Participatory Politics and the Discussion of the 1936 Draft Constitution* (London: Routledge, 2018), 15–16.

54. Lomb, *Stalin's Constitution*, 14.

55. "Konstitutsiia (Osnovnoi zakon) Soiuza Sovetskikh Sotsialisticheskikh Respublik (utverzhdena postanovleniem Chrezvychainogo VIII S"ezda Soiuza Sovetskikh Sotsial-isticheskikh Respublik ot 5 Dekabria 1936 g.)," Sait Konstitutsii Rossiiskoi Federatsii, http://www.constitution.garant.ru/history/ussr-rsfsr/1936/red_1936/3958676.

56. "Konstitutsiia (Osnovnoi zakon) Soiuza Sovetskikh Sotsialisticheskikh Respub-lik (priniata na vnecherednoi sed'moi sessii Verkhogno Soveta deviatogo sozyva 7 Ok-tiabria 1977 g.)," Sait Konstitutsii Rossiiskoi Federatsii, http://www.constitution.garant.ru/history/ussr-rsfsr/1977/red_1977/5478732/.

57. For a discussion of the limitations of the rights in the 1977 constitution, see Pomeranz, *Law and the Russian State*, 100–105; and Olimpiad S. Ioffe, "Soviet Attitudes toward International Human Rights Law," *Connecticut Journal of International Law 2*, no. 2 (1987): 361–65.

58. Geoffrey A. Hosking, Jonathan Aves, and Peter J. S. Duncan, *The Road to Post-Communism: Independent Political Movements in the Soviet Union, 1985–1991* (London: Pinter, 1992), 2.

59. Hosking, Aves, and Duncan, *Road to Post-Communism*, 2.

60. Aleksandra Andreevna Dorskaia, "Universal'nye mezhdunarodno-pravovye standarty v obespechenii prav cheloveka i pravovye traditsii Rossii," *Iuridicheskaia nauka* 5 (2016): 135.

61. Inna Vladimirovna Logvinova, "Mezhdunarodnye pakty o pravakh cheloveka 1966 g. v kontekste razvitiia obshchepriznannykh prav i svobod lichnosti," *Mezhdun-arodnoe Pravo i Mezhdunarodnye Organizatsii* 1 (2017): 56–64. Also, I. A. Aggeeva, "Dzhon Khamfri i Sovetskii Soiuz," *Kanadskii Ezhegodnik* 19 (2015): 24.

62. Aggeeva, "Dzhon Khamfri," 20.

63. Dorskaia, "Universal'nye mezhdunarodno-pravovye standarty," 137.

64. For a statement to this effect, see John Quigley, "Human Rights Study in Soviet Academia," *Human Rights Quarterly* 11, no. 3 (1989): 455.

65. Aggeeva, "Dzhon Khamfri," 36–47.

66. Thomas, *Helsinki Effect*, 62.

67. Thomas, *Helsinki Effect*, 64–85.

68. "Conference on Security and Cooperation in Europe, Final Act," Helsinki, 1975, https://www.osce.org/files/f/documents/5/c/39501.pdf.

69. Pavel Litvinov, "O dvizhenii za prava cheloveka v SSSR," in Litvinov, Meerson-Aksenov and Shragin, *Samosoznanie*, 78, 86.

70. Valery Chalidze, *The Soviet Human Rights Movement: A Memoir* (New York: Jacob Blaustein Institute for the Advancement of Human Rights, 1984), 4.

71. Nathans, "Dictatorship of Reason," 656–57.

72. Nathans, "Dictatorship of Reason," 631.

73. Gilligan, *Defending Human Rights*, 28.

74. Amalrik, *Will the Soviet Union Survive?*, 13.

75. Chalidze, *Soviet Human Rights Movement*, 7, 13.

76. Chalidze, *Soviet Human Rights Movement*, 5.

77. Serguei Alex Oushakine, "The Terrifying Mimicry of Samizdat," *Public Culture* 13, no. 2 (2001): 199.

78. Oushakine, "Terrifying Mimicry of Samizdat," 207.

79. Michael Meerson-Aksenov, "Rozhdenie novoi intelligentsii," in Litvinov, Meerson-Aksenov, and Shragin, *Samosoznanie*, 114; Dmitrii Nelidov, "Ideokraticheskoe soznanie i'," in Litvinov, Meerson-Aksenov, and Shragin, *Samosoznanie*, 140; and Sergei Kovalev, cited in Boobbyer, *Conscience, Dissent and Reform*, 76.

80. Chalidze, *Soviet Human Rights Movement*, 27.

81. Litvinov, "O dvizhenii," 79.

82. Ivan Sablin, "Parliaments and Parliamentarism in the Works of Soviet Dissidents, 1960s–80s," *Parliaments, Estates and Representation* 40, no. 1 (2020): 79.

83. Sablin, "Parliaments and Parliamentarism," 88; Abraham Rothberg, *The Heirs of Stalin: Dissidence and the Soviet Regime 1953–1970* (Ithaca, NY: Cornell University Press, 1971), 294–95.

84. Sablin, "Parliaments and Parliamentarism," 89.

85. Nathans, "Coming to Terms with Late Soviet Liberalism," 179.

86. Andrei Sakharov, "Progress, Coexistence, and Intellectual Freedom," in Andrei D. Sakharov, *Sakharov Speaks* (New York: Alfred A. Knopf, 1974), 108.

87. Peter Dornan, "Andrei Sakharov: The Conscience of a Liberal Scientist," in Tokes, *Dissent in the USSR*, 383.

88. Sakharov, *My Country and the World* (New York: Alfred A. Knopf, 1976), 102.

89. Sakharov, "On Aleksandr Solzhenitsyn's *Letter*," 297–98.

90. Sakharov, *My Country*, 55.

91. Sakharov, *Memoirs*, 644.

92. Valentin Turchin, "Chto takoe bespristrastnost'?" in Litvinov, Meerson-Aksenov, and Shragin, *Samosoznanie*, 310.

93. Litvinov, "O dvizhenii," 65.

94. Litvinov, "O dvizhenii," 66.

95. Kojima, "Russian Liberal Visions," 55–76.

96. Kojima, "Russian Liberal Visions," 62–63.

97. Kojima, "Russian Liberal Visions," 65.

98. Yevsei Liberman, "The Soviet Economic Reform," *Foreign Affairs* 46, no. 1 (1967): 58.

99. Paul Robinson and Jay Dixon, *Aiding Afghanistan: A History of Soviet Assistance to a Developing Country* (London: Hurst, 2013), 40.

100. R. N. Andreasian and L. N. Vinogradrova, "Razvivaiushchiesia strany: Gorno-dobyvaiushchaia promyshlennost' i problemy industrializatsii," *Narody Azii i Afriki* 5 (1970): 29.

101. A. I. Dinkevich, "O strategii ekonomicheskogo razvitiia stran 'tret'ego mira,'" *Narody Azii i Afriki* 1 (1975): 9, 10.

102. Dinkevich, "O strategii ekonomicheskogo razvitiia," 9.

103. Dinkevich, "O strategii ekonomicheskogo razvitiia," 12.

104. English, *Russia and the Idea of the West*, 99–100.

105. English, *Russia and the Idea of the West*, 144–45. See also English and Svyatets, "Soviet Elites and European Integration," 225–26.

106. English, *Russia and the Idea of the West*, 96.

107. English, *Russia and the Idea of the West*, 99.

108. Amalrik, *Will the Soviet Union Survive?*, 12.

109. Nathans, "Human Rights Defenders within Soviet Politics," 66.

110. Zinoviev, *Reality of Communism*, 199.

111. Iurii Orlov, "Vozmozhen li sotsializm ne totalitarnogo tipa?," in Litvinov, Meerson-Aksenov, and Shragin, *Samosoznanie*, 280.

112. Orlov, "Vozmozhen li sotsializm," 282.

113. Orlov, "Vozmozhen li sotsializm," 288–89.

114. Orlov, "Vozmozhen li sotsializm," 299–301.

115. Sakharov, "Progress, Coexistence," 97.

116. Sakharov, "Progress, Coexistence," 104–5.

117. Sakharov, *Memoirs*, 629.

118. Sakharov, *My Country*, 100-102.

119. Zubok, *Zhivago's Children*, 265.

9. Perestroika

1. William Taubman, *Gorbachev: His Life and Times* (New York: W. W. Norton, 2017), 215. Georgy Arbatov commented that "the overwhelming majority of reformers and dissidents started with a belief in the age-old promises of communism"; Arbatov, *The System*, 309. Svetlana Savranskaya, "Gorbachev's New Thinking: A Post-Liberal Program for the Soviet Union," in Cucciolla, *Dimensions and Challenges*, 109-110.

2. Anatoly S. Chernyaev, *My Six Years with Gorbachev* (University Park: Pennsylvania State University Press, 2000), 71, 97.

3. Mikhail Gorbachev, *Perestroika: New Thinking for Our Country and the World* (London: Collins, 1987), 36.

4. Gorbachev, *Perestroika*, 17, 24.

5. Boobbyer, *Conscience, Dissent, and Reform*, 207.

6. Quigley, "Human Rights Study," 452. Geoffrey Hosking, *The Awakening of the Soviet Union* (London: Heinemann, 1990), 144–45.

7. Marc Nuttall, "Tipping Points and the Human World: Living with Change and Thinking about the Future," *Ambio* 41, no. 1 (2012): 97–98.

8. Alexander Lukin, *The Political Culture of the Russian "Democrats"* (Oxford: Oxford University Press, 2000), 161.

9. Lukin, *Political Culture of the Russian "Democrats"*, 153, 158.

10. Aleksandr Tsipko, for instance, commented that "in the ideology espoused by the authors of *Vekhi* and in the works of Sergei Bulgakov, Nikolai Berdyaev, and Semen Frank I discovered my own brand of liberal patriotism. . . . The patriotism of

Pyotr Struve became my patriotism." Alexander S. Tsipko, "The Collapse of Marxism-Leninism," in *The Destruction of the Soviet Economic System*, ed. Michael Ellman and Vladimir Kontorovich (London: Routledge, 2015), 172.

11. Lukin, *Political Culture of the Russian "Democrats"*, 151.

12. Gorbachev, *Perestroika*, 197, 209.

13. Taubman, *Gorbachev*, 467.

14. Gorbachev, *Perestroika*, 137, 188.

15. Leonid Batkin, "Turn to Be Europe," *XX Century and Peace* 8 (1988): 31.

16. Batkin, "Turn to Be Europe," 32.

17. Batkin, "Turn to Be Europe," 33.

18. For a discussion of the national question in the late Soviet Union, see Gail W. Lapidus, "Transforming the 'National Question': New Approaches to Nationalism, Federalism and Sovereignty," in *The Demise of Marxism-Leninism in Russia*, ed. Archie Brown (Basingstoke: Palgrave, 2004), 139.

19. Vera Tolz, *The USSR's Emerging Multiparty System* (New York: Praeger, 1990), 71.

20. Geoffrey Hosking, "The Beginnings of Independent Political Activity," in Hosking, Aves, and Duncan, *Road to Post-Communism*, 78.

21. Chernyaev, *My Six Years with Gorbachev*, 254.

22. Peter J. S. Duncan, "The Rebirth of Politics in Russia," in Hosking, Aves, and Duncan, *Road to Post-Communism*, 91.

23. Duncan, "Rebirth of Politics," 67.

24. Chernyaev, *My Six Years with Gorbachev*, 321.

25. Duncan, "Rebirth of Politics," 105.

26. Pipes, *Alexander Yakovlev*, 31. See also Aleksandr Yakovlev, "Perestroika or the 'Death of Socialism,'" in *Voices of Glasnost: Interviews with Gorbachev's Reformers*, ed. Stephen F. Cohen and Katrina Vanden Heuvel (New York: W. W. Norton, 1989), 33–75.

27. Alexander Yakovlev, "The Memorandum of December 1985," in Pipes, *Alexander Yakovlev*, 119–28.

28. Alexander M. Yakovlev, *Striving for Law in a Lawless Land: Memoirs of a Russian Reformer* (Armonk, NY: M. E. Sharpe, 1996), 56, 62–63.

29. Gorbachev, *Perestroika*, 105.

30. Hosking, "The Beginnings," 13.

31. Sauvé, *Subir la victoire*, 119–21.

32. Lukin, *Political Culture of the Russian "Democrats"*, 75.

33. Tolz, *USSR's Emerging Multiparty System*, 57.

34. Lukin, *Political Culture of the Russian "Democrats"*, 186.

35. M. Steven Fish, *Democracy from Scratch: Opposition and Regime in the New Russian Revolution* (Princeton: Princeton University Press, 1995). 108. Hosking, "The Beginnings," 20.

36. Boobbyer, *Conscience, Dissent, and Reform*, 212.

37. Tolz, *USSR's Emerging Multiparty System*, 75–76.

38. Sauvé, *Subir la victoire*, 144.

39. Sauvé, *Subir la victoire*, 146–47.

40. Fish, *Democracy from Scratch*, 116.

41. Fish, *Democracy from Scratch*, 88–89; Duncan, "Rebirth of Politics,"101.

42. Yitzhak M. Brudny, "The Dynamics of 'Democratic Russia,' 1990–1993," *Post-Soviet Affairs* 9, no. 2 (1993): 151.

43. Lukin, *Political Culture of the Russian "Democrats"*, 105.

44. Fish, *Democracy from Scratch*, 117.

45. Fish, *Democracy from Scratch*, 114.

46. Duncan, "Rebirth of Politics," 98.

47. Duncan, "Rebirth of Politics," 99.

48. Lukin, *Political Culture of the Russian "Democrats"*, 208–9.

49. Sauvé, "Subir la victoire," 226.

50. Lukin, *Political Culture of the Russian "Democrats"*, 62.

51. A. Migranyan, "The Long Road to the European Home," *Current Digest of the Soviet Press* 41, no. 42 (1989): 6.

52. Migranyan, "The Long Road," 8.

53. "Nuzhna li zheleznaia ruka?" *Vremia i my* 107 (1989): 127. For a discussion of Migranian's and Kliamkin's views, see Sauvé, *Subir la victoire*, 160–90.

54. "Nuzhna li zheleznaia ruka?" 125.

55. "Nuzhna li zheleznaia ruka?" 126.

56. Barry Sautman, "The Devil to Pay: The 1989 Debate and the Intellectual Origins of Yeltsin's 'Soft Authoritarianism,'" *Communist and Post-Communist Studies* 28, no. 1 (1995): 138.

57. For example, see Alexei Yemelyanov, "Economic and Political Perestroika," *Cato Journal* 11, no. 2 (1991): 273.

58. Gulnaz Sharafutdinova, "Was There a 'Simple Soviet' Person? Debating the Politics and Sociology of 'Homo Sovieticus,'" *Slavic Review* 78, no. 1 (2019): 178.

59. Lukin, *Political Culture of the Russian "Democrats"*, 202, 212.

60. "Zhestkim kursom: Analiticheskaia zapiska ASEN," LiveJournal, June 1990, https://aillarionov.livejournal.com/470196.html.

61. Lukin, *Political Culture of the Russian "Democrats"*, 62.

62. Tobias Rupprecht, "Formula Pinochet: Chilean Lessons for Russian Liberal Reformers during the Soviet Collapse, 1970–2000," *Journal of Contemporary History* 51, no. 1 (2016): 174.

63. Alfred Koch and Igor Svinarenko, *A Crate of Vodka* (New York: Enigma, 2000), 44, 285.

64. Sautman, "Devil to Pay," 139–40; Duncan, "Rebirth of Politics," 112–13.

65. Tat'iana I. Zaslavskaia, "The Novosibirsk Report," in *A Voice of Reform: Essays by Tat'iana I. Zaslavskaia*, ed. Murray Yanowitch (Armonk, NY: M. E. Sharpe, 1989), 159.

66. For more on this, see Vadim Medvedev, "Under Andropov and Gorbachev," in Ellman and Kontorovich, *Destruction of the Soviet Economic System*, 95–96.

67. Zaslavskaia, "Novosibirsk Report," 168, 162.

68. Tatyana Zaslavskaya, "Socialism with a Human Face," in Cohen and Vanden Heuvel, *Voices of Glasnost*, 123.

69. Nikolai Shmelev, "Avansy i dolgy," *Novyi Mir* 6 (1987): 147.

70. Shmelev, "Avansy i dolgy," 154.

71. Nikolai Shmelyov, "Rebirth of Common Sense," in Cohen and Vanden Heuvel, *Voices of Glasnost*, 151.

72. Shmelyov, "Rebirth of Common Sense," 151.

73. Shmelyov, "Rebirth of Common Sense," 153.

74. Gorbachev, *Perestroika*, 36, 83.

75. Vladimir Mozhin, "It Was about Enterprise Autonomy," in Ellman and Kontorovich, *Destruction of the Soviet Economic System*, 137.

76. Rupprecht, "Formula Pinochet," 174.

77. Yevgenii Yasin, "Getting the Details Wrong," in Ellman and Kontorovich, *Destruction of the Soviet Economic System*, 145.

78. Larisa Piyasheva, "Economic Reform: A Great Bubble or a Faint Chance to Survive?," *Cato Journal* 11, no. 2 (1991): 293.

79. Koch and Svinarenko, *Crate of Vodka*, 193.

80. A. Popkova, "Gde pyshnee pirogi?" *Novyi Mir* 5 (1987): 239.

81. Popkova, "Gde pyshnee pirogi?" 239.

82. Popkova, "Gde pyshnee pirogi?" 240.

83. Boris Pinsker and Larisa Piiasheva, "Sobstvennost' i svoboda," *Novyi Mir* 11 (1989): 191.

84. Pinsker and Piiasheva, "Sobstvennost' i svoboda," 196–97.

85. Yasin, "Getting the Details Wrong," 150.

86. Yakovlev, "Perestroika or the 'Death of Socialism,'" 57.

87. Abel G. Aganbegian, "The Program of Radical Restructuring," *Problems of Economics* 31, no. 5 (1988): 8, 17, 18.

88. Yevgenii Yasin, "Unintended Consequences at Work," in Ellman and Kontorovich, *Destruction of the Soviet Economic System*, 157.

89. Taubman, *Gorbachev*, 450.

90. Yevgenii Yasin, "The Parade of Market Transformation Programs," in Ellman and Kontorovich, *Destruction of the Soviet Economic System*, 228.

91. Yasin, "The Parade," 235–36.

92. Chernyaev, *My Six Years with Gorbachev*, 286. Taubman, *Gorbachev* 528.

93. Taubman, *Gorbachev*, 529.

94. Joachim Zweynert, "Economic Ideas and Institutional Change: Evidence from the Soviet Economic Debates, 1987–1991," *Europe-Asia Studies* 58, no. 2 (2006): 190.

95. Sauvé, *Subir la victoire*, 84-86.

96. Zweynert, "Economic Ideas," 191.

97. E. Iasin, "Problems of Making the Transition to a Regulated Market Economy," *Problems of Economics* 33, no. 12 (1991): 12.

98. Iasin, "Problems of Making the Transition," 13.

99. Iasin, "Problems of Making the Transition," 21–23.

100. Iasin, "Problems of Making the Transition," 29.

101. Anatoly A. Sobchak, "Transition to a Market Economy," *Cato Journal* 11, no. 2 (1991): 196.

102. Sobchak, "Transition to a Market Economy," 197.

103. Sobchak, "Transition to a Market Economy," 198.

104. Graham Allison and Grigory Yavlinsky, *Window of Opportunity: The Grand Bargain for Democracy in the Soviet Union* (New York: Pantheon, 1991), 35.

105. "Zhestkim kursom."

106. Iasin, "Problems of Making the Transition," 18.

107. Allison and Yavlinsky, *Window of Opportunity*, 33–34.

108. Igor Timofeyev, "The Development of Russian Liberal Thought since 1985," in Brown ed., *Demise of Marxism-Leninism*, 92–93.

109. Zweynert, "Economic Ideas," 192.

110. Zweynert, "Economic Ideas," 191–92.

10. Russian Liberalism under Yeltsin

1. Boris Yeltsin, *Against the Grain: An Autobiography* (London: Jonathan Cape, 1990); Boris Yeltsin, *The Struggle for Russia* (New York: Times Books, 1994).

2. Timothy J. Colton, *Yeltsin: A Life* (New York: Basic Books, 2008), 219.

3. Colton, *Yeltsin*, 8.

4. Gennadi Kazakevitch, "Yegor Gaidar: Pragmatic Economist or Romantic Revolutionary?," *Agenda: A Journal of Policy Analysis and Reform* 17, no. 1 (2010): 128.

5. Olga Malinova, "Encounters with Liberalism in Post-Soviet Russia," in *In Search of European Liberalisms: Concepts, Languages, Ideologies*, ed. Michael Freeden, Javier Fernandez-Sebastian, and Jörn Leonhard (New York: Berghahn, 2019), 284.

6. Hilary Appel, *A New Capitalist Order: Privatization and Ideology in Russia and Eastern Europe* (Pittsburgh: University of Pittsburgh Press, 2004), 167.

7. Padma Desai, *Conversations on Russia: Reform from Yeltsin to Putin* (Oxford: Oxford University Press, 2006), 194, 198.

8. Yegor Gaidar, *Days of Defeat and Victory* (Seattle: University of Washington Press, 1996), 191.

9. Yegor Gaidar, *Russia: A Long View* (Cambridge, MA: MIT Press, 2012), xiv.

10. Yegor Gaidar, *State and Evolution: Russia's Search for a Free Market* (Seattle: University of Washington Press, 2003), 5.

11. Gaidar, *State and Evolution* 53, 116.

12. David White, *The Russian Democratic Party Yabloko: Opposition in a Managed Democracy* (Aldershot: Ashgate, 2006), 73.

13. Grigory Yavlinsky, "Where Is Russia Headed? An Uncertain Prognosis," *Journal of Democracy* 8, no. 1 (1997): 4.

14. Yavlinsky, "Where Is Russia Headed?" 5.

15. Gilligan, *Defending Human Rights*, 4.

16. Gilligan, *Defending Human Rights*, 169.

17. Gaidar, *Days of Defeat and Victory*, 283.

18. Malinova, "Encounters," 290.

19. Herbert J. Ellison, *Boris Yeltsin and Russia's Democratic Transformation* (Toronto: University of Toronto Press, 2006), 202.

20. Grigory Yavlinsky, "Russia's Phony Capitalism," *Foreign Affairs* 77, no. 3 (1998): 76–77.

21. Dmitry Sokolov-Mitrich, "The Russia They Lost," *Slavyangrad*, September 24, 2014, https://slavyangrad.org/2014/09/24/the-russia-they-lost/.

22. Anatol Lieven, "How the West Lost," *Prospect*, August 31, 2020, https://www.prospectmagazine.co.uk/magazine/how-the-west-lost-victory-communism-moral-defeat.

23. Ellison, *Boris Yeltsin*, 208.

24. Desai, *Conversations*, 79-80.

25. Anders Åslund, *How Russia Became a Market Economy* (Washington, DC: Brookings Institution, 1995), 87; Chrystia Freeland, *Sale of the Century: Russia's Wild Ride from Communism to Capitalism* (Toronto: Doubleday, 2000), 45–46.

26. Gaidar, *Days of Defeat and Victory*, 257.

27. Ellison, *Boris Yeltsin*, 149.

28. Lynn D. Nelson and Irina Y. Kuzes, *Property to the People: The Struggle for Radical Economic Reform in Russia* (Armonk, NY: M. E. Sharpe, 1994), 110

29. Yakovlev, *Striving for Law*, 147.

30. Ellison, *Boris Yeltsin*, 93.

31. Gilligan, *Defending Human Rights*, 116–17.

32. Gilligan, *Defending Human Rights*, 117.

33. Valeriia Novodvorskaia, "Na toi edinstvennoi, grazhdanskoi," *Ogonek* 2–3 (1994), 26–27.

34. Sauvé, *Subir la Victoire*, 218–19.

35. Gaidar, *Days of Defeat*, 252.

36. Sergei Chuprinin, "Choice: Notes of a Russian Liberal: The Experience of Self-Identification," *Russian Politics and Law* 32, no. 5 (1994): 33.

37. Peter Reddaway and Dmitri Glinski, *The Tragedy of Russia's Reforms: Market Bolshevism against Democracy* (Washington, DC: United States Institute of Peace, 2001), 300.

38. Rupprecht, "Formula Pinochet," 182.

39. Lieven, "How the West Lost."

40. Reddaway and Glinski claim that the referendum passed due only to "government voter fraud": Reddaway and Glinski, *Tragedy of Russia's Reforms*, 432.

41. "Konstitutsiia Rossiiskoi Federatsii," 1993, http://www.constitution.ru/.

42. "Konstitutsiia Rossiiskoi Federatsii."

43. Vladimir Mau, "Macroeconomic Stabilization as a Sociopolitical Problem," in *The Economics of Transition*, ed. Yegor Gaidar (Cambridge, MA: MIT Press, 2003), 101–2.

44. Marcia A. Weigle, *Russia's Liberal Project: State-Society Relations in the Transition from Communism* (University Park: Pennsylvania State University Press, 2000), 227, 236.

45. Guillaume Sauvé, "The Lessons from Perestroika and the Evolution of Russian Liberalism (1995–2005)," in Cucciolla, *Dimensions and Challenges*, 165; White, *Russian Democratic Party Yabloko*, 53, 71; V. Sogrin, "Liberalizm v Rossii: Peripetii i perspektivy," *Obshchestvennye nauki i sovremennost'* 1 (1997): 17–21. A. V. Golovchenko divides the strands of liberal thought into three, those of Gaidar-Chubais, Nemtsov, and Yavlinsky: A. V. Golovchenko, "Postsovetskie liberal'nye politiki: Politicheskaia tselesoobraznost' ili moral'nyi imperativ?" *Vestnik Moskovskogo gosudarstvennogo oblastnogo universiteta* 3 (2018): 3–20.

46. Weigle, *Russia's Liberal Project*, 397–409.

47. Weigle, *Russia's Liberal Project*, 410.

48. Gaidar, *Days of Defeat*, 289–93.

49. White, *Russian Democratic Party Yabloko*, 90.

50. Yavlinsky, "Where Is Russia Headed?" 7.

51. Peter Rutland, "Grigorii Yavlinskii: The Man Who Would Be King," *Problems of Post-Communism* 46, no. 5 (1999): 48.

52. White, *Russian Democratic Party Yabloko*, 129.

53. M. Steven Fish, "The Predicament of Russian Liberalism: Evidence from the December 1995 Parliament Elections," *Europe-Asia Studies* 49, no. 2 (1997): 207.

54. Fish, "Predicament of Russian Liberalism," 210.

55. White, *Russian Democratic Party Yabloko*, 113.

56. White, *Russian Democratic Party Yabloko*, 166.

57. Freeland, *Sale of the Century*, 116-118.

58. White, *Russian Democratic Party Yabloko*, 170.

59. Freeland, *Sale of the Century*, 133. Reddaway and Glinski, *Tragedy of Russia's Reforms*, 499.

60. Reddaway and Glinski, *The Tragedy of Russia's Reforms*, 495.

61. Koch and Svinarenko, *A Crate of Vodka*, 479.

62. Yavlinsky, "Russia's Phony Capitalism," 73.

63. Reddaway and Glinski, *Tragedy of Russia's Reforms*, 566.

64. Reddaway and Glinski, *Tragedy of Russia's Reforms*, 565.

65. Reddaway and Glinski, *Tragedy of Russia's Reforms*, 566.

66. Reddaway and Glinski, *Tragedy of Russia's Reforms*, 503, 514.

67. Reddaway and Glinski, *Tragedy of Russia's Reforms*, 514.

68. Andre Mommen, "Boris Nemtsov, 1959–2015: The Rise and Fall of a Provincial Democrat," *Demokratizatsiya* 24, no. 1 (2016): 15.

69. Lynn D. Nelson and Irina Y. Kuzes, *Radical Reform in Yeltsin's Russia: Political, Economic, and Social Dimensions* (Armonk, NY: M. E. Sharpe, 1995), 66.

70. Nelson and Kuzes, *Radical Reform*, 141–42.

71. Egor Gaidar, "At the Beginning of a New Phase: An Economic Review," *Problems of Economics* 34, no. 6 (1991): 21.

72. Gaidar, "At the Beginning," 13-14.

73. Yegor Gaidar, "Russian Reform," in Yegor Gaidar and Karl Otto Pohl, *Russian Reform/International Money* (Cambridge, MA: MIT Press, 1995), 19, 26.

74. Gaidar, "Russian Reform," 29, 31–32; Gaidar, *Days of Defeat*, 80-83.

75. Åslund, *How Russia Became a Market Economy*, 142.

76. Åslund, *How Russia Became a Market Economy*, 143, 145.

77. Ellison, *Boris Yeltsin*, 155; Åslund, *How Russia Became a Market Economy*, 150, 169; William Tompson, "Was Gaidar Really Necessary? Russian 'Shock Therapy' Reconsidered," *Problems of Post-Communism* 49, no. 4 (2002): 17.

78. Tompson, "Was Gaidar Really Necessary?," 17; Åslund, *How Russia Became a Market Economy*, 172, 221, 313.

79. Ellison, *Boris Yeltsin*, 157.

80. Ellison, *Boris Yeltsin*, 73–74.

81. "Yavlinsky Criticizes Russia's Reform Policy," *Current Digest of the Post-Soviet Press* 44, no. 23 (1908): 10.

82. Nelson and Kuzes, *Radical Reform*, 95.

83. Desai, *Conversations*, 192.

84. Nelson and Kuzes, *Property to the People*, 42.

85. Appel, *New Capitalist Order*, 82.

86. Nelson and Kuzes, *Property to the People*, 46–51.

87. Nelson and Kuzes, *Property to the People*, 62–68.

88. Desai, *Conversations*, 89.

89. Nelson and Kuzes, *Property to the People*, 125–27; Appel, *New Capitalist Order*, 84.

90. Freeland, *Sale of the Century*, 87.

91. Freeland, *Sale of the Century*, 67.

92. Appel, *New Capitalist Order*, 96.

93. Daniel Treisman, "'Loans for Shares,' Revisited," *Post-Soviet Affairs* 26, no. 3 (2010): 215.

94. Treisman, "'Loans for Shares,' Revisited," 218.

95. Freeland, *Sale of the Century*, 163.

96. Ellison, *Boris Yeltsin*, 160.

97. Desai, *Conversations*, 90.

98. Desai, *Conversations*, 36.

99. Freeland, *Sale of the Century*, 162.

100. Freeland, *Sale of the Century*, 163.

101. Reddaway and Glinski, *Tragedy of Russia's Reforms*, 552.

102. Peter Reddaway and Dmitri Glinski, "What Went Wrong in Russia? The Ravages of Market Bolshevism," *Journal of Democracy* 10, no. 2 (1999): 27.

103. Mommen, "Boris Nemtsov," 17.

104. Reddaway and Glinski, *Tragedy of Russia's Reforms*, 552.

105. Malinova, "Encounters," 292.

106. Gutorov, "Rossiiskii liberalizm," part II, 26-27; Shelokhaev, "Russian Liberalism," 26–27.

107. Fish, "The Predicament of Russian Liberalism," 209.

108. Golovchenko, "Postsovetskie liberal'nye politiki," 5.

109. Koch and Svinarenko, *Crate of Vodka*, 490, 492.

110. Gaidar, "Russian Reform," 51–52.

111. Tompson, "Was Gaidar Really Necessary?" 15.

112. Tompson, "Was Gaidar Really Necessary?" 20.

113. For instance, Nelson and Kuzes, *Property to the People*, 178, 192–93.

114. Ellison, *Boris Yeltsin*, 263.

115. Colton, *Yeltsin*, 8.

116. Lilia Shevstova, "Post-Communist Russia: A Historic Opportunity Missed," *International Affairs* 83, no. 5 (2007): 893.

117. Gulnaz Sharafutdinova, *The Red Mirror: Putin's Leadership and Russia's Insecure Identity* (Oxford: Oxford University Press, 2020), 127.

118. Sauvé, *Subir la Victoire*, 233.

11. Russian Liberalism under Putin

1. Richard Sakwa, *Russia's Futures* (Cambridge: Polity, 2019), 9, 26.

2. Elena Chebankova, *Political Ideologies in Contemporary Russia* (Montreal: McGill-Queen's University Press, 2020), 16.

3. Sakwa, *Russia's Futures*, 93.

4. Chebankova, "Contemporary Russian Liberalism," 344.

5. Kara-Murza, "O natsional'nykh variantakh liberalizma," 28.

6. Kara-Murza and Zhukova, "Political Philosophy of Russian Liberalism," 37.

7. Aleksandr S. Tsipko, "Tsennosti svobody i rossiiskoi gosudarstvennosti," *Nezavisimaia Gazeta*, November 16, 2020, https://www.ng.ru/ideas/2020-11-16/7_8015_freedom.html.

8. Lien Verpoest and Eva Claessen, "Liberalism in Russia: From the Margins of Russian Politics to an Instrument of Geopolitical Othering," *Global Affairs* 3, nos. 4–5 (2017): 345.

9. Mikhail Khodorkovsky, *Novaia Rossiia, ili Gardarika*, February 2020, 102, https://gardarika-book.org.

10. Grigory Yavlinsky, *The Putin System: An Opposing View* (New York: Columbia University Press, 2019), 6.

11. "Yavlinsky Attacks Regime from the Outside," *Current Digest of the Russian Press* 69, no. 28 (2017): 9.

12. "Programma 'Demokraticheskii manifest' (2012)," *Yabloko*, June 17, 2012, https://www.yabloko.ru/content/programma_demokraticheskij_manifest.

13. Dmitry Gubin, "Zachem liubit' Rodinu? Russkii patriotizm kak stokgol'mskii sindrom," *Republic*, January 5, 2021, https://republic.ru/posts/99195.

14. Iuliia Latynina, "Esli my ne zapad, to kto my?," Ekho Moskvy, September 12, 2014, https://www.lrt.lt/ru/novosti/17/63885/iuliia-latynina-esli-my-ne-zapad-to-kto-my-kommentarii.

15. Griory Yavlinsky, *Realeconomik: The Hidden Cause of the Great Recession (and How to Avert the Next One)* (New Haven, CT: Yale University Press, 2011), 104.

16. Iuliia Latynina, 'Evropa, ty ofigela!" *Novaia Gazeta*, August 16, 2011, https://novayagazeta.ru/articles/2011/08/16/45476-yuliya-latynina-171-evropa-ty-ofigela-187.

17. Iuliia Latynina, "Zabludilis' v trekh narrativakh: Diskussiia," *Novaia Gazeta*, August 3, 2020, https://novayagazeta.ru/articles/2020/08/03/86505-zabludilis-v-treh-narrativah-diskussiya.

18. Kimberly St. Julian-Varnon, "The Curious Case of 'Russian Lives Matter,'" *Foreign Policy*, July 11, 2020, https://foreignpolicy.com/2020/07/11/the-curious-case-of-russian-lives-matter/#.

19. Konstantin Eggert, "Letter to Dr Niblett," https://twitter.com/kvoneggert/status/1458379001593008128.

20. Konstantin Bogomolov, "Pokhishchenie Evropy 2.0," *Novaia Gazeta*, February 10, 2021, https://novayagazeta.ru/articles/2021/02/10/89120-pohischenie-evropy-2.

21. Bogomolov, "Pokhishchenie Evropy 2.0."

22. Jan Surman and Ella Rossman, "New Dissidence in Contemporary Russia: Students, Feminism and New Ethics," *New Pespectives* 30, no. 1 (2022): 32.

23. Surman and Rossman, "New Dissidence," 33.

24. Surman and Rossman, "New Dissidence," 32–33.

25. Latynina, "Zabludilis' v trekh narrativakh."

26. Viktor Shenderovich, "Podniat' ili opustit,'" *Colta*, July 21, 2020, https://colta.ru/articles/society/24960-viktor-shenderovich-novaya-etika-znakomye-motivy.

27. Rossen Djagalov, "Racism: The Highest State of Anti-Communism," *Slavic Review* 80, no. 2 (2021): 297.

28. Djagalov, "Racism," 297.

29. Sergei Medvedev, *The Return of the Russian Leviathan* (Cambridge: Polity, 2020), 27.

30. Oleg Kashin, *Reaktsiia Putina: Chto takoe khorosho i chto takoe plokho* (Moscow: Algoritm, 2013), 14.

31. Rossen Djagalov, "Racism," 297.

32. Jan Matti Dollbaum, Morvan Lallouet, and Ben Noble, *Navalny: Putin's Nemesis, Russia's Future?* (Oxford: Oxford University Press, 2021), 65. Marlene Laruelle, "Alexei Navalny and Challenges in Reconciling 'Nationalism' and 'Liberalism,'" *Post-Soviet Affairs* 30, no. 4 (2014): 281.

33. Dollbaum, Lallouet, and Noble, *Navalny*, 66.

34. Dollbaum, Lallouet, and Noble, *Navalny*, 69, 70.

35. Laruelle, "Alexei Navalny," 279.

36. Felix Light and Pjotr Sauer, "True Beliefs and Opportunism: Navalny's Tangled Political Development," *Moscow Times*, February 1, 2021, https://www.themoscowtimes.com/2021/02/01/true-beliefs-and-opportunism-navalnys-tangled-political-development-a72797.

37. Laruelle, "Alexei Navalny," 279.

38. Geir Flikke, "Canaries in a Coal Mine: The Uphill Struggle of Russia's Non-System Liberals," *Demokratizatsiya* 24, no. 3 (2016): 296.

39. Masha Gessen, "The Evolution of Alexey Navalny's Nationalism," *New Yorker*, February 15, 2021, https://www.newyorker.com/news/our-columnists/the-evolution-of-alexey-navalnys-nationalism.

40. A collection of these can be found at https://twitter.com/kazbek/status/1351563359762718725.

41. Laruelle, "Alexei Navalny," 279–80.

42. Sergei Abashin, "Samyi slozhnyi vopros, ili Den' natsional'nogo edinstva protiv migrantov," *Fond Liberal'naia Missiia*, November 8, 2021, https://liberal.ru/migration/samyj-slozhnyj-vopros-ili-den-naczionalnogo-edinstva-protiv-migrantov.

43. Vladimir Pastukhov, "Spoiler Rossii budushchego," *Novaia Gazeta*, August 7, 2021, https://novayagazeta.ru/articles/2021/08/07-vladimir-pastukhov-spoiler-rossii-budushchego.

44. Pastukhov, "Spoiler Rossii budushchego."

45. "Programma 'Demokraticheskii manifest' (2012)."

46. A. V. Golovchenko, "Inversii liberal'nogo patriotizma," *Izvestiia Saratovskogo Universiteta* 14, no. 4 (2014): 99.

47. Golovchenko, "Inversii liberal'nogo patriotizma," 99.

48. Medvedev, *Return*, 248.

49. Vera Slavtcheva-Petkova, *Russia's Liberal Media: Handcuffed but Free* (New York: Routledge, 2018), 61.

50. Slavtcheva-Petkova, *Russia's Liberal Media*, 147.

51. Igor' Kliamkin, *Kakaia doroga idet k pravu?* (Moscow: Mysl', 2018), 21.

52. Igor Romanov, "Yabloko Identifies Its Enemies," *Current Digest of the Russian Press* 60, no. 13 (2008): 14.

53. V. I. Golovchenko, "Ideologicheskii factor v deiatel'nosti RODP 'Iabloko' v sovremennoi Rossii," *Izvestiia Saratovskogo Universiteta* 18, no. 2 (2018): 202.

54. Golovchenko, "Inversii liberal'nogo patriotizma," 100.

55. D. V. Redchenko, "Prisoedinenie Kryma k Rossii v 2014 g.: Pozitsiia rossiiskoi ob"edinennoi demokraticheskoi partii 'Iabloko,'" *Izvestiia Saratovskogo Universiteta* 17, no. 2 (2017): 218

56. Redchenko, "Prisoedinenie," 218.

57. Gary Kasparov, *Winter is Coming: Why Vladimir Putin and the Enemies of the Free World Must Be Stopped* (New York: Public Affairs, 2015), 237.

58. Kasparov, *Winter is Coming*, 247, 262. Yulia Kurnyshova, "Boris Nemtsov: A Ukrainian Afterword," *Demokratizatiya* 24, no. 1 (2016): 42.

59. Dollbaum, Lallouet, and Noble, *Navalny*, 97

60. "Predvybornaia programma partii 'Iabloko' 'Uvazhenie k cheloveku,' 2016 goda," Yabloko, 2016, https://www.yabloko.ru/program.

61. Redchenko, "Prisoedinenie," 216.

62. Ol'ga Sedakova, "'Neotlichenie zla,' Interv'iu Iulii Muchnik," http://olgasedakova.com/interview/1780.

63. Alexander V. Obolensky, "Ethical Liberal Values vs. the Soviet Political and Administrative Heritage from the 1980s to the Present," in Cucciolla, *Dimensions and Challenges*, 156.

64. Medvedev, *Return*, 219–20.

65. Ilya A. Matveev, "The 'Two Russias' Culture War: Constructions of the 'People' during the 2011–2013 Protests," *South Atlantic Quarterly* 113, no. 1 (2014): 188.

66. Viktor Sheinis, "Chto tam—za povorotom?" In *Politicheskii stroi Rossii: Vchera, segodnia, zavtra*, ed. Viktor Sheinis (Moscow: Mysl', 2019), 53–54.

67. Boris Nemtsov, *Ispoved' buntaria* (Moscow: Partizan, 2007), 71–72.

68. Lipovetsky, "Poetics of ITR Discourse," 128.

69. Medvedev, *Return*, 157–58.

70. Masha Gessen, "What Russians Crave: Cheese." *New York Times*, July 4, 2015, https://www.nytimes.com/2015/07/05/opinion/sunday/what-the-russians-crave-cheese.html.

71. Irina Prokhorova, "Totalitarnoe soznanie i missiia intellektuala," *New Times*, May 28, 2018, https://newtimes.ru/articles/detail/165063.

72. Nemtsov, *Izpoved' buntaria*, 116.

73. Valeriia Novodvorskaia, "Takoi narod pust' vymiraet, ne zhalko," *Newsland*, October 18, 2012, http://newsland.com/news/detail/id/1058648/.

74. Medvedev, *Return*, 137, 144, 235.

75. Andrei Kovalev, *Russia's Dead End: An Insider's Testimony from Gorbachev to Putin* (Lincoln, NE: Potomac, 2017), 9.

76. Gubin, "Zachem liubit' Rodinu?" The term "liberast" is a pejorative term for liberals, combining the words "liberal" and "pederast."

77. Ol'ga Sedakova, "'Net khuda bez dobra.' O nekotorykh osobennostiakh otnosheniia k zlu v russkoi traditsii," http://olgasedakov.com/Moralia/282.

78. Sedakova, "Net khuda bez dobra."

79. Sedakova, "Net khuda bez dobra."

80. Kovalev, *Russia's Dead End*, 11.

81. Sharafutdinova, "Was There a 'Simple Soviet' Person?," 189.

82. Ol'ga Sedakova, "Razgovor o svobode. Beseda s Aleksandrom Kyrlezhevym," http://olgasedakova.com/interview/129.

83. Sedakova, "Razgovor o svobode."

84. Medvedev, *Return*, 213.

85. "Predvybornaia programma." For a further statement by Yabloko on this topic, see "O prizyvakh golosovat' za KPRF," *Yabloko*, October 18, 2021, https://www.yabloko.ru/reshenija_politicheskogo_komiteta/2021/10/18-3.

86. Partiia Narodnoi Svobody PARNAS, "Osnovnye napravleniia sistemnoi dekommunizatsii Rossii," June 5, 2018, https://parnasparty.ru/news/457.

87. Medvedev, *Return*, 198–99.

88. Kashin, *Reaktsiia Putina*, 58.

89. Chebankova, *Political Ideologies*, 36.

90. Chebankova, *Political Ideologies*, 37.

91. Gavriil Popov, "Vyzyvaiu dukh generala Vlasova," *Novaia Gazeta*, September 9, 2007, https://novayagazeta.ru/articles/2007/09/10/32026-gavriil-popov-vyzyvayu -duh-generala-vlasova.

92. Redchenko, "Prisoedinenie," 218.

93. "Odobrenie deiatel'nosti Vladimira Putina', *Levada Tsentr*, June 2022, https:// www.levada.ru/indikatory/. "Konflikt s Ukrainoi," *Levada Tsentr*, September 29, 2022, https://www.levada.ru/2022/0/29/konflikt-s-ukrainoj-sentyabr-2022-goda/.

94. Dmitry Muratov, "Rossiia. Bombit. Ukrainu," *Novaia Gazeta*, February 25, 2022. The online version of this editorial statement is no longer available.

95. Sindikat-100, "Bol', gnev, styd. Eta voina—avantiura," *Novaia gazeta*, February 24, 2022. This article was taken down soon after publication and is no longer available.

96. Free Russia Forum, "Defeat Putin's War Machine," September 29, 2022, https:// www.forumfreerussia.org/en/documents-en/2022-09-28/defeat-putins-war-machine.

97. "Russian Reporter Put under House Arrest over War Criticism," *CTV News*, August 11, 2022, https://www.ctvnews.ca/world/russian-reporter-put-under-house -arrest-over-war-criticism-1.6023281.

98. Iuliia Latynina, "Mir prosto razdelitsia na svobodnykh—i nas," *Novaia Gazeta*, February 24, 2022. This article was taken down soon after publication and is no longer available.

99. Ivan Davydov, "Kto takie liberaly i est' li oni v rossiiskoi politike?," *Otkrytye Media*, April 4, 2019, https://openmedia.io/news/kto-takie-liberaly-i-est-li-oni-v-rossijskoj -politike/.

100. Riccardo Mario Cucciolla, "Introduction: The Many Dimensions of Russian Liberalism," in Cucciolla, *Dimensions and Challenges*, xxxiv.

101. Boris Nemtsov, "Strana gotova snova vpast' v rabskoe sostoianie," *Kommersant-Vlast'*, March 5, 2002, https://nemtsov-most-org/2017/12/29/boris-nemtsov-the -country-is-ready-to-fall-into-slavery-again/.

102. White, *Russian Democratic Party Yabloko*, 194–95.

103. Romanov, "Yabloko Identifies Its Enemies," 10.

104. Grigorii Iavlinskii, "Vtoroe iiulia. Politicheskaia situatsiia v Rossii posle 1 iiulia, zadachi demokraticheskogo dvizheniia i perspektivy razvitiia partii," *Yabloko*, August 31, 2020, https://www.yabloko.ru/publikatsii/2020/08/31.

105. Ol'ga Sedakova, "Khristianskogo golosa eta vlast' ne slyshat', Interv'iu Antonu Zhelnovu dlia 'The New Times,'" http://olgasedakova.com/interview/1122.

106. White, *Russian Democratic Party Yabloko*, 171–72.

107. Dmitry Azarov, "A Question of National Sovereignty," *Meduza*, March 1, 2021, https://meduza.io/en/feature/2021/03/01/a-question-of-national-sovereignty.

108. David White, "Russian Liberalism in Crisis? Khodorkovsky Revisited," *Studies of Transition States and Societies 5*, no. 1 (2013): 78.

109. For an examination of these, see Slavtcheva-Petkova, *Russia's Liberal Media*.

110. Nobel Prize, "Dmitry Muratov," https://www.nobelprize.org/prizes/peace /2021/muratov/facts/.

111. Alexey Gorbachev, "New Generation of Russian Protestors Harnesses Social Media," *VOA*, February 4, 2021, https://www.voanews.com/a/press-freedom_new -generation-russian-protesters-harnesses-social-media/6201632.html.

112. Flikke, "Canaries," 309.

113. Flikke, "Canaries," 313.

114. Flikke, "Canaries," 314.

115. Nicolai Petro, "Are We Reading Russia Right?," *Fletcher Forum of World Affairs* 42, no. 2 (2018): 134.

116. Mary McAuley, *Human Rights in Russia: Citizens and the State from Perestroika to Putin* (London: I. B. Tauris, 2015), 130–33.

117. McAuley, *Human Rights*, 133.

118. McAuley, *Human Rights*, 151.

119. Kirsti Stuvøy, "'The Foreign Within': State-Civil Society Relations in Russia," *Europe-Asia Studies* 72, no. 7 (2020): 1104.

120. Stuvøy, "Foreign Within," 1110.

121. Stuvøy, "Foreign Within," 1114.

122. Stuvøy, "Foreign Within," 1119.

123. Alfred B. Evans, "Vladimir Putin's Design for Civil Society," in *Russian Civil Society: A Critical Assessment*, ed. Alfred B. Evans, Laura A. Henry, and Lisa McIntosh Sundstrom (Armonk, NY: M. E. Sharpe, 2006), 149.

124. Agnès Wenger, "Return of the *Voenkor*: The Military as a New Opinion Leader in Russia?" *Russia.Post*, August 15, 2022, https://www.russiapost.info/politics/voenkor.

125. "Programma 'Demokraticheskii manifest' (2012)."

126. White, "Russian Liberalism in Crisis?," 70.

127. White, "Russian Liberalism in Crisis?," 79.

128. White, "Russian Liberalism in Crisis?," 80.

129. Flikke, "Canaries," 304.

130. Dollbaum, Lallouet, and Noble, *Navalny*, 90–92.

131. "Partiia rosta," https://rost.ru/.

132. Boris Berezovsky, "Manifest rossiiskogo liberalizma," *Nezavisimaia Gazeta*, April 11, 2002, parts 1 and 2, http://www.ng.ru/ideas/2002-04-11/1_berezovskiy.html and http://www.ng.ru/ideas/2002-04-11/11_berezovskiy.html.

133. Nemtsov, "Strana gotova."

134. Desai, *Conversations*, 136.

135. Nemtsov, *Izpoved' buntaria*, 72.

136. Nemtsov, *Izpoved' buntaria*, 91.

137. Grigorii Iavlinskii, "Bez putinizma i populizma," *Yavlinsky.ru*, February 6, 2021, https://www.yavlinsky.ru/article/bez-putinizma-i-populizma/.

138. "'Ia v tsentre uragana': Aleksei Naval'nyi—v proekte 'Russkie norm!'" *The Bell*, December 11, 2019, https://thebell.io/ya-v-tsentre-uragana-aleksej-navalnyi-v-proekte-russkie-norm/.

139. Anders Åslund and Leonid Gozman, "Russia after Putin: How to Rebuild the State," Atlantic Council, February 24, 2021, 4, https://www.atlanticcouncil.org/in-depth-research-reports/report/russia-after-putin-report/.

140. Iavlinskii, "Bez putinizma."

141. Khodorkovsky, *Novaia Rossiia*, 99.

142. Flikke, "Canaries," 306.

143. Kasparov, *Winter is Coming*, 148.

144. "O prizyvakh golosovat' za KPRF."

145. "Predvybornaia programma."

146. "O situatsii v Rossii," *Yabloko*, October 18, 2021, https://www.yabloko.ru/reshenija_politicheskogo_komiteta/2021/10/18-0.

147. D. V. Redchenko, "RODP 'Iabloko' i razvitie 'Arabskoi vesny' v Livii i Sirii v 2011–2013 gg.," *Izvestiia Saratovskogo Universiteta* 16, no. 2 (2016): 204.

148. Iavlinskii, "Bez putinizma."

149. Dmitrii Muratov, "Pro Venediktova i'," *Novaia Gazeta*, September 29, 2021, https://novayagazeta.ru/articles/2021/09/29/pro-venediktova-i-nenavist.

150. "O prizyvakh golosovat' za KPRF."

151. Vladimir Gel'man, "Tupik avtoritarnoi modernizatsii," Moskovskii Tsentr Karnegi, February 23, 2010, https://polit.ru/article/2010/02/23/gelman/#_ednref10.

152. Vladimir Pastukhov, "Gosudarstvo diktatury liumpen-proletariata," *Novaia Gazeta*, August 13, 2012, https://novayagazeta.ru/articles/2012/08/13/50971-gosudarstvo-diktatury-lyumpen-proletariata.

153. Gel'man, "Tupik avtoritarnoi modernizatsii."

154. "Roundtable: The Constitutional Agenda of the Russian Democratic Opposition from 2011 to 2020," ASEES Convention, online, November 7, 2020.

155. Kliamkin, *Kakaia doroga*, 34.

156. Khodorkovsky, *Novaia Rossiia*, 38, 40.

157. Vladimir Inozemtsev, "Different or the Same? Is Navalny a Good Alternative to Putin?" *Current Digest of the Russian Press* 69, no. 28 (2017): 8.

158. Partiia Narodnoi Svobody PARNAS, "Zo chto my boremsia i k chemu stremimsia? Kratkaia programma PARNAS," https://parnasparty.ru/news/353.

159. "Predvybornaia programma."

160. "Predvybornaia programma."

161. Petro, "Are We Reading Russia Right?" 1367.

162. Kathryn Hendley, "The Role of Law," in *Return to Putin's Russia: Past Imperfect, Future Uncertain*, ed. Stephen K. Wegren (Lanham: Rowman and Littlefield, 2013), 93.

163. Hendley, "Role of Law," 95.

164. Hendley, "Role of Law," 98.

165. Hendley, "Role of Law," 87.

166. "Meeting on Liberalisation of Criminal Law," President of Russia, October 21, 2010, http://en.kremlin.ru/events/president/news/9305.

167. Maxim Nikonov and Ol'ga Shepeleva, "Development of Russia's Criminal Justice System: Vectors, Reform Measures, and Major Players," *Statutes and Decisions* 51, no. 4 (2017): 457, 459.

168. "Russia's Prison Population Is Now Lower than at Any Point in Modern History," *Meduza*, December 14, 2018, https://meduza.io/en/news/2018/12/14/russia-s-prison-population-is-now-lower-than-at-any-point-in-modern-history; "Russia's Prison Population Falls to a Record Low," *RT*, August 13, 2020, https://www.rt.com/russia/497907-russia-prison-population-record-low/.

169. McAuley, *Human Rights*, 264.

170. McAuley, *Human Rights*, 204, 207.

171. McAuley, *Human Rights*, 208–9.

172. Hendley, "Role of Law," 83.

173. Vladimir Ryzhkov, "Russian Democracy in Eclipse: The Liberal Debacle," *Journal of Democracy* 15, no. 3 (2004): 53.

174. Peter Rutland, "Neoliberalism and the Russian Transition," *Review of International Political Economy* 20, no. 2 (2013): 354. Desai, *Conversations*, 163–64.

175. Ilya A. Matveev, "Gibridnaia neoliberalizatsiia: Gosudarstvo, legitimnost' i neoliberalizm v putinskoi Rossii," *Politiia* 79, no. 4 (2015): 33–34.

176. Alfred B. Evans, "Civil Society and Protest," in Wegren, *Return to Putin's Russia*, 108–9.

177. Matveev, "Gibridnaia neoliberalizatsiia," 31.

178. Matveev, "Gibridnaia neoliberalizatsiia," 31–32.

179. Vladimir Putin, "Poslanie Presidenta Federal'nomu Sobraniiu", President of Russia, December 4, 2014, http://kremlin.ru/events/president/news/47173.

180. Vladimir Putin, "Zasedanie mezhregional'nogo foruma ONF," President of Russia, January 25, 2016, http://kremlin.ru/events/president/news/51206.

181. Vladimir Putin, "Poslanie Presidenta Federal'nomu Sobraniiu," President of Russia, April 21, 2021, http://www.kremlin.ru/events/president/news/65418.

182. Sakwa, *Russia's Futures*, 96.

183. "Domestic Demand Will Not Push Our Economic Growth to 3–4%," *Realnoe Vremya*, July 5, 2017, https://realnoevremya.com/articles/1610-domestic-demand-will-not-push-our-economic-growth-to-3-4.

184. "Domestic Demand."

185. "Putin Fires Apparent Warning Salvo at Russian Federation Accounts Chamber Head Kudrin," *Memri TV*, February 27, 2020, https://www.memri.org/reports/putin-fires-apparent-warning-salvo-russian-federation-accounts-chamber-head-kudrin.

186. "Kudrin predlozhil Putinu zaniat'sia obrazovaniem i zdorov'em," *Vedemosti*, September 6, 2017, https://www.vedemosti.ru/economics/articles/2017/09/06/732485-kudrin-putinu-obrazovaniem-zdorovem?

187. "Russia Needs New Wave of Privatization to Slash Public Sector & Sell Off 'Inefficient' State Companies: Putin Confidant Kudrin," *RT*, September 7, 2021, https://www.rt.com/russia/534161-kudrin-privatization-financial-benefits/.

188. "Putin Fires Apparent Warning Salvo."

189. Kasparov, *Winter is Coming*, 150.

190. Light and Sauer, "True Beliefs." Dollbaum, Lallouet, and Noble, *Navalny*, 96.

191. Khodorkovsky, "Liberalism in Crisis."

192. Khodorkovsky, *Novaia Rossiia*, 57.

193. Khodorkovsky, *Novaia Rossiia*, 62.

194. Khodorkovsky, *Novaia Rossiia*, 65.

195. "Programma 'Demokraticheskii manifest' (2012)."

196. "Programma 'Demokraticheskii manifest' (2012)."

197. Yavlinsky, *Realeconomik*, 113.

198. Aleksei Polukhin, "Grigory Yavlinsky: 'The Economy Cannot Survive Such Political Decisions,'" *Current Digest of the Russian Press* 67, no. 6 (2015): 14.

199. "Rossiiskii liberal'nyi manifest (Programma politicheskoi partii 'Soiuz pravykh sil') [2001 g.]," in *Prava i svobody cheloveka v programmnykh dokumentakh osnovnykh politicheskikh partii i ob"edinenii Rossii xx vek* (Moscow: Rosspen, 2002), 484.

200. White, *Russian Democratic Party Yabloko*, 75.

201. Partiia rosta, "Progamma partii," 2020, http://www.rost.ru/about/programma-partii/.

202. Latynina, "Evropa, ty ofigela!"

203. Nemtsov, *Ispoved'*, 173–74.

204. Sakwa, *Russia's Futures*, 127.

205. Sergei Abashin, "Sushchestvuet li migratsionnaia politika v Rossii?," *Fond Liberal'naia Missiia*, April 19, 2021, https://liberal.ru/migration/sushhestvuet-li -migraczionnaya-politika-v-rossii. See also Vera Michlin-Shapir, *Fluid Russia: Between the Global and the National in the Post-Soviet Era* (DeKalb: Northern Illinois University Press, 2021).

206. Chebankova, *Political Ideologies*, 233.

207. Chebankova, *Political Ideologies*, 248.

208. Chebankova, *Political Ideologies*, 257–58.

209. Surman and Rossman, "New Dissidence," 31, 36.

210. "Predvybornaia programma."

211. Samantha Berkhead, "Russian Women Are Ready to Reclaim Once-Forbidden Jobs," *Moscow Times*, March 6, 2020, https://www.themoscowtimes.com/2020/03/06 /ruissian-women-are-ready-to-reclaim-once-forbidden-jobs-a69544.

212. Royce Kurmelovs, "Raising Hell: Q and A: Who the Hell Is Alexei Navalny?," *Raising Hell*, January 27, 2021, https://roycekurmelovs.substack.com/p/whoisnavalny; also Dollbaum, Lallouet, and Noble, *Navalny*, 12.

213. Medvedev, *Return*, 137.

214. Kashin, *Reaktsiia Putina*, 135.

215. Chebankova, *Political Ideologies*, 217.

216. Medvedev, *Return*, 132–34.

217. Valeriy Solovey, "Liberals or Technocrats? Liberal Ideas and Values in the Mindset of the Russian Political Elite," in Cucciolla, *Dimensions and Challenges*, 179.

218. Gutorov, "Rossiiskii liberalizm" (part 1), 10.

219. White, "Russian Liberalism in Crisis?," 78.

220. Loredana Maria Simionov and Ramona Tiganasu, "Historical Incrementalism and Its Effects on the (Mis)Perception of Liberalism in Russia. Guidance from In-Country Experts," *Europolity* 12, no. 2 (2018): 142.

221. Olga Malinova, "Konstruirovanie 'liberalizma' v postsovetskoi Rossii: Nasledie 1990-kh v ideologicheskikh bitvakh 2000-kh," *Politiia* 84, no. 1 (2017): 18.

222. Solovey, "Liberals or Technocrats?," 161.

223. P. M. Kozyreva and A. M. Smirnov, "Doverie v nestabil'noi rossiiskom obshchestve," *Polis. Politicheskie Issledovaniia* 5 (2019): 142.

224. VTsIOM, "Zhiznennye prioritety rossiian," *VTSIOM*, June 7, 2017, https:// wciom.ru/analytical-reviews/analiticheskii-obzor/zhiznennye-prioritety-rossiyan -semya-dengi-ili-tvorchestvo.

225. "Gosudarstvennyi paternalizm," *Levada Tsentr*, February 25, 2020, https:// www.levada.ru/2020/02/25/gosudarstvennyj-paternalizm/.

226. "Kakoi dolzhna byt' Rossiia v predstavlenii rossiian?," *Levada Tsentr*, September 10, 2021, https://www.levada.ru/2021/09/10/kakoj-dolzhna-byt-rossiya-v-predstav lenii-rossiyan/.

227. "Pomogat' i nakazyvat'," *Kommersant*, April 20, 2020, http://www.kommersant .ru/doc/4326252.

228. Lev Gudkov et al., *Russia's Generation Z: Attitudes and Values 2019/2020* (Moscow: Friedrich-Ebert-Stiftung, 2020), http://library.fes.de/pdf-files/bueros/moskau/16134.pdf.

Conclusion

1. "In Russia, It's either Putin or Navalny," *Meduza*, September 16, 2020, https:// meduza.io/en/feature/2020/09/16/in-russia-it-s-either-putin-or-navalny.

2. Partiia Novye Liudi, "Programma partii," https://newpeople.ru/progam _newpeople.

Bibliography

Abashin, Sergei. "Samyi slozhnyi vopros, ili Den' natsional'nogo edinstva protiv migrantov." *Fond Liberal'naia Missiia*, November 8, 2021. https://liberal.ru /migration/samyj-slozhnyj-vopros-ili-den-naczionalnogo-edinstva-protiv -migrantov.

——. "Sushchestvuet li migratsionnaia politika v Rossii?" *Fond Liberal'naia Missiia*, April 19, 2021. https://liberal.ru/migration/sushhestvuet-li-migraczionnaya -politika-v-Rossii.

Abramov, M. A. "Liberalizm v SSSR." In Abramov, *Opyt russkogo liberalizma*, 441–46.

——, ed. *Opyt russkogo liberalizma: Antologiia*. Moscow: Kanon, 1996.

Aganbegian, Abel G. "The Program of Radical Restructuring." *Problems of Economics* 31, no. 5 (1988): 6–22.

Aggeeva, I. A. "Dzhon Khamfri i Sovetskii Soiuz." *Kanadskii Ezhegodnik* 19 (2015): 18–47.

Airapetov, O. R. *Generaly, liberaly i predprinimateli: Rabota na front i na revolutsiiu [1907–1917]*. Moscow: Tri kvadrata, 2003.

Ajani, Gianmaria. "Russian Liberalism and the Rule of Law: Notes from Underground." In Cucciolla, *Dimensions and Challenges*, 39–50.

Akhiezer, Aleksandr. "Russian Liberalism in the Face of Crisis." *Russian Social Science Review* 36, no. 2 (1995): 56–70.

Aleksandrov, S. A. *Lider rossiiskikh kadetov P. N. Miliukov v emigratsii*. Moscow: AIRO-XX, 1996.

Allison, Graham, and Grigory Yavlinsky. *Window of Opportunity: The Grand Bargain for Democracy in the Soviet Union*. New York: Pantheon, 1991.

Amalrik, Andrei. "An Open Letter to A. Kuznetsov." In Meerson-Aksenov and Shragin, *Political, Social, and Religious Thought*, 165–76.

——. *Will the Soviet Union Survive until 1984?* New York: Harper and Row, 1970.

Andreasian, R. N., and L. N. Vinogradova. "Razvivaiushchiesia strany: Gorno-dobyvaiushchaia promyshlennost' i problemy industrializatsii." *Narody Azii i Afriki* 5 (1970): 29–40.

Antonenko, Natal'ia Viktorovna. "Emigrantskie liberal'nye konseptsii resheniia natsional'nogo voprosa v Rossii." *Vestnik TGU* 93, no. 1 (2011): 259–63.

Appel, Hilary. *A New Capitalist Order: Privatization and Ideology in Russia and Eastern Europe*. Pittsburg: University of Pittsburgh Press, 2004.

Arbatov, Georgi. *The System: An Insider's Life in Soviet Politics*. New York: Times Books, 1992.

Arslanov, R. A. "Istoriia rossiiskogo gosudarstva v kontseptsii K. D. Kavelina." *Vestnik RUDN* 1 (2007): 37–47.

Ascher, Abraham. *P. A. Stolypin: The Search for Stability in Late Imperial Russia.* Stanford, CA: Stanford University Press, 2001.

Åslund, Anders. *How Russia Became a Market Economy.* Washington, DC: Brookings Institution, 1995.

Åslund, Anders, and Leonid Gozman. "Russia after Putin: How to Rebuild the State." Atlantic Council, February 24, 2021. https://www.atlanticcouncil.org /in-depth-research-reports/report/russia-after-putin-report/.

Azarov, Dmitry. "A Question of National Sovereignty." *Meduza*, March 1, 2021. https://meduza.io/en/feature/2021/03/01/a-question-of-national-sovereignty.

Baranov, N. A. "Liberal'no-konservativnyi sintez v Rossii: Istoriia i perspektivy." *Problemnyi analiz i gosudarstvenno-upravlencheskoe proektirovanie* 5 (2010): 90–102.

Barber, Lionel, and Henry Foy. "Vladimir Putin Says Liberalism Has 'Become Obsolete.'" *Financial Times*, June 27, 2019. https://www.ft.com/content /670039ec-98f3-11e9-9573-ee5cbb98ed36.

Batkin, Leonid. "Turn to Be Europe." *XX Century and Peace* 8 (1988): 29–33.

Beer, Daniel. *Renovating Russia: The Human Sciences and the Fate of Liberal Modernity, 1880–1930.* Ithaca, NY: Cornell University Press, 2008.

Belinsky, Vissarion Grigorevich. "Letters to V. P. Botkin 1840–1841 (Extracts)." In Leatherbarrow and Offord, *Documentary History of Russian Thought*, 124–29.

Bell, Duncan. "What Is Liberalism?" *Political Theory* 42, no. 6 (2004): 682–715.

Bennett, Vincent. *A History of Russian Economic Thought.* London: Routledge, 2013.

Berdiaev, Nikolai. "Philosophical Verity and Intelligentsia Truth." In Berdiaev et al., *Landmarks*, 1–16.

Berdiaev, Nikolai, Sergei Bulgakov, Mikhail Gershenzon, A. S. Izgoev, Bogdan Kistiakovskii, Peter Struve, and Semen Frank. *Landmarks. Vekhi: A Collection of Essays about the Russian Intelligentsia.* Armonk, NY: M. E. Sharpe, 1994.

Berdyaev, Nicolas. *Freedom and the Spirit.* London: Geoffrey Bles, 1948.

——. *Slavery and Freedom.* New York: Charles Scribner's Sons, 1944.

Berest, Julia. *The Emergence of Russian Liberalism: Alexander Kunitsyn in Context, 1783–1840.* New York: Palgrave, 2011.

Berezovaia, L. G. "Interpretatsiia liberalizma v obshchestvennoi mysli russkoi emigratsii." In Shelokhaev, *Rossiiskii liberalizm*, 74–84.

Berezovskii, Boris. "Manifest rossiiskogo liberalizma." *Nezavisimaia Gazeta*, April 11, 2002, parts 1 and 2. http://www.ng.ru/ideas/2002-04-11/1_berezovskiy.html; http://www.ng.ru/ideas/2002-04-11/11_berezovskiy.html.

Bergman, Jay. "Soviet Dissidents on the Russian Intelligentsia, 1956–1985: The Search for a Usable Past." *Russian Review* 51, no. 1 (1992): 16–35.

Berkhead, Samantha. "Russian Women Are Ready to Reclaim Once-Forbidden Jobs." *Moscow Times*, March 6, 2020. https://www.themoscowtimes.com /2020/03/06/russian-women-are-ready-to-reclaim-once-forbidden-jobs -a69544.

Berlin, Isaiah. *Russian Thinkers.* London: Penguin, 2008.

——. "Two Concepts of Liberty." In *Liberty*, 166–217. Oxford: Oxford University Press, 2002.

Berlov, A. V. "Predstaviteli liberal'noi ekonomicheskoi shkoly russkoi emigratsii 1920–1930–kh gg. o putiakh resheniia krest'ianskogo voprosa v Rossii v nachale xx veka." *Prostranstvo i vremia* 1, no. 15 (2014): 161–64.

Bogomolov, Konstantin. "Pokhishchenie Evropy 2.0." *Novaia Gazeta*, February 10, 2021. https://novayagazeta.ru/articles/2021/02/10/89120-pohischenie -evropy-2-0.

Boobbyer, Philip. *Conscience, Dissent, and Reform in Soviet Russia.* London: Routledge, 2005.

——. "Russian Liberal Conservatism." In *Russian Nationalism Past and Present*, edited by Geoffrey Hosking and Robert Service, 34–53. Basingstoke: Macmillan, 1998.

Bradley, Joseph. "Associations and the Development of Civil Society in Tsarist Russia." *Social Science History* 41, no. 1 (2017): 19–42.

Brown, Archie, ed. *The Demise of Marxism-Leninism in Russia.* Basingstoke: Palgrave Macmillan, 2004.

——. "The Rise of Non-Leninist Thinking about the Political System." In Brown, *Demise of Marxism-Leninism*, 19–40.

Brudny, Yitzhak. "The Dynamics of 'Democratic Russia,' 1990–1993." *Post-Soviet Affairs* 9, no. 2 (1993): 141–70.

Brutskus, Boris. "Narodnoe khoziastvo sov. Rossiii, ego priroda i ego sud'by." *Sovremennye Zapiski* 38 (1929): 401–32 (part 1); 39 (1929): 428–74 (part 2).

Brutzkus, Boris. *Economic Planning in Soviet Russia.* London: Routledge, 1935.

Budnitskii, Oleg V., and Robin Ganev. "Russian Liberalism in War and Revolution." *Kritika: Explorations in Russian and Eurasian History* 5, no. 1 (2004): 149–68.

Budraitkis, Ilya. "Russia, George Floyd, and the End of the Imaginary West." *Open Democracy*, June 12, 2020. https://www.opendemocracy.net/en/odr/russia -floyd-imaginary-west.

Bulgakov, Sergei N. "Basic Problems of the Theory of Progress." In Poole, *Problems of Idealism*, 85–123.

——. "Heroism and Asceticism: Reflections on the Religious Nature of the Russian Intelligentsia." In Berdiaev et al., *Landmarks*, 17–49.

Bunyan, Paul. "Re-Conceptualizing Civil Society: Towards a Radical Understanding." *Voluntas* 25, no. 2 (2014): 538–52.

Butler, Eamonn. *Classical Liberalism: A Primer.* London: Institute of Economic Affairs, 2015.

Chalidze, Valery. *The Soviet Human Rights Movement: A Memoir.* New York: Jacob Blaustein Institute for the Advancement of Human Rights, 1984.

Chamberlain, Lesley. *The Philosophy Steamer: Lenin and the Exile of the Intelligentsia.* London: Atlantic, 2006.

Chamberlin, William Henry. "The Short Life of Russian Liberalism." *Russian Review* 26, no. 2 (1967): 144–52.

Chebankova, Elena. "Competing Ideologies of Russia's Civil Society." *Europe-Asia Studies* 67, no. 2 (2015): 244–68.

——. "Contemporary Russian Liberalism." *Post-Soviet Affairs* 30, no. 5 (2014): 341–69.

——. *Political Ideologies in Contemporary Russia.* Montreal: McGill-Queen's University Press, 2020.

Chernyaev, Anatoly S. *My Six Years with Gorbachev.* University Park: Pennsylvania State University Press, 2000.

Chernyshevsky, Nikolai. "[On Liberalism]." In Leatherbarrow and Offord, *Documentary History of Russian Thought*, 203–206.

Chicherin, Boris N. "Contemporary Tasks of Russian Life." In Chicherin, *Liberty, Equality, and the Market*, 110–40.

——. "Excerpts from 'On Popular Representation.'" In Chicherin, *Liberty, Equality, and the Market*, 149–206.

——. "Excerpts from 'Property and the State.'" In Chicherin, *Liberty, Equality, and the Market*, 351–424.

——. "Konstitutsionnyi vopros Rossii." In Abramov, *Opyt russkogo liberalizma*, 52–76.

——. *Liberty, Equality, and the Market: Essays*. New Haven, CT: Yale University Press, 1998.

——. "On Serfdom." In Chicherin, *Liberty, Equality, and the Market*, 69–109.

——. "Razlichnye vidy liberalizma." In Abramov, *Opyt russkogo liberalizma*, 38–51.

Chubais, Anatolii. "Missiia Rossii v xxi veke." *Nezavisimaia Gazeta*, October 1, 2003. https://www.ng.ru/ideas/2003-10–01/1_mission.html.

Chuprinin, Sergei. "Choice: Notes of a Russian Liberal: The Experience of Self-Identification." *Russian Politics and Law* 32, no. 5 (1995): 32–55.

Cohen, Stephen F., and Katrina vanden Heuvel, eds. *Voices of Glasnost: Interviews with Gorbachev's Reformers*. New York: W. W. Norton, 1989.

Colburn, Ben. *Autonomy and Liberalism*. New York: Routledge, 2010.

Colton, Timothy J. *Yeltsin: A Life*. New York: Basic Books, 2008.

"Conference on Security and Cooperation in Europe, Final Act." Helsinki, 1975. https://www.osce.org/files/f/documents/5/c/39501.pdf.

Conroy, Mary Schaeffer. "Civil Society in Late Imperial Russia." In Evans, Henry, and Sundstrom, *Russian Civil Society*, 11–27.

Cucciolla, Riccardo Mario, ed. *Dimensions and Challenges of Russian Liberalism: Historical Drama and New Prospects*. Cham: Springer, 2019.

Dahlmann, D. "Liberals in the Provinces: The Kadets and the Duma Elections in Saratov, 1906–1912." In *Emerging Democracy in Late Imperial Russia: Case Studies on Local Self-Government (the Zemstvos), State Duma Elections, the Tsarist Government, and the State Council before and during World War I*, edited by Mary Schaeffer Conroy, 88–111. Niwot: University Press of Colorado, 1998.

Daniel, Wallace L. *Russia's Uncommon Prophet: Father Aleksandr Men and His Times*. DeKalb: Northern Illinois University Press, 2016.

Davydov, Ivan. "Kto takie liberaly i est' li oni v rossiiskoi politike?" *Oktrytye Media*, April 4, 2019. https://openmedia.io/news/kto-takie-liberaly-i-est-li-oni-v -rossijskoj-politike/.

Desai, Padma. *Conversations on Russia: Reform from Yeltsin to Putin*. Oxford: Oxford University Press, 2006.

Dinkevich, A. I. "O strategii ekonomicheskogo razvitiia stran 'tret'ego mira.'" *Narody Azii i Afriki* 1 (1975): 7–19.

Djagalov, Rossen. "Racism: The Highest Stage of Anti-Communism." *Slavic Review* 80, no. 2 (2021): 290–98.

Dollbaum, Jan Matti, Morvan Lallouet, and Ben Noble. *Navalny: Putin's Nemesis, Russia's Future?* Oxford: Oxford University Press, 2021.

"Domestic Demand Will Not Push Our Economic Growth to 3–4%." *Realnoe Vremya*, July 5, 2017. https://realnoevremya.com/articles/1610-domestic -demand-will-not-push-our-economic-growth-to-3-4.

Dornan, Peter. "Andrei Sakharov: The Conscience of a Liberal Scientist." In Tokes, *Dissent in the USSR*, 354–417.

Dorskaia, Aleksandra Andreevna. "Universal'nye mezhdunarodno-pravovye standarty v obespechenii prav cheloveka i pravovye traditsii Rossii." *Iuridicheskaia Nauka* 5 (2016): 133–38.

Dowler, Wayne. "The Intelligentsia and Capitalism." In *A History of Russian Thought*, edited by William Leatherbarrow and Derek Offord, 263–85. Cambridge: Cambridge University Press, 2000.

Duncan, Peter J. S. "The Rebirth of Politics in Russia." In Hosking, Aves, and Duncan, *Road to Post-Communism*, 67–119.

Edmonson, Linda Harriet. *Feminism in Russia, 1900–17*. Stanford, CA: Stanford University Press, 1984.

Eggert, Konstantin. "Letter to Dr Niblett," November 4, 2021. https://twitter.com /kvoneggert/status/1458379001593008128.

Egorov, Andrei N. "'A Democrat by Mistake': Political Activity of Anton Kartashev during the Russian Civil War." *Historia Provinciae: The Journal of Regional History* 4, no. 3 (2020): 929–72.

———. "Kadety i P. A. Stolypin: Problema vsaimootnosheniia." In *Sergei Andreevich Muromtsev*, 197–207.

Ekhina, Natal'ia Aleksandrovna. "Transformatsiia politicheskikh pozitsii kadetskoi intelligentsii v 1917—pervoi polovine 1930 gg." PhD diss., Moskovskii Gosudarstvennyi Universitet (Moscow State University), 2012.

Ellison, Herbert J. *Boris Yeltsin and Russia's Democratic Transformation*. Toronto. University of Toronto Press, 2006.

Ellman, Michael, and Vladimir Kontorovich, eds. *The Destruction of the Soviet Economic System*. London: Routledge, 2015.

Emmons, Terrence. "The Beseda Circle, 1899–1905." *Slavic Review* 32 (1973): 461–90.

———. *The Russian Landed Gentry and the Peasant Emancipation of 1861*. Cambridge: Cambridge University Press, 1968.

———. "The Statutes of the Union of Liberation." *Russian Review* 33, no. 1 (1974): 80–85.

English, Robert D. *Russia and the Idea of the West: Gorbachev, Intellectuals, and the End of the Cold War*. New York: Columbia University Press, 2000.

English, Robert David, and Ekaterina (Kate) Svyatets. "Soviet Elites and European Integration: From Stalin to Gorbachev." *European Review of History* 21, no. 2 (2014): 219–33.

Enticott, Peter. *The Russian Liberals and the Revolution of 1905*. London: Routledge, 2016.

Epstein, Mikhail. *The Phoenix of Philosophy: Russian Thought of the Late Soviet Period (1953–1991)*. New York: Bloomsbury Academic, 2019.

Evans, Alfred B. "Civil Society and Protest." In Wegren, *Return to Putin's Russia*, 103–24.

———. "Vladimir Putin's Design for Civil Society." In Evans, Henry, and Sundstrom, *Russian Civil Society*, 147–58.

Evans, Alfred B., Laura A. Henry, and Lisa McIntosh Sundstrom, eds. *Russian Civil Society: A Critical Assessment*. Armonk, NY: M. E. Sharpe, 2006.

Fawcett, Edmund. *Liberalism: The Life of an Idea*. Princeton, NJ: Princeton University Press, 2018.

Fedotov, Georgy P. "Nasha demokratiia." *Novyi Grad* 9 (1934): 11–25.

——. "Oni i my." *Sovremennye Zapiski* 70 (1940): 219–34.

——. "Problemy budushchei Rossii." *Sovremennye Zapiski* 43 (1931): 406–37 (part 1); 45 (1931): 475–90 (part 2); 46 (1931): 378–95 (part 3).

——. "Zachem my zdes'?" *Sovremennye Zapiski* 58 (1935): 433–44.

Fedyashin, Anton A. "Humane Modernization as a Liberal Ideal: Late Imperial Russia on the Pages of the 'Herald of Europe,' 1891–1904." *The Historian* 71, no. 4 (2009): 780–804.

——. *Liberals under Autocracy: Modernization and Civil Society in Russia, 1866–1904*. Madison: University of Wisconsin Press, 2012.

Ferro, Marc. *The Russian Revolution of February 1917*. London: Routledge and Kegan Paul, 1972.

Field, Daniel. "Kavelin and Russian Liberalism." *Slavic Review* 32, no. 1 (1973): 59–78.

Figes, Orlando. *The Europeans: Three Lives and the Making of a Cosmopolitan Culture*. New York: Metropolitan, 2019.

Fischer, George. *Russian Liberalism: From Gentry to Intelligentsia*. Cambridge, MA: Harvard University Press, 1958.

Fish, M. Steven. *Democracy from Scratch: Opposition and Regime in the New Russian Revolution*. Princeton, NJ: Princeton University Press, 1995.

——. "The Predicament of Russian Liberalism: Evidence from the December 1995 Parliamentary Elections." *Europe-Asia Studies* 49, no. 2 (1997): 192–220.

Fleischhauer, Ingeborg. "The Agrarian Program of the Russian Constitutional Democrats." *Cahiers du monde russe et soviétique* 20, no. 2 (1979): 173–201.

Flikke, Geir. "Canaries in a Coal Mine: The Uphill Struggle of Russia's Non-System Liberals." *Democratizatsiya* 24, no. 3 (2016): 291–325.

Frank, Semen. "The Ethic of Nihilism: A Characterization of the Russian Intelligentsia's Moral Outlook." In Berdiaev et al., *Landmarks*, 131–55.

Free Russia Forum. "Defeat Putin's War Machine," September 29, 2022. https://www.forumfreerussia.org/en/documents-en/2022-09-28/defeat-putins-war -machine.

Freeden, Michael. *Liberalism: A Very Short Introduction*. Oxford: Oxford University Press, 2015.

——. *The New Liberalism: An Ideology of Social Reform*. Oxford: Clarendon Press, 1986.

Freeland, Chrystia. *Sale of the Century: Russia's Wild Ride from Communism to Capitalism*. Toronto: Doubleday Canada, 2000.

Freeze, Gregory L. "A National Liberation Movement and the Shift in Russian Liberalism, 1901–1903." *Slavic Review* 28, no. 1 (1969): 81–91.

Friedgut, Theodore. "The Democratic Movement: Dimensions and Perspectives." In Tokes, *Dissent in the USSR*, 116–36.

Gaida, F. A. "Osobennosti natsional'nogo politicheskogo opyta rossiiskogo liberala nachala xx v." In Shelokhaev, *Rossiiskii liberalizm*, 174–84.

Gaidar, Egor. "At the Beginning of a New Phase: An Economic Review." *Problems of Economics* 34, no. 6 (1991): 6–23.

——. "The Most Correct Policy Is a Responsible Policy, Not Populism." *Problems of Economic Transition* 37, no 4 (1994): 5–13.

Gaidar, Yegor. *Days of Defeat and Victory.* Seattle: University of Washington Press, 1996.

——. *Russia: A Long View.* Cambridge, MA: MIT Press, 2012.

——. "Russian Reform." In Yegor Gaidar and Karl Otto Pohl, *Russian Reform/ International Money,* 1–54. Cambridge, MA: MIT Press, 1995.

——. *State and Evolution: Russia's Search for a Free Market.* Seattle: University of Washington Press, 2003.

Galai, Shmuel. "The Impact of War on the Russian Liberals in 1904–5." *Government and Opposition* 1, no. 1 (1965): 85–109.

——. "The Kadets in the Second Duma." *Revolutionary Russia* 23, no. 1 (2010): 1–28.

——. *The Liberation Movement in Russia, 1900–1905.* New York: Cambridge University Press, 1973.

——. "The True Nature of Octobrism." *Kritika: Explorations in Russian and Eurasian History* 5, no. 1 (2004): 137–47.

Galas, Marina. "'Respublikansko-demokraticheskoe ob"edinenie' rossiiskoi emigratsii: Organizatiia, strategiia i taktika." *Vlast'* 6 (2008): 81–84.

Gaut, Greg. "A Practical Unity: Vladimir Solov'ev and Russian Liberalism." *Canadian Slavonic Papers* 42, no. 3 (2000): 295–314.

Gel'man, Vladimir. "Tupik avtoritarnoi modernizatsii." Moskovskii Tsentr Karnegi, February 23, 2010. https://polit.ru/article/2010/02/23/gelman/#_ednref10.

Gerschenkron, Alexander. "The Problem of Economic Development in Russian Intellectual History of the Nineteenth Century." In Simmons, *Continuity and Change,* 11–39.

Gessen, Masha. "The Evolution of Alexey Navalny's Nationalism." *New Yorker,* February 15, 2021. https://www.newyorker.com/news/our-columnists/the-evolution-of-alexey-navalnys-nationalism.

——. "What Russians Crave: Cheese." *New York Times,* July 4, 2015. https://www.nytimes.com/2015/07/05/opinion/sunday/what-the-russians-crave-cheese.html.

Geuss, Raymond. "Liberalism and Its Discontents." *Political Theory* 30, no. 3 (2002): 320–38.

Giffin, Frederick C. "The Formative Years of the Russian Factory Inspectorate." *Slavic Review* 25, no. 4 (1966): 641–50.

Gilligan, Emma. *Defending Human Rights in Russia: Sergei Kovalyov, Dissident and Human Rights Commissioner, 1969–2003.* London: Routledge, 2004.

Glebov, Serguei. "'Congresses of Russia Abroad' in the 1920s and the Politics of Émigré Nationalism: A Liberal Survival." *Ab Imperio* 2000, no. 3 (2000): 159–85.

Glinski, Dmitri, and Peter Reddaway. "What Went Wrong in Russia?" *Journal of Democracy* 10, no. 2 (1999): 19–34.

Gnatiuk, O. L. "Konservativnyi ('okhranitel'nyi') liberalizm B. N. Chicherina." *Filosofskie Traditsii i Sovremennost'* 2 (2013): 22–29.

Golovchenko, A. V. "Ideologicheskii faktor v deiatel'nosti RODP 'Iabloko' v sovremennoi Rossii." *Izvestiia Saratovskogo Universiteta* 18, no. 2 (2018): 200–204.

——. "Inversiia oppozitsionnogo statusa partii 'Iabloko' v usloviakh obostreniia mezhdunarodnykh otnoshenii." *Izvestiia Saratovskogo Universiteta* 16, no. 2 (2016): 196–200.

——. "Inversii liberal'nogo patriotizma v sovremennoi Rossii." *Izvestiia Saratovskogo Universiteta* 14, no. 4 (2014): 98–102.

——. "Postsovetskie liberal'nye politiki: Politicheskaia tselesoobrasnost' ili moral'nyi imperativ?" *Vestnik Moskovskogo Gosudarstvennogo Oblastnogo Universiteta* 3 (2018): 3–20.

Gooding, John. "The Liberalism of Michael Speransky." *Slavonic and East European Review* 64, no. 3 (1986): 401–24.

Gopnik, Adam. *A Thousand Small Sanities: The Moral Adventure of Liberalism.* New York: Basic, 2019.

Gorbachev, Alexey. "New Generation of Russian Protestors Harnesses Social Media." *VOA*, February 4, 2021. https://www.voanews.com/a/press-freedom _new-generation-russian-protesters-harnesses-social-media/6201632.html.

Gorbachev, Mikhail. *Perestroika: New Thinking for Our Country and the World.* London: Collins, 1987.

Gorlov, A. V. "Dva 'vzgliada' russkogo liberala XIX veka: K. D. Kavelin o razvitii instituta sobstvennosti v Rossii." *Vestnik Gosudarstvennogo i Munitsipal'nogo Upravleniia* 3 (2012): 39–49.

Gorskii, V. "Russian Messianism and the New National Consciousness." In Meerson-Aksenov and Shragin, *Political, Social, and Religious Thought,* 353–93.

"Gosudarstvennyi paternalizm." *Levada Tsentr*, February 25, 2020. https://www .levada.ru/2020/02/25/gosudarstvennyj-paternalizm/.

Gray, John. *Black Mass: Apocalyptic Religion and the Death of Utopia.* Toronto: Doubleday Canada, 2007.

——. *Liberalism.* Minneapolis: University of Minnesota Press, 1986.

Grishnova, E. E. "Politicheskii liberalizm v Rossii: Uroki istorii." *Sotsialno-Politicheskie Nauki* 3 (2016): 63–67.

Gubin, Dmitry. "Zachem liubit' Rodinu? Russkii patriotizm kak stokgol'mskii sindrom." *Republic*, January 5, 2021. https://republic.ru/posts/99195.

Gudkov, Lev, Natalia Zorkaya, Ekaterina Kochergina, Karina Pipiya, and Alexandra Ryseva. *Russia's Generation Z: Attitudes and Values 2019/2020.* Moscow: Friedrich-Ebert-Stiftung, 2020. http://library.fes.de/pdf-files/bueros/moskau/16134.pdf.

Gusev, V. A. *Russkii konservatizm: Osnovnye napravleniia i etapy razvitiia.* Tver: Tverskii Gosudarstvennyi Universitet, 2001.

Gutorov, V. A. "Rossiiskii liberalizm v politiko-kul'turnom ismerenii: Opyt sravnitel'nogo teoreticheskogo i istoricheskogo analiza." *Politeks* 13, no. 1 (2017): 4–36 (part 1); 13, no. 2 (2017): 4–42 (part 2); 13, no. 3 (2017): 4–26 (part 3).

Hamburg, Gary M. *Boris Chicherin and Early Russian Liberalism, 1828–1866.* Stanford, CA: Stanford University Press, 1992.

——. "Boris Chicherin and Human Dignity in History." In Hamburg and Poole, *A History of Russian Philosophy,* 111–30.

——. "Peasant Emancipation and Russian Social Thought: The Case of Boris N. Chicherin." *Slavic Review* 50, no. 4 (1991): 890–904.

——. *Russia's Path toward Enlightenment: Faith, Politics, and Reason, 1500–1801.* New Haven, CT: Yale University Press, 2016.

Hamburg, Gary M., and Randall A. Poole. "Introduction: The Humanist Tradition in Russian Philosophy." In Hamburg and Poole, *History of Russian Philosophy,* 1–23.

Hamburg, Gary M., and Randall A. Poole, eds. *A History of Russian Philosophy, 1830–1930: Faith, Reason, and the Defense of Human Dignity.* Cambridge: Cambridge University Press, 2010.

Hayek, Friedrich von. *The Constitution of Liberty: The Definitive Edition*. Chicago: University of Chicago Press, 2011.

Hendley, Kathryn. "The Role of Law." In Wegren, *Return to Putin's Russia*, 83–102.

Hickey, Michael C. "Discourses of Public Identity and Liberalism in the February Revolution: Smolensk, Spring 1917." *Russian Review* 55, no. 4 (1996): 615–37.

Hosking, Geoffrey. *The Awakening of the Soviet Union*. London: Heinemann, 1990.

——. "The Beginnings of Independent Political Activity." In Hosking, Aves, and Duncan, *Road to Post-Communism*, 1–28.

Hosking, Geoffrey, Jonathan Aves, and Peter J. S. Duncan. *The Road to Post-Communism: Independent Political Movements in the Soviet Union, 1985–1991*. London: Pinter, 1992.

Huntington, W. Chapin. *The Homesick Million: Russia-out-of-Russia*. Boston: Stratford, 1933.

"'Ia v tsentre uragana': Aleksei Naval'nyi—v proekte 'Russkie norm!'" *The Bell*, December 11, 2019. https://thebell.io/ya-v-tsentre-uragana-aleksej-navalyj-v -proekte-russkie-norm/.

Iasin, E. "Problems of Making the Transition to a Regulated Market Economy." *Problems of Economics* 33, no. 12 (1991): 7–32.

Iavlinskii, Grigorii. "Bez putinizma i populizma." *Yavlinsky.ru*, February 6, 2021. https://www.yavlinsky.ru/article/bez-putinizma-i-populizma/.

——. "Vtoroe iiulia: Politicheskaia situatsiia v Rossii posle 1 iiulia, zadachi de-mokraticheskogo dvizheniia i perspektivy razvitiia partii." *Yabloko*, August 31, 2020. https://www.yabloko.ru/publikatsii/2020/08/31.

"Ideologicheskie orientiry i programmnye ustanovki." *Yabloko*, 2003. https://www .yabloko.ru/Elections/2003/History_Yabloko/yabloko_history004.html.

Il'in, Ivan A. *Nashi zadachi: Stat'i 1948–1954 gg.* Paris: Izdanie Russkogo Obshche-Voinskogo Soiuza, 1956.

"In Russia, It's either Putin or Navalny." *Meduza*, September 16, 2020. https:// meduza.io/en/feature/2020/09/16/in-russia-it-s-either-putin-or-navalny.

Inozemtsev, Vladimir. "Different or the Same? Is Navalny a Good Alternative to Putin?" *Current Digest of the Russian Press* 69, no. 28 (2017): 7–8.

Ioffe, Olimpiad S. "Soviet Attitudes toward International Human Rights Law." *Connecticut Journal of International Law* 2, no. 2 (1987): 361–65.

Ivanov, V. F. *Russkaia intelligentsia i masontsvo: Ot Petra I do nashikh dnei*. Moscow: Moskva, 1997.

Johnson, Robert H. *New Mecca, New Babylon: Paris and the Russian Exiles, 1920–1945*. Montreal: McGill-Queen's University Press, 1988.

"Kakoi dolzhna byt' Rossiia v predstavlenii rossiian?" *Levada Tsentr*, September 10, 2021. https://www.levada.ru/2021/09/10/kakoj-dolzhna-byt-rossiya-v -predstavlenii-rossiyan/.

Kantor, Vladimir. "Semen Liudvigovich Frank." In Kara-Murza, *Rossiiskii liberalizm*, 853–63.

Kapeliushnikov, Rostislav. "Rossiiskii liberalizm: Byt' ili ne byt'?" *Colta*, July 16, 2019. https://www.colta.ru/articles/specials/21886-rossiyskiy-liberalizm-byt-ili-ne -byt.

Kara-Murza, Aleksei. "Liberalizm protiv khaosa. Osnovnye tendentsie liberal'noi ideologii na zapade i Rossii." http://libertarium.ru/l_lib_LiberChaos.

——. "Nekotorye voprosy genezisa i typologii russkogo liberalizma." *Istoriia filosofii* 21, no. 2 (2016): 69–76.

——. "O natsional'nykh variantakh liberalizma i russkoi modeli v chastnosti." In Shelokhaev, *Rossiiskii liberalizm: Itogi i perspektivy izucheniia*, 28–38.

——, ed. *Rossiiskii liberalizm: Idei i liudi.* Moscow: Fond Liberal'naia Missiia, 2007.

——. *Svoboda i poriadok: Iz istorii russkoi politicheskoi mysli xix–xx vv.* Moscow: Moskovskaia Shkola Politicheskikh Issledovanii, 2009.

Kara-Murza, Alexey, and Olga Zhukova. "The Political Philosophy of Russian Liberalism." In Cucciolla, *Dimensions and Challenges*, 27–38.

Kara-Murza, Vladimir. "Andrei Dmitrievich Sakharov." In Kara-Murza, *Rossiiskii liberalizm*, 887–95.

——. "Boris Nemtsov: From Kremlin Heir to Dissident." *Demokratizatsiya* 24, no. 1 (2016): 31–34.

Karipov, B. N. "Liberaly Rossii: K analyzu kontseptsii ravnovesiia i vzaimodopolneniia v otnosheniiakh mezhdu grazhdanskim obshchestvom i gosudarstvom." *Izvestii Saratovskogo Universiteta* 14, no. 1 (2014): 91–94.

——. "Sushchnost' i osnovnye cherty russkogo liberal'nogo klassicheskogo diskursa." *Vestnik Moskovskogo Universiteta* 12, no. 2 (2008): 89–101.

Karpachev, Mikhail. "Andrei Ivanovich Shingarev." In Kara-Murza, *Rossiiskii liberalizm*, 716–22.

Karpovich, Michael. "Two Types of Russian Liberalism: Maklakov and Miliukov." In Simmons, *Continuity and Change*, 129–43.

Kashin, Oleg. *Reaktsiia Putina: Chto takoe khorosho i chto takoe plokho.* Moscow: Algoritm, 2013.

Kasparov, Gary. *Winter Is Coming: Why Vladimir Putin and the Enemies of the Free World Must Be Stopped.* New York: Public Affairs, 2015.

Kavelin, Konstantin Dmitrievich. "Chto nam byt'?" In Abramov, *Opyt russkogo liberalizma*, 78–122

——. "Dvorianstvo i osvobozhdenie krest'ian." http://dugward.ru/library/kavelin /kavelin_dvoranstvo_i_osvobojdenie.html.

——. "Vzgliad na iuridicheskii byt drevnei Rossii." In *Nash umstvennyi stroi: Stat'i po filosofii russkoi istorii i kul'tury*, 11–67. Moscow: Pravda, 1989.

Kavelin, Konstantin Dmitrievich, and Boris N. Chicherin. "Pis'mo k izdatel'stvu." In Abramov, *Opyt russkogo liberalizma*, 21–37.

Kazakevitch, Gennadi. "Yegor Gaidar: Pragmatic Economist or Romantic Revolutionary?" *Agenda: A Journal of Policy Analysis and Reform* 17, no. 1 (2010): 121–30.

Kelly, Aileen. "Byl' li Gertsen liberalom?" *Gor'kii media* 6 (2002). https://magazines .gorky.media/nlo/2002/6/byl-li-gerczen-liberalom.html.

——. "'What Is Real Is Rational': The Political Philosophy of B. N. Chicherin." *Cahiers du monde russe et soviétique* 18, no. 3 (1977): 195–222.

Kelly, Paul. *Liberalism.* Cambridge: Polity, 2005.

Khailova, Nina B. "'Drug poriadka, osnovannogo na svobode i prave': M. M. Kovalevskii protiv P. A. Stolypina." In *Sergei Andreevich Muromtsev*, 207–17.

——. "Mikhail Matveevich Stasiulevich." In Kara-Murza, *Rossiiskii liberalizm*, 307–20.

Khefner, Liutz, and A. Kaplunovskogo. "'Konstitutsionno-demokraticheskaia partiia ne menee tverdo derzhitsia printsipa edinstva i nerazdel'nosti Rossii':

Liberalizm i natsionalizm v Rossiiskoi provintsii, 1905–1914 gg." *Ab Imperio* 2000, no. 3 (2000): 91–126.

Khevrolina, V. M. "Russian Liberalism's Views on Foreign Policy at the End of the Nineteenth Century." *Russian Studies in History* 37, no. 3 (1998): 66–92.

Khodorkovskii, Mikhail. *Novaia Rossiia, ili Gardarika.* February 2020. https://gardarika-book.org.

Khodorkovsky, Mikhail. "Liberalism in Crisis: What Is to Be Done?" *Moscow Times,* April 1, 2004. https://khodorkovsky.com/liberalism-in-crisis-what-is-to-be-done.

Kiriakin, Aleksandr Viktorich. "Politicheskii, ekonomicheskii i sotsial'nyi liberalizm B. N. Chicherina." *Vestnik TGU* 2, no. 2 (2015): 59–65.

Kiselev, A. F., ed. *Politicheskaia istoriia russkoi emigratsii, 1920–1940 gg.: Dokumenty i materialy.* Moscow: Gumanitarnyi Izdatel'skii Tsentr, 1999. http://www.rus-sky.com/history/library/emigration.

Kistiakovskii, Bogdan. "In Defense of Law: The Intelligentsia and Legal Conscious-ness." In Berdiaev et al., *Landmarks,* 91–113.

Kitaev, V. A. "The Unique Liberalism of Vestnik Evropy, 1870–1880." *Russian Studies in History* 46, no. 1 (2007): 43–61.

Kliamkin, Igor'. *Kakaia doroga idet k pravu?* Moscow: Mysl', 2018.

Klimina, Anna. "Ideas of Constructed Market in Late Imperial Russia: Constructivist Liberalism of Peter Struve (1870–1944)." *Economics Bulletin* 31, no. 3 (2011): 2041–52.

Koch, Alfred, and Igor Svinarenko. *A Crate of Vodka.* New York: Enigma, 2009.

Kojima, Shuichi. "Exiled Russian Economists and the USSR: Brutzkus and Prokopo-vich." In *Economics in Russia: Studies in Intellectual History,* edited by Joachim Zweynert, 123–40. London: Routledge, 2008.

——. "Russian Liberal Visions of Agricultural Development at the Beginning of the Twentieth Century: Litoshenko and Brutzkus." *Oeconomica* 4, no. 1 (2014): 55–76.

"Konflikt s Ukrainoi." *Levada Tsentr,* September 29, 2022. https://www.levada.ru/2022/09/29/konflikt-s-ukrainoj-sentyabr-2022-goda/.

"Konstitutsiia (Osnovnoi zakon) Rossiiskoi Sotsialisticheskoi Federativnoi Sovetskoi Respubliki (priniata V Vserossiiskim S"ezdom Sovetov v zasedanii ot 10 iiulia 1918 g.)." Sait Konstitutsii Rossiiskoi Federatsii. http://www.constitution.garant.ru/history/ussr-rsfsr/1918/.

"Konstitutsiia (Osnovnoi zakon) Soiuza Sovetskikh Sotsialisticheskikh Respublik (priniata na vneocherednoi sed'moi sessii Verkhovnogo Soveta deviatogo sozyva 7 oktiabria 1977g.)." Sait Konstitutsii Rossiiskoi Federatsii. http://www.constitution.garant.ru/history/ussr-rsfsr/1977/red_1977/5478732.

"Konstitutsiia (Osnovnoi zakon) Soiuza Sovetskikh Sotsialisticheskikh Respublik (utverzhdena postanovleniem Chrezvychainogo VIII S"ezda Sovetov Soiuza Sovetskikh Sotsialisticheskikh Respublikh ot 5 dekabria 1936 g.)." Sait Konstitutsii Rossiiskoi Federatsii. http://www.constitution.garant.ru/history/ussr-rsfsr/1936/red_1936/3958676/.

"Konstitutsiia Rossiiskoi Federatsii." 1993. http://www.constitution.ru.

Kotel'nitskii, N.A. "Obshchestvennaia deiatel'nost' I. I. Petrunkevicha na Chernigov-shchine (1868–1879)." *Vestnik RUDN, ser. Istoriia Rossii* 4 (2010): 5–24.

Kotliarevskii, S. A. "Predposylki demokratii." In Abramov, *Opyt russkogo liberalizma*, 215–39.

Kovalev, Andrei. *Russia's Dead End: An Insider's Testimony from Gorbachev to Putin.* Lincoln, NE: Potomac, 2017.

Kovalevskii, M. M. "Uchenie o lichnykh pravakh." In Abramov, *Opyt russkogo liberalizma*, 168–212.

Kozyreva, P. M., and A. M. Smirnov. "Doverie v nestabil'noi rossiiskom ob-shchestve." *Polis. Politicheskie Issledovaniia* 5 (2019): 134–47.

Kramer, David J. "Boris Nemtsov: A Variety of Perspectives." *Demokratizatsiya* 24, no. 1 (2016): 29–31.

"Kudrin predlozhil Putinu zaniat'sia obrazovaniem i zdorov'em." *Vedomosti*, September 6, 2017. https://www.vedomosti.ru/economics/articles/2017/09/06/732485-kudrin-putinu-obrazovaniem-zdorovem?

Kurmelovs, Royce. "Raising Hell: Q and A: Who the Hell Is Alexei Navalny?" *Raising Hell*, January 27, 2021. https://roycekurmelovs.substack.com/p/whoisn avalny.

Kurnyshova, Y. "Boris Nemtsov: A Ukrainian Afterword." *Demokratizatsiya* 24, no. 1 (2016): 41–43.

Lapidus, Gail W. "Transforming the 'National Question': New Approaches to Nationalism, Federalism and Sovereignty." In Brown, *Demise of Marxism-Leninism*, 119–77.

Laruelle, Marlene. "Alexei Navalny and Challenges in Reconciling 'Nationalism' and 'Liberalism.'" *Post-Soviet Affairs* 30, no. 4 (2014): 276–97.

Latynina, Iuliia. "Donbass v N'iu-Iorke." *Novaia Gazeta*, June 3, 2020. https://novayagazeta.ru/articles/2020/06/03/85679-donbass-v-nyu-yorke.

——. "Esli my ne Zapad, to kto my?" *Ekho Moskvy*, September 12, 2014. https://www.lrt.lt/ru/novosti/17/63885/iuliia-latynina-esli-my-ne-zapad-to-kto-my-kommentarii.

——. "Evropa, ty ofigela!" *Novaia Gazeta*, August 16, 2011. https://novayagazeta.ru/articles/2011/08/16/45476-yuliya-latynina-171-evropa-ty-ofigela-187.

——. "Mir prosto razdelitsia na svobodnykh—i nas." *Novaia Gazeta*, February 24, 2022. (This article is no longer available.)

——. "Zabludilis' v trekh narrativakh: Diskussiia." *Novaia Gazeta*, August 3, 2020. https://novayagazeta.ru/articles/2020/08/03/86505-zabludilis-v-trekh-narrativah-diskussiya.

Leatherbarrow, William, and Derek Offord, eds. *A Documentary History of Russian Thought from the Enlightenment to Marxism.* Ann Arbor, MI: Ardis, 1987.

Leontovitsch, Victor. *The History of Liberalism in Russia.* Pittsburgh, PA: University of Pittsburgh Press, 2012.

Liberman, Yevsei. "The Soviet Economic Reform." *Foreign Affairs* 46, no. 1 (1967): 53–63.

Lieven, Anatol. "How the West Lost." *Prospect*, August 31, 2020. https://www.prospectmagazine.co.uk/magazine/how-the-west-lost-victory-communism-moral-defeat.

Light, Felix, and Pjotr Sauer. "True Beliefs and Opportunism: Navalny's Tangled Political Development." *Moscow Times*, February 1, 2021. https://www

.themoscowtimes.com/2021/02/01/true-beliefs-and-opportunism-navalnys
-tangled-political-development-a72797.

Lincoln, W. Bruce. *The Great Reforms: Autocracy, Bureaucracy, and the Politics of Change in Imperial Russia.* DeKalb: Northern Illinois University Press, 1990.

———. *In the Vanguard of Reform: Russia's Enlightened Bureaucrats, 1825–1861.* DeKalb: Northern Illinois University Press, 1982.

Lindenmeyr, Adele. *Citizen Countess: Sofia Panina and the Fate of Revolutionary Russia.* Madison: University of Wisconsin Press, 2019.

Liubeznova, E. V. "Kadety Sibiri v poiskakh form organizatsii vlasti v pervyi god grazhdanskoi voiny." *Omskii nauchnyi vestnik* 2 (2011): 23–26.

Lipovetsky, Mark. "The Poetics of ITR Discourse in the 1960s and Today." *Ab Imperio* 2013, no. 1 (2013): 109–39.

Litvinov, Pavel. "O dvizhenii za prava cheloveka v SSSR." In Litvinov, Meerson-Aksenov, and Shragin, *Samosoznanie,* 63–88.

Litvinov, Pavel, Mikhail Meerson-Aksenov, and Boris Shragin. "Ot sostavitelei." In Litvinov, Meerson-Aksenov, and Shragin, *Samosoznanie,* 5–9.

———, eds. *Samosoznanie: Sbornik statei.* New York: Khronika, 1976.

Logvinova, Inna Vladimirovna. "Mezhdunarodnye pakty o pravakh cheloveka 1966 g. v kontekste razvitiia obshchepriznannykh prav i svobod lichnosti." *Mezhdunarodnoe Pravo i Mezhdunarodnye Organizatsii* 1 (2017): 56–64.

Lomb, Samantha. *Stalin's Constitution: Soviet Participatory Politics and the Discussion of the 1936 Draft Constitution.* London: Routledge, 2018.

Lukin, Alexander. *The Political Culture of the Russia "Democrats."* Oxford: Oxford University Press, 2000.

Maklakov, V. A. "Iz proshlogo." *Sovremennye Zapiski* 38 (1929): 276–314 (part 1); 40 (1930): 291–334 (part 2); 41 (1930): 232–75 (part 3).

Malinova, Olga. "Encounters with Liberalism in Post-Soviet Russia." In *In Search of European Liberalisms: Concepts, Languages, Ideologies,* edited by Michael Freeden, Javier Fernandez-Sebastian, and Jörn Leonhard, 278–301. New York: Berghahn, 2019.

———. "Konstruirovanie 'liberalizma' v postsovetskoi Rossii: Nasledie 1990-kh v ideologicheskikh bitvakh 2000-kh." *Politiia* 84, no. 1 (2017): 6–28.

Mamardashvili, Merab. "The 'Third' State." In Slaughter and Sushytska, *Spy for an Unknown Country,* 165–76.

Manent, Pierre. "The Greatness and Misery of Liberalism." *Modern Age* (Summer 2010): 176–83.

Matveev, Ilya A. "The 'Two Russias' Culture War: Constructions of the 'People' during the 2011–2013 Protests." *South Atlantic Quarterly* 113, no. 1 (2014): 186–95.

———. "Gibridnaia neoliberalizatsiia: Gosudarstvo, legitimnost', i neoliberalizm v putinskoi Rossii." *Politiia* 79, no. 4 (2015): 25–47.

Mau, Vladimir. "Macroeconomic Stabilization as a Sociopolitical Problem." In *The Economics of Transition,* edited by Yegor Gaidar, 89–104. Cambridge, MA: MIT Press, 2003.

Mazour, Anatole G., *The First Russian Revolution, 1825: The Decembrist Movement, Its Origins, Development, and Significance.* Stanford, CA: Stanford University Press, 1963.

McAuley, Mary. *Human Rights in Russia: Citizens and the State from Perestroika to Putin.* London: I. B. Tauris, 2015.

McCloskey, H. J. "Liberalism." *Philosophy* 49, no. 187 (1974): 13–32.

McKenzie, Kermit E. "The Political Faith of Fedor Rodichev." In Timberlake, *Essays on Russian Liberalism,* 42–61.

Medushevskii, Andrei. "Byt' liberalom v Rossii: o svobodnom obraze myshleniia i ego kritikakh." In Shelokhaev, *Rossiiskii liberalizm,* 38–57.

———. "The Constitutional Projects of Russian Liberalism and Its Political Strategy." *Russian Studies in History* 37, no. 3 (1998): 32–65.

———. "Pavel Ivanovich Novgorodtsev." In Kara-Murza, *Rossiiskii liberalizm,* 628–38.

Medushevsky, Andrey N. *Russian Constitutionalism: Historical and Contemporary Development.* London: Routledge, 2006.

Medvedev, Sergei. *The Return of the Russian Leviathan.* New York: Polity, 2020.

Medvedev, Vadim. "Under Andropov and Gorbachev." In Ellman and Kontorovich, *Destruction of the Soviet Economic System,* 94–97.

Meerson-Aksenov, Michael. "Rozhdenie novoi intelligentsii." In Litvinov, Meerson-Aksenov, and Shragin, *Samosoznanie,* 89–116.

Meerson-Aksenov, Michael, and Boris Shragin, eds. *The Political, Social, and Religious Thought of Russian "Samizdat": An Anthology.* Belmont: Nordland, 1977.

"Meeting on Liberalisation of Criminal Law." President of Russia, October 21, 2010. http://en.kremlin.ru/events/president/news/9305.

Men, Alexander. "Christianity." http://www.alexandermen.com/Christianity.

———. "Interview on the State of the Russian Church." http://www.alexandermen .com/Interview_on_the_state_of_the_Russian_Church.

———. "On Christ and the Church." http://www.alexandermen.com/On_Christ_and _the_Church.

———. "Two Understandings of Christianity." http://www.alexandermen.com/Two _Understandings_of_Christianity.

Michelson, Patrick Lally. "Freedom of Conscience and the Limits of the Liberal Solovyov." *Solov'evskie issledovaniia* 41, no. 1 (2014): 25–45.

Michlin-Shapir, Vera. *Fluid Russia: Between the Global and the National in the Post-Soviet Era.* DeKalb: Northern Illinois University Press, 2021.

Migranyan, Andranik. "The Long Road to a European Home." *Current Digest of the Soviet Press* 41, no. 42 (1989): 6–32.

Miliukov, Pavel N. "Chto delat' posle Krymskoi katastrophy?" In *Protokoly Tsentral'nogo Komiteta i zagranichnykh grupp konstitutsionno-demokraticheskoi partii, 1905—seredina 1930–kh gg.,* 4:76–83. Moscow: Rosspen, 1996.

———. *Emigratsiia na pereput'e.* Paris: Izdanie Respublikansko-Demokraticheskikh Ob"edinenii, 1926

———. "Liberalizm, radikalizm, i revolutsiia." *Sovremennye Zapiski* 47 (1935): 285–315.

———. "Sud nad kadetskim 'liberalizmom.'" *Sovremennye Zapiski* 41 (1930): 347–71.

———. *Tri platformy Respublikansko-Demokraticheskikh Ob"edinenii (1922–24 gg.).* Paris: Izdanie Respublikansko-demokraticheskogo ob"edeneiia, 1925.

Milyoukov, Paul. *Russia and Its Crisis.* Chicago: University of Chicago Press, 1906.

Mommen, Andre. "Boris Nemtsov, 1959–2015: The Rise and Fall of a Provincial Democrat." *Demokratizatsiya* 24, no. 1 (2016): 5–28.

Mozhin, Vladimir. "It Was about Enterprise Autonomy." In Ellman and Kontorovich, *Destruction of the Soviet Economic System*, 136–38.

Muratov, Dmitry. "Pro Venediktova i nenavist'." *Novaia Gazeta*, September 29, 2021. https://novayagazeta.ru/articles/2021/09/29/pro-venediktova-i-nenavist.

——. "Rossiia. Bombit. Ukrainu." *Novaia Gazeta*, September 25, 2022.

Muravev, Nikita Mikhailovich. "A Project for a Constitution (Extracts)." In Leatherbarrow and Offord, *Documentary History of Russian Thought*, 42–50.

Nathans, Benjamin. "Coming to Terms with Late Soviet Liberalism." *Ab Imperio* 2013, no. 1 (2013): 175–82.

——. "Human Rights Defenders within Soviet Politics." In Cucciolla, *Dimensions and Challenges*, 87–96.

——. "The Dictatorship of Reason: Aleksandr Vol'pin and the Idea of Rights under 'Developed Socialism.'" *Slavic Review* 66, no. 4 (2007): 630–63.

Naval'nii, Aleksei. "Gde prikhodit 'orgiia tolerantnosti'?" *Navalny.com*, November 16, 2015. https://navalny.com/t/92/.

Nazarov, Mikhail. *Missiia russkoi emigratsii*. Stavropol: Kavkazskii krai, 1992.

Nelidov, Dmitrii. "Ideokraticheskoe soznanie i lichnost'." In Litvinov, Meerson-Aksenov, and Shragin, *Samosoznanie*, 117–50.

Nelson, Lynn D., and Irina Y. Kuzes. *Property to the People: The Struggle for Radical Economic Reform in Russia*. Armonk, NY: M. E. Sharpe, 1994.

——. *Radical Reform in Yeltsin's Russia: Political, Economic, and Social Dimensions*. Armonk, NY: M. E. Sharpe, 1995.

Nemtsov, Boris. *Ispoved' buntaria*. Moscow: Partizan, 2007.

——. "Strana gotova snova vpast' v rabskoe sostoianie." *Kommersant-Vlast'*, March 5, 2002. https://nemtsov-most.org/2017/12/29/boris-nemtsov-the-country-is-ready-to-fall-into-slavery-again/.

Nikonov, Maxim, and Ol'ga Shepeleva. "Development of Russia's Criminal Justice System: Vectors, Reform Measures, and Major Players." *Statutes and Decisions* 51, no. 4 (2017): 455–517.

Nintsieva, Galina Vasil'evna. "Osnovnye techeniia ekonomicheskoi mysli russkoi emigratsii 20–50–x godov xx stoletiia." PhD diss., Kandidat ekonomicheskikh nauk, Sankt-Peterburgskii Gosudarstvennyi Universitet Ekonomiki i Finansov, 2004.

Nobel Prize. "Dmitry Muratov." https://www.nobelprize.org/prizes/peace/2021/muratov/facts/.

Nove, Alec. "The Rise of Non-Leninist Thinking on the Economy." In Brown, *Demise of Marxism-Leninism*, 42–50.

Novgorodtsev, P. I. "Ethical Idealism in the Philosophy of Law (On the Question of the Revival of Natural Law)." In Poole, *Problems of Idealism*, 274–324.

——. "Idealy partii narodnoi svobody i sotsializm." In Abramov, *Opyt russkogo liberalizma*, 284–99.

——. "Pravo na dostoinoe chelovecheskoe sushchestvovanie." In P. I. Novgorodtsev and I. A. Pokrovskii, *O prave na sushchestvovanie: Sotsial'no-filosofskie etiudy*, 1–13. St Petersburg: Izdanie T-va M. O. Vol'f, 1911.

Novikova, Lidiia, and Irina Sizemskaia, "Ideinye istoki russkogo liberalizma." *Obshchestvennye Nauki i Sovremennost'* 3 (1993): 124–34.

Novodvorskaia, Valeriia. "Na toi edinstvennoi, grazhdanskoi." *Ogonek* 2–3 (1994): 26–27.

——. "Takoi narod pust' vymiraet, ne zhalko." *Newsland*, October 18, 2012. https://newsland.com/post/1614524-esli-takovoi-narod-vymret-to-chestnoe-slovo-naplevat-i-zabyt

Nuttall, Marc. "Tipping Points and the Human World: Living with Change and Thinking about the Future." *Ambio* 41, no. 1 (2012): 97–98.

"Nuzhna li zheleznaia ruka?" *Vremia i Mir* 107 (1989): 123–31.

Obolensky, Alexander V. "Ethical Liberal Values vs. the Soviet Political and Administrative Heritage from the 1980s to the Present." In Cucciolla, *Dimensions and Challenges*, 147-62

"Odobrenie deiatel'nosti Vladimira Putina." *Levada Tsentr*, June 2022. https://www.levada.ru/indikatory/.

Offord, Derek. "*Lichnost'*: Notions of Individual Identity." In *Constructing Russian Identity in the Age of Revolution, 1881–1940*, edited by Catriona Kelly and David Shepherd, 13–25. Oxford: Oxford University Press, 1998.

O'Meara, P. *The Decembrist Pavel Pestel: Russia's First Republican*. Basingstoke: Palgrave, 2003.

"O prizyvakh golosovat' za KPRF." *Yabloko*, October 18, 2021. https://www.yabloko.ru/reshenija_politicheskogo_komiteta/2021/10/18-3.

Orlov, Iurii. "Vozmozhen li sotsializm ne totalitarnogo tipa?" In Litvinov, Meerson-Aksenov, and Shragin, *Samosoznanie*, 279–303.

"O situatsii v Rossii." *Yabloko*, October 18, 2021. https://www.yabloko.ru/reshenija_politicheskogo_komiteta/2021/10/18-0/.

Oushakine, Serguei. "The Terrifying Mimicry of Samizdat." *Public Culture* 13, no. 2 (2001): 191–214.

Pabst, Adrian. "Liberalism." In *Handbook on the Economics of Reciprocity and Social Enterprise*, edited by Luigno Bruni and Stefano Zamagni, 217–26. Cheltenham: Edward Elgar, 2013.

Partiia Narodnoi Svobody PARNAS. "Osnovnye napravleniia sistemnoi dekommunizatsii Rossii." June 5, 2018. https://partyparnas.ru/news/457.

——. "Za chto my boremsia i k chemu stremimsia. Kratkaia programma PARNAS." April 20, 2017. https://partyparnas.ru/news/353.

Partiia Novye Liudi. "Programma partii." https://newpeople.ru/progam_newpeople.

Partiia rosta. "Progamma partii." http://www.rost.ru/about/programma-partii/.

Pastukhov, Vladimir. "Gosudarstvo diktatury liumpen-proletariata." *Novaia Gazeta*, August 13, 2012. https://novayagazeta.ru/articles/2012/08/13/50971-gosudarstvo-diktatury-lyumpen-proletariata.

——. "Spoiler Rossii budushchego." *Novaia Gazeta*, August 7, 2021. https://novayagazeta.ru/articles/2021/08/07/vladimir-pastukhov-spoiler-rossii-budushchego.

Pearson, Raymond. *The Russian Moderates and the Crisis of Tsarism, 1914–1917*. London: Macmillan, 1977.

Pestel, Pavel Ivanovich. "Russian Law (Extracts)." In Leatherbarrow and Offord, *Documentary History of Russian Thought*, 51–58.

Petrazycki, Leon. *Law and Morality*. New Brunswick, NJ: Transaction, 2011.

Petro, Nicolai. "Are We Reading Russia Right?" *Fletcher Forum of World Affairs* 42, no. 2 (2018): 131–54.

Pinsker, Boris, and Larisa Piiasheva. "Sobstvennost' i svoboda." *Novyi Mir* 11 (1989): 184–98.

Pipes, Richard. *Alexander Yakovlev: The Man Whose Ideas Delivered Russia from Communism*. DeKalb: Northern Illinois University Press, 2015.

——. *Struve: Liberal on the Left, 1870–1905*. Cambridge, MA: Harvard University Press, 1970.

——. *Struve: Liberal on the Right, 1905–1944*. Cambridge, MA: Harvard University Press, 1980.

Piyasheva, Larisa. "Economic Reform: A Great Bubble or a Faint Chance to Survive?" *Cato Journal* 11, no. 2 (1991): 293–98.

Polukhin, Aleksei. "Grigory Yavlinsky: 'The Economy Cannot Survive Such Political Decisions.'" *Current Digest of the Russian Press* 67, no. 6 (2015): 13–15.

Polunov, A. *Russia in the Nineteenth Century: Autocracy, Reform, and Social Change, 1814–1914*. Armonk, NY: M. E. Sharpe, 2005.

Pomerants, Grigorii. "Chelovek niotkuda." http://www.liv.piramidin.com/publ /Pomerants_G/chelovek_niotkuda.html.

——. "Modernizatsiia nezapadnykh stran." In Litvinov, Meerson-Aksenov, and Shragin, *Samosoznanie*, 209–42.

Pomeranz, William E. *Law and the Russian State: Russia's Legal Evolution from Peter the Great to Vladimir Putin*. London: Bloomsbury, 2019.

"Pomogat' i nakazyvat'." *Kommersant*, April 20, 2020. http://www.kommersant.ru /doc/4326252.

Poole, Randall A. "Editor's Introduction: Philosophy and Politics in the Russian Liberation Movement." In Poole, *Problems of Idealism*, 1–78.

——. "Nineteenth-Century Russian Liberalism: Ideals and Realities." *Kritika: Explorations in Russian and Eurasian History* 16, no. 1 (2015): 157–81.

——, ed. *Problems of Idealism: Essays in Russian Social Philosophy*. New Haven, CT: Yale University Press, 2005.

——. "Religion, War, and Revolution: E. N. Trubetskoi's Liberal Construction of Russian National Identity, 1912–20." *Kritika: Explorations in Russia and Eurasian History* 7, no. 2 (2006): 195–240.

——. "Religious Toleration, Freedom of Conscience, and Russian Liberalism." *Kritika: Explorations in Russian and Eurasian History* 13, no. 3 (2012): 611–34.

Popkova, A. "Gde pyshnee pirogi?" *Novyi Mir* 5 (1987): 239–41.

Popov, Gavriil. "The Goals and the Mechanism." *Problems of Economics* 31, no. 11 (1989): 33–47.

——. "Vyzyvaiu dukh generala Vlasova," *Novaia Gazeta*, September 9, 2007. https://novayagazeta.ru/articles/2007/09/10/32026-gavriil-popov-vyzyvayu -duh-generala-vlasova.

Popova, A. V. "Sotsialisticheskoe uchenie kak sostavnaia chast' neoliberal'noi politiko-pravovoi doktriny na rubezhe xix–xx vv." *RUDN Journal of Law* 3 (2012): 5–13.

Prava i svobody cheloveka v programmnykh dokumentakh osnovnykh politicheskikh partii i ob"edinenii Rossii xx vek. Moscow: Rosspen, 2002.

"Predvybornaia programma partii 'Iabloko' 'Uvazhenie k cheloveku,' 2016 god."
    Yabloko, 2016. https://www.yabloko.ru/program.
Procyk, Anna. *Russian Nationalism and Ukraine: The Nationality Policy of the Volunteer
    Army during the Civil War.* Edmonton, AB: Canadian Institute of Ukrainian
    Studies Press, 1995.
"Programma 'Demokraticheskii manifest' (2012)." *Yabloko*, June 17, 2012. https://
    www.yabloko.ru/content/programma_demokraticheskij_manifest.
"Programma obshchestvennogo ob"edineniia 'Iabloko.'" In *Prava i svobody cheloveka*,
    475–83.
"Programma partii 'Demokraticheskii vybor Rossii.'" In *Prava i svobody cheloveka*, 464–73.
Prokhorova, Irina. "Totalitarnoe soznanie i missiia intellektuala." *New Times*,
    May 28, 2018. https://newtimes.ru/articles/detail/165063.
Pursglove, Michael. "Introduction." In Ivan Turgenev, *Smoke*, xi–xix. London: Alma
    Classics, 2013.
"Putin Fires Apparent Warning Salvo at Russian Federation Accounts Chamber
    Head Kudrin." Memri TV, February 27, 2020. https://www.memri.org
    /reports/putin-fires-apparent-warning-salvo-russian-federation-accounts
    -chamber-head-kudrin.
Putin, Vladimir. "Poslanie Presidenta Federal'nomu Sobraniiu." President of Russia
    December 4, 2014. http://kremlin.ru/events/president/news/47173.
——. "Poslanie Presidenta Federal'nomu Sobraniiu." President of Russia, April 21,
    2021. http://www.kremlin.ru/events/president/news/65418.
——. "Zasedanie mezhregional'nogo foruma ONF." President of Russia, January 25,
    2016. http://kremlin.ru/events/president/news/51206.
Putnam, George. "P. B. Struve's View of the Russian Revolution of 1905." *Slavonic
    and East European Review* 45, no. 105 (1967): 457–63.
——. *Russian Alternatives to Marxism: Christian Socialism and Idealistic Liberalism in
    Twentieth-Century Russia.* Knoxville: University of Tennessee Press, 1977.
Pyziur, Eugene. "Mikhail N. Katkov: Advocate of English Liberalism in Russia."
    Slavonic and East European Review 45, no. 105 (1967): 439–56.
Quigley, John. "Human Rights Study in Soviet Academia." *Human Rights Quarterly*
    11, no. 3 (1989): 452–58.
Rabow-Edling, Susanna. *Liberalism in Pre-Revolutionary Russia: State, Nation, Empire.*
    Abingdon: Routledge, 2019.
Radishchev, Aleksandr N. "[On Autocracy]." In Leatherbarrow and Offord, *Documen-
    tary History of Russian Thought*, 17.
Raeff, Marc. *The Decembrist Movement.* Englewood Cliffs, NJ: Prentice-Hall, 1966.
——. *Michael Speransky: Statesman of Imperial Russia, 1772–1839.* The Hague: Nijhoff,
    1957.
——. "A Reactionary Liberal: M. N. Katkov." *Russian Review* 11, no. 3 (1952): 157–67.
——. *Russia Abroad: A Cultural History of the Russian Emigration, 1919–1939.* Oxford:
    Oxford University Press, 1990.
——. "Some Reflections on Russian Liberalism." *Russian Review* 18, no. 3 (1959):
    218–30.
——. "What Became of the Liberal Tradition? Comments on Samosoznanie." *Slavic
    Review* 37, no. 1 (1978): 116–19.

Rampton, Vanessa. *Liberal Ideas in Tsarist Russia: From Catherine the Great to the Russian Revolution*. Cambridge: Cambridge University Press, 2020.

Redchenko, D. V. "Prisoedinenie Kryma k Rossii v 2014 g.: Pozitsiia rossiiskoi ob"edinennoi demokraticheskoi partii 'Iabloko.'" *Izvestiia Saratovskogo Universiteta* 17, no. 2 (2017): 216–22.

——. "RODP 'Iabloko' i razvitie 'Arabskoi vesny' v Livii i Sirii v 2011–2013 gg." *Izvestiia Saratovskogo Universiteta* 16, no. 2 (2016): 201–5.

Reddaway, Peter, and Dmitri Glinski. *The Tragedy of Russia's Reforms: Market Bolshevism against Democracy*. Washington, DC: United States Institute of Peace, 2000.

Rey, Marie-Pierre. *Alexander I: The Tsar Who Defeated Napoleon*. DeKalb: Northern Illinois University Press, 2012.

Rieber, Alfred J. "Interest-Group Politics in the Era of the Great Reform." In *Russia's Great Reforms, 1855–1881*, edited by Ben Eklof, John Bushnell, and Larissa Zakharova, 58–83. Bloomington: Indiana University Press, 1994.

Riha, Thomas. *A Russian-European: Paul Miliukov in Russian Politics*. Notre Dame, IN: University of Notre Dame Press, 1969.

Robinson, Paul. *Grand Duke Nikolai Nikolaevich: Supreme Commander of the Russian Army*. DeKalb: Northern Illinois University Press, 2014.

——. *Russian Conservatism*. DeKalb: Northern Illinois University Press, 2019.

Robinson, Paul, and Jay Dixon. *Aiding Afghanistan: A History of Soviet Assistance to a Developing Country*. London: Hurst, 2013.

Rodichev, Fedor. "The Veteran of Russian Liberalism: Ivan Petrunkevich." *Slavonic and East European Review* 7, no. 20 (1929): 316–26.

Rodichev, Fedor, and J. E. S. C. "The Liberal Movement in Russia (1855–1891)." *Slavonic Review* 2, no. 4 (1923): 1–13.

Romanov, Igor. "Yabloko Identifies Its Enemies." *Current Digest of the Post-Soviet Press* 60, no. 13 (2008): 10.

Roosevelt, Priscilla Reynolds. *Apostle of Russian Liberalism: Timofei Granovsky*. Newtonville, MA: Oriental Research Partners, 1986.

Rosenberg, William G. *Liberals in the Russian Revolution: The Constitutional Democratic Party, 1917–1921*. Princeton, NJ: Princeton University Press, 1974.

——. "Representing Workers and the Liberal Narrative of Modernity." *Slavic Review* 55, no. 2 (1996): 245–69.

—— "Russian Liberals and the Bolshevik Coup." *Journal of Modern History* 40, no. 3 (1968): 328–47.

Rosenblum, Nancy L. "Civil Societies, Liberalism and the Moral Uses of Pluralism." *Social Research* 61, no. 3 (1994): 539–62.

"Rossiiskii liberal'nyi manifest (Programma politicheskoi partii 'Soiuz pravykh sil') [2001 g.]." In *Prava i svobody cheloveka*, 483–85.

Rossiiskii Zarubezhnyi S"ezd 1926 Parizh: Dokumenty i materialy. Moscow: Russkii Put', 2006.

Rothberg, Abraham. *The Heirs of Stalin: Dissidence and the Soviet Regime, 1953–1970*. Ithaca, NY: Cornell University Press, 1972.

"Roundtable. The Constitutional Agenda of the Russian Democratic Opposition from 2011 to 2020." ASEEES Convention, November 7, 2020.

Rupprecht, Tobias. "Formula Pinochet: Chilean Lessons for Russian Liberal Reformers during the Soviet Collapse, 1970–2000." *Journal of Contemporary History* 51, no. 1 (2016): 165–86.

"Russia Needs New Wave of Privatization to Slash Public Sector & Sell Off 'Inefficient' State Companies: Putin Confidant Kudrin." *RT*, September 7, 2021. https://www.rt.com/russia/534161-kudrin-privatization-financial-benefits/.

"Russian Reporter Put under House Arrest over War Criticism." *CTV News*, August 11, 2022. https://www.ctvnews.ca/world/russian-reporter-put-under-house-arrest-over-war-criticism-1.6023281.

"Russia's Prison Population Falls to a Record Low." *RT*, August 13, 2020. https://www.rt.com/russia/497907-russia-prison-population-record-low/.

"Russia's Prison Population Is Now Lower than at Any Point in Modern History." *Meduza*, December 14, 2018. https://meduza.io/en/news/2018/12/14/russia-s-prison-population-is-now-lower-than-at-any-point-in-modern-history.

Rutland, Peter. "Grigorii Yavlinskii: The Man Who Would Be King." *Problems of Post-Communism* 46, no. 5 (1999): 48–54.

——. "Neoliberalism and the Russian Transition." *Review of International Political Economy* 20, no. 2 (2013): 332-62.

Ryzhkov, Vladimir. "Russian Democracy in Eclipse: The Liberal Debacle." *Journal of Democracy* 15, no. 3 (2004): 52–58.

Sablin, Ivan. "Parliaments and Parliamentarism in the Works of Soviet Dissidents, 1960s–80s." *Parliaments, Estates and Representation* 40, no. 1 (2020): 78–96.

Saburova, T. A. "'Revolutsionnyi i konservativnyi liberalizm': Vospominaniia russkikh liberalov o vsaimootnosheniiakh vlasti i obshchestva v Rossii nachala xx v." *Vestnik Omskogo Universiteta: Seriia "Istoricheskie Nauki"* 8, no. 4 (2015): 51–58.

Sakharov, Andrei. *Memoirs*. New York: Vintage, 1992.

——. *My Country and the World*. New York: Alfred A. Knopf, 1976.

——. "On Aleksandr Solzhenitsyn's *Letter to the Soviet Leaders*." In Meerson-Aksenov and Shragin, *Political, Social, and Religious Thought*, 291–301.

——. "Progress, Coexistence, and Intellectual Freedom." In Sakharov, *Sakharov Speaks*, 55–114. New York: Alfred A. Knopf, 1974.

Sakwa, Richard. *Russia's Futures*. Cambridge: Polity, 2019.

Sautman, Barry. "The Devil to Pay: The 1989 Debate and the Intellectual Origins of Yeltsin's 'Soft Authoritarianism.'" *Communist and Post-Communist Studies* 28, no. 1 (1995): 131–51.

Sauvé, Guillaume. "The Lessons from Perestroika and the Evolution of Russian Liberalism (1995–2005)." In Cucciolla, *Dimensions and Challenges*, 163–75.

——. *Subir la victoire: Essor et chute de l'intelligentsia libérale en Russie (1987–1993)*. Montreal: Les Presses de l'Université de Montréal, 2019.

Savranskaya, Svetlana. "Gorbachev's New Thinking: A Post-Liberal Program for the Soviet Union." In Cucciolla, *Dimensions and Challenges*, 97–111

Sedakova, Ol'ga. "Khristianskogo golosa eta vlast' ne slyshat'. Interv'iu Antonu Zhelnovu dlia 'The New Times.'" http://olgasedakova.com/interview/1122.

——. "'Neotlichenia zla.' Interv'iu Iulii Muchnik." http://olgasedakova.com/interview/1780.

——. "'Net khuda bez dobra.' O nekotorykh osobennostiakh otnosheniia k zlu v russkoi traditsii." http://olgasedakova.com/Moralia/282.

——. "O fenomene sovetskogo cheloveka. Interv'iu Elene Kudriavtsevoi." http://
olgasedakova.com/interview/903.

——. "O lozhnoi gordosti za stranu. Interv'iu Anne Danilovoi." http://olgasedakova
.com/interview/2041.

——. "Razgovor o svobode. Beseda s Aleksandrom Kyrlezhevym." http://olgased
akova.com/interview/129.

Sedugin, V. I. "Liberaly tsentral'noi Rossii i rabochii klass." *Izvestiia Vysshikh
Uchebnykh Zavedenii: Povolzhskii Region* 3 (2008): 19–27.

Sekirinskii, Sergei. "Petr Berngardovich Struve." In Kara-Murza, *Rossiiskii liberalizm*,
449–55.

Seleznev, F. A. "Partiia kadetov v gody grazhdanskoi voiny: Problemnye voprosy
istoriografii." In Shelokhaev, *Rossiiskii liberalizm*, 142–50.

Semyonov, Alexander. "Russian Liberalism and the Problem of Imperial Diversity."
In *Liberal Imperialism in Europe*, edited by Matthew P. Fitzpatrick, 67–89. New
York: Palgrave, 2012.

*Sergei Andreevich Muromtsev—Predsedatel' pervoi gosudarstvennoi dumy: Politika, uchenyi,
pedagog.* Orel: Orlik, 2010.

Shamkhalov, Shamil'. "Osobennosti ideino-politicheskikh programmnykh ustanovok
kadetov." *Vlast'* 11 (2010): 81–84.

——. "Sushchnostnye kharakteristiki novogo liberalizma kak ideino-politicheskoi
platformy kadetov." *Vlast'* 4 (2011): 58–62.

Sharafutdinova, Gulnaz. "Was There a 'Simple Soviet' Person? Debating the Politics
and Sociology of 'Homo Sovieticus.'" *Slavic Review* 78, no. 1 (2019): 173–95.

Sheinis, Viktor. "Chto tam—za povorotom?" In *Politicheskii stroi Rossii: Vchera,
segodnia, i zavtra*, edited by Viktor Sheinis, 20–61. Moscow: Mysl', 2019.

Shelokhaev, Valentin. "Ariadna Vladimirovna Tyrkova." In Kara-Murza, *Rossiiskii
liberalizm*, 737–44.

——. *Konstitutsionno-demokraticheskaia partiia v Rossii i emigratsii.* Moscow: Rosspen,
2015.

——. *Liberal'naia model' pereustroistva Rossii.* Moscow: Rosspen, 1996.

——. "Liberalizm v Rossii: Perspektivy izucheniia." In Shelokhaev, *Rossiiskii
liberalizm*, 16–28.

——. "Russian Liberalism as a Historiographical and Historico-Philosophical
Problem." *Russian Studies in History* 37, no. 3 (1998): 7–31.

Shelokhaev, Valentin, ed. *Rossiiskii liberalizm: Itogi i perspektivy izucheniia.* "X
Muromtsevskie chteniia." Orel. Orlik, 2018.

Shelokhaev, Valentin, and K. A. Solov'ev. "Rossiiskie liberaly o Pervoi mirovoi
voine." *Noveishaia Istoriia Rossii* 3 (2014): 184–195.

Shenderovich, Viktor. "Podniat' ili opustit'." *Colta*, July 21, 2020. https://colta.ru
/articles/24960-viktor-shenderovich-novaya-etika-znakomye-motivy.

Shkarenkov, L. K. *Agoniia beloi emigratsii.* Moscow: Mysl', 1986.

Shmelev, Nikolai. "Avansy i dolgi." *Novyi Mir* 6 (1987): 142–58.

Shmelyov, Nikolai. "Rebirth of Common Sense." In Cohen and Vanden Heuvel,
Voices of Glasnost, 141–56.

Shneider, Konstantin, and David C. Fisher. "Was There an 'Early Russian Liberalism'? Perspectives from Russian and Anglo-American Historiography." *Kritika:
Explorations in Russian and Eurasian History* 7, no. 4 (2006): 825–41.

Shragin, Boris. "Oppozitsionnye nastroeniia v nauchnykh gorodakh." *SSSR: Vnutrennie protivorechiia* 1 (1981): 100–120.

——. "Toska po istorii." In Litvinov, Meerson-Aksenov, and Shragin, *Samosoznanie*, 243–77.

Simionov, Loredana Maria, and Ramona Tiganasu. "Historical Incrementalism and Its Effects on the (Mis)Perception of Liberalism in Russia: Guidance from In-Country Experts." *Europolity* 12, no. 2 (2018): 135–50.

Simmons, Ernst J., ed. *Continuity and Change in Russian and Soviet Thought.* New York: Russell and Russell, 1955.

Sindikat-100. "Bol', gnev, styd. Eta voina—avantiura." *Novaia Gazeta*, February 24, 2022. (This article is no longer available.)

Slaughter, Alisa, and Julia Sushytska. "Introduction." In Slaughter and Sushytska, *Spy for an Unknown Country*, 17–52.

——, eds. *A Spy for an Unknown Country: Essays and Lectures by Merab Mamardashvili.* Stuttgart: Ibidem-Verlag, 2020.

Slavtcheva-Petkova, Vera. *Russia's Liberal Media: Handcuffed but Free.* New York: Routledge, 2018.

Smagina, S. M. "Rossiiskii liberalizm nachala xx veka: Teoriia i praktika. Istoriograficheskie siuzhety." *Gumanitarnye i iuridicheskie issledovaniia* 94, no. 47 (2014): 36–43.

Sobchak, Anatoly. "Transition to a Market Economy." *Cato Journal* 11, no. 2 (1991): 195–205.

Sogrin, V. "Liberalizm v Rossii: Perepetii i perspektivy." *Obshchestvennye Nauki i Sovremennost'* 1 (1997): 13–23.

Sokolov-Mitrich, Dmitry. "The Russia They Lost." *Slavyangrad*, September 24, 2014. https://slavyangrad.org/2014/09/24/the-russia-they-lost/.

Solov'ev, A. I. "Liberalizm: Logika istorii i problemy sovremennogo diskursa." *Problemnyi analiz i gosudarstvenno upravlencheskoe proektirovanie* 5 (2010): 66–83.

Solov'ev, Kirill. "Lev Iosifovich Petrazhitskii." In Kara-Murza, *Rossiiskii liberalism*, 683–89.

Solovey, Valeriy. "Liberals or Technocrats? Liberal Ideas and Values in the Mindset of the Russian Political Elite." In Cucciolla, *Dimensions and Challenges*, 179–88.

Soloviev, Vladimir S. "Law and Morality." In Soloviev, *Politics, Law, and Morality*, 131–212.

——. "Morality and Politics." In Soloviev, *Politics, Law, and Morality*, 6–19.

——. "Nationality from a Moral Point of View." In Soloviev, *Politics, Law, and Morality*, 37–53.

——. "Pan Mongolism." http://max.mmlc.northwestern.edu/mdenner/Demo/texts/panmongolism.html.

——. *Politics, Law, and Morality: Essays by V. S. Soloviev.* New Haven, CT: Yale University Press, 2000.

——. "The Social Question in Europe." In Soloviev, *Politics, Law, and Morality*, 32–36.

Solovyov, Vladimir Sergeyevich. *The Justification of the Good: An Essay on Moral Philosophy.* New York: Cosimo, 2010.

Spirova, E. M. "Konservatizm vs liberalizm." *Vek Globalizatsii* 9 (2016): 12–22.

Stepun, F. A. "O svobode (Demokratiia, diktatura i 'Novyi Grad')." In Abramov, *Opyt russkogo liberalizma*, 349–86.

Stepanov, Valerii. "Nikolai Khristianovich Bunge." In Kara-Murza, *Rossiiskii liberalizm*, 264–74.

St. Julian-Varnon, Kimberly. "The Curious Case of 'Russian Lives Matter.'" *Foreign Policy*, July 11, 2020. https://foreignpolicy.com/2020/07/11/the-curious-case-of-russian-lives-matter/#.

Stolypin, Peter. "We Need a Great Russia." In *Readings in Russian Civilization*. Vol. 2, *Imperial Russia, 1700–1917*, edited by Thomas Riha, 456–64. Chicago: University of Chicago Press, 1969.

Stremoukhov, A. V. "Evolutsiia prav cheloveka v sovetskoi i postsovetskoi Rossii." https://cyberleninka.ru/article/n/evolyutsiya-prav-cheloveka-v-sovetskoy-i-postsovetskoy-rossii/viewer.

Sizemskaia, Irina, and Lidiia Novikova. "Novyi liberalizm v Rossii." *Obshchestvennye nauki i sovremennost'* 5 (1993): 132–40.

Struve, Petr B. "Chto zhe takoe Rossiia?" *Russkaia mysl'*, January 1911, 175–78. http://az.lib.ru/s/struwe_p_b/text_1911_chto_takoe_rossia.shtml.

——. "Istoricheskii smysl' russkoi revolutsii i natsional'nye zadachi." In *Iz glubiny: Sbornik statei o russkoi revolutsii*, edited by S. A. Askol'dov, 285–306. Paris: YMCA Press, 1967.

——. "Otryvki o gosudarstve." In Abramov, *Opyt russkogo liberalizma*, 266–83.

——. "The Intelligentsia and Revolution." In Berdiaev et al., *Landmarks*, 115–29.

——. "Toward Characterization of Our Philosophical Development." In Poole, *Problems of Idealism*, 143–60.

——. "V chem zhe istinnyi natsionalizm?" In Petr Struve, *Na raznye temy (1893–1901 gg.): Sbornik stat'ei*, 526–55. St. Petersburg: Tipografiia Doma Prizren. Maloleti. Bedn., 1902.

——. "Velikaia Rossiia: Iz razmyshlenii o probleme russkogo mogushchestva." *Russkaia Mysl'* 1 (1908): 143–57. https://www.yabloko.ru/Themes/History/struve.htm.

Stuvøy, Kirsti. "'The Foreign Within': State-Civil Society Relations in Russia." *Europe-Asia Studies* 72, no. 7 (2020): 1103–24.

Surman, Jan, and Ella Rossman. "New Dissidence in Contemporary Russia: Students, Feminism and New Ethics." *New Perspectives* 30, no. 1 (2022): 27–46.

Swoboda, Philip J. "Semen Frank's Expressive Humanism." In Hamburg and Poole, *History of Russian Philosophy*, 205–23.

Tamarenkova, E. A. "Konstitutsionnye demokraty i 'ukrainsky vopros' v 1917 g.: Problemy preodoleniia kompleksov." In Shelokhaev, *Rossiiskii liberalizm*, 341–59.

Tartak, Elias L. "The Liberal Tradition in Russia: A. Herzen and V. Soloviev." In *European Ideologies: A Survey of 20th Century Political Ideas*, edited by Feliks Gross, 310–23. New York: Philosophical Library, 1948.

Taubman, William. *Gorbachev: His Life and Times*. New York: W. W. Norton, 2017.

Taylor, Charles. "The Politics of Recognition." In *Multiculturalism: Examining the Politics of Recognition*, edited by Amy Gutmann, 25–73. Princeton, NJ: Princeton University Press, 1994.

Thomas, Daniel C. *The Helsinki Effect: International Norms, Human Rights, and the Demise of Communism*. Princeton, NJ: Princeton University Press, 2001.

Thurston, Robert W. *Liberal City, Conservative State: Moscow and Russia's Urban Crisis, 1906–1914*. New York: Oxford University Press, 1987.

Timberlake, Charles. "Introduction: The Concept of Liberalism in Russia." In Timberlake, *Essays on Russian Liberalism*, 1–17.

——. "Ivan Il'ich Petrunkevich: Russian Liberalism in Microcosm." In Timberlake, *Essays on Russian Liberalism*, 18–41.

——, ed. *Essays on Russian Liberalism*. Columbia: University of Missouri Press, 1972.

Timofeyev, Igor. "The Development of Russian Liberal Thought since 1985." In Brown, *Demise of Marxism-Leninism*, 51–118.

Tokes, Rudolf L., ed. *Dissent in the USSR: Politics, Ideology, and People*. Baltimore: Johns Hopkins University Press, 1975.

Tolz, Vera. *The USSR's Emerging Multiparty System*. New York: Praeger, 1992.

Tompson, William. "Was Gaidar Really Necessary? Russian 'Shock Therapy' Reconsidered." *Problems of Post-Communism* 49, no. 4 (2002): 12–21.

Tongour, Nadia. "Diplomacy in Exile: Russian Émigrés in Paris, 1918–1925." PhD diss., Stanford University, 1979.

Treadgold, Donald. "The Constitutional Democrats and the Russian Liberal Tradition." *American Slavic and East European Review* 10, no. 2 (1951): 85–94.

Treisman, Daniel. "'Loans for Shares' Revisited." *Post-Soviet Affairs* 26, no. 3 (2010): 207–27.

Tsipko, Aleksandr S. "The Collapse of Marxism-Leninism." In Ellman and Kontorovich, *Destruction of the Soviet Economic System*, 169–86.

——. "Liberal'nyi konservatizm Nikolaia Berdiaeva i Petra Struve i zadachi dekommunizatsii sovremennoi Rossii." *Tetradi po konservatizmu* 2, no. 1 (2014): 31–39.

——. "Tsennosti svobody i rossiiskoi gosudarstvennosti." *Nezavisimaia Gazeta*, November 16, 2020. https://www.ng.ru/ideas/2020-11-16/7_8015_freedom.html.

Tsonchev, Tsoncho. "Person and Communion: The Political Theology of Nikolai Berdyaev." PhD diss., McGill University, 2020.

Tsygankov, Pavel A., and Andrei P. Tsygankov. "Dilemmas and Promises of Russian Liberalism." *Communist and Post-Communist Studies* 35, no. 1 (2004), 53–70.

Turchin, Valentin. "Chto takoe bespristrastnost'?" In Litvinov, Meerson-Aksenov, and Shragin, *Samosoznanie*, 305–16.

Turgenev, Ivan. *Smoke*. London: Alma Classics, 2013.

Tyrkova-Williams, Ariadna. *From Liberty to Brest-Litovsk: The First Year of the Russian Revolution*. London: Macmillan, 1919.

——. "Russian Liberalism." *Russian Review* 10, no. 1 (1951): 3–14.

"Uregulirovanie na Donbasse: 10 punktov." *Za Yavlinskogo*, 2018. https://2018.yavlinsky.ru/donbass/.

Valliere, Paul. *Modern Russian Theology: Bukharev, Soloviev, Bulgakov: Theology in a New Key*. Grand Rapids, MI: Willian B. Eerdmans, 2000.

Ventsov, Lev. "To Think!" In Meerson-Aksenov and Shragin, *Political, Social, and Religious Thought*, 148–64.

Verpoest, Lien, and Eva Claessen. "Liberalism in Russia: From the Margins of Russian Politics to an Instrument of Geopolitical Othering." *Global Affairs* 3, nos. 4–5 (2017): 337–52.

Volkova, N. K. "Miliukov: Istorik, politik." *Vestnik Rossiiskogo Universiteta Kooperatsii* 2 (2015): 126–34.

Von Laue, Theodore H. "The Prospects of Liberal Democracy in Tsarist Russia." In Timberlake, *Essays on Russian Liberalism*, 164–81.

Vostrikova, Vlada V. "Gosudarstvo i pravo v teoriakh rossiiskikh liberalov nachala xx v." *Izvestiia Vysshikh Uchebnykh Zavedenii. Povolzhskii Region* 3 (2010): 36–42.

——. "Rossiiskie liberaly o roli gosudarstva v obshchestvennom razvitii." *Izvestiia Vysshikh Uchebnykh Zavedenii. Povolzhskii Region* 1 (2008): 20–27.

——. "Vlast' v predstavlenii rossiiskikh liberalov nachala xx v." *Vlast'* 1 (2010): 67–69.

VTsIOM. "Zhizhnennye prioritety rossiian: Sem'ia, den'gi ili tvorchestvo?" *VTsIOM*, June 7, 2017. https://wciom.ru/analytical-reviews/analiticheskii-obzor/zhiznennye-prioritety-rossiyan-semya-dengi-ili-tvorchestvo.

Wagner, William G. "Family Law, the Rule of Law, and Liberalism in Late Imperial Russia." *Jahrbücher für Geschichte Osteuropas* 43, no. 4 (1995): 519–35.

Waldron, Jeremy. "Theoretical Foundations of Liberalism." *Philosophical Quarterly* 37, no. 147 (1987): 127–50.

Walicki, Andrzej. *The Flow of Ideas: Russian Thought from the Enlightenment to the Religious-Philosophical Renaissance*. Frankfurt: Peter Lang, 2015.

——. *Legal Philosophies of Russian Liberalism*. Oxford: Oxford University Press, 1987.

——. "Russian Political Thought of the Nineteenth Century." In *The Cambridge History of Nineteenth Century Political Thought*, edited by Gareth Stedman Jones and Gregory Claeys, 811–34. Cambridge: Cambridge University Press, 2011.

Wartenweiler, David. *Civil Society and Academic Debate in Russia, 1905–1914*. Oxford: Oxford University Press, 2011.

Wegren, Stephen K., ed. *Return to Putin's Russia: Past Imperfect, Future Uncertain*. Lanham, MD: Rowman and Littlefield, 2013.

Weigle, Marcia A. "Political Liberalism in Postcommunist Russia." *Review of Politics* 58, no. 3 (1996): 469–503.

——. *Russia's Liberal Project: State-Society Relations in the Transition from Communism*. Philadelphia: Pennsylvania State University Press, 2000

Wenger, Agnès. "Return of the *Voenkor*: The Military as a New Opinion Leader in Russia?" *Russia.Post*, August 15, 2022. https://www.russiapost.info/politics/voenkor.

White, David. *The Russian Democratic Party Yabloko: Opposition in a Managed Democracy*. Aldershot: Ashgate, 2006.

——. "Russian Liberalism in Crisis? Khodorkovsky Revisited." *Studies of Transition States and Societies* 5, no. 1 (2013): 69–84.

Wilhelm, John Howard. "The Soviet Economic Failure: Brutzkus Revisited." *Europe-Asia Studies* 45, no. 2 (1993): 343–57.

Williams, Robert C. *Culture in Exile: Russian Émigrés in Germany, 1881–1941*. Ithaca, NY: Cornell University Press, 1972.

Williams, Stephen F. *Liberal Reform in an Illiberal Regime: The Creation of Private Property in Russia, 1906–1915*. Stanford, CA: Hoover Institution Press, 2006.

——. *The Reformer: How One Liberal Fought to Preempt the Russian Revolution*. New York: Encounter, 2017.

Wortman, Richard. *The Development of a Russian Legal Consciousness*. Chicago: University of Chicago Press, 1976.

Yasin, Yevgenii. "Getting the Details Wrong." In Ellman and Kontorovich, *Destruction of the Soviet Economic System*, 143–51.

——. "The Parade of Market Transformation Programs." In Ellman and Kontorovich, *Destruction of the Soviet Economic System*, 228–37.

——. "Unintended Consequences at Work." In Ellman and Kontorovich, *Destruction of the Soviet Economic System*, 156–58.

Yakovlev, Alexander. "The Memorandum of December 1985." In Pipes, *Alexander Yakovlev*, 115–28.

——. "Perestroika or the 'Death of Socialism.'" In Cohen and Vanden Heuvel, *Voices of Glasnost*, 33–75.

——. *Striving for Law in a Lawless Land: Memoirs of a Reformer*. Armonk, NY: M. E. Sharpe, 1996.

Yavlinsky, Grigory. *The Putin System: An Opposing View*. New York: Columbia University Press, 2019.

——. *Realeconomik: The Hidden Cause of the Great Recession (and How to Avert the Next One)*. New Haven, CT: Yale University Press, 2011.

——. "Russia's Phony Capitalism." *Foreign Affairs* 77, no. 3 (1998): 67–79.

——. "Where Is Russia Headed? An Uncertain Prognosis." *Journal of Democracy* 8, no. 1 (1997): 3–11.

"Yavlinsky Attacks Regime from the Outside," *Current Digest of the Russian Press* 69, no. 28 (2017): 8–9.

"Yavlinsky Criticizes Russia's Reform Policy: I." *Current Digest of the Soviet Press* 44, no. 23 (1992): 6–10.

Yeltsin, Boris. *Against the Grain: An Autobiography*. London: Jonathan Cape, 1990.

——. *The Struggle for Russia*. New York: Times Books, 1994.

Yemelyanov, Alexei. "Economic and Political Perestroika." *Cato Journal* 11, no. 2 (1991): 269–76.

Yevlampiev, Igor. "Man and Mind in the Philosophy of Boris N. Chicherin." *Studies in East European Thought* 61, no. 2/3 (2009): 113–21.

"Zapiska Moskovskikh liberalov gr. Loris-Melikovu, nachal'niku verkhovnoi rasporiaditel'noi komissii." In Abramov, *Opyt russkogo liberalizma*, 123–39.

Zaslavskaia, Tat'iana I. "The Novosibirsk Report." In *A Voice of Reform: Essays by Tat'iana I. Zaslavskaia*, edited by Murray Yanowitch, 158–83. Armonk, NY: M. E. Sharpe, 1989.

Zaslavskaya, Tatyana. "Socialism with a Human Face." In Cohen and Vanden Heuvel, *Voices of Glasnost*, 115–39.

Zelensky, Elizabeth Kristofovich. "*Bud' gotov razvedchik delu chestomu* / 'Be Prepared Scout for Honorable Deeds': Russian Scouting as a School for Liberalism." *Russian History* 41, no. 2 (2014): 241–54.

Zharikov, A. A. "Zashchita idei pravoporiadka predstaviteliami liberal'noi filosofii prava v dorevolutsionnoi Rossii." *Mezhdunarodnyi Nauchno-Issledovatel'skii Zhurnal* 53, no. 11 (2016): 84–86.

Zharkov, Vasilii. "Liberaly v SSSR i RF." *Russkii Zhurnal*, April 7, 2009. http://www.russ.ru/Mirovaya-povestka/Liberaly-v-SSSR-i-RF.

"Zhestkim kursom. Analiticheskaia zapiska ASEN." *LiveJournal*, June 1990. https://aillarionov.livejournal.com/470196.html.

Zhidkova, Elena Nikolaevich. "Vozzreniia A. D. Gradkovskogo na publichnoe pravo." *Vestnik TGU* 10, no. 114 (2012): 326–31.

Zinoviev, Alexander. *The Reality of Communism*. New York: Schocken, 1984.

Zolotarev, S. P., and T. N. Zolotareva. "Vozniknovenie i razvitie liberalizma v Rossii." *Nauchnye Vedomosti* 45, no. 3 (2018): 573–80.

Zolotukhina, E. K. "Bor'ba za prava cheloveka: Konstitutsionno-demokraticheskaia partiia i partiia demokraticheskikh reform v pervoi gosudarstvennoi dume." In *Sergei Andreevich Muromtsev*, 231–41.

Zubok, Vladislav. *Zhivago's Children: The Last Russian Intelligentsia*. Cambridge, MA: Belknap Press of Harvard University Press, 2009.

Zweynert, Joachim. "Economic Ideas and Institutional Change: Evidence from the Soviet Economic Debates, 1987–1991." *Europe-Asia Studies* 58, no. 2 (2006): 169–92.

INDEX

www.ingramcontent.com/pod-product-compliance
Lightning Source LLC
Chambersburg PA
CBHW031514210225
22341CB00004B/378